HOW TO PHOTOGRAPH
ABSOLUTELY EVERYTHING

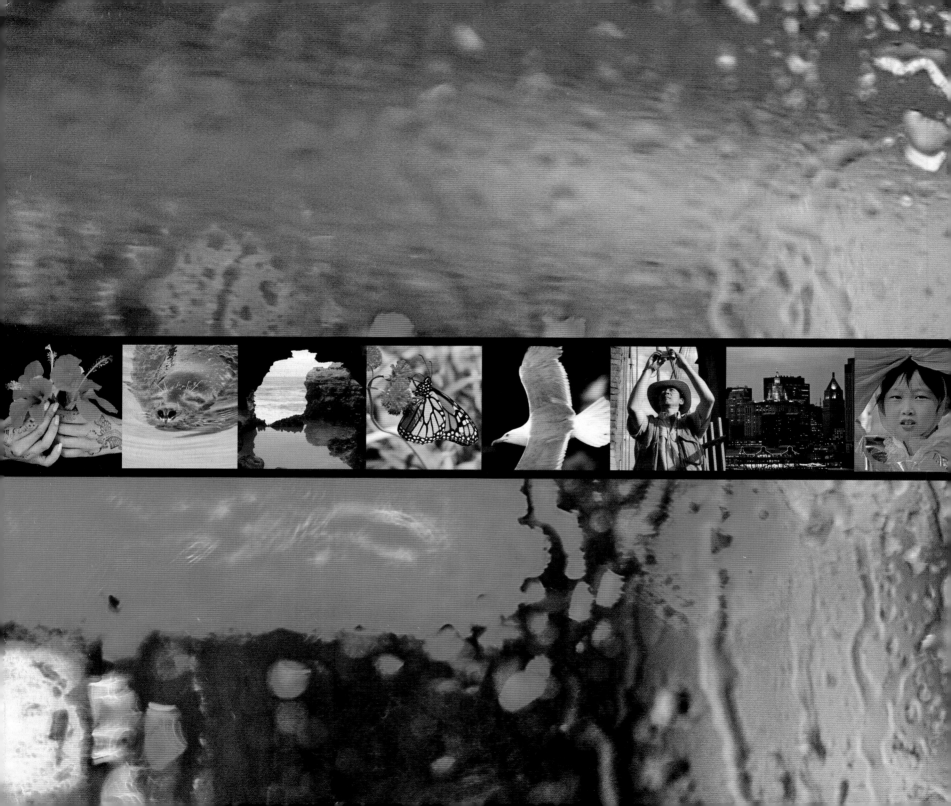

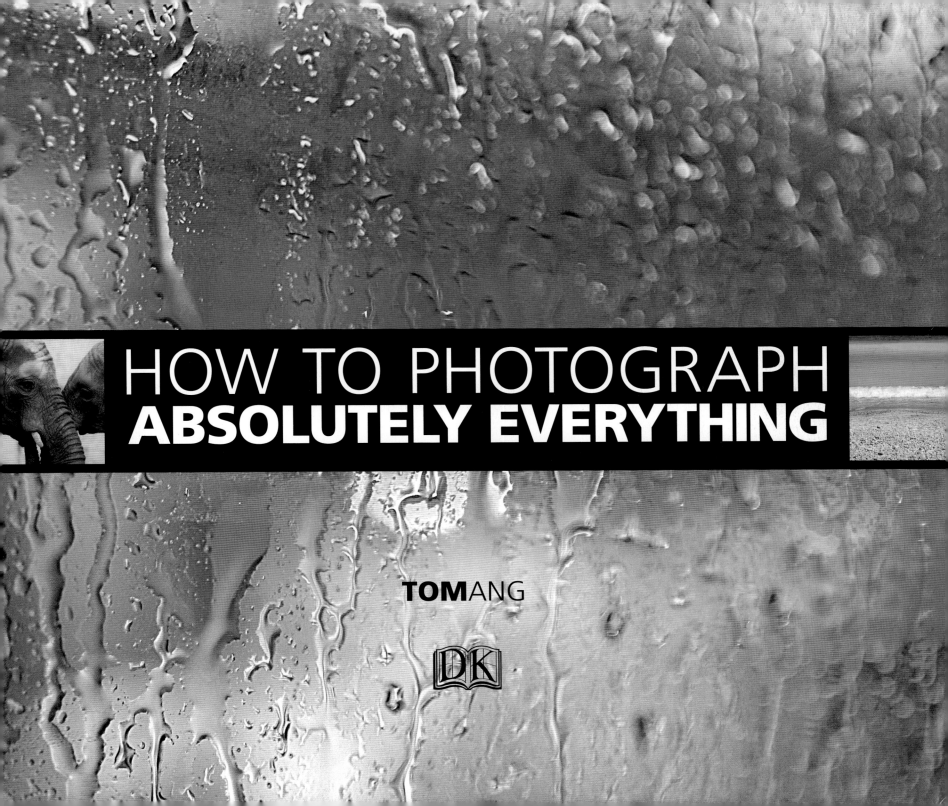

HOW TO PHOTOGRAPH
ABSOLUTELY EVERYTHING

TOMANG

DK

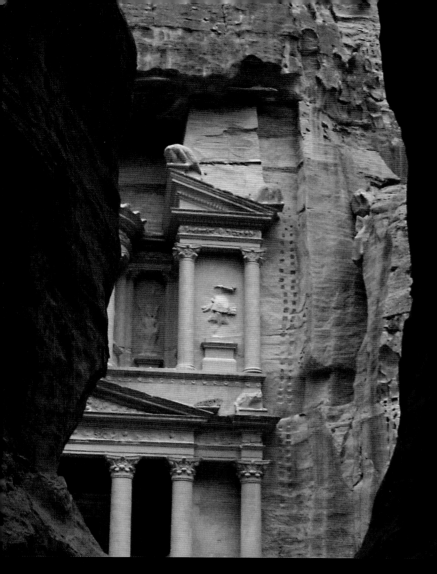
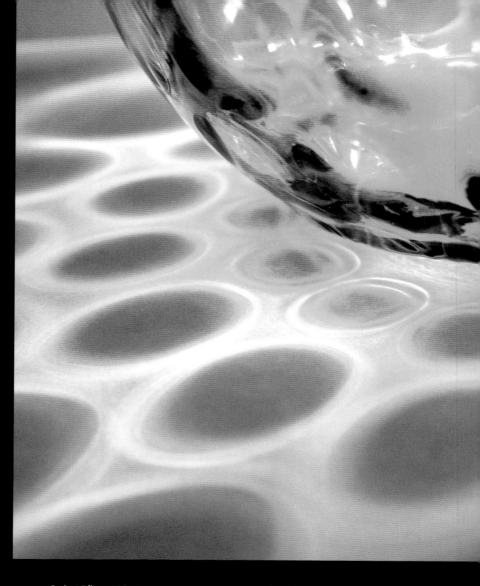
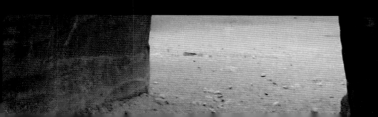

 DK
LONDON, NEW YORK, MELBOURNE,
MUNICH, AND DELHI

for Wendy

Project Editor Nicky Munro
Project Art Editor Jenisa Patel
Designer Sarah-Anne Arnold
Production Editor Vania Cunha
Production Controller Melanie Dowland
Managing Editor Stephanie Farrow
Managing Art Editor Lee Griffiths

Produced on behalf of Dorling Kindersley by
Sands Publishing Solutions
4 Jenner Way, Eccles,
Aylesford, Kent ME20 7SQ

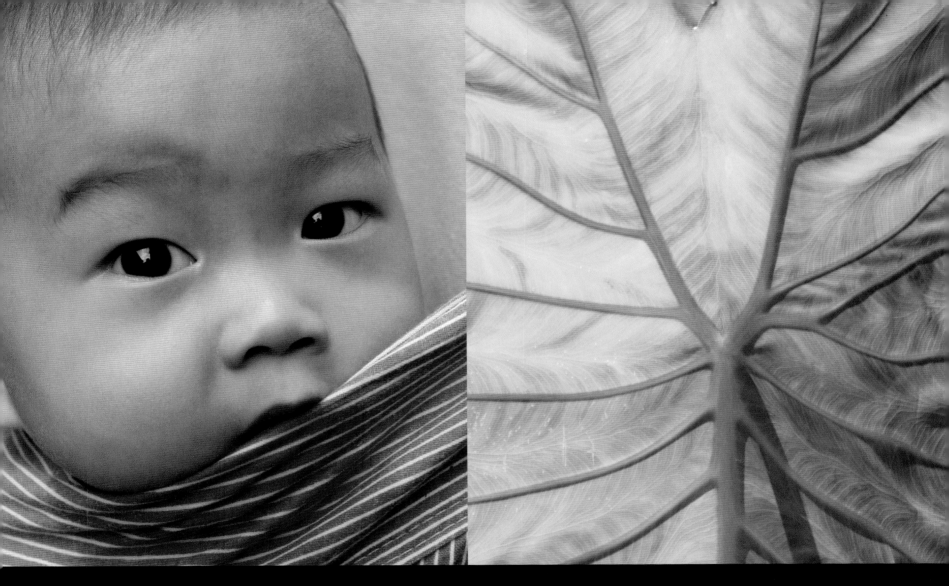

First American Edition 2007

Published in the United States by
DK Publishing
375 Hudson Street
New York, New York 10014

07 08 09 10 11   10 9 8 7 6 5 4 3 2 1

Published in Great Britain by Dorling Kindersley Limited

This edition published in 2010

A catalog record for this book is available from
the Library of Congress

DK books are available at special discounts when purchased
in bulk for sales promotions, premiums, fund-raising, or
educational use. For details, contact: DK Publishing Special
Markets, 375 Hudson Street, New York, New York 10014 or
SpecialSales@DK.com

ISBN: 978 0 7566 4308 9

Printed and bound in China, by Leo Paper
Color reproduction by MDP in the UK

Discover more at
www.dk.com

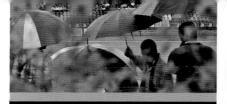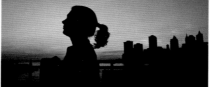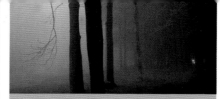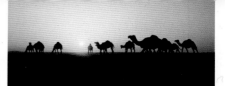

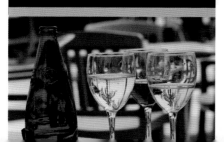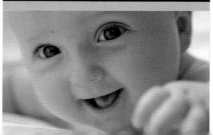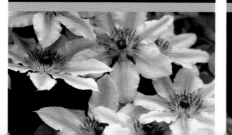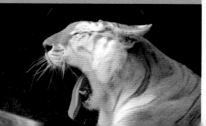

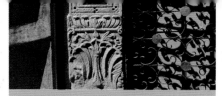
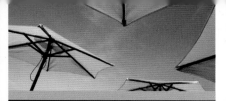
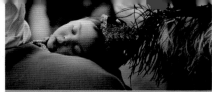
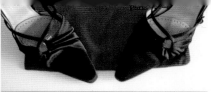

5 Architecture

6 Events

7 Artistic expression

8 Other applications

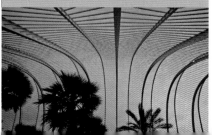
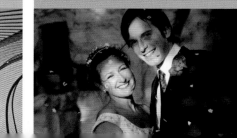
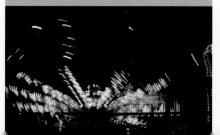
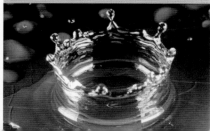

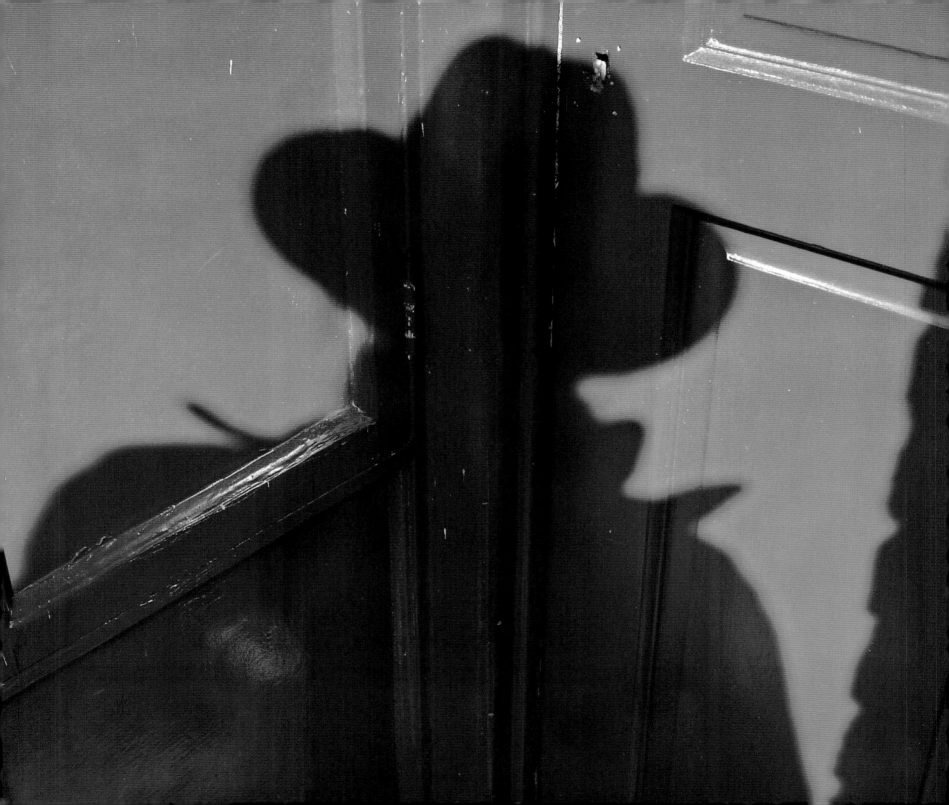

Introduction

This is a unique book, with a unique aim and daring ambition. I want to help you to know how to photograph any subject or situation you may encounter. Of course, it is essential to learn the basic techniques of photography. But that is like learning basic cooking techniques such as chopping, stir-frying, boiling. You have nothing edible until you add the ingredients. And to make a tasty meal you have to follow a recipe which works with and responds to the character of the ingredients to make the best use of them. This is a photographic recipe book. It shows how to create pictures by working with the basic ingredients of color, light, and space—then "cooking" them up using techniques such as exposure, framing, and focus. By following the step-by-step recipes, you will steadily gain the ability to photograph absolutely everything. At the same time, the book brings together numerous tricks and tips that you may apply to a vast range of photographic challenges, empowering you to make the most of every photographic opportunity.

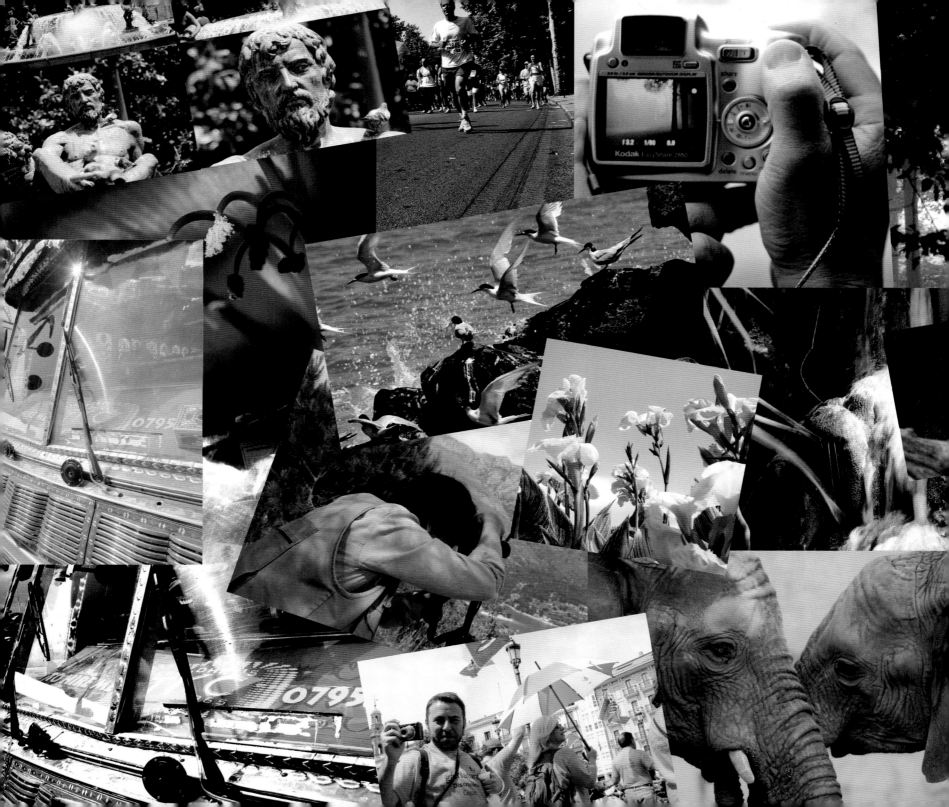

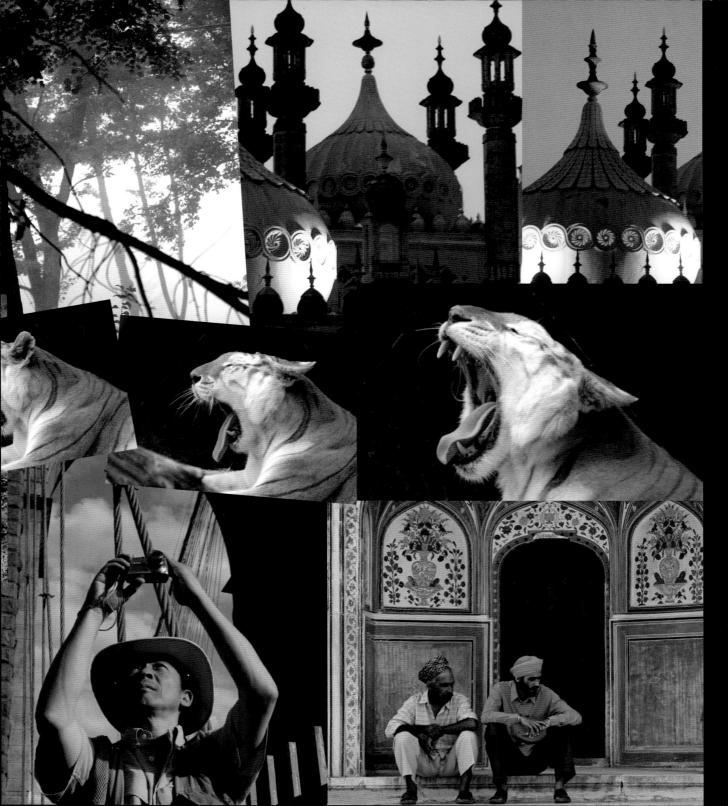

Elements of Photography

12345678

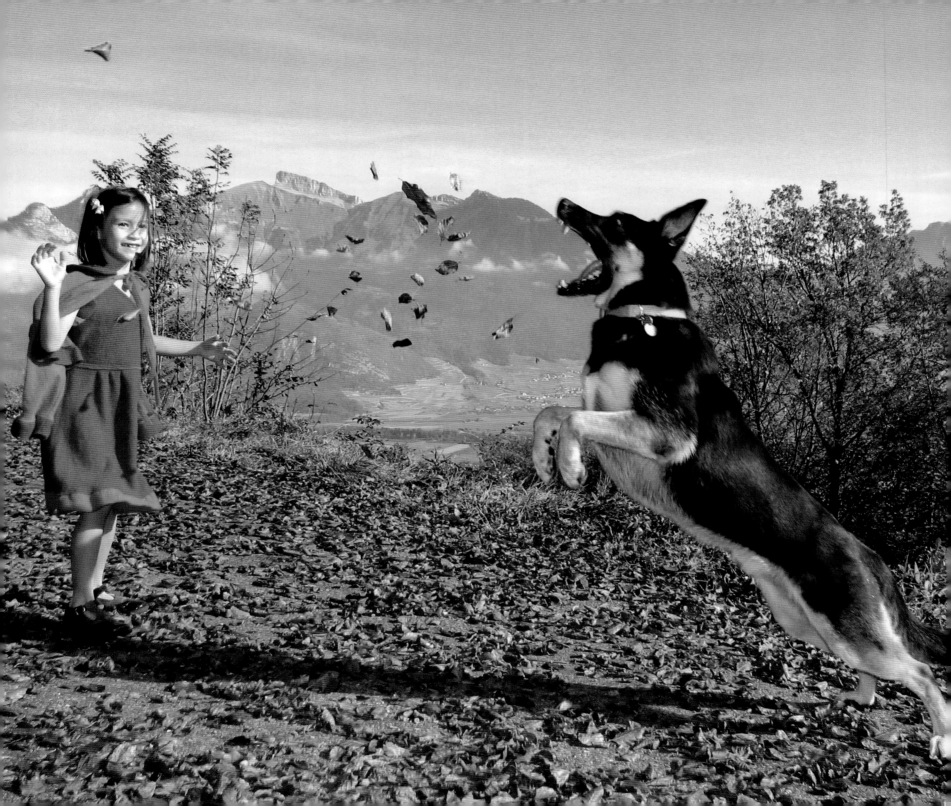

Elements of photography describes the building blocks that make up all photographs. Whether snapped on the simplest camera, crafted in the finest professional model, or made with scientific instruments, all photographs are created with light. And to create any image you must control the quantity of light and bring it into focus, while composing and timing the shot with precision. Here you will learn how to combine focusing, exposure, zooming, and framing with the ingredients of space, time, light, and color, discovering how to make your camera work for you. You will also see how software can enhance your images by refining their shape, exposure, color balance, contrast, and sharpness.

Which digital camera do I choose?

Today's digital cameras are universally capable of producing excellent results and offer a wide range of controls designed to make photography easy and fun. Cameras for the beginner fall broadly in to the simple point-and-shoot cameras with 3–4 megapixels and basic controls. Next up are those offering greater resolution—5–7 megapixels—with more advanced controls and faster operating speed. Some of these models concentrate on quality with a zoom lens of limited range, while others offer a greater zoom range with a reduction in other features. More costly cameras will offer even greater resolution as well as more flexible camera and image controls or better lenses.

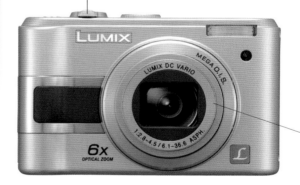

CONTROL SWITCH for changing camera mode or zoom setting (varies with camera model).

ZOOM LENS with versatile zoom range.

LCD SCREEN is the main interface with the camera, controlling framing as well as display of menu options.

INTERFACE HATCH covers the jacks for connecting to a computer or TV screen.

SHUTTER BUTTON initiates the exposure sequence; good cameras respond quickly to pressure on the button.

NAVIGATION ROSETTE is used to move through the menu and make settings.

FUNCTION BUTTONS are used to select display modes and delete images (varies with camera model).

MID-RANGE COMPACT

Modern compact cameras offer zoom lenses with at least 3x range (the longest focal length is 3x longer than the shortest) with sensors carrying 6 or more megapixels. In addition, all offer auto-focus, have a built-in flash, removable memory, LCD viewfinder (some have see-through viewfinders too), and a choice of different auto-exposure modes.

ADVANTAGES

>> Compact and lightweight
>> Easy to use
>> Capable of high-quality images
>> Inexpensive to use

DISADVANTAGES

>> Battery life may be limited
>> Display may be difficult to read
>> Range of accessories limited
>> Zoom action may not be smooth

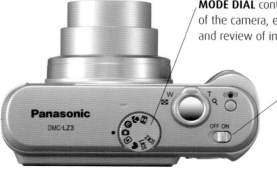

MODE DIAL controls the operational mode of the camera, exposure metering, set-up and review of images.

POWER SWITCH for turning camera on and off; good models turn on quickly.

FREQUENTLY ASKED QUESTIONS

  WHAT KIND OF VIEWFINDER IS BEST FOR ME?

Liquid crystal display (LCD) viewfinders that flip out are useful for awkward angles. The larger the screen, the easier it is to use. Cameras with optical (see-through) viewfinders provide a small view but one that is easy to use in bright light and does not rely on batteries.

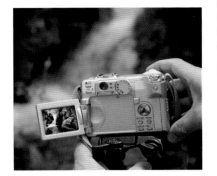

WHAT EXACTLY ARE MEGAPIXELS?

Pixels are the picture's elements—the more you have available, the greater the capacity to record detail. The image sensor is made up of individual picture elements, so an 8-megapixel sensor is covered with 8 million individual elements.

HOW MANY PIXELS DO I NEED TO HAVE?

3–5 megapixels are ample for web use and for average-sized prints, while 8 or more megapixels are sufficient for many professional uses. However, the number of pixels does not guarantee good image quality—much depends on the lens quality and image processing.

MODE DIAL sets scene modes and other functions.

ELECTRONIC VIEWFINDER is a small LCD screen under a magnifier.

ZOOM LENS is much larger and offers greater zoom range and quality.

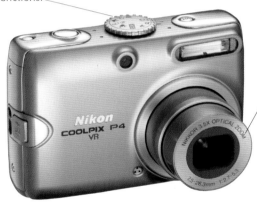

ZOOM LENS with limited zoom range.

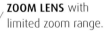

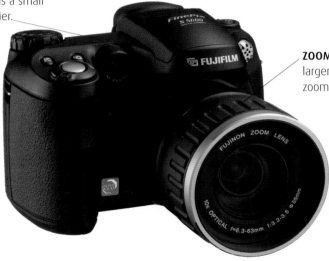

BEGINNER'S COMPACT

Modern entry-level compacts suitable for the beginner represent exceptional value-for-money. They combine very good image quality with real ease of use in extremely compact and stylishly designed bodies. Some models offer moisture-proof bodies, some are extremely thin, others are chunkier for the larger hand. The range is broad and you can select with confidence.

ADVANTAGES

» Inexpensive to purchase
» Inexpensive to use
» Very easy to use
» Very lightweight and compact

DISADVANTAGES

» Zoom range may be limited
» May not accept accessories
» May be slow in operation
» May limit you as you progress

PROSUMER

Cameras that bridge the consumer and professional ranges—the prosumer—are capable of professional quality images, and offer a good range of photographic controls. They sacrifice sturdy construction in order to keep weight low and reduce size. Prosumer cameras accept flash and lens accessories as well as featuring high-performance lenses.

ADVANTAGES

» High-quality images
» Wider zoom range
» Accepts accessory flash unit
» May be rapid in operation

DISADVANTAGES

» Bulkier and heavier than point-and-shoot compacts
» More costly to purchase
» More complicated to use

What else to consider?

As your photographic experience grows, you may want to extend the range of your photography. As your confidence in your skills grows, you may start to stretch the capabilities of your camera. This is when you will begin to think about adding accessories to your camera. Some, such as a tripod or data storage, can be applied to any camera. Others, such as an accessory flash or a larger zoom lens, will depend on the facilities of your camera.

USING AN EXTRA FLASH

If you want to take photographs at parties, clubs, or other events that take place indoors or at night, you will need an accessory flash. Your camera must have a way to connect the flash—usually through a hot-shoe in the top. Flash units with heads you can swivel and point in different directions provide the most control of the quality of light.

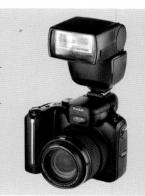

INCREASING ZOOM RANGE

If your camera has a modest zoom range—between 3x and 5x—it will not be long before you wish for an extension of this range. Just as with digital SLRs, in many cameras, zoom range may be extended by screwing on lens adaptors: wide-angle adaptors increase the field of view; tele adaptors increase the telephoto end of the range.

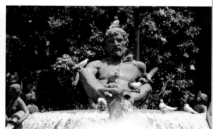

WIDE ANGLE

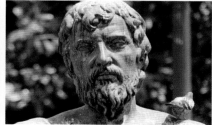

STANDARD

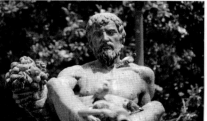

TELEPHOTO

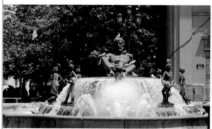

EXTENDED TELEPHOTO

USING A TRIPOD

There is no doubt that a tripod is the best way to ensure sharp, high-quality images. Tripods also reduce the strain when you are waiting for a photographic moment, whether it is a setting sun or an animal moving across a landscape. A ball-and-socket head (above right) is light and easy to use, but a 3-way head (far right) gives the most control. Purchase the sturdiest tripod you can comfortably carry.

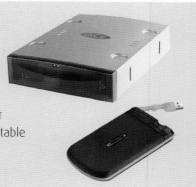

STORING DATA

The more you photograph, the more you will want to store. Modern data storage is amazingly affordable. You can back up images onto CDs or DVDs using inexpensive writers and disks. For more rapid access, store images on portable hard-disk drives.

MEMORY CARD OPTIONS

Digital cameras store images on removable memory cards. The cards supplied with cameras are usually adequate for only a handful of images, so you will need to buy your own. Get the largest capacity you can afford, but you do not have to purchase the fastest cards, as these are designed for professional cameras. It's a good idea to keep a spare card—deleting images as you go in order to make space is a practice guaranteed to result in you losing important pictures.

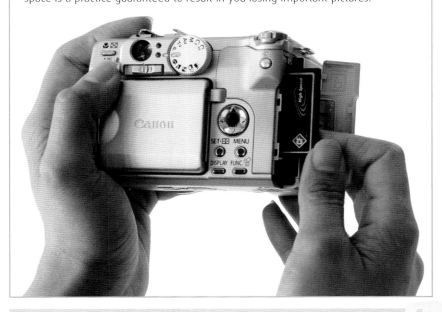

Q HOW CAN I BACK UP IMAGES WHILE TRAVELING?

A Use portable hard-disk drives with built-in card readers. Insert your memory card, press a button, and the drive copies the contents of the card. When the operation is over, you can erase the card's data and start again.

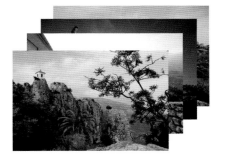

Q HOW DO I DOWNLOAD PHOTOS?

A One method is to install the camera's software on your computer, then you will be able to connect it via a cable to transfer data. Alternatively, connect a card reader to the computer: remove the card from your camera, insert it into the reader and copy the files to the computer.

Q WHAT IS THE BEST WAY TO ORGANIZE MY PICTURES?

A Create a "Pictures" folder if you do not already have one. Then create another folder named according to the location and date. Copy your pictures to that folder. When you open a picture to alter it in any way, immediately "save as" under a different name so you always preserve the original image.

PRINTING

Modern printers produce excellent quality images and are inexpensive, but printing materials are often costly. Some printers connect directly with cameras, others read the memory cards. Both methods eliminate the need for a computer.

» **DYE-SUBLIMATION PRINTERS** produce small prints of superb quality very quickly and easily.

» **INK-JET PRINTERS** can produce very large prints but require you to prepare the image. Also, color control may be tricky.

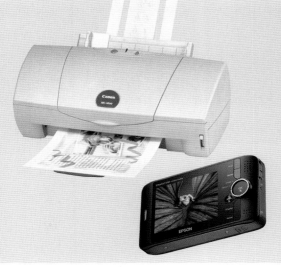

PRESENTING

There are numerous ways in which you can show your pictures to family, friends and, indeed, the whole world. Picture viewers store numerous images and display them on a screen.

» **PICTURE-SHARING SITES** allow you to upload images from any part of the world for storage and for others to view.

» **PERSONAL WEBSITES** can be constructed to show off your photographs in ways that you personally design and control.

Camera settings

Modern cameras emerge from their box with basic settings that will suit most photographers. But as you become more experienced and demanding in your photography, you will want your camera to do more. This means learning about its different settings and their effects.

USE YOUR CAMERA'S P FOR "PROGRAM" MODE. This gives you a high level of automation but allows you to make corrections or alter settings. The fully automatic mode—usually a green square or symbol—shuts off many adjustments, so is best avoided.

IF YOUR CAMERA OFFERS SCENE MODES—settings designed for situations such as landscapes, close-ups or sports—use them. They save a lot of button-pressing and scrolling through menus.

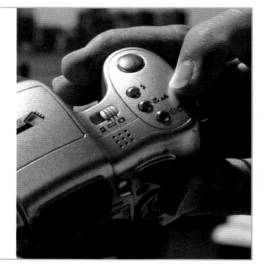

USE THE CAMERA'S HIGHEST QUALITY SETTING, but avoid the RAW or TIFF settings unless you have a specific need for these formats, such as printing large images. You can always reduce the size of the image but you cannot put back quality that is not already in the image.

IF YOUR CAMERA HAS ONE, USE THE BRACKETING SETTING to make sure you get the right exposure for your image. The camera will usually take three separate images at three slightly different exposures, and one of these should be correct.

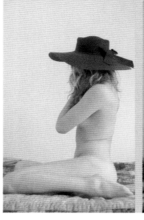 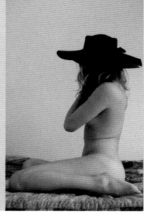 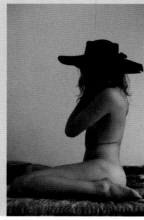

CHANGE THE ISO OR SENSITIVITY SETTING OF YOUR CAMERA when working in dim lighting conditions. Raising the ISO number will make your camera more sensitive to light and enable you to use faster shutter speeds.

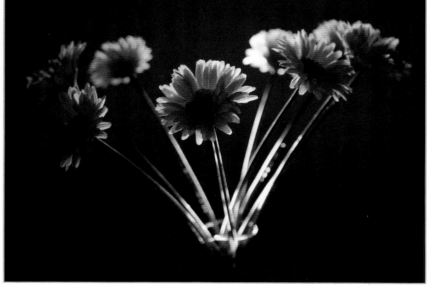

SET THE CAMERA TO SERIES EXPOSURE, RATHER THAN SINGLE EXPOSURE, if possible. This readies the camera to respond quickly if you need to make a number of exposures in rapid succession. If you don't need a series of images, you can just lift your finger off the shutter button.

USE THE AV (APERTURE VALUE) PRIORITY SETTING when the depth of field is an important aspect of your photograph. A high AV setting will capture a scene with a large depth of field; a low AV setting will produce an image with a narrow depth of field.

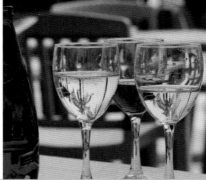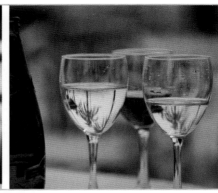

IF YOU HAVE TRAVELED TO ANOTHER TIME ZONE, remember to change the time setting on the camera. Accurate local time stamps on your images will help you to keep track of your pictures and store them in order when you return home.

SET THE CAMERA TO USE ADOBE RGB (if available on your camera) and set color saturation (richness) and sharpness to increase by a notch or two in the camera's image adjustment menu to save work on your computer.

USE THE TV (TIME VALUE) PRIORITY SETTING when short or long exposures are necessary to suit the subject. You should use short shutter times such as $\frac{1}{500}$ second for action, and longer times such as 1 second or more for blurred light trails at night. TV settings are represented as fractions of a second and can range from $\frac{1}{8000}$ second to several seconds.

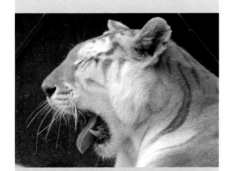

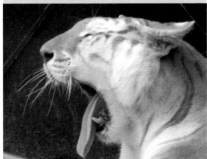

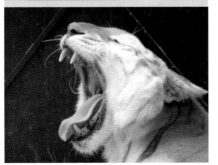

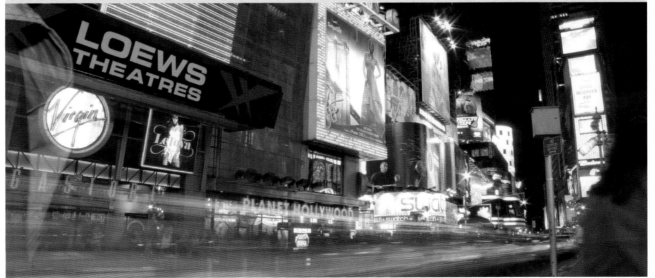

Finding focus

Virtually all modern cameras have auto-focus systems that almost guarantee the sharpness of some part of your image. But is the image sharp where you want it to be? The key to focusing is not just to focus the lens but to control where the sharpness lies. Most cameras will focus, by default, on the very center of the image. While this is handy in most situations, it may lead to improperly focused images if the main subject of your image is not in the center of the frame.

IF IN DOUBT, SHOOT ANYWAY. It is better to risk an unsharp image than having no image at all. If your image is a little bit on the soft side, you can always use your editing software to improve its sharpness.

DECIDE ON WHAT NEEDS TO BE SHARP AND FORGET THE REST. If you worry too much about technicalities like depth of field (how much of the scene appears sharp), your photography will be slowed down unnecessarily.

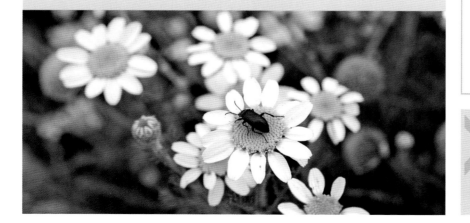

LEARN TO FOCUS ON ONE PART OF THE SUBJECT, hold down the button to keep focus, and re-compose for the shot. The more easily you can do this, the more your photography will improve.

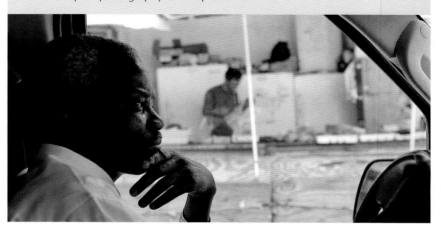

IF YOUR CAMERA OFFERS A CHOICE BETWEEN MULTIPLE OR SINGLE FOCUSING POINTS, choose the single, central point. This allows you to focus more precisely and to focus past near obstructions such as railings or the leaves of a tree. In addition, the camera may work faster when set to a single focusing point, rather than several.

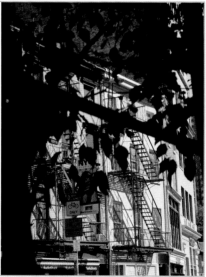

IF YOUR CAMERA IS UNABLE TO FOCUS, for example, because the subject lacks detail or is too high in contrast, point the focusing spot at another object that is the same distance away as your subject, before re-framing your shot and taking the picture.

IF POSSIBLE, SET YOUR CAMERA'S AUTO-FOCUS TO SERVO OR CONTINUOUS MODE when there is lots going on around you, or when your subject is moving irregularly and constantly changing its distance from you.

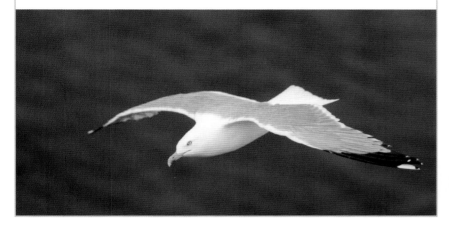

WHEN WORKING VERY CLOSE TO YOUR SUBJECT, it may be easier to keep it in focus by maintaining the distance between yourself and the subject by moving the camera backward and forward (nearer and further away) rather than by adjusting focus.

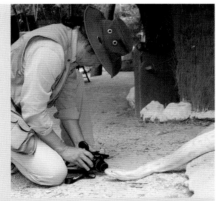

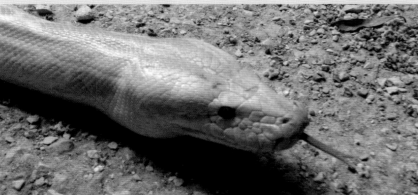

IF YOU SET THE AUTO-FOCUS TO SINGLE-SHOT or one-shot mode, the camera will expose only when it determines that focus has been found. This helps ensure sharp images but may slow down photography in fast-changing situations.

IF YOU HAVE MANUAL FOCUSING CONTROLS on your camera or lens, learn to use them. The controls on some point-and-shoot cameras may be very limited to setting focus by distance, rather than by watching the sharpness of the image. Manual control is useful when photographing close-up as it allows you to make precise adjustments in focus.

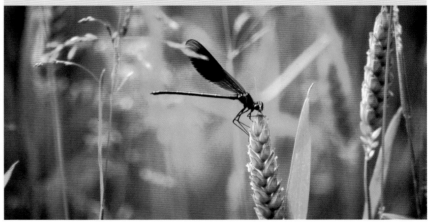

FOR SELF-TIMER SHOTS—where you set up the camera to include yourself in a group shot—ensure that the camera is not only framed correctly, but also focused on the group before you set off the self-timer. Alternatively, it may be easier to set the focus manually.

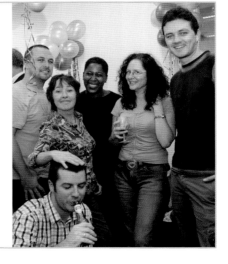

Judging exposure

Modern cameras and image manipulation techniques are close to making exposure problems a thing of the past. Many cameras actually analyze the scene and compare it with a database of known scenes to work out the best exposure. The result is that badly under-exposed images (too dark) or heavily over-exposed images (too light) are now much less common than before. But that is no consolation if one of your images has been incorrectly exposed. The key is to learn how to help the camera get the result you want.

IN TRICKY LIGHTING CONDITIONS, learn to obtain the exposure from the part of the scene you want exposed correctly, such as the face. Select the section of the image in the viewfinder, then hold the reading and re-compose the shot. This is the fastest way to ensure correct exposure.

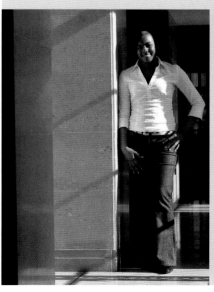 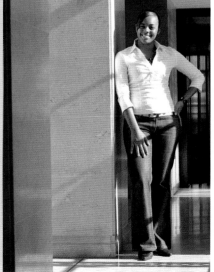

IF IN DOUBT, MAKE THE EXPOSURE ANYWAY. It is better to have something that is not perfectly exposed than no image at all. You can always adjust the image later using editing software.

THE EASIEST LIGHTING SITUATION to expose for is when the subject is lit from the front, and the sun is behind you. However, such lighting does not give the most interesting textures.

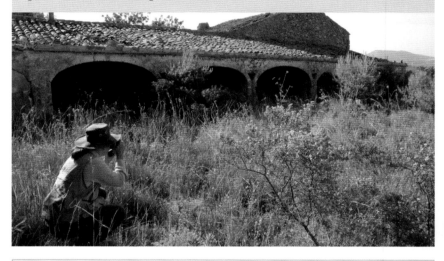

WITH DIGITAL CAMERAS IT IS BETTER TO ERR ON THE SIDE OF UNDER-EXPOSURE. While even slight over-exposure tends to make colors look faded and washed out, under-exposure can actually make colors (especially paler colors) look richer in tone.

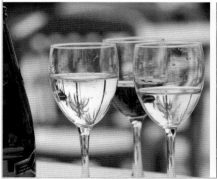 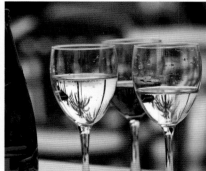

TO REFINE YOUR EXPOSURE TECHNIQUE, use the center-weighted or spot-metering mode to determine exposure. These read only a limited part of the scene, and you will learn by evaluating the results and making adjustments.

IN SUNNY SITUATIONS, try to position yourself so that the sun is to one side, so that you see your subject partially lit and partially in shadow. An exposure that takes in both the sunny and the shadowy areas is likely to be correct.

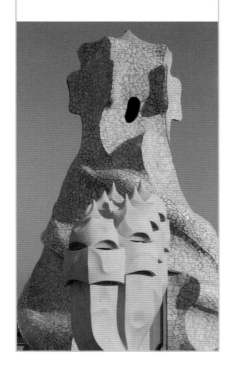

THE MOST DEMANDING LIGHTING CONDITIONS—against the light or high-contrast lighting, for example—make it difficult to obtain the correct exposure. If you have the opportunity, check the image and repeat the shot with extra or reduced exposure (using the override controls or manual exposure settings) as you need.

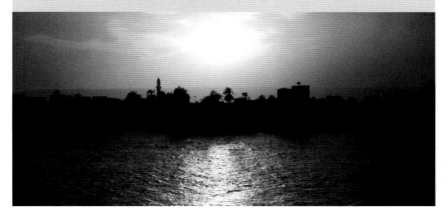

WHEN SHOOTING IN POOR LIGHT CONDITIONS, or if you or your subject is moving, you can reduce exposure times by adjusting your camera's sensitivity—the ISO setting. Raising it may enable you to take pin-sharp photos with little reduction in image quality.

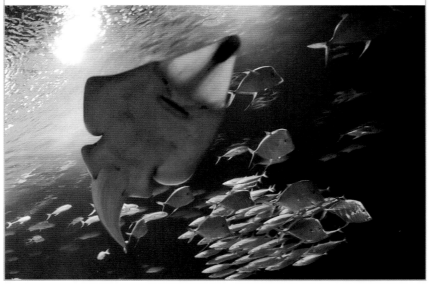

EXPOSURE METERS WORK BEST MEASURING FROM MID-TONES—roughly half-way between lightest and darkest. Learn to recognize what mid-tones look like—lightly tanned Caucasian skin, green grass in half-shade, deep blue sky—and measure from that.

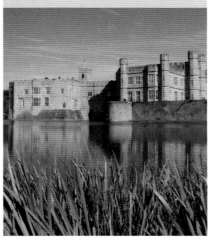

WHETHER AN IMAGE IS PROPERLY EXPOSED OR NOT depends on the type of image you want to create. You will have a key tone—a face, or flower, or patch of landscape, for example—that must look right, so expose for that. The rest of the image can fall in where it will.

Zoom settings

The combination of low price, top performance, and compact design in modern zoom lenses is one of the cornerstones of the success of modern photography. They put great optical powers into your hands, with the exciting prospect of being able to take command of all picture-making possibilities.

IF YOU HAVE A DIGITAL SLR, ADD MOVEMENT TO YOUR IMAGES by experimenting with the zoom effect. Set your camera to a slow shutter speed and, while the shutter is open, either zoom in to or out from the subject. For best effects, you will need to keep your camera as still as possible so that the motion lines are straight.

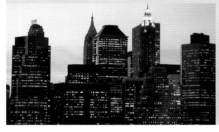 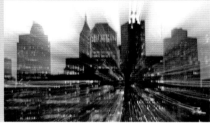

THE BEST WAY TO USE THE ZOOM is to decide what kind of picture or what part of the scene you want, then set the zoom to suit. Often you will want either the widest or the longest setting, but when you compose the image you can make small adjustments if you have time.

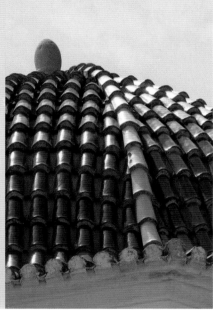

TRY SETTING THE ZOOM TO A FAVORITE FOCAL LENGTH, for example, very long or very wide or halfway between, and leave it there for the day if your camera allows. You will find you can photograph more quickly and decisively when you are not always adjusting the zoom.

WHEN USING THE LONG END OF A ZOOM, be extra careful to hold the camera steady, since the chance of camera shake grows as focal length increases.

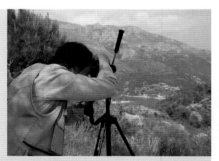

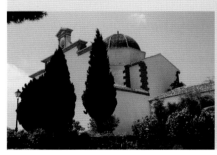

WALKING TOWARD OR AWAY FROM THE SUBJECT IS OFTEN BETTER THAN ZOOMING IN OR OUT. It helps you to experience and explore changes in perspective, and keeps you actively looking for the best picture.

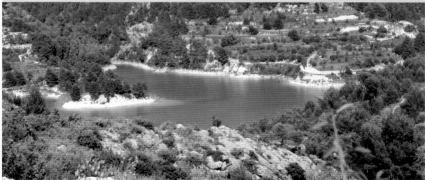

IF IN DOUBT, SHOOT AT A WIDER ANGLE and take in more of the scene. You can always crop an image afterward, but you can't add to it once you leave.

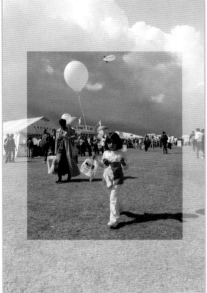

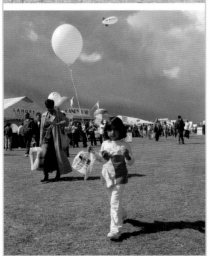

AVOID USING THE DIGITAL ZOOM WHENEVER POSSIBLE. This is where the camera zooms as far as the lens will go, then increasingly small sections of the center of image are enlarged for greater zoom. The results from digital zoom may disappoint, as the resolution is reduced.

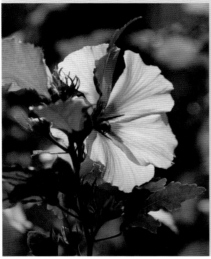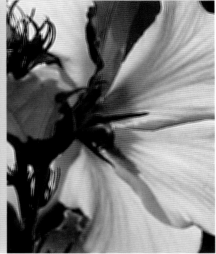

IF YOU WANT THE LINES IN AN IMAGE TO BE AS STRAIGHT AS POSSIBLE, for example, when photographing buildings, use the lens at around the middle of the range of zoom settings. Lenses tend to distort (bend) lines less at mid-range settings.

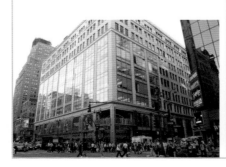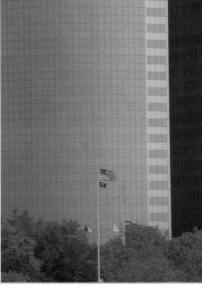

IN DIM LIGHT, USE THE WIDEST ZOOM SETTING AVAILABLE as zoom lenses can gather more light (have a larger maximum aperture) at wide settings than at longer settings.

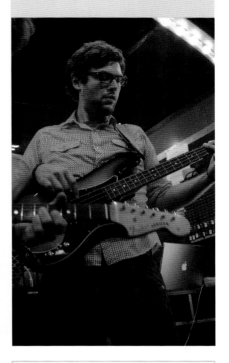

KEEP YOUR ZOOM LENS CLEAN. The lenses of modern compact cameras are very small, so the slightest smudge can have a significant effect on the quality of the image projected by the lens.

Framing images

Aiming the camera directly at a subject will ensure that it is "caught" in the picture. But exactly how you frame it is what can make the difference between a snap and a photograph. Framing is the process of choosing a camera position to create a composition that is visually effective. It is about ensuring that the elements in the picture, including colors and shapes, complement each other so that the picture communicates with the viewer in the way you envisaged.

>> **MAKE SURE YOU HOLD YOUR CAMERA LEVEL**—so that the horizon is level—unless you have a special framing effect in mind. In that case tilt the horizon strongly and obviously.

>> **KEEP MOVING IN YOUR SEARCH FOR VIEWPOINTS,** changing perspectives and variety in picture framing. If you are static, your pictures will also feel static and lacking in dynamism.

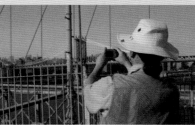
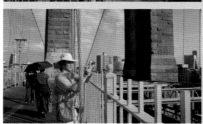
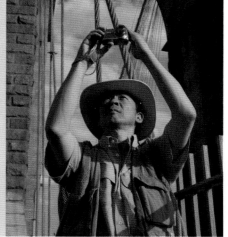

>> **WHEN PHOTOGRAPHING SCENES WITH PEOPLE** it is almost always better to be too close than to be too far away, so move in closer and keep up with the action.

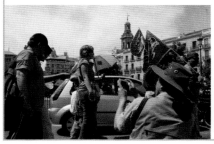
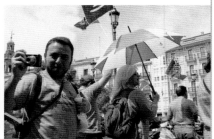

>> **TRY TO FILL THE FRAME** right up to the corners. It is a good approach to keep visual interest going across the whole the image as far as possible, to give the viewer lots to look at.

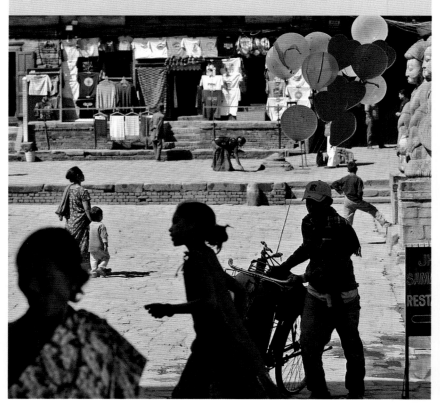

PLACING THE MAIN SUBJECT OFF-CENTER, closer to one side or the other, is usually (but not always) more effective than placing them in the dead center. A useful starting point is to place your main subject roughly a third of the way into the image.

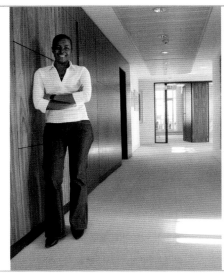

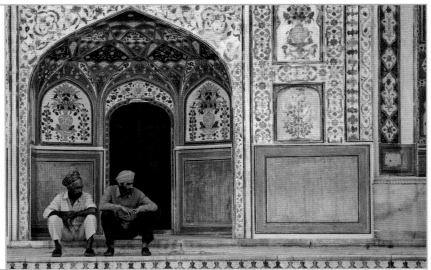

USE FRAMING DEVICES SUCH AS DOORWAYS, overhanging leaves, and out-of-focus features to form a natural frame to shape your picture. This helps to emphasize the subject, and give it context. It is also useful for hiding unwanted or distracting elements in the scene.

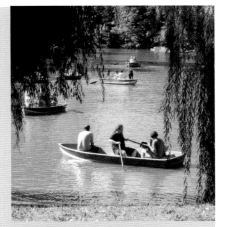

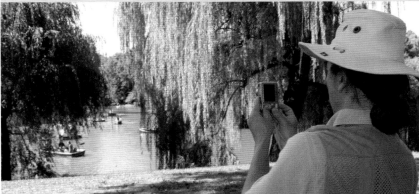

IF OBJECTS IN YOUR PICTURE ARE SIMILAR IN COLOR OR DARKNESS, frame to keep them separate—with some of the background in between them. Otherwise, their shapes may become confused.

WHEN COMPOSING VISTAS OR SCENICS, try to place elements in the foreground; this gives a sense of scale and dynamic space. Allow the foreground interest to be out of focus to draw attention to the background.

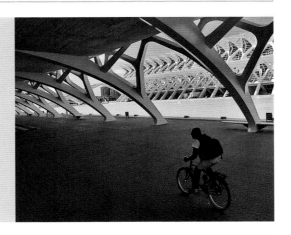

IF THE OBJECTS IN YOUR SCENE ARE EASY TO DISTINGUISH FROM EACH OTHER—for example, one is dark, another is light-colored—you can try to overlap them, to give a sense of scale and receding distance.

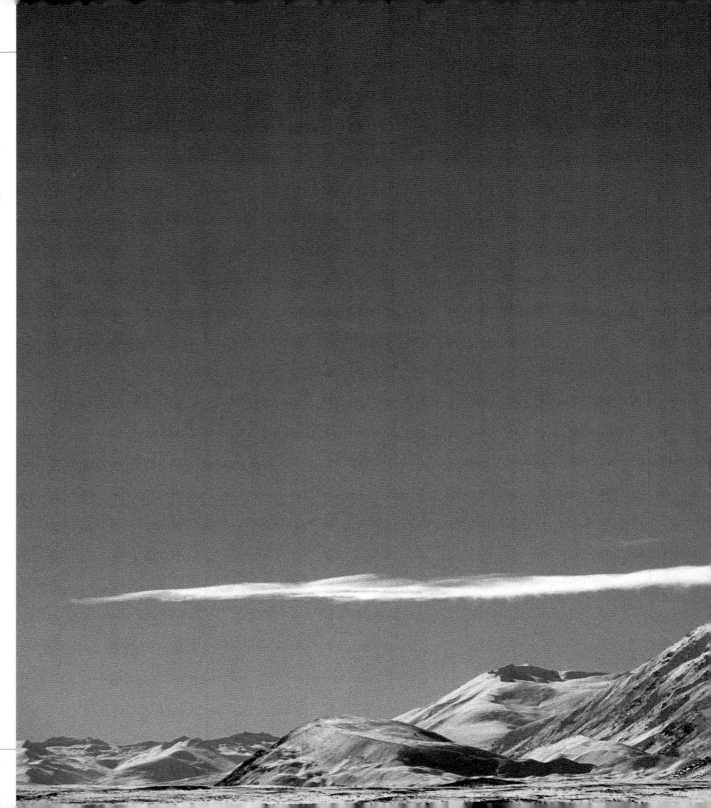

WHEN SHOOTING LANDSCAPES, try pointing the camera high so there is only a narrow strip of land in the bottom of the picture—this helps give a sense of open space. Don't be afraid of exaggerating the difference in proportions in your picture.

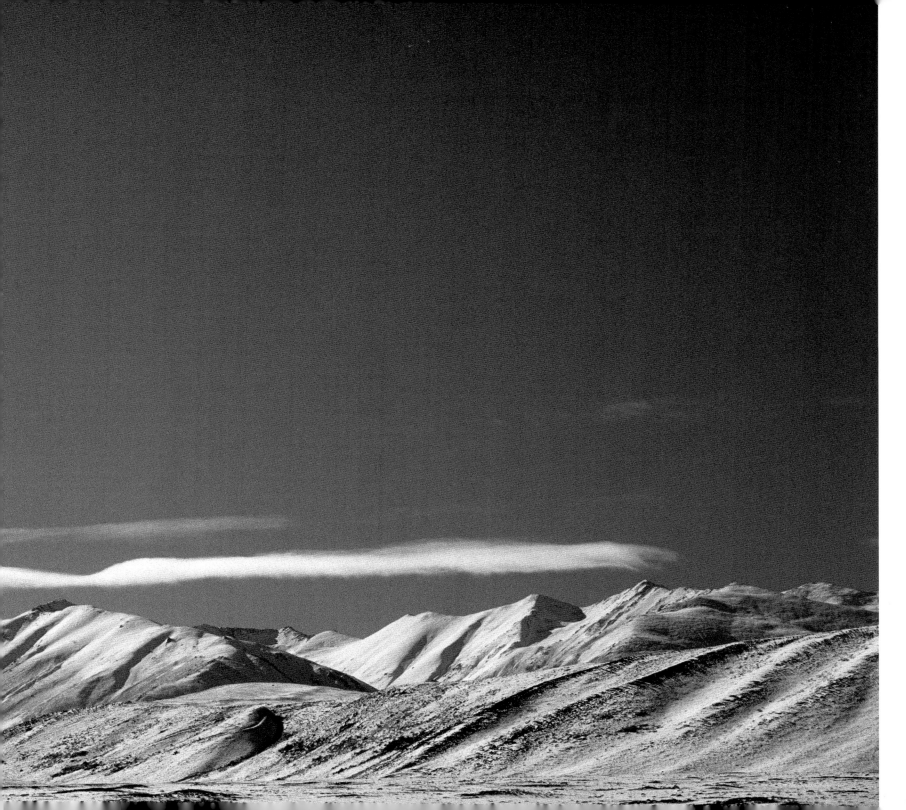

Picture space

Photographs are records of scenes that occupy three-dimensional space. As a photograph—whether it is on paper or on a screen—stretches only over two dimensions, photographers must somehow capture a sense of depth and space for the viewer. The tricks of composition help you to convey a sense of space in your pictures, while choosing your viewpoint carefully can help the viewer to interact with your picture.

"NEGATIVE SPACE" is a photographic term for empty space that contains no subject matter. You can use common examples of negative space, such as sky or water, to help define or give a backdrop to the main subject of your photographs.

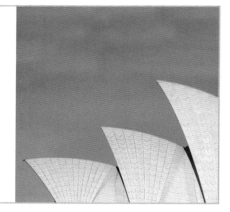

ENCLOSE YOUR MAIN SUBJECT IN A FRAME such as an archway, window, or branches of a tree. In this way you will guide the viewer's eyes toward the main subject. Because your subject is shown to be further away than the frame, this will give an impression of traveling through the picture.

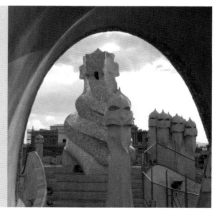

THE EASIEST WAY TO SHOW THAT ONE OBJECT IS CLOSER THAN ANOTHER is to capture it overlapping and partially covering the furthest object. Control of overlap is a powerful way to convey space and describe spatial relationships.

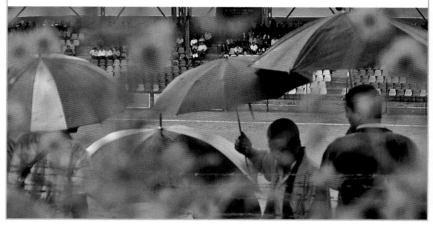

ANOTHER WAY TO SHOW DIFFERENCES IN DISTANCE—and hence the space between subjects—is through differences in focus. Focusing on the main subject in the midground, and throwing the background and foreground out of focus, helps locate the subject.

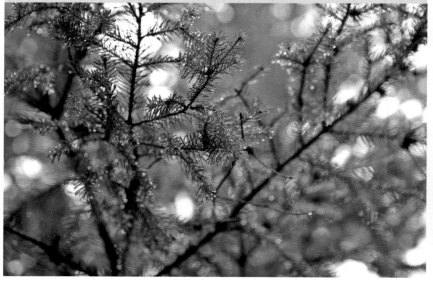

LINES CURVING THROUGH THE IMAGE SPACE lead the viewer's eye on a journey through the picture. This helps give a lively sense of composition, and keeps the viewer's attention.

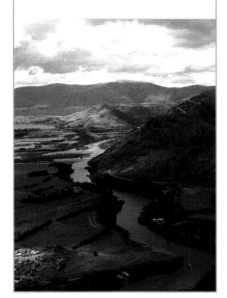

YOU CAN REDUCE THE SENSE OF SPACE between elements in your picture by using the longest focal length setting. This gives a magnified view of a distant part of the scene, which compresses space, making objects appear to be almost touching when, in fact, they are far apart.

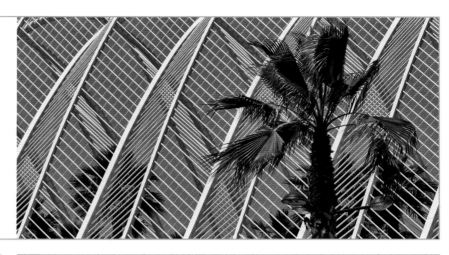

USE RECEDING LINES such as railings, a road, a wall, or a railroad line to lead the eye from the foreground to the background. The convergence of parallel lines gives very strong clues about depth in the picture.

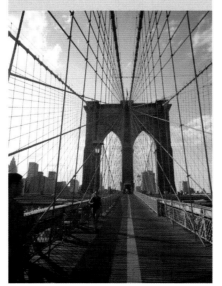

WHEN PHOTOGRAPHING A DISTANT OBJECT, such as a building or structure, one effective trick is to find something very close to you and position yourself so that the nearby object is in frame and out of focus, with the main subject in focus. Creating foreground interest in this way helps exaggerate the sense of space and distance.

WHEN TAKING LANDSCAPE PHOTOGRAPHS YOU CAN EVOKE WIDE-OPEN SPACES and the majesty of the landscape by filling most of the frame with an open sky.

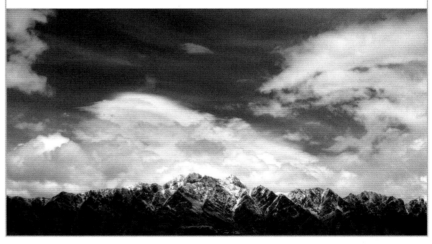

FOR SOME SUBJECTS, SUCH AS BUILDINGS OR MONUMENTS, IT CAN BE USEFUL TO ALLOW SPACE ON ALL SIDES OF THE PHOTOGRAPH to frame your image. Too tight a crop on the subject's outline can make it feel trapped and have an unpleasing effect on the eye. By giving your subject space to breathe you can also add context to your image.

Time tips

Photographers are masters of time: we use and control time at two levels. There is the broader, larger time-scale of days, weeks, and months that determines the seasons of our photography. The low light either side of winter offers soft effects and long shadows, but short days. In contrast the long days of high summer sun give us hard light and high contrasts. Then there is the small-scale time – the fractions of a second that determine whether our images are sharp, or catch the smile or peak of action. Some photographs depend on waiting long hours or even months for the right lighting, but the precise timing is not so vital. Other photographs depend entirely on split-second timing for their success.

THE BEST TIME TO TAKE PHOTOGRAPHS IS WHEN YOU FIRST SEE THE OPPORTUNITY. Many modern digital cameras are so small and light that you can carry them with you everywhere. You can be ready to take photographs at any time, without delay, without having to promise yourself that you will return the next day with your camera.

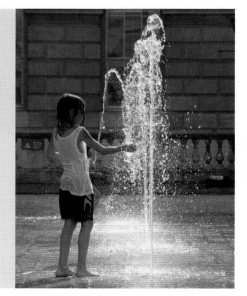

WHEN YOU TAKE ANY PHOTOGRAPH YOU ARE FREEZING A MOMENT IN TIME, but this is particularly evident in action shots. To capture sharp images of moving subjects your exposure should be as short as possible—no longer than $^1/_{250}$ second, but preferably $^1/_{500}$ second for subjects like action sports or moving animals.

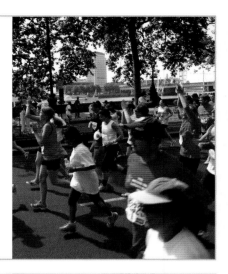

THE BEST TIMES OF DAY FOR TAKING PHOTOGRAPHS OUTSIDE ARE THE "GOLDEN" HOURS just after sunrise and just before sunset. At these times the sunlight is softened by the atmosphere, giving it a warm hue that makes landscapes and buildings glow.

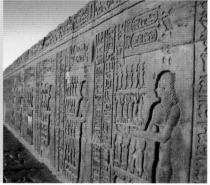

TRY SHOOTING MOVING WATER AT SLOW SHUTTER TIMES. You will find that scenes of waterfalls, mountain streams, or lapping tides are transformed from being frozen and static to being alive and evocative.

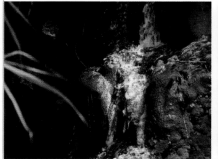
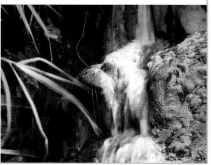

EACH TIME AND SEASON OFFERS ITS OWN KIND OF LIGHT. Work with whatever light is offered to you: whether it is hard or soft, colored or neutral, plentiful or scarce, all light is wonderful.

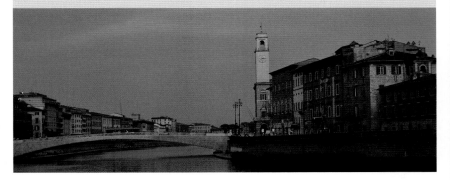

USE THE "BULB" SETTING ON YOUR CAMERA TO ACHIEVE VERY LONG EXPOSURE TIMES. These are particularly effective when taking photographs at night, when over a period of a few minutes you can capture star trails as they move across the sky, forked lightning during storms, or fireworks as they explode one after another.

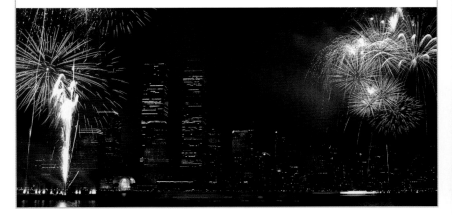

YOUR CAMERA MAY BE SLOW TO RESPOND to being turned on or to the press of the shutter button. You may need to account for any delays by leaving the camera on stand-by rather than turning it off, or by releasing the shutter a little before you want the exposure.

WHEN TRYING TO CAPTURE A MOMENT OR EVENT, your sense of timing is vital. Try to anticipate the action by watching and learning repeated or regular patterns of behavior or occurrences.

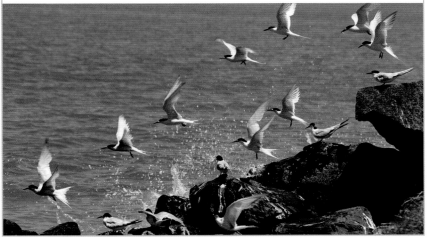

WHEN TAKING PHOTOGRAPHS OF A MOVING SUBJECT, you can capture the sense of movement by choosing a longer shutter time. As the subject moves through the frame its image will blur in the direction of its path. Alternatively, using the same shutter setting, you can pan along with your subject, so that it remains sharp but the background is blurred.

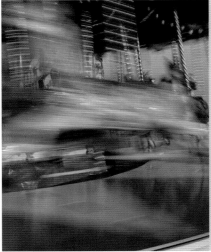
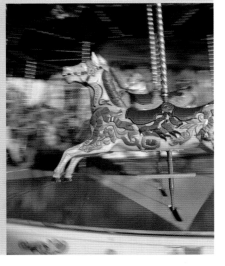

Capturing light

For some people, photography is primarily about capturing light itself, and the subject comes second. In some instances light can turn even the most mundane scene into a visually captivating image. While you may not be able to control the weather, nor position the sun to order, you can wait for the light, or position yourself to make the best of it. Lighting is intimately linked to camera exposure: correct exposure brings out the best in dull lighting but inaccurate exposure can ruin great lighting.

SHAFTS OF LIGHT, such as those cast through a forest canopy, create natural spotlights that you can use to capture subjects with dramatic effect.

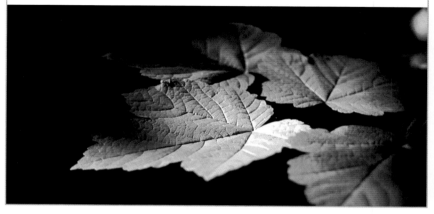

HIGH-CONTRAST LIGHTING— where the difference between light and dark areas is great—can give you striking results, but is tricky to expose for. Shoot lots of frames at different exposure settings to learn which give the best results.

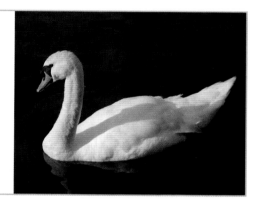

USE STRONG SHADOWS produced by harsh sunlight to create interesting patterns or balance your compositions. You can also use shadows to create an impression of depth or space, and to lead the eye.

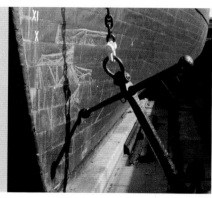

FOR THE MOST INTERESTING LIGHTING, try facing the light and place your subject in between. In these contre-jour ("against the day") situations you can obtain dramatic silhouettes, place the sun in shot for flare effects, and experiment with dramatic, dark skies.

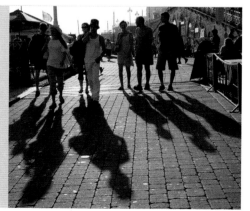

WHEN SHOOTING PORTRAITS, it is very little trouble to ask the subject to move close to a window or out of the direct sun. Soft but directional light gives the most satisfying results in portraiture.

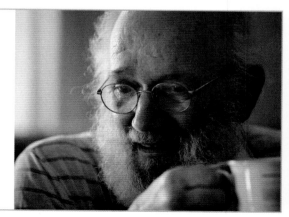

IN VERY BRIGHT CONDITIONS, USE THE FLASH TO REDUCE SHADOWS. Set the fill-in flash or synchro-sun mode (modern point-and-shoot cameras do this automatically) and turn the flash on. This can help reveal details and colors that would have been otherwise hidden.

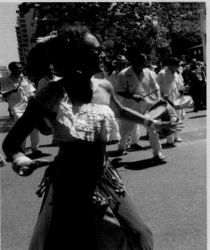
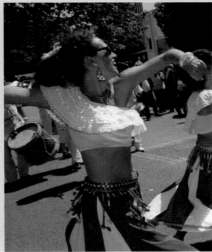

USE YOUR HAND TO CAST A SHADOW OVER YOUR LENS. This reduces the effect of the sun shining into the lens, which causes flare—distracting reflections in the image. This may be necessary as many point-and-shoot cameras do not have effective lens hoods. But make sure your hand does not intrude into wide-angle shots.

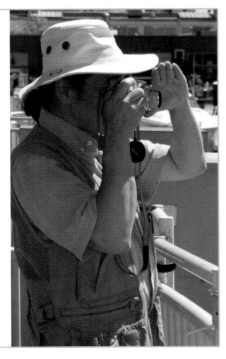

WHEN THE LIGHTING IS TRICKY, and it is important that you have the correct exposure, try different settings to make sure you get the shot. You can take a look at the images after each exposure and delete those that you are not completely happy with.

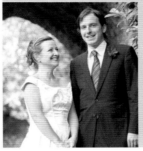
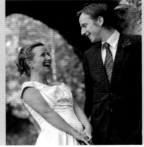
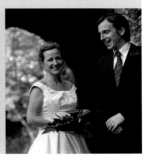

WHEN TAKING CLOSE-UP PHOTOGRAPHS in full sunlight, use a piece of paper to diffuse and soften the light. This helps to deliver rich colors and delicate textures.

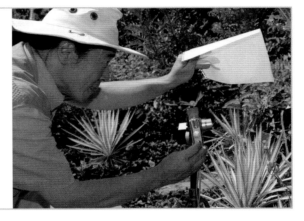

PHOTOGRAPHS CAN BE TAKEN IN THE DULLEST LIGHT. Even if the scene looks unpromising and too dark, shoot anyway. The results may surprise and delight you because the camera can see more colors at night than you can.

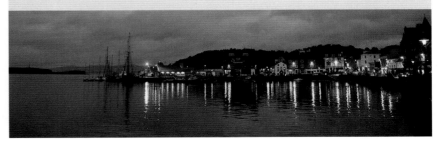

Using color

One of the steps to being able to photograph anything is being able to separate your experience of color from the recording of color in a photograph. This will help you to appreciate that the way in which a camera senses and records colors differs from the way that we see them—a captured image is never quite the same as we perceive it. But, more importantly, your versatility as a photographer improves the more you see color as a subject in itself, not something that is only a feature of your subject.

COLOR CAN BE ONE OF THE STRONGEST COMPOSITIONAL TOOLS IN PHOTOGRAPHY. Try isolating a strong color against a muted background to emphasize the shape of an object or the perspective in a scene. You might also try picking out a small area of color within a sea of contrasting colors and use it as a focal point.

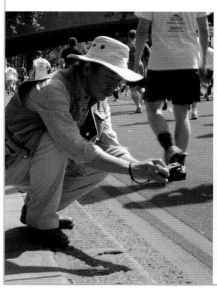 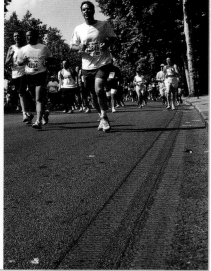

COMPOSE YOUR IMAGE SO THAT THE RANGE OF COLORS IS LIMITED to similar hues—different shades of green, or a variety of warm colors, for example. The colors will compose your image and give it internal harmony.

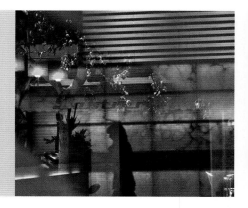

IF YOU PHOTOGRAPH A SCENE CONTAINING A RIOT OF DIFFERENT COLORS, try to organize it so that very strong lines of composition run through it, or try to group the colors together. Alternatively, capture colors against a dull background such as gray or black—this is particularly effective in city scenes.

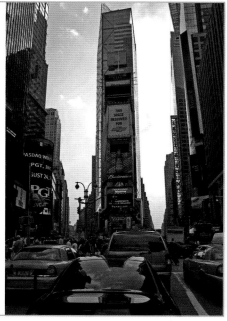

COLORS ARE USUALLY AT THEIR MOST VIVID or saturated in semi-diffused light, such as that on a partially cloudy day. This is because the diffused light prevents strong highlights or glossy surfaces from causing a reduction in color richness.

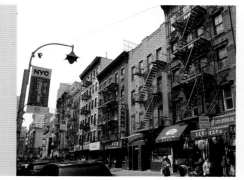

SLIGHT UNDEREXPOSURE CAN IMPROVE COLORS in photographs taken using a digital camera. This applies particularly to light, bold colors such as yellows and reds, which can otherwise appear washed out and faded.

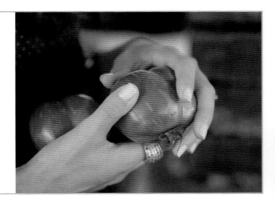

ALTHOUGH YOU CAN CORRECT THE COLOR BALANCE of your photographs using image manipulation software, try to use the white balance setting on your camera to avoid either yellow-orange or bluish hues.

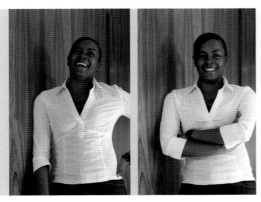

YOU CAN STRENGTHEN COLORS—that is, make them more saturated—using a camera setting. This setting may be called "Enhanced" color. However, some cameras produce strong colors by default, so it is best to experiment with the settings to find the results you like most. If you can get it right "in camera" this will save you having to work on the images on a computer later.

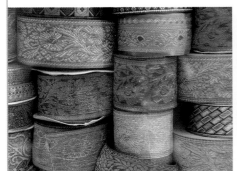
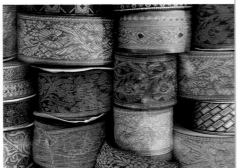

COLORS ARE KEY TO CONVEYING MOOD AND EMOTION. A limited, muted color scheme, such as cool blues and greens, can give an overall feeling of peace and tranquility. Highly contrasting bright colors can give an instant impression of high-energy and excitement.

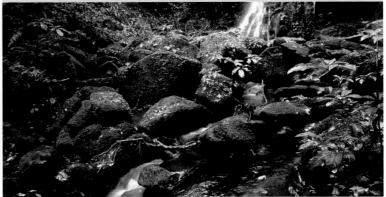

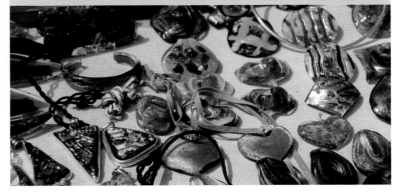

THE JUXTAPOSITION OF PRIMARY COLORS can provide your images with great visual potency. Mix swatches of blue, red, and yellow to produce dramatic images that make a statement.

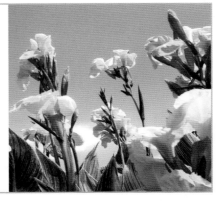

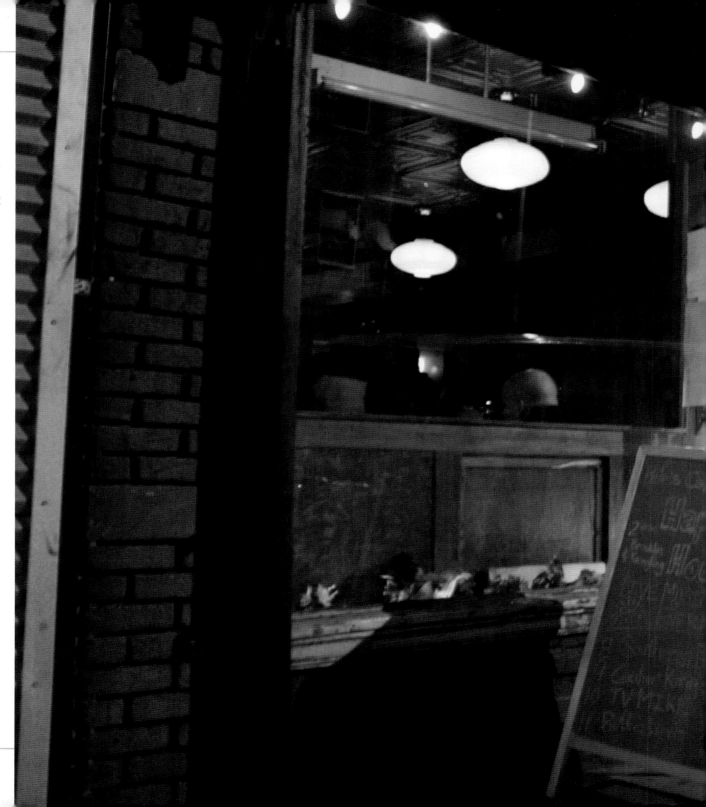

COLORS THAT ARE NOT VISIBLE OR THAT APPEAR WEAK AT NIGHT CAN REGISTER STRONGLY IN AN IMAGE. This is because when our eyes are adapted to night vision they are not able to distinguish colors easily, but neither film nor digital cameras have problems with picking out different colors.

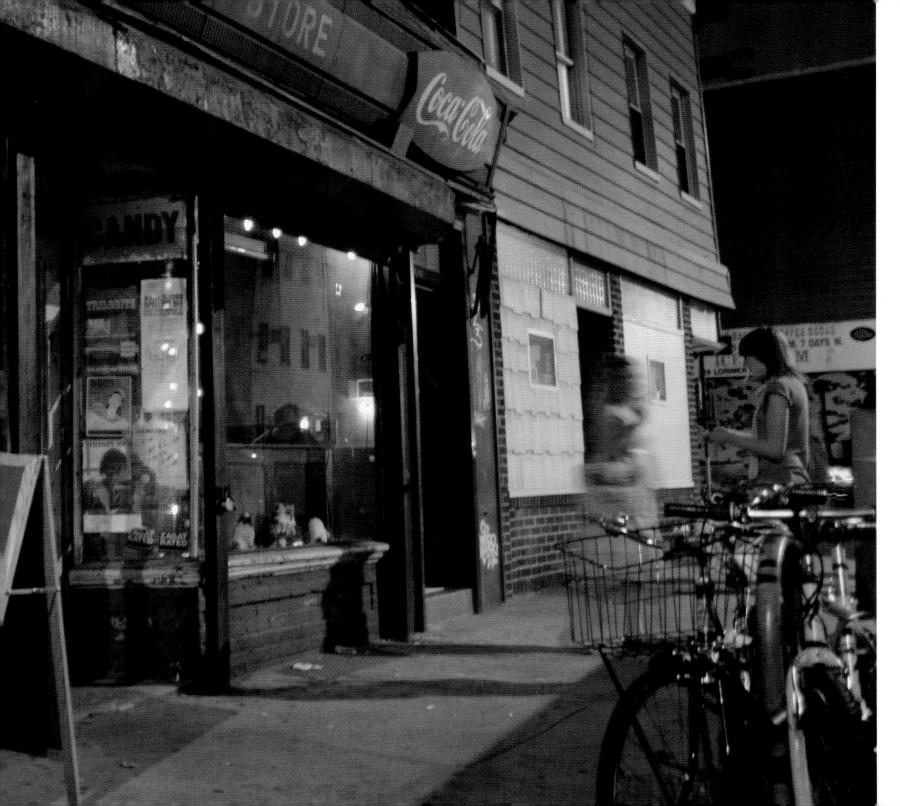

Brightness and Levels

Exposure controls the overall brightness of an image. Ideally you should not need to alter this using image manipulation software as the camera should have got it right in the first place. But the way you want the image to look often does not match what the camera has produced. So you need the Levels adjustment to make the broad changes in overall brightness. The Levels control also enables you to adjust the contrast—how quickly gray changes to white or to black.

IT IS ACCEPTABLE FOR SOME IMAGES TO LOOK VERY DARK OR NEAR BLACK. These include night shots, of course, but also shots that emphasize a focus of light on small areas of an image, such as a face, for example.

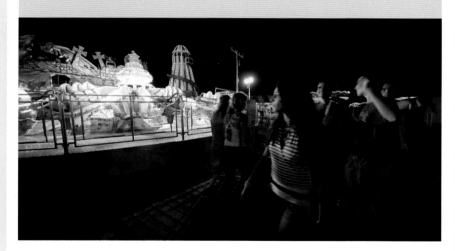

THE AUTO LEVELS COMMAND CAN OFTEN FIX AN IMAGE INSTANTLY, but manual levels adjustments will yield more controlled results.

LEVELS CAN CONTROL THE MID-TONE CONTRAST by changing the relationship between black and white. This either compresses white and black close together to give you high-contrast or spreads them out to give you more gentle tonal transitions.

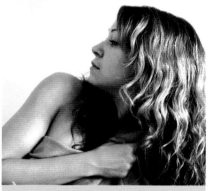

HIGH CONTRAST

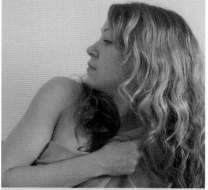

LOW CONTRAST

MANY CAMERAS CAN DISPLAY A HISTOGRAM when pictures are reviewed, and all image manipulation applications show a similar display in the Levels control. It represents what proportion of the picture is at different tonal ranges, which helps you work out what to do with the image. Here, to compensate for any over-exposure you would move the middle slider towards the peak of the histogram.

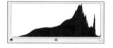

IF THE HISTOGRAM SHOWS MANY INDIVIDUAL NARROW BARS, like the teeth of a broken comb, the image is of poor quality. Further manipulation will not improve it, and it may print with colors markedly different from those on screen (neither your printer nor screen is faulty in this case).

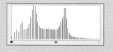

IT IS ACCEPTABLE FOR SOME IMAGES TO LOOK VERY BRIGHT or near white. Pictures such as a bride in her white outfit, white pottery on a white background, or snow scenes, are naturally light and not necessarily over-exposed. However, for very bright images it is always a good idea to experiment with contrast and brightness, to see if you can improve the image.

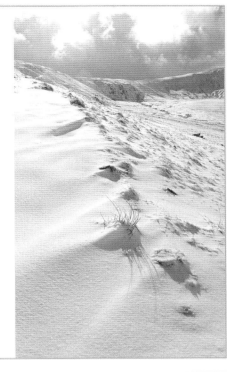

AN UNDER-EXPOSED IMAGE LOOKS DARKER THAN AVERAGE. Shadows will show little detail and highlights may not be bright. Colors may look gray and dark, but colors in bright light may look deep and rich.

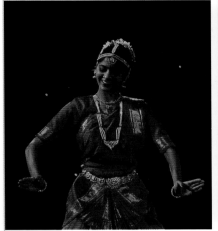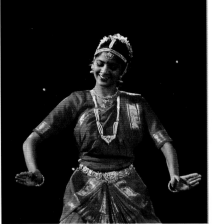

ORIGINAL IMAGE

ADJUSTED IMAGE

AN OVER-EXPOSED IMAGE LOOKS BRIGHTER THAN AVERAGE. Shadows will show a lot of detail but bright parts of the image will look bleached out, offering weak colors. Note that after adjustment, the white areas still look too bright.

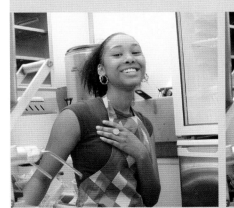

ORIGINAL IMAGE

ADJUSTED IMAGE

ADJUST THE BLACKS SO THAT THEY LOOK BLACK. This ensures that you have nicely solid shadow densities when you print out the image. Lack of good blacks makes a print look washed-out.

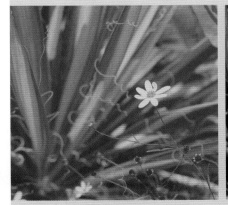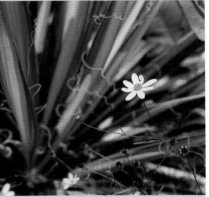

ORIGINAL IMAGE

ADJUSTED IMAGE

Color balance and saturation

Balancing colors is important as it helps ensure that the colors in your image are true to life. The key is to ensure that colors which everyone can recognize are accurate. Of these, the most important is skin color: any visible variation from what is expected will make the whole image look wrong. The other key colors are the so-called "achromats": white, black, and gray. As the name suggests, these tones should be without color or tint for color reproduction to be accurate.

MODERN COMPUTER MONITORS ARE FAIRLY ACCURATE AT REPRODUCING COLORS, but if you find that the prints from your printer are very different from the image as seen on your monitor you will need to use the monitor control panel or system preferences in your computer's operating system to calibrate the screen.

SKIN TONES, IF PRESENT, ARE THE KEY TO COLOR BALANCE. If skin appears too cold or too warm you can be sure the rest of the image is unbalanced. Adjust the balance control in your software until skin appears natural.

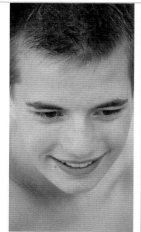
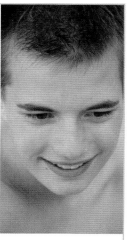

ORIGINAL IMAGE   ADJUSTED IMAGE

DECREASING SATURATION BRINGS COLORS CLOSER TO SHADES OF GRAY, BLACK, AND WHITE. Reducing color saturation completely leaves you with a black-and-white, or monochrome, picture.

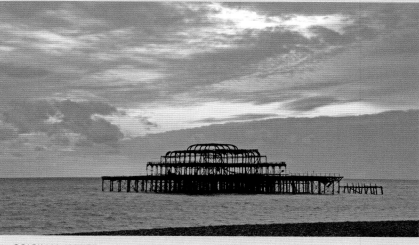

ORIGINAL IMAGE

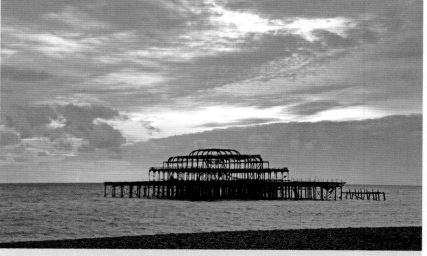

ADJUSTED IMAGE

THE EASIEST WAY TO ADJUST COLOR BALANCE IS TO USE THE VARIATIONS COMMAND. This shows, at a glance, the effect of different settings. All you have to do is click on the one that looks most natural or closest to the colors as you remember them.

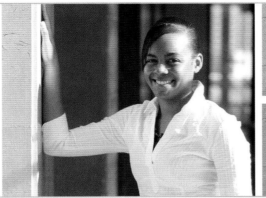 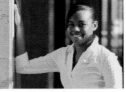 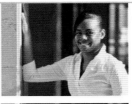 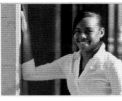 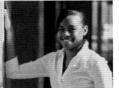 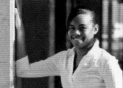 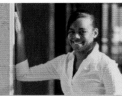

COLORS OR HUES CAN BE DELIBERATELY DISTORTED to give a strongly graphic effect. All colors are distorted by the same degree, so, for example, blues become greens and reds turn mauve.

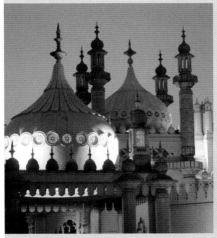 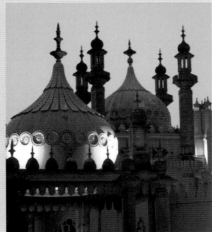

ORIGINAL IMAGE   ADJUSTED IMAGE

TRY TO SET THE CAMERA UP SO THAT YOU HAVE TO DO AS LITTLE COLOR ADJUSTMENT AS POSSIBLE AFTER MAKING THE EXPOSURE. Many digital cameras allow you to adjust color richness, as well as the contrast and sharpness that is applied to the image when it is saved on the memory card. Use these features to optimize your pictures for viewing or printing to save time and effort.

COLORS LOOK MORE LIVELY AND PUNCHY when you increase their saturation. However, colors that are too highly saturated may look brilliant on a monitor screen but cannot be printed accurately. Prints on paper may appear pale because some printers cannot reproduce the brightest colors.

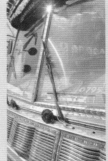 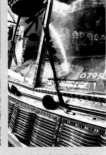

ORIGINAL IMAGE   OVERSATURATED

YOU CAN REMOVE COLOR FROM PICTURES BY USING THE SATURATION (OR SPONGE) TOOL TO DESATURATE—that is to reduce the strength of color. This is effective at reducing the impact of a busy or colorful background that distracts from the main subject.

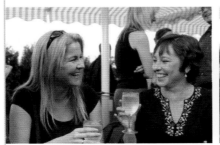 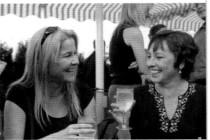

ORIGINAL IMAGE   ADJUSTED IMAGE

Contrast and tone

Contrast is the relationship between the middle grays and the whites and blacks—how the middle tones relate to the lightest and darkest tones in a picture. Contrast is largely the product of the lighting at the time you make the exposure, but it is also something that is easily altered on a computer, using image manipulation software. The careful adjustment of contrast and its suitability for the subject is a hallmark of fine photography.

HIGH-CONTRAST IMAGES SHOW AREAS OF DEEP SHADOWS and areas of bright white, with sharp transitions in-between. These images exhibit hard lighting, such as when directly lit by bright sun.

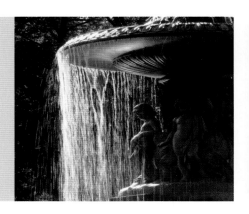

MOST PICTURE-EDITING SOFTWARE PROGRAMS have a contrast menu option with a slider for adjusting the contrast. However, you can alter the contrast and tone with more control by adjusting the Levels settings.

SOFTEN THE CONTRAST of images shot on brilliantly sunny days to bring back details into the brighter mid-tones and lighter shadows. This will make the printed image look more natural.

IMAGES WITH NORMAL CONTRAST show mostly middle-tones—grays about half-way between white and black—with some bright white tones plus some deep black, and with transitional tones in between.

LOW-CONTRAST IMAGES show large areas of middle or gray tones, with little that is either very dark or very bright—the look of a foggy day, for example. These images are said to be flat.

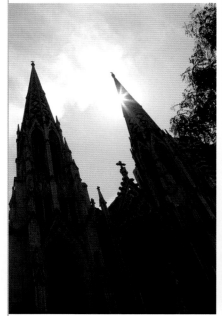

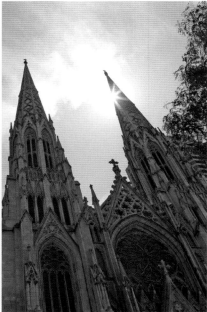

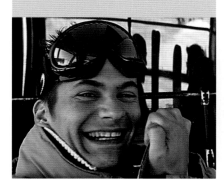

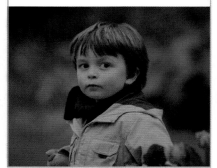

ORIGINAL IMAGE

ADJUSTED IMAGE

INCREASE THE CONTRAST IN BLACK-AND-WHITE IMAGES to produce a stronger, more graphic picture. If the original is in color, first convert it to black and white. Then increase the contrast until you achieve the desired effect. This technique works well with silhouettes with clear outlines, and with objects with geometrical shapes or strong patterns.

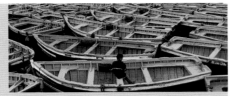

ORIGINAL IMAGE

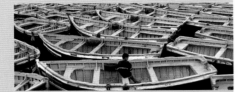

BLACK-AND-WHITE IMAGE

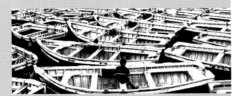

ADJUSTED IMAGE

INCREASE THE CONTRAST IN IMAGES SHOT IN DULL OR OVERCAST CONDITIONS to restore tonal depth and richness. You will find that, as well as making colors bolder and brighter, this will increase definition and bring out details in your subject.

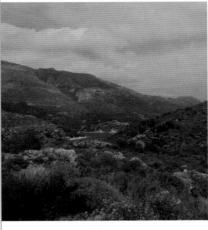

ORIGINAL IMAGE   ADJUSTED IMAGE

IF YOU INCREASE THE BRIGHTNESS OF AN IMAGE, you alter the relationship between grays, blacks, and whites, so a compensation in contrast may also be necessary. Look at each image on its own merits, and adjust the brightness and contrast until you are happy with the result.

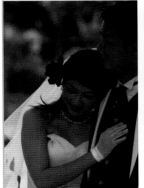
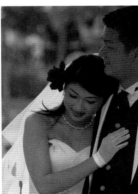
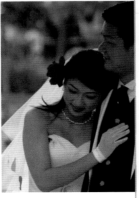

ORIGINAL IMAGE   BRIGHTER IMAGE   ADJUSTED IMAGE

AN IMAGE THAT IS HIGH IN CONTRAST, will appear to be sharper than one that is lower in contrast. This is because the margin between a white and a black area is seen as an edge, so the more marked the difference, the sharper the edge appears to be.

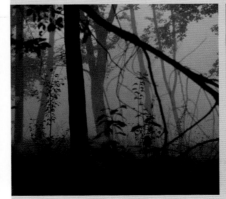
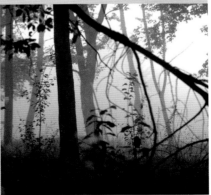

ORIGINAL IMAGE   ADJUSTED IMAGE

Removing distractions and sharpening

The best way to deal with distractions in your pictures is, of course, to avoid them in the first place. Care taken when you position yourself and point the camera to compose a picture will save you much effort later. But image manipulation software usually offers powerful tools for removing unwanted objects or unsightly elements. Once you have removed distractions, you may wish to sharpen the image, as this can help improve the appearance of your photograph, even if you have focused it correctly.

A STANDARD FEATURE IN MOST IMAGE MANIPULATION SOFTWARE IS A CLONE OR CLONE STAMP TOOL. This is one of the best ways of removing unwanted elements or distractions from your images. It works by copying or sampling one part of an image and pasting it onto another. For example, you can place a sample of sky onto tree branches or electricity pylons to make them disappear.

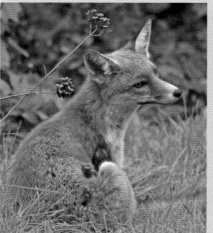

ORIGINAL IMAGE   ADJUSTED IMAGE

INSTEAD OF SPENDING TIME REMOVING DISTRACTIONS, try blurring them (using a blurring or smudge tool) in order to make them less sharply delineated and obvious. This is effective because the eye favors objects with sharp contours or edges. To blur a section of an image, first you will need to select it using one of the selection tools.

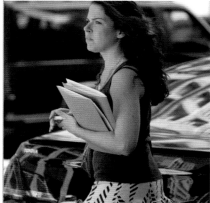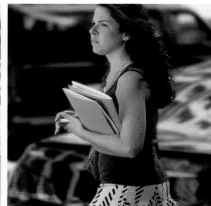

ORIGINAL IMAGE   ADJUSTED IMAGE

ANOTHER KIND OF DISTRACTION IS NOISE, which is a by-product of setting very high sensitivities (high ISO ratings such as 800 or greater). It gives a grainy look to the image. Many image manipulation software packages contain filters that can remove noise from an image, including dust and scratches.

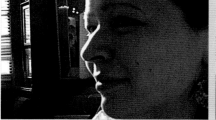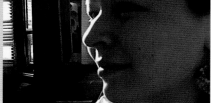

ORIGINAL IMAGE   ADJUSTED IMAGE

IF YOUR IMAGE IS A LITTLE SOFT OR BLURRED, USE A SHARPEN FILTER TO INCREASE THE SHARPNESS OF YOUR IMAGES. You can sharpen the image by as much or as little as you like by adjusting filter settings.

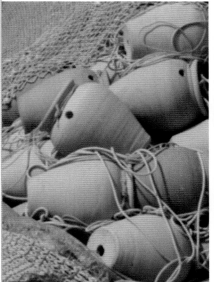

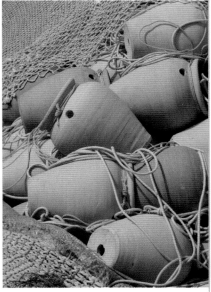

ORIGINAL IMAGE

ADJUSTED IMAGE

WHEN SHARPENING AN IMAGE FOR PRINTING, it should look slightly over-sharpened on the screen, so that artifacts such as exaggerated borders are only just visible at full size (viewing at 100 percent). For on-screen use, for example, in websites, sharpen your images only until they look right on screen.

INCREASING THE CONTRAST OF AN IMAGE GIVES AN IMPRESSION OF INCREASED SHARPNESS. Ensure that the image is at the correct contrast before using a filter to increase sharpness.

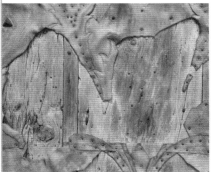

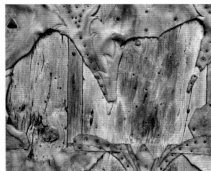

ORIGINAL IMAGE

ADJUSTED IMAGE

IF YOUR CLONING PRODUCES AN UNNATURALLY SMOOTH-LOOKING AREA, you may need to introduce some noise to make it look more natural. Select the area to be worked on and apply the noise filter. Alternatively try changing the settings on the clone tool such as the hardness of the brush edge and also the opacity—how strongly the clone is applied to the image.

GENERALLY, SHARPENING SHOULD BE THE VERY LAST FILTER YOU APPLY—following other manipulations such as cropping, resizing, and adjusting levels—because of its very strong effects on image data. After applying the sharpening, check the image at 100 percent magnification for any defects which the sharpening may have revealed.

USE SHARPENING FILTERS SPARINGLY. These filters sharpen pictures in a magical way, and reduce the effect of mild blur, but too much of a good thing can cause artifacts, such as contrasting haloes and exaggerated borders, to appear around your subject. It can also exaggerate noise, making the image look as if it is composed of rounded grains of sand.

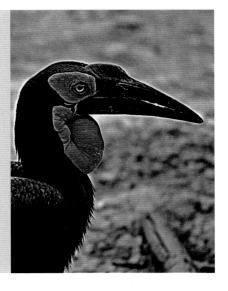

Cropping and resizing

One of the most basic things you do with a digital image is ensure that it is the size you need it to be. Changing the size of an image does not alter its appearance, but can make it easier to send over the internet, or to ensure that it comes out the right size for the printing paper you use. You will also need to crop the image a little if you need to straighten out horizons that are not quite level.

CROPPING REDUCES THE SIZE OF AN IMAGE, and throws away information, so severe crops should be reserved for large images. When you crop an image and then try to view it at the same size as it was before it was cropped you will notice that the pixels are larger.

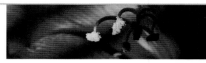

ORIGINAL IMAGE

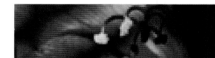

ADJUSTED IMAGE

THE FIRST THING TO DO WITH YOUR IMAGE BEFORE YOU WORK ON IT IS TO MAKE A COPY. Duplicating your image before you make any changes prevents you from accidentally saving any changes onto the original file and closing it, which loses the original forever.

CROPPING IS AN EFFECTIVE AND SIMPLE WAY TO ENLARGE PART OF AN IMAGE. In this way you can focus attention on the main subject if there is too much space around the edges.

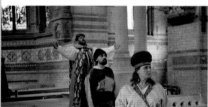
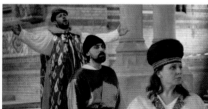

ORIGINAL IMAGE   ADJUSTED IMAGE

YOU CAN CROP AN IMAGE TO REDUCE FILE SIZE, particularly if you are sure you do not need the elements you are removing. Even removing a narrow margin from a large image can offer a significant saving in file size.

CROPPING AND STRAIGHTENING CAN CORRECT TITLED HORIZONS. Draw a narrow crop near the horizon and rotate the crop so that it lines up with the horizon. Then extend the corners of the crop to the edge of the picture – two of the corners will meet the picture edge, but the opposite corners will be inside the picture. When you crop, the picture will be rotated correctly.

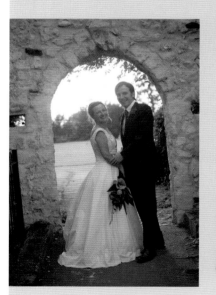
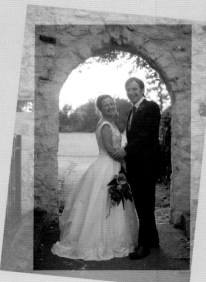

ORIGINAL IMAGE   ADJUSTED IMAGE

TO MAINTAIN THE ORIGINAL PICTURE'S SIZE RATIO, choose the crop tool, click and drag over the whole image (as if you want to crop the entire image), then hold down shift key and drag the crop box to the desired size. (This trick works for most image manipulation programs.)

CROP OUT DISTRACTING ELEMENTS or anything that doesn't add to the image, such as dominant colors, as the eye is drawn to bright objects first.

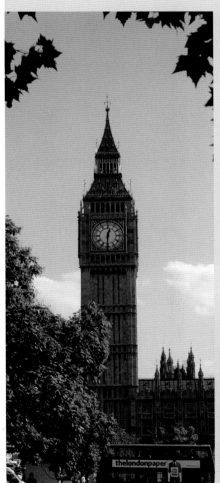
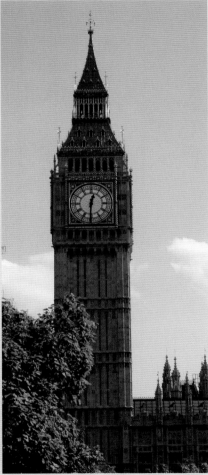

ORIGINAL IMAGE   ADJUSTED IMAGE

IF YOU CHANGE THE SHAPE OF YOUR IMAGE expect large borders—especially if you're having your pictures printed at an outlet—as these generally print only in standard shapes and sizes.

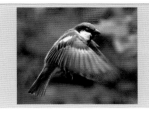

ADJUSTED IMAGE

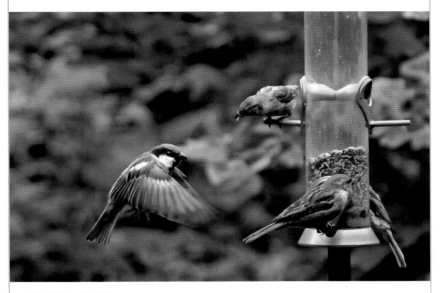

ORIGINAL IMAGE

RESIZE THE IMAGE TO SUIT THE TASK. If you want to share images, either on the internet or by email, they seldom need to be more than 500 pixels wide, and at most 1280 pixels wide. This will give you very high quality for viewing on monitors. If you wish to make prints, you need to ensure that two settings are correct. Firstly, make sure that you have enough pixels for the size: a rule of thumb is to have around 300 pixels for every 1 inch of print. For example, a 5 x 4in (12 x 10cm) print needs an image measuring about 1500 x 1200 pixels – well within the capacity of all modern digital cameras. The other measure you need is the output size. This should be the size of print that you want, and it should fit the paper that you're using. Check this measurement in the image software.

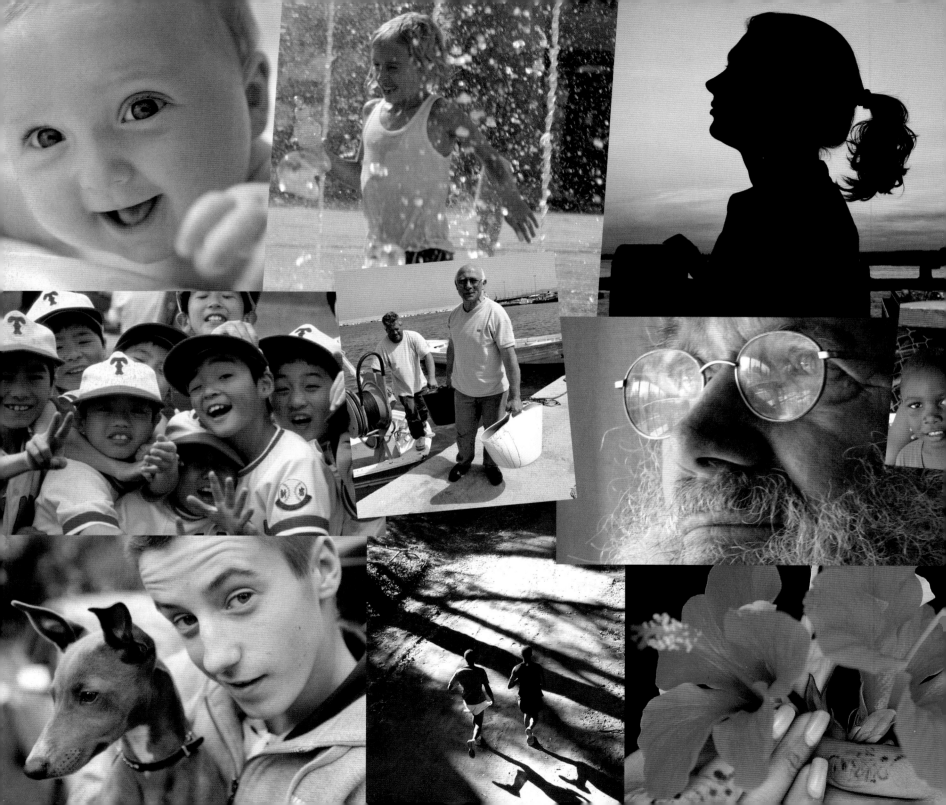

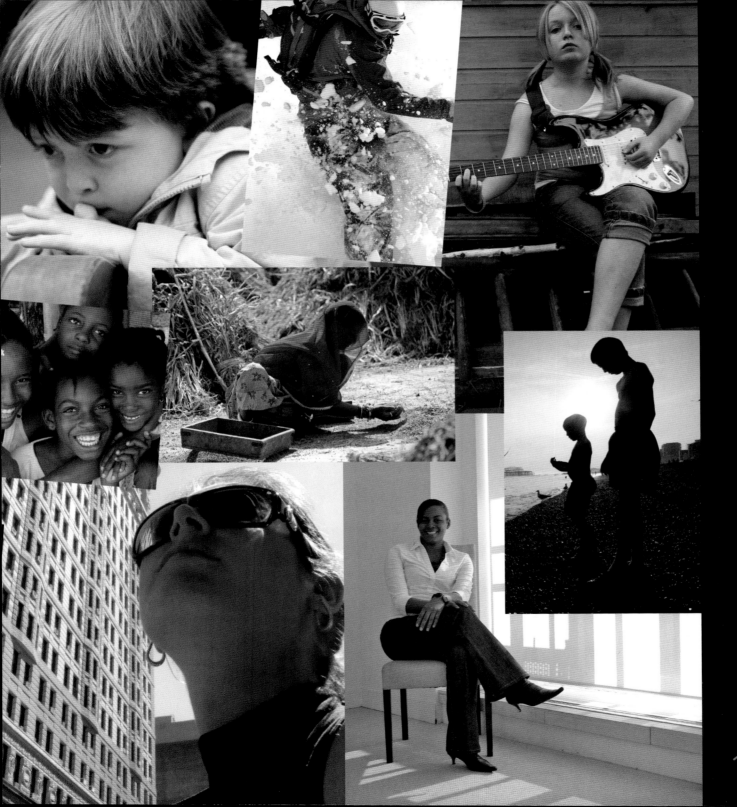

People

12345678

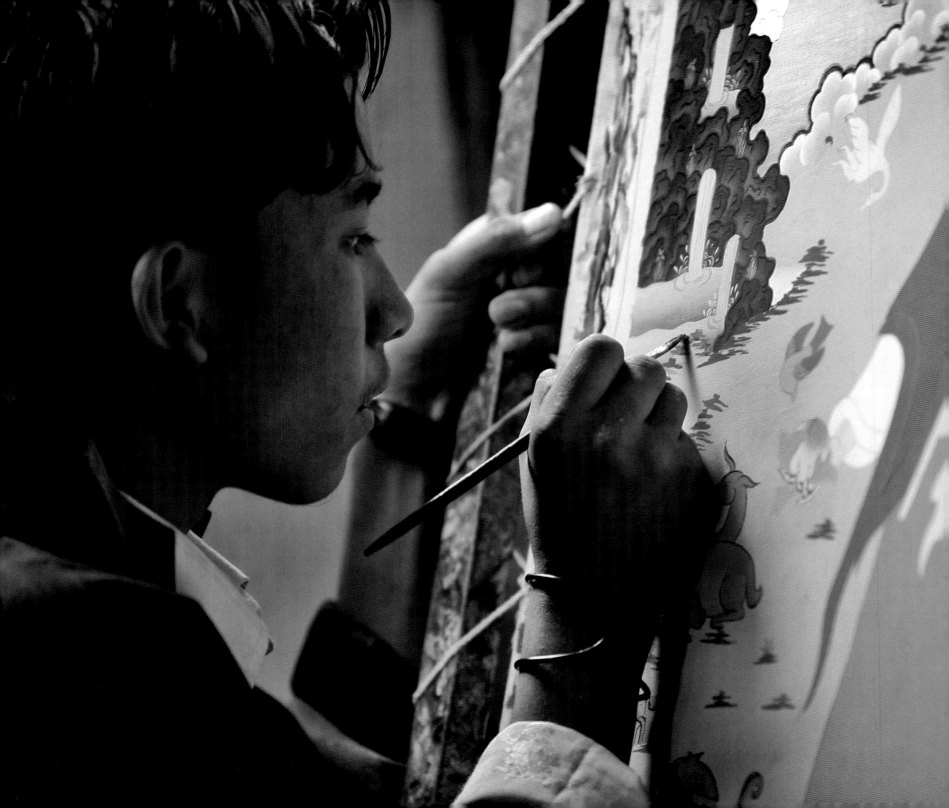

People are the most rewarding and richest—and by far the most popular—subjects for photography. Perhaps because they mean so much on a personal level, when pictures of people disappoint, the impact is usually greater than with other subjects. This chapter shows you how to utilize the basic elements of photography to make satisfying, sensitive, and engaging pictures of people. You will work with light and exposure, use composition and zoom settings, choose backgrounds, and learn how to relax and pose your subject. You will also discover the different approaches for photographing children and older people, and for formal portraits and candid shots.

Portraits on sunny days

The natural home for the portrait is a photographer's studio, but outdoor spaces offer unlimited light and lots of space. This location, a Spanish town square, offered a variety of backgrounds—from old doors, to distant walls. And the lighting varied from hard, full sunlight, to the softest light in the shadows of buildings. The color of the light varied, too—from bluish shaded light, to a warm light reflected from the stonework.

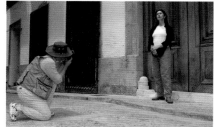
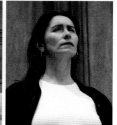

Photographing from below eye level can make for a dramatic shot, but it is often unflattering to the subject. This perspective tends to be best reserved for cinematic portraits – to show strong character traits, for example.

1 EXPLORE THE LIGHTING

Soft light is usually – but not always – best for portraiture because it is kindest to facial features. Bright sunlight can lead to too much shadow on the face.

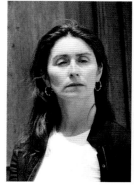
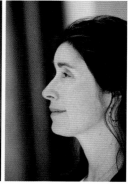

2 VARY BACKGROUNDS

As you search for the best light for your shot, experiment with different backgrounds, too. A busy background can be interesting or distracting; a plain one may be neutral but dull. By trying both, you will learn which work best.

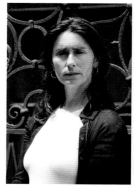
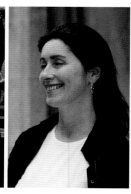

3 CONSIDER THE FORMAT

Decide how much of the subject you want to show. Full-length shots put more emphasis on the clothes and allow the person to express their character through their pose. Closer views naturally emphasize more of the face and its expression.

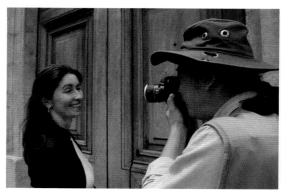
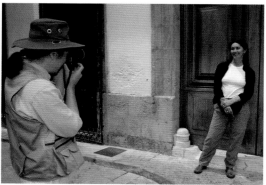

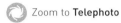

FOR THIS SHOT

I set the zoom to a long focal length. The background offered colors that contrasted with skin tones, which were warmed by light reflected from a stone wall. I used a low ISO setting for the best image quality.

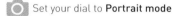

CAMERA MODE

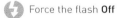 Set your dial to **Portrait mode**

LENS SETTING

Zoom to **Telephoto**

SENSOR/FILM SPEED

Use a **Low** ISO setting

FLASH

Force the flash **Off**

4 SHOOT A VARIETY OF POSES

Encourage your subject to move naturally, as if in conversation. Keep shooting all the time to ensure that you capture the nuances of expression.

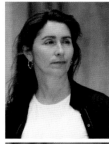
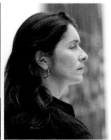
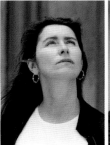
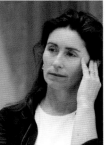

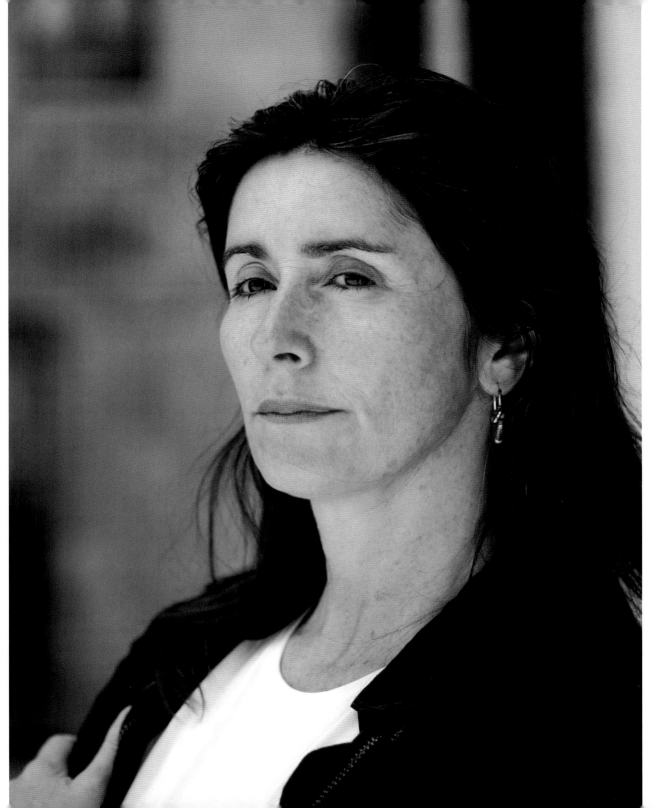

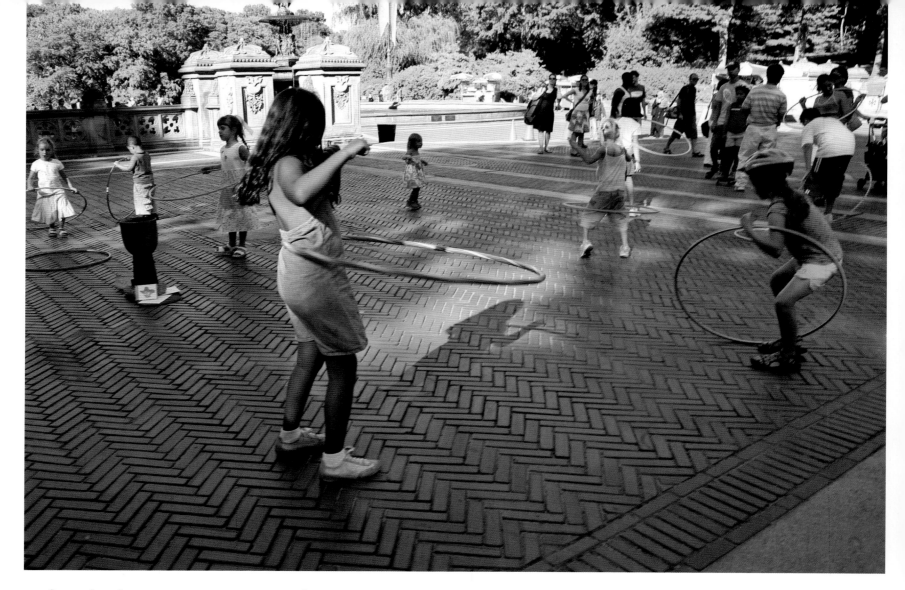

Children at play

Unstructured activities, such as children getting together to play in a city park, offer the chance to capture beautiful, and sometimes amusing, moments. However, the window of opportunity is usually small: there is an early stage when the activity grows as more and more people take part; then the interest peaks before tailing off. At the right moment, light and motion come together to create interesting compositions. Here, one girl had just worked her way into the light.

FOR THIS SHOT

The wide-angle setting was the natural choice, but a normal setting can also be very effective, since it concentrates the view more. I achieved a short shutter time and maximum depth of field with a high sensitivity setting.

CAMERA MODE

Set your dial to **Sports mode**

LENS SETTING

Zoom to **Wide Angle**

SENSOR/FILM SPEED

Use a **High** or **Medium** ISO setting

FLASH

Force the flash **Off**

USE LIGHT AND SHADE

Depending on the time of day and location, there may be patterns of light and shade falling on the scene. This interplay can make it hard to balance exposures between bright and dark, but it also brings some structure to the composition.

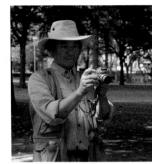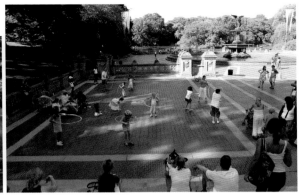

SET YOUR CAMERA

In order to freeze rapid movement, you should set a high ISO. Do this despite the bright natural light. A wide-angle setting and large aperture will help to keep shutter times short.

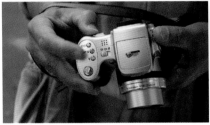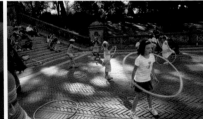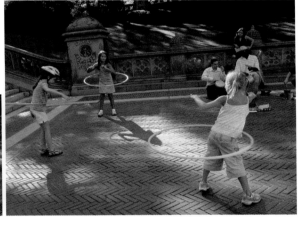

CONSIDER COMPOSITION

Bring your composition to life by selecting a group of characters. From within that group, you can then single out a main character. In this case, this little girl had begun to distinguish herself with her hula-hoop skills.

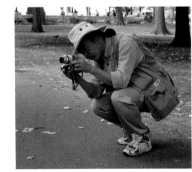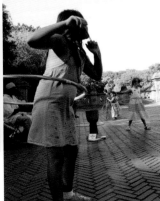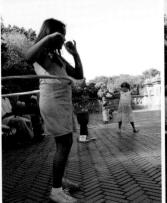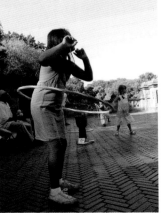

People in action

Action photography is an area in which photography excels above any other art. The camera's ability to freeze dynamic movement and then open it to the most detailed scrutiny is unsurpassed by even video recording. These days, some consumer cameras offer shutter times as short as $1/4{,}000$ of a second, bringing action photography within easy reach of anyone.

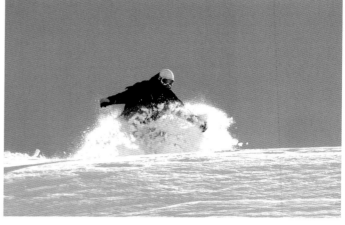

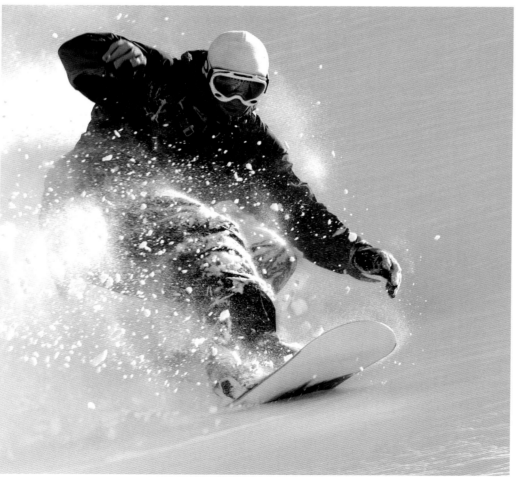

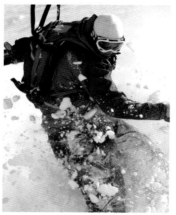

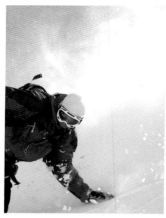

RAPID SHOOTING

Some action sequences—such as a snowboarder hurtling down a slope—start and end so rapidly that there is hardly any time to respond at all. The best you can do is to start photographing before the action begins and keep shooting until it is all over.

1 If you can't see the subject approaching, ask someone to act as lookout.

2 If you can, set your camera to continuous exposure, and servo, or follow, auto-focus.

3 Some cameras permit the use of faster memory cards for action shots. Utilize this option if you are able.

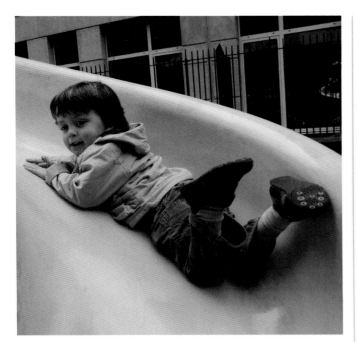

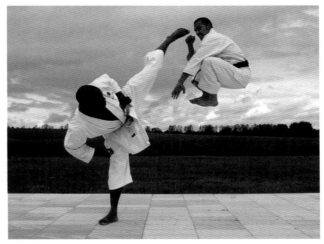

Martial arts such as karate, and kickboxing are highly photogenic subjects. If possible, shoot outdoors to provide a more interesting background other than a gym.

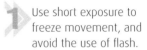 Use short exposure to freeze movement, and avoid the use of flash.

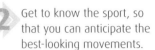 Get to know the sport, so that you can anticipate the best-looking movements.

PANNING WITH THE ACTION

If rapid action takes place in low-light conditions, you can still make a good attempt at recording it. The trick is to follow the movement during the course of a long exposure to keep at least part of the subject sharp.

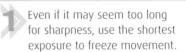 Even if it may seem too long for sharpness, use the shortest exposure to freeze movement.

For best results using flash, select the "second-curtain flash" mode, if it is available on your camera.

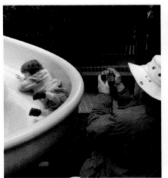

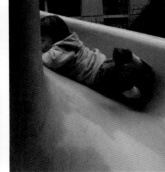

PLANNING AND TIMING

Even the shyest of children will lose their inhibitions about being photographed if they are busy amusing themselves, playing with other children, or engaged in a fun activity, such as coming down a slide.

Position yourself so you can focus on a spot and wait for the child's arrival.

Press the shutter button as soon as the child comes into view.

Be patient: it might take a few shots to get right, but the child is sure to oblige.

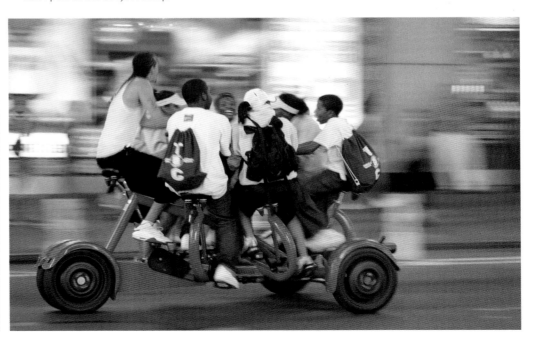

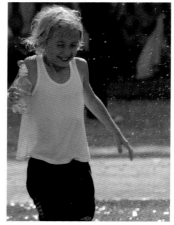
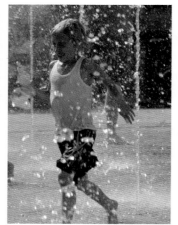
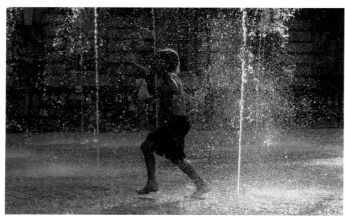

WATER AND LIGHT

Children love to splash around in water, and this scene at a public fountain was a delight to photograph. If you concentrate on only one or two children, it is best that they are your own. Otherwise, ask the parents' permission.

1 Position yourself so that you face the sun; this will bring out the sparkle of the water.

2 Set a long zoom and sports or action mode to freeze movement.

3 Use fill-in flash if the sun's brilliance is causing harsh shadows.

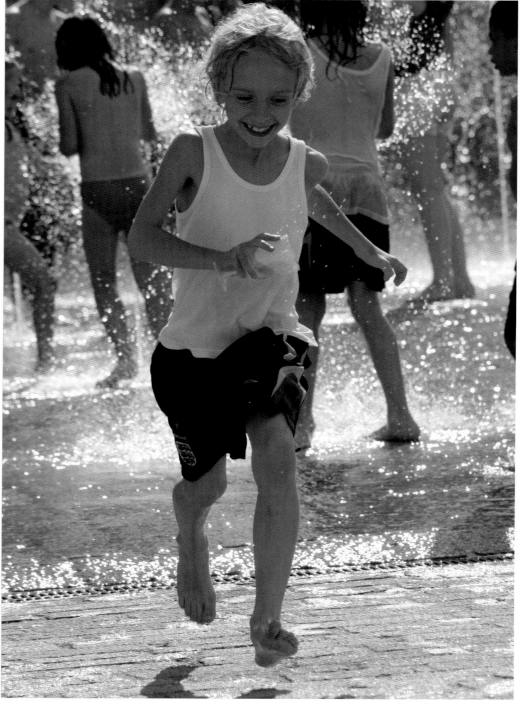

AVOIDING BLUR

Freezing rapid movement, like the swish of a skipping rope, can be a challenge. Keep trying until you get it.

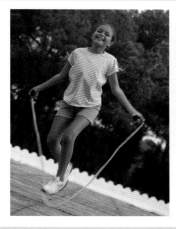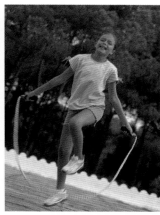

1. Try tilting the camera to one side for an unusual framing of the subject.

2. Use a short exposure to avoid movement blur, and turn off the flash to preserve the scene's natural light.

TELLING SHADOWS

A shot showing the shadow of an action rather than the action itself may be more telling than a direct picture. Set to action mode and use short exposures to capture movement.

1. Frame your composition so that there is enough space for the action to move into.

2. Try unusual viewpoints— high up and low down, for example.

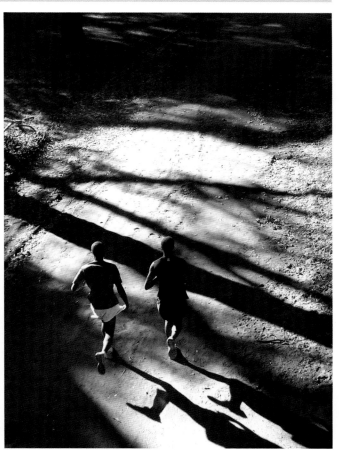

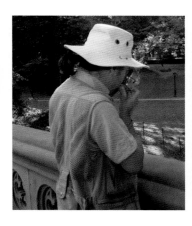

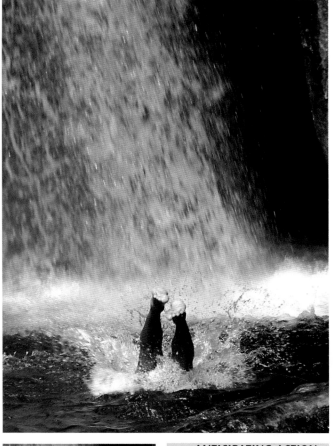

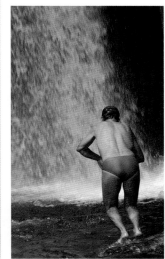

ANTICIPATING ACTION

Being able to anticipate movement and behavior is the key to capturing pictures of people in action.

1. Listen and watch: there may be only small clues to what is about to happen.

2. If possible use the serial-exposure, or motor-drive, mode to shoot several pictures in a short time.

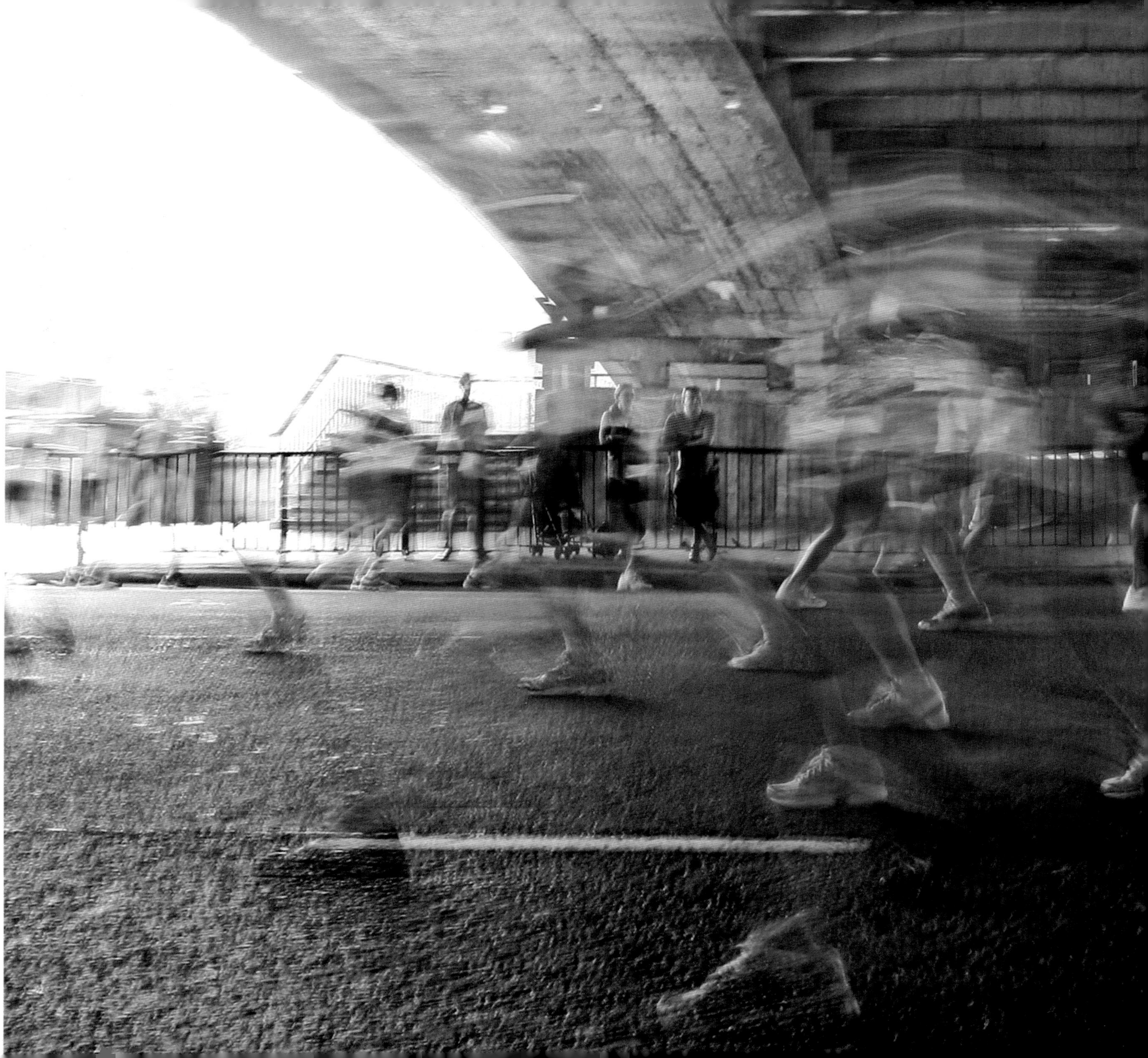

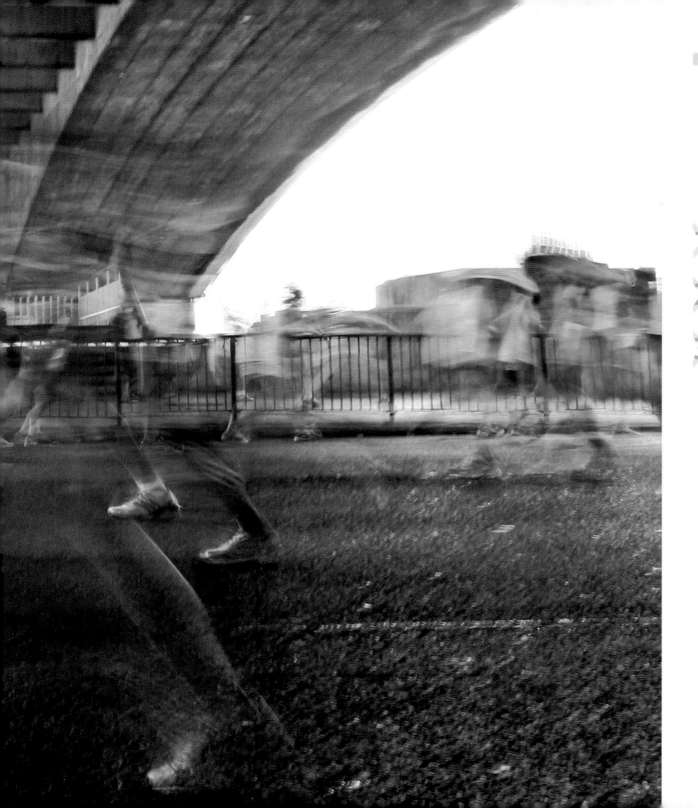

RUNNERS IN MOTION

You can push movement blur to convey the pace of people in motion. Setting a longer-than-normal exposure reduced these runners to a mere blur. However, the feet, which were momentarily on the ground during exposure, are much more defined.

1 Choose a position that offers strong composition potential: in this case, under a bridge.

2 For this shot, I set a shutter time of 1/3 second, an aperture of f/16, and a wide zoom.

3 Take several shots with various shutter settings, and review your pictures to decide which works best.

Vacation highlight

For many, the most important vacation picture is the one that says, "I was there," positioned in front of a famous landmark or view. It may not matter that it is not a great photograph, so long as the record is made. However, it is more satisfying to create a picture that stands on its own merits. One approach is to combine the landmark in a visually organic way with your subject. You can do this through pose, viewpoint, or perspective.

 BE CREATIVE
Popular locations attract many people, all looking for the perfect shot. If the landmark is in the center of the town, the issue is further compounded by passing traffic. If you don't wish to include the crowds in your shot, you need to find creative solutions.

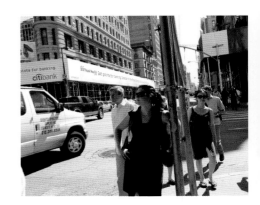

 ZOOM IN
To eliminate the crowds, you can try zooming in close to your subject, throwing the background out of focus. However, this technique has an obvious drawback: you lose the sense of location.

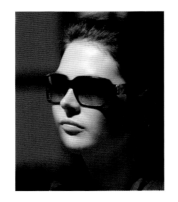

 LOSE THE FOREGROUND
The usual way to remove surrounding crowds from the composition is to point the camera upward, crouching close to your subject. However, you will need to look out for other elements entering the picture, such as street furniture or overhanging foliage.

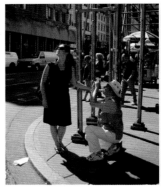 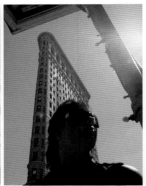

 AVOID DIRECT SUNLIGHT
Another problem with shooting upward arises if the sun is behind the subject. From the camera's point of view, the subject's face will be in shadow. Setting the exposure for the girl would leave the building too bright, while exposing for the building would produce a silhouette-like effect on her. Fill-in flash would leave her face unnaturally bright. This issue can be overcome by having her lift her face upward.

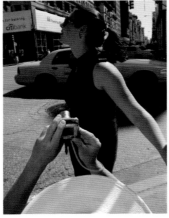 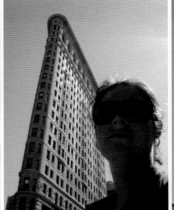 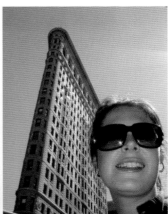

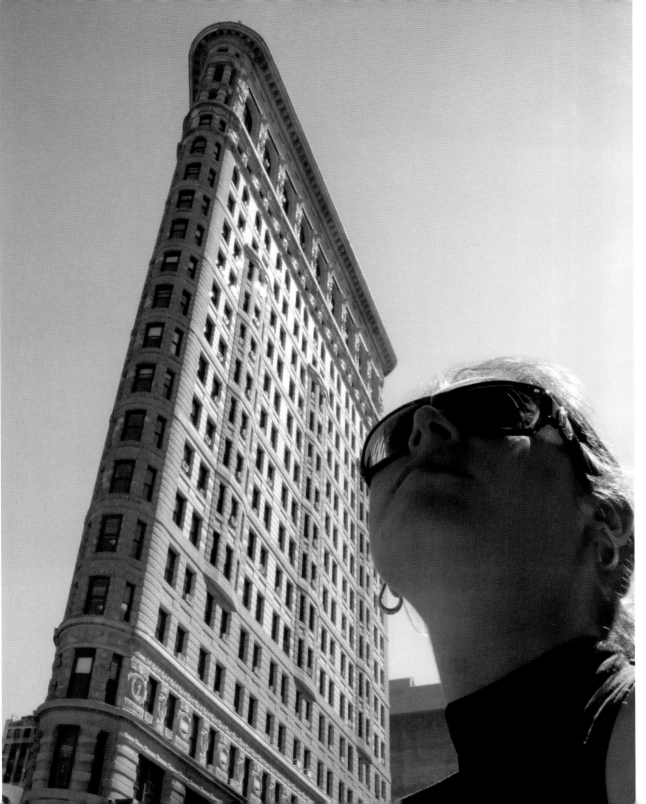

>> FOR THIS SHOT

I asked my model to tilt her face in order to catch as much light as possible. For the greatest depth of field, I set the smallest aperture and chose the widest-angle zoom, which also allowed me to get the entire building into the shot.

CAMERA MODE

 Set your dial to **Aperture Priority**

LENS SETTING

Zoom to **Widest Angle**

SENSOR/FILM SPEED

Use a **Medium** to **High** ISO setting

FLASH

Force the flash to **Fill-in mode**

5 GET THE SETTINGS RIGHT

Make sure that the camera settings give you enough depth of field to keep both the subject and the landmark sharp.

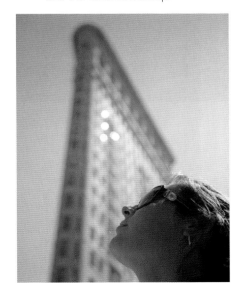

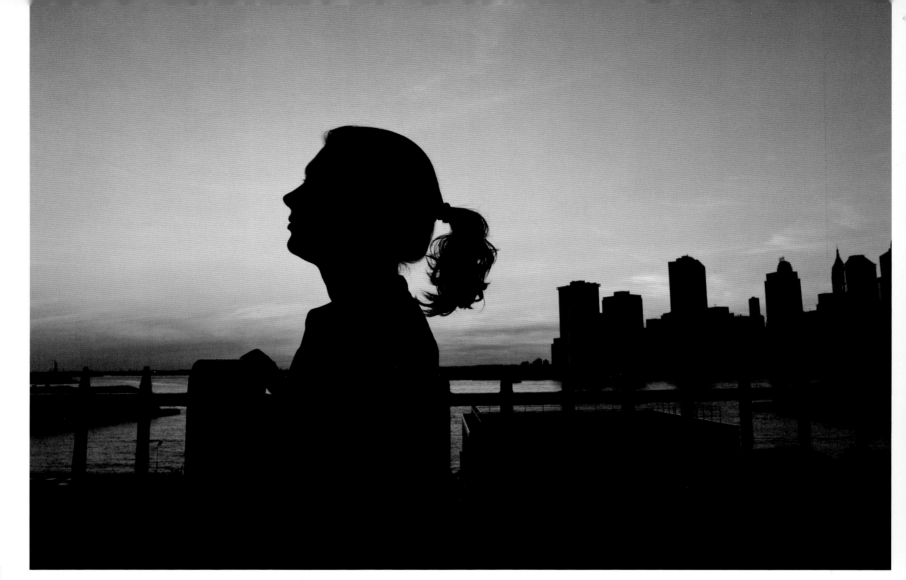

Creating a silhouette

Before the days of photography, the painted silhouette was a classic way to depict a profile. Silhouette portraits look simple, stripped as they are of any unnecessary detail, yet dramatic and strong. Achieving this effect in photography depends on a combination of lighting, exposure control, and careful choice of subject. Sunset is a good time for such a shot, since the sun is low in the sky, allowing the background to be lit without light falling on the foreground.

FOR THIS SHOT

I chose a moderately wide-angle setting to take in both the silhouette of the face and that of the city skyline. I also wanted a good expanse of sky, which I exposed for, to make the foreground completely black.

CAMERA MODE

Set your dial to **any exposure mode**

LENS SETTING

Zoom to **Normal** to **Wide Angle**

SENSOR/FILM SPEED

Use a **Medium** to **High** ISO setting

FLASH

Force the flash **Off**

POSITION YOUR SUBJECT

For the best silhouettes, place your subject directly between yourself and the light source. If the subject is too far to one side, you can see light on her face; if she stands too far back, the sun will creep into the picture.

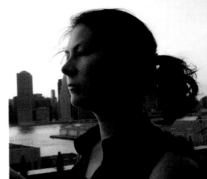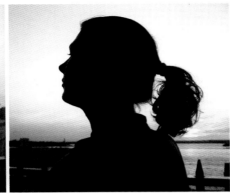

GET THE PROFILE RIGHT

Make sure you get the entire profile of the subject in your picture. A silhouette portrait is one of the few situations in which you need to pose your subject and get them to stay still. Here, a slight movement of the head ruined the effect.

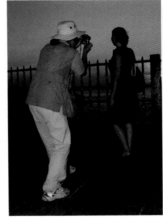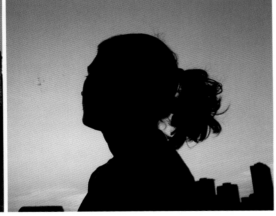

TRY DIFFERENT EFFECTS

The choice between pinning long hair up or letting it loose can have quite an impact on the image. Be also aware that the sun is a distraction when visible in a silhouette portrait, as are other elements, such as buildings. Make sure there is some empty space between your subject and any background elements.

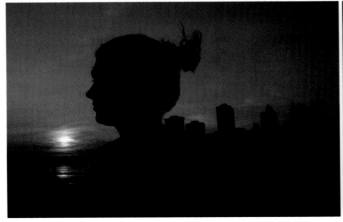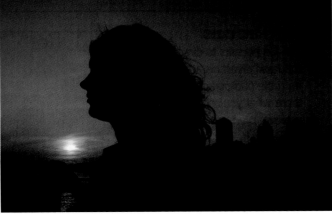

CREATING A SILHOUETTE >> PEOPLE **67**

Informal child portraits

The best portraits of children are those that are taken in an informal setting, but you need to have patience, stamina, and quick reflexes. In order to avoid having to run around after the child, try to find something that they are interested in doing so you can take photographs while they happily entertain themselves. This gives a lovely, natural feel to the photograph and also reveals something of the child's character at the same time.

KEEPING CHILDREN HAPPY

Before you start the photo session, make sure the child has had something to eat and drink. A hungry child is less willing to cooperate. It is a good idea, however, to avoid sugary or fatty foods and sweet drinks, since these are likely to make the child overactive or drowsy.

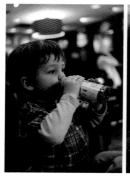
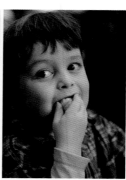

1 ENGAGE WITH THE CHILD
Children can be shy around cameras, especially if a fuss is made about them being the sole subject of the shoot. Get them to cooperate by making the exercise fun and involving them – for example, show them their picture on the LCD screen, or allow them to take a picture of you.

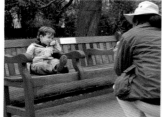
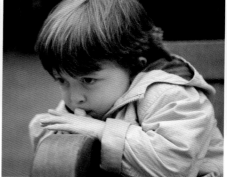
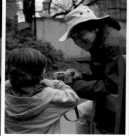
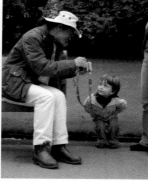

2 DIRECT THE CHILD
Use fun pursuits to direct the child and divert his attention from the photography. Tell them what you are trying to achieve. Even young children will enjoy being part of a team effort.

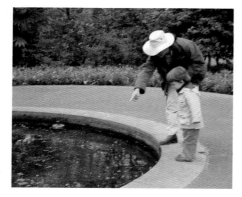

3 LET THE CHILD GET USED TO THE CAMERA
If you wait until a significant moment, the camera may distract the child. Make sure you take lots of pictures before you start the actual shoot. This will get the child used to the sounds of the camera. Soon, he'll be ignoring you and what you're doing.

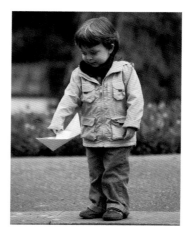

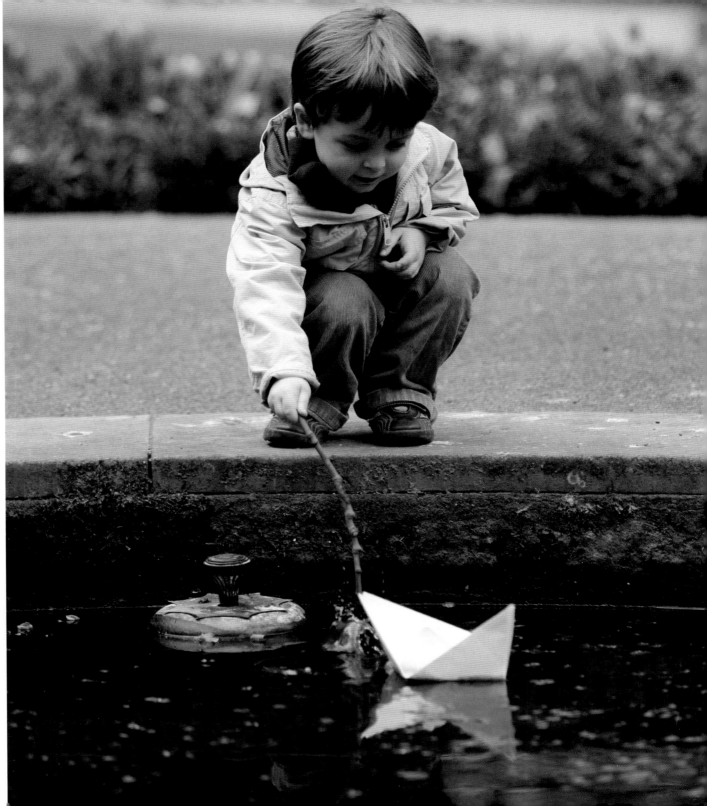

FOR THIS SHOT

I set a long focal length to zoom in on the child and to throw the background out of focus. Knowing he wouldn't stay still for long, I set the sports mode to give the short shutter times and quick camera responses needed for capturing action.

CAMERA MODE

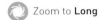 Set your dial to **Sports mode**

LENS SETTING

Zoom to **Long**

SENSOR/FILM SPEED

 Use a **Medium** to **High** ISO setting

FLASH

Force the flash **Off**

KEEP YOUR DISTANCE

By taking pictures of the child from a distance and zooming in, you are more likely to obtain natural poses. Ensure an adult is standing by to watch over the child; they do not have to be in the shot.

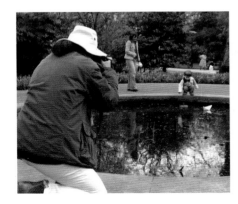

Candid snaps

The key to a successful portrait is to capture and reveal some aspect of the sitter's personality, their life, or their interests. Candid portraiture is an approach that espouses non-intervention: you simply stand back and observe, you do not interfere or give directions. It is akin to wildlife photography in that it calls for patience in waiting and watching, as well as quick reflexes to catch a telling gesture or moment.

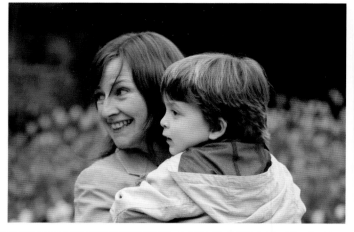

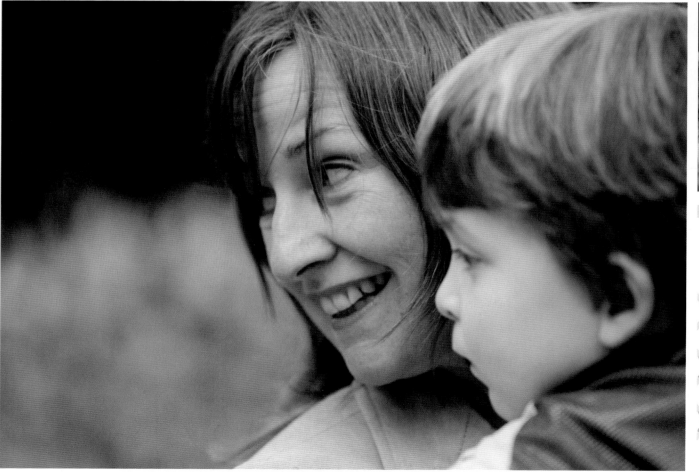

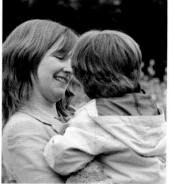

WOMAN AND CHILD

A candid shot taken from a distance prevents family portraits from looking posed or staged.

1 Stand at a distance and zoom in to blur the background.

2 Focus on the eyes of one of the subjects; everything else can be unsharp.

3 Try different zoom settings for variety in the way the subject fills in the frame.

DRIVER AT THE WHEEL

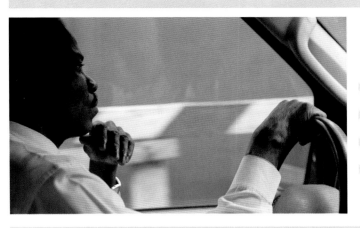

Opportunities for candid portraits abound, even when you are sitting in a car.

1 Look for a suitable background to create an interesting composition.

2 Turn off the flash and any camera sounds so you don't distract the driver.

HUMOROUS MOMENT

Many amusing scenes build up slowly: learn to read this lead-in process and seize the moment.

1 Use the serial-exposure, or motor-drive, setting instead of single-shot.

2 Freeze movement and catch the peak of the action with short exposure.

3 Turn off the flash: it can spoil a candid moment by advertising your presence.

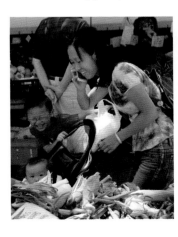

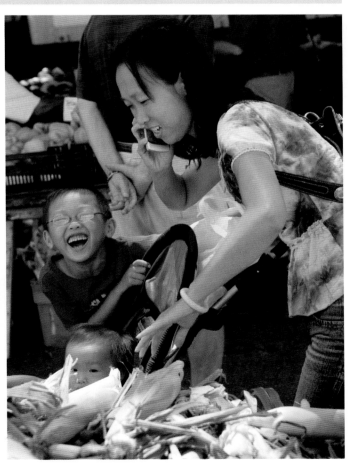

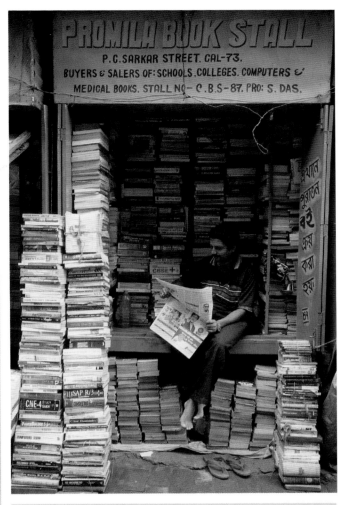

FRAMING THE SHOT

One of the neatest and most effective compositional devices is the frame. This confines and organizes the space in your shot, creating a visually logical stage for your subject.

1 For the best results, position yourself square on to the frame.

2 Hold the camera level to keep verticals parallel to the picture frame.

3 Start with long to medium focal lengths since these are easiest to work with.

PEOPLE AT WORK

Candid photography aims to record people unposed and natural, going about their business without altering their normal behavior because of the camera. This does not mean, however, that they have to be unaware of you.

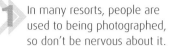
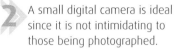
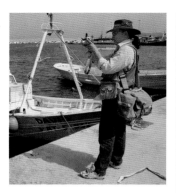

1 In many resorts, people are used to being photographed, so don't be nervous about it.

2 A small digital camera is ideal since it is not intimidating to those being photographed.

3 If anyone looks at you, just smile and make eye contact. You can still make the picture.

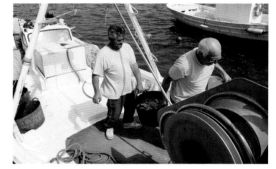
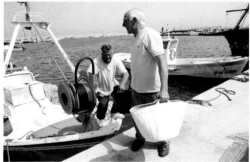

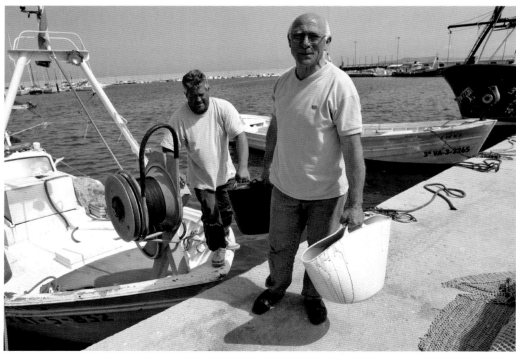

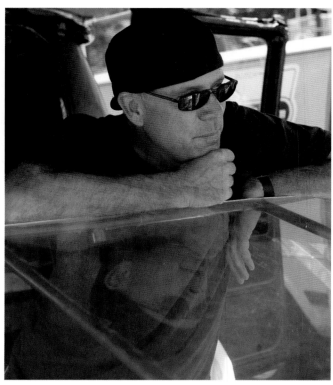

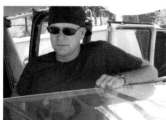
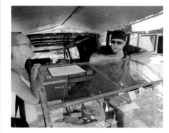

CONVERSATIONAL PORTRAIT

Don't feel shy about asking people for permission to photograph them. Most will agree and simply continue with their conversation or activity.

1 A normal to moderately long zoom works well for portraits.

2 Turn off unnecessary camera noises to avoid distracting your subjects.

3 Use the surroundings to frame and contain the subject of your photograph.

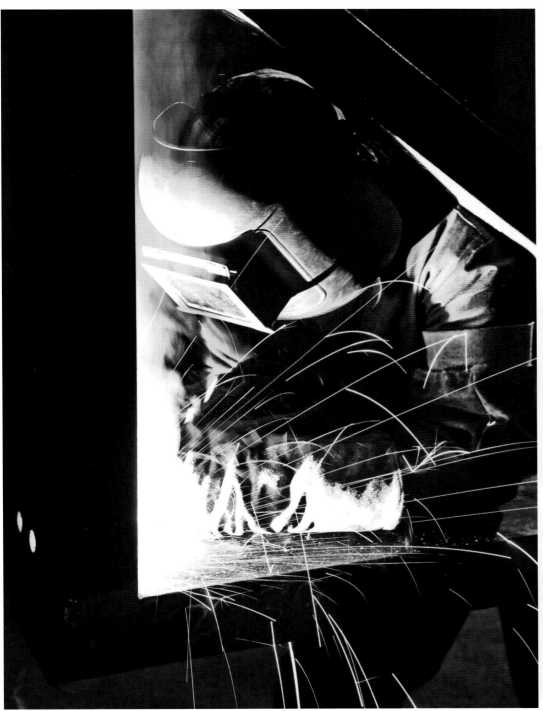

INDUSTRIAL PORTRAIT

Skilled people at work are often inspiring to watch and to photograph. This welder makes a particularly photogenic subject, thanks to the flying sparks and dramatic light of his working environment.

1 Follow all safety rules when working in industrial sites, and watch where you step.

2 Experiment with different shutter times to catch the action in the most effective way.

3 Look for areas with interesting contrasts in lighting to add drama to your composition.

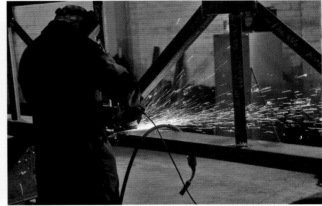

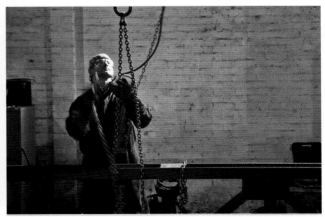

Using dramatic lighting

Being adventurous with lighting when shooting a portrait can be very rewarding, creating effects that you might not have anticipated. All you need to do is work a little with positioning and framing. Some harsh lighting from a street lamp may appear unflattering at first, but a few moments' posing and fine-tuning can reveal its real potential. Often the result is dramatic and cinematic in character. A long lens setting can throw unwanted background into blur.

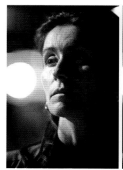
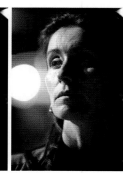

1 EXPERIMENT A LITTLE

The situation may not look ideal, but sit your subject comfortably while you experiment with various camera settings. Explore positions carefully to work out how to make the best use of the available lighting.

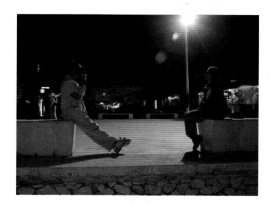

2 CHANGE ISO SETTINGS

If the light levels are very low, as they are here, set the highest ISO for maximum sensitivity. The resulting image may be "noisy," with a grainy look, but you can use that to help give character to the image.

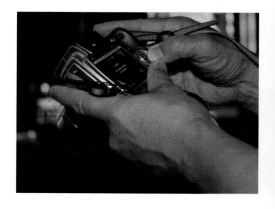

3 VARY THE POSES

Try out various positions and angles. In this kind of lighting, even small changes in the position of the face in the frame can make a big difference. Try to keep a solid stance. My position here was unsteady and led to unsharp images.

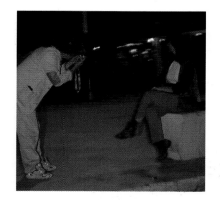

4 GET IN CLOSER

Zoom in close so that you emphasize the chiaroscuro—that is, the subtle changes in shade between light and dark—of the face.

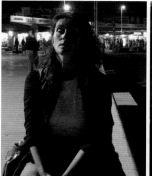
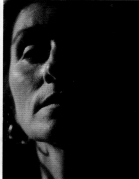

FOR THIS SHOT

I zoomed to a mid- to telephoto length to find a comfortable perspective on the face, and used the available light to sculpt the face. The maximum aperture allows the background to be blurred.

CAMERA MODE

 Set your dial to **Night mode**

LENS SETTING

 Zoom to **Medium Telephoto**

SENSOR/FILM SPEED

 Use the **Maximum** ISO setting

FLASH

 Force the flash **Off**

5 TRY VARIOUS POSES

Changing the position of the head is like moving a lamp around: here, a tiny change lights up the whole face but loses the chiaroscuro.

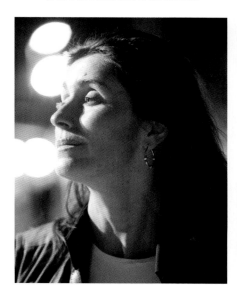

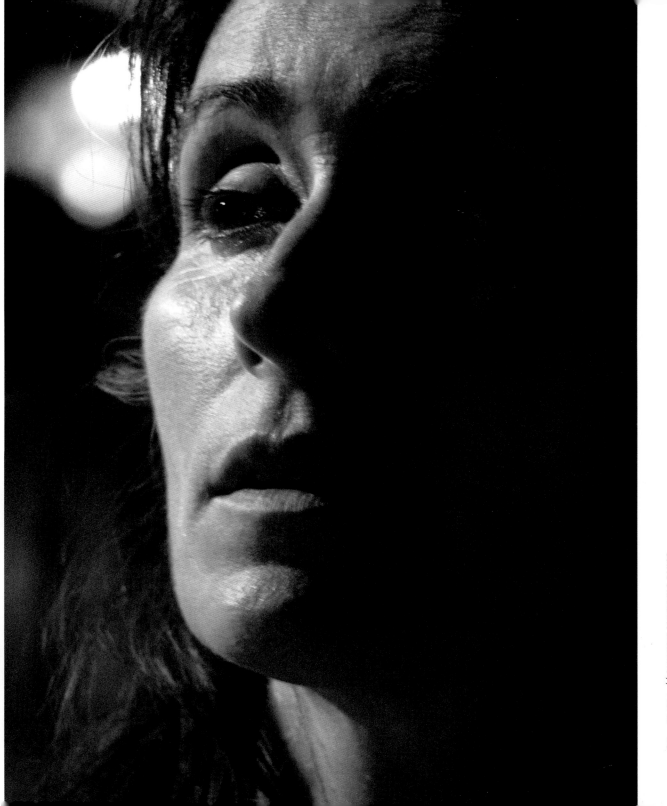

Posed child portraits

Any formal portrait benefits from an investment in effort. The resulting images will be perceived as having greater value if they have been, literally, taken seriously. When working with children, the effort must come from both the photographer and the subject, who may not be used to sitting quietly for any length of time. Your responsibility is to reward the child's patience with a picture that captures their essence without subduing their character.

1 SELECT THE SETTINGS
Children have a low boredom threshold, so plan the shot and make your camera settings before involving the child. Set the color balance and high image quality, and turn off the flash.

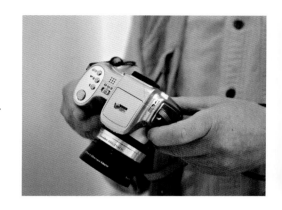

2 WORK WITHIN THE AVAILABLE SPACE
In the majority of homes, space is fairly limited. Give yourself as much working space as possible by photographing from one corner of the room to the one diagonally opposite.

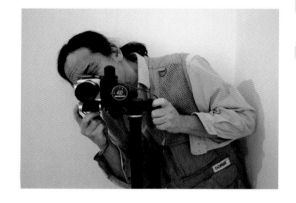

3 GET THE POSE RIGHT
Slight adjustments to a pose can make a huge difference. Here, by simply turning the chair around, the child's posture is greatly improved. It also allows her hands to be part of the portrait.

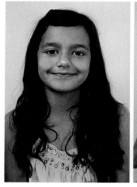
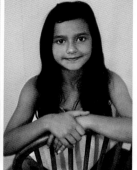

4 POSE AND COMPOSE
If possible, try to maintain eye contact with your subject. However, if the child feels self-conscious, suggest that she looks slightly to one side. It may be helpful for her to focus on a friend or relative nearby.

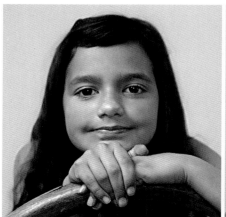
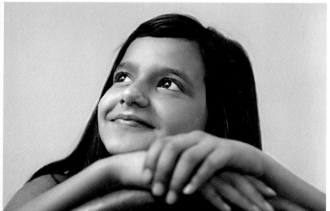

FOR THIS SHOT

I set up on a tripod so that I could direct and communicate with the sitter without having to hold the camera. I turned off the flash, selected high image quality, a low ISO setting, and a medium to long telephoto on the zoom.

CAMERA MODE

Set your dial to **Aperture Priority**

LENS SETTING

Zoom to **Medium** to **Long Telephoto**

SENSOR/FILM SPEED

Use a **Low** ISO setting

FLASH

Force the flash **Off**

5 FOCUS ON THE EYES

In the vast majority of portraits, the crucial area of focus is the eyes. Unless you have a very good reason—such as to make a statement about the sitter's hands—the eyes should always be shape.

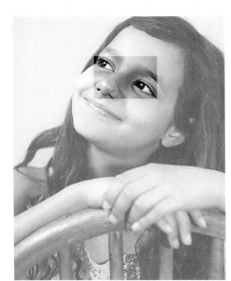

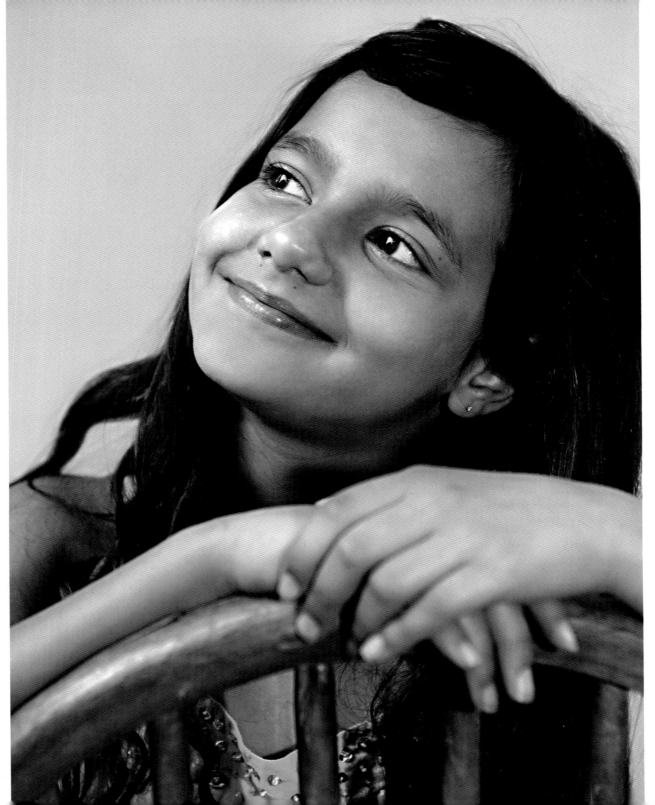

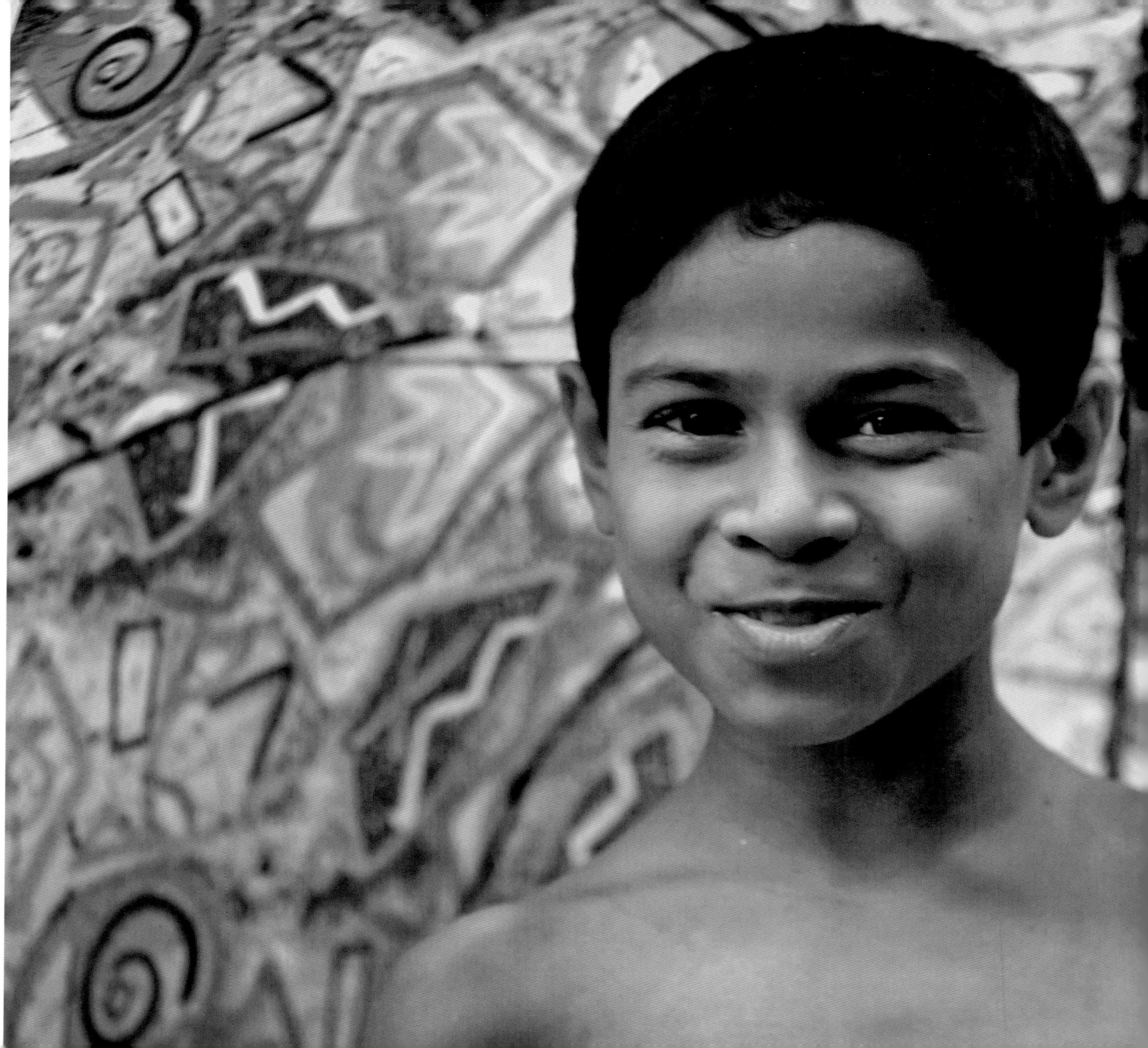

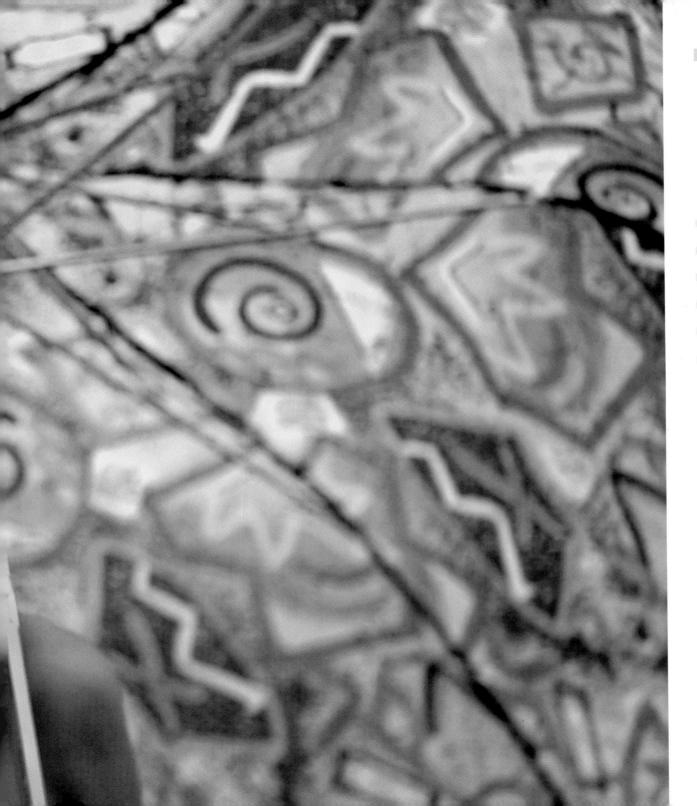

SMILING EYES

Black-and-white photography is perhaps the natural medium for portraits. In color, the patterned umbrella provided a brilliant backdrop, but in monochrome, attention is immediately drawn to the boy's friendly, smiling face.

1. A long focal length crops the image so that the umbrella entirely frames the face.

2. In very bright sunlight, set the flash to automatic in order to fill in shadows.

3. Shoot black-and-white portraits if you wish to remove the distractions of color.

Alternative portraiture

Some physical details, such as hands, can reveal as much about the character and lifestyle of a person as their face. When taking a portrait shot, it is worth considering this approach, especially if the sitter is not confident in front of the camera. These henna-decorated hands are obviously highly photogenic, but all hands are expressive – whether they belong to a baby or to an aged farmer. Giving the hands something to hold makes for a more natural pose.

TRY A FULL PORTRAIT
Start with a conventional portrait. This might bring to light individual aspects that are worth focusing on. In this case, for example, the background of the dark shirt is perfect for the flowers and clearly suggests an alternative approach.

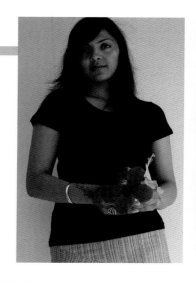

MOVE CLOSER
Experiment with close-up views with a short focal length, as well as from a greater distance with a longer lens setting to decide on what works best for the subject. Use a low ISO setting for the best image quality.

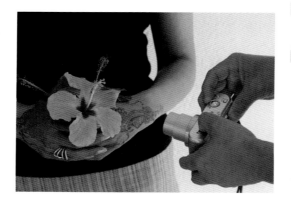

VARY THE BACKGROUND
For subjects with delicate textures and subtle tones, try to work in subdued lighting. Try different backgrounds, too. Here, the warm tones of a wall complement the flowers and hands, but it is clear that an even simpler approach will be best.

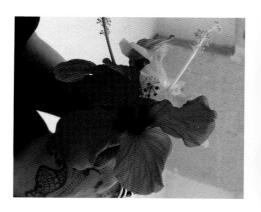

DIRECT YOUR SUBJECT
Try the hands with jewelry and without, and ask the sitter to change the position of their hands, but to do so slowly. Meanwhile, keep shooting: the hands will look most natural when they are not deliberately posed.

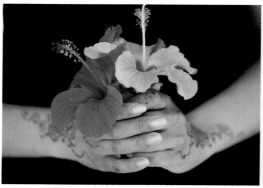
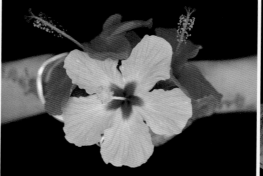
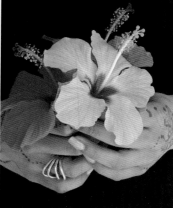

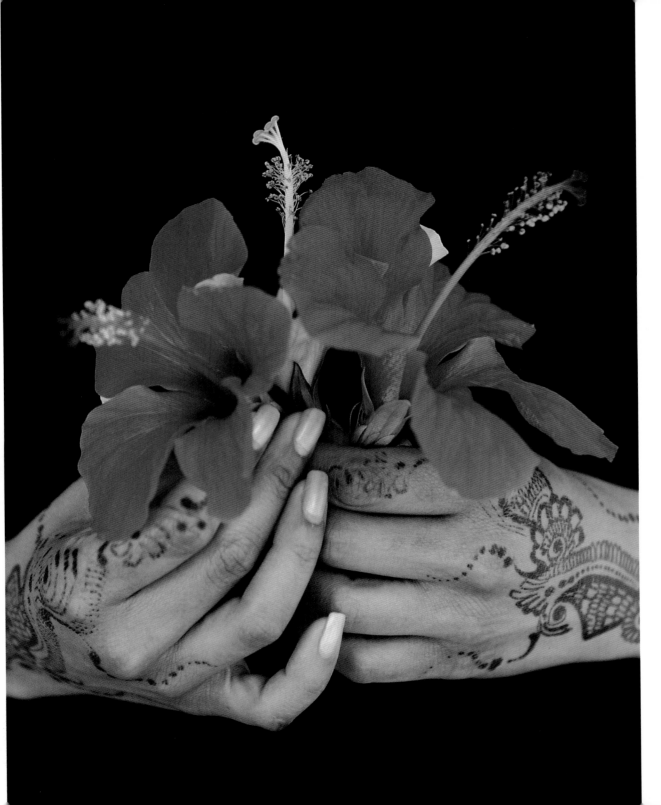

 FOR THIS SHOT

I zoomed in to create a slightly distant look. Low sensitivity gives high quality and a short shutter time offers sharpness. I made many exposures in a short time to ensure that I achieved a graceful, telling composition.

CAMERA MODE

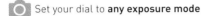 Set your dial to **any exposure mode**

LENS SETTING

Zoom to **Maximum Telephoto**

SENSOR/FILM SPEED

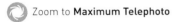 Use a **Low** to **Medium** ISO setting

FLASH

Force the flash **Off**

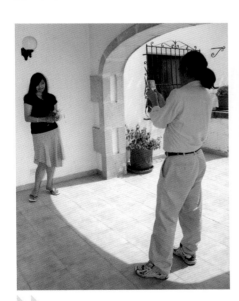

5 USE AVAILABLE LIGHT

Here, the subject of the portrait is standing in semi-shade, with light bouncing off the floor to illuminate her hands from below.

Beautiful baby pictures

Every parent longs for a picture that perfectly captures their baby's personality. However, babies and small children can be challenging subjects to photograph. Their movements are often unpredictable, as are their moods, which can switch from smiles to tears in the space of a few seconds. Careful and patient preparation will allow you to work quickly when the circumstances come together, creating a picture you will treasure forever.

1 PREPARE THE SET
Babies will benefit from being photographed against a neutral background and bathed in diffused light, which is kindest to soft features. A white sheet reflects light to fill the shadows under your subject. It also reflects in the baby's eyes.

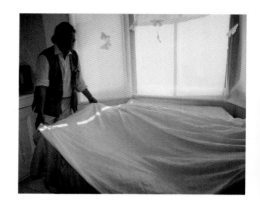

2 INVOLVE THE BABY
Let the baby touch the camera – after all, you are playing with it, so why shouldn't the baby? Let them get used to the camera. It will not be long until they lose interest in it.

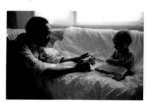
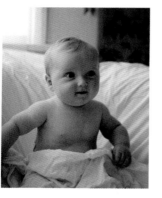

3 CHOOSE A POSITION
Try the baby in different positions. Some are likely to be more comfortable than others, depending on the child's age and inclination. You need to discover which one works best.

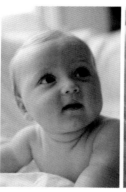
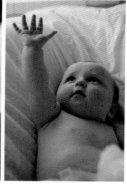

4 KEEP SHOOTING
You may not notice the subtleties in expression while shooting, so don't waste time reviewing your shots at the time, especially if the baby is cooperating. If you take your eye off a rapidly changing situation to check your images, you are sure to miss a great shot.

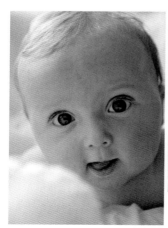
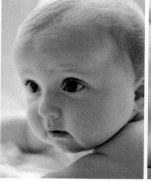
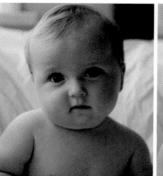
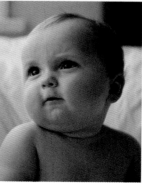

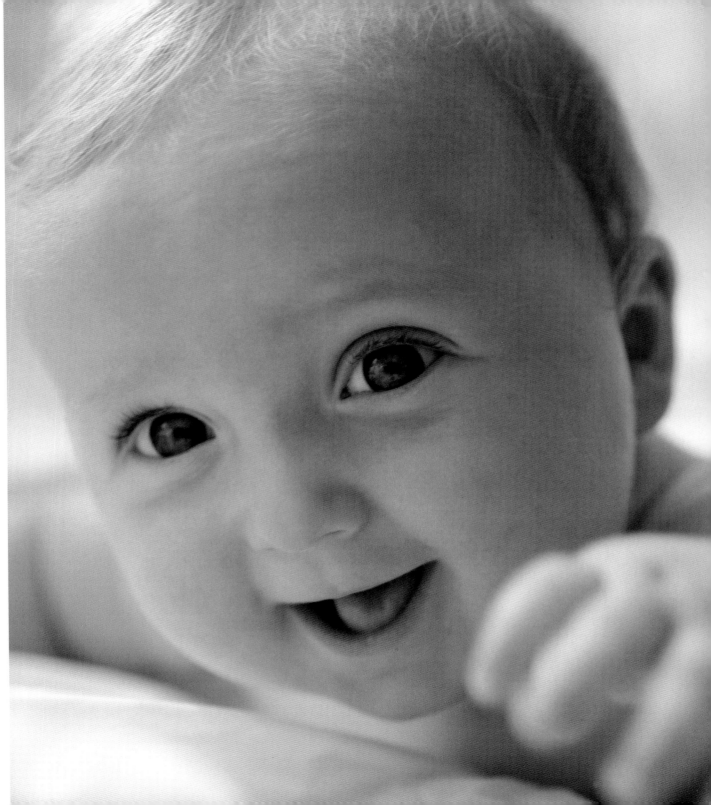

 FOR THIS SHOT
I set the zoom medium telephoto and close-up mode, so that the baby's face filled the frame. By quick-firing I took some 100 pictures in 6 minutes, giving a good choice of expressions. (For this you may need to set a small image size.)

CAMERA MODE

 Set your dial to **Portrait mode**

LENS SETTING

 Zoom to **Medium Telephoto**

SENSOR/FILM SPEED

 Use a **Medium** to **High** ISO setting

FLASH

 Force the flash **Off**

5 USE ASSISTANCE
Get someone to help keep the baby entertained and smiling. However, if you want the child to look directly into the camera, you might have to do a little entertaining yourself, as well as taking the photographs.

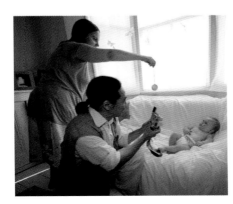

Children year by year

Most parents experience a similar pattern when it comes to photographing their own children: they dive in with great enthusiasm at the start, taking hundreds of photos of the newborn baby. Then, as the child grows, the number of pictures drops dramatically. One way to keep up a consistent photographic record is to think of your child's development as a project whose key stages need to be documented.

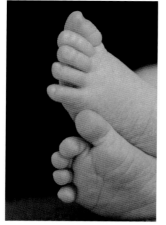

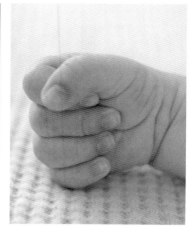

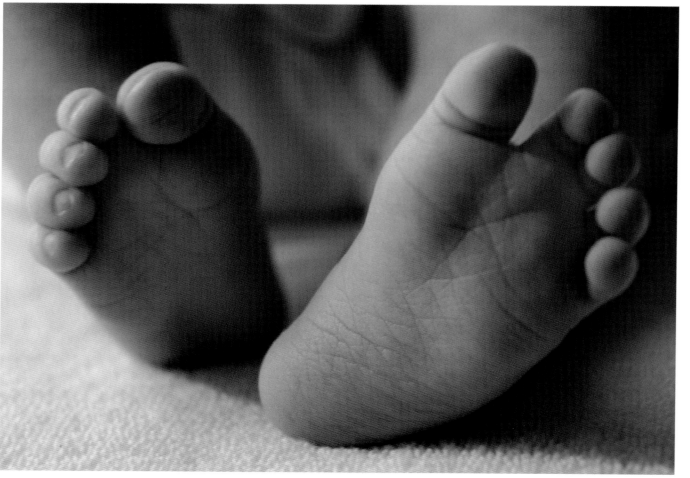

FOCUS ON THE DETAILS

While, of course, you will want to record the varied and ever-changing facial expressions of your newborn, remember that other parts of the baby's body undergo equally rapid – and astonishing – changes.

1 Take the baby close to a window to avoid having to use the flash.

2 Use close-up mode to zoom as close as possible to the baby's tiny hands and feet.

3 Try a range of backgrounds. Pastel tones complement the baby's skin, while dark tones offer contrast.

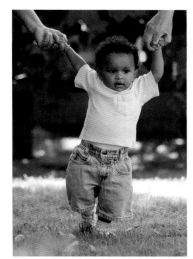

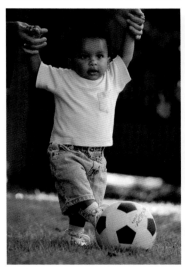

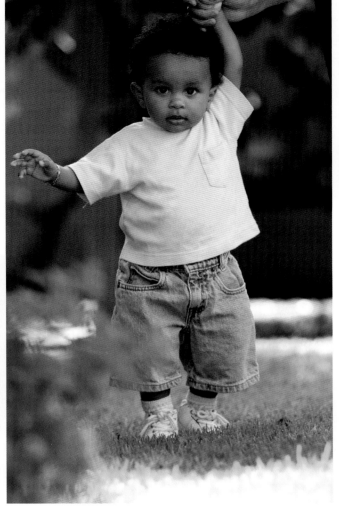

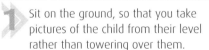

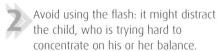

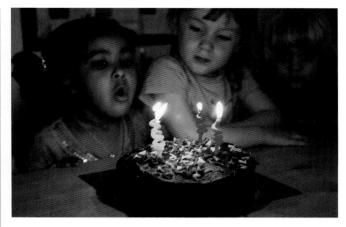

CANDLES AND LOW LIGHT

Different societies celebrate children's birthdays in different ways. The tradition of the birthday cake symbolizes good wishes to ensure a healthy year ahead.

1 If the celebration takes place in low light, use all the available light.

2 Use a tripod to steady the camera, since flash would ruin the candlelit effect.

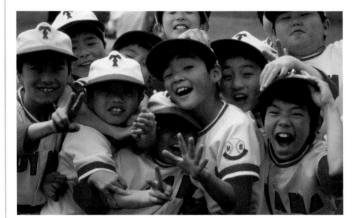

TEAM SPIRIT

Your child's growing social life is reflected in their taking part in team sports at school and outside. They will treasure your pictures as records of their teammates.

1 Encourage the team to pose, but don't make the shot too formal – it should be fun.

2 Take several pictures in rapid succession to ensure that you catch everyone.

BABY STEPS

A child's first faltering steps are an emotionally charged moment for any parent: as well as being inordinately proud of their achievements, you are also aware that with growing confidence come mobility and freedom.

1 Sit on the ground, so that you take pictures of the child from their level rather than towering over them.

2 Avoid using the flash: it might distract the child, who is trying hard to concentrate on his or her balance.

3 If possible, work outside in good light, keeping to open shade and avoiding direct sunlight.

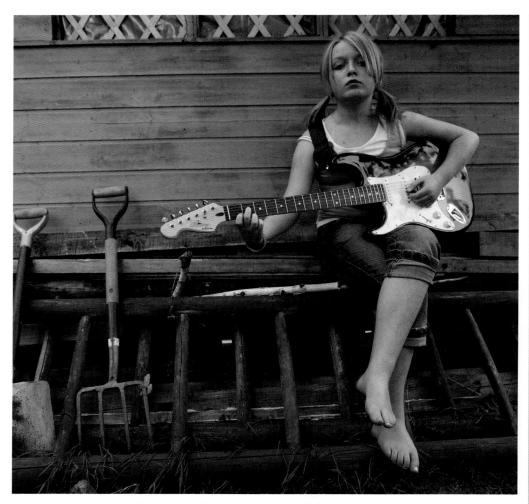

Children feel more relaxed in front of the camera if they are surrounded by their friends. They are more likely to reveal their personalities if you let them pose together.

> Go along with the kids' pranks and sense of fun for the session, it's the most natural approach.

> Instead of lining them up on a bench, look for a spot where you can experiment with grouping.

> Work rapidly. Children bore easily, and once they've lost interest, it will be almost impossible to persuade them to cooperate.

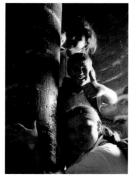

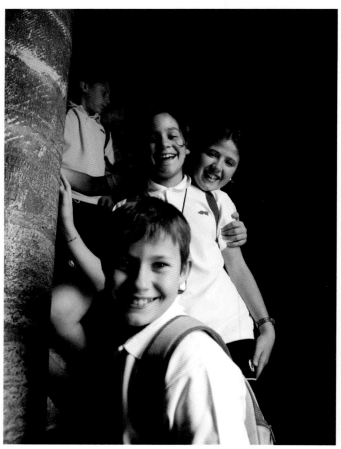

FAVORITE HOBBY

Many children who are shy around the camera will agree to pose to show off something they are proud of or passionate about, such as their musical instrument.

> Focus your portrait as much on the object of the child's passion as on their face.

> Try formal as well as informal poses, with different zoom settings from different positions.

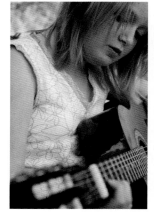

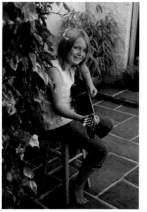

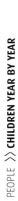

DEEP IN THOUGHT

The toughest portrait subject is the reluctant subject, and teenagers are notoriously reluctant to pose for the family album. The key is to accept them as they are: they do not have to pose, they do not have to smile; in fact, they do not have to make any effort at all.

1 Work quietly, quickly, and discreetly, and avoid giving instructions.

2 Don't ask your subject to smile unless he or she is enjoying being photographed.

3 Convert the image to black-and-white to convey the subject's mood and intensity.

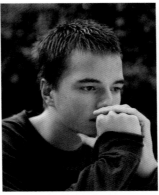
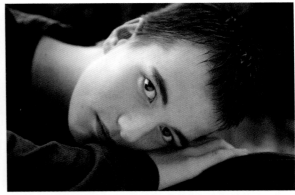

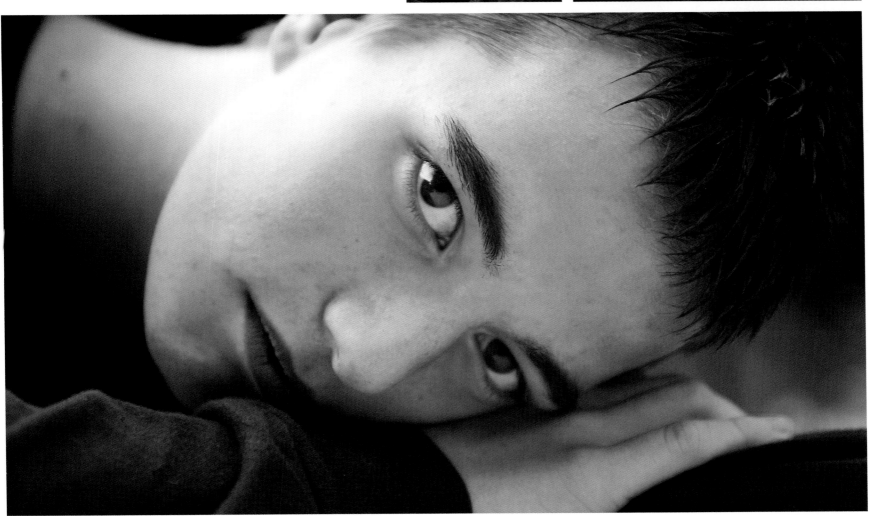

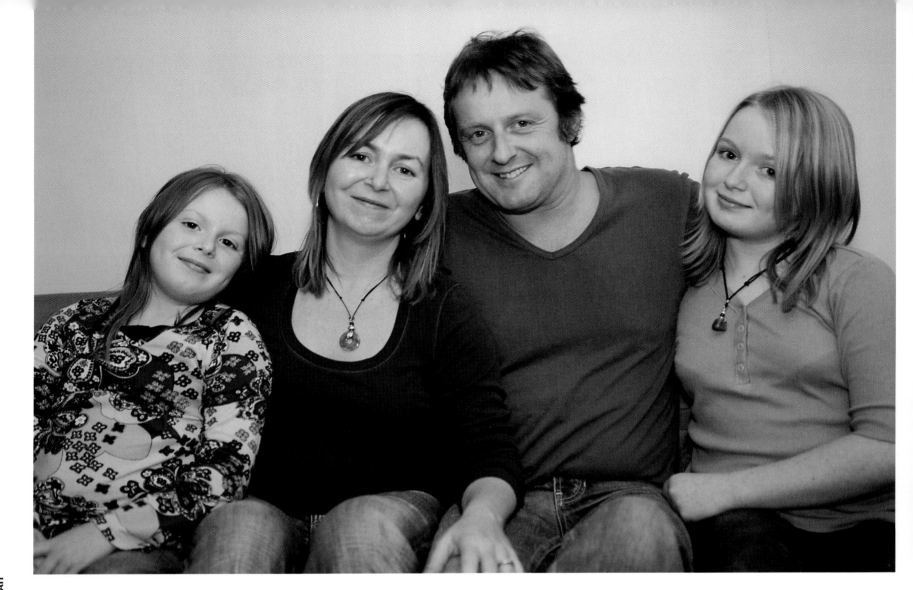

Family self-portrait

A family self-portrait—to send to distant relatives and friends, for a Christmas card, or just for yourself—can be surprisingly difficult to organize: it may take time to get everyone in the same place and in the right frame of mind to sit for a group shot. It is helpful that digital cameras allow you to see the image right away. This not only gives immediate feedback on your settings, it also encourages everyone to work together to make an appealing picture.

FOR THIS SHOT

The camera was set to a moderate zoom and a low ISO then placed on a tripod. Flash was used to fill in dark areas, creating a mixture of ambient lighting and flash to give a softer effect.

CAMERA MODE

Set your dial to **Program mode**

LENS SETTING

Zoom to **Medium Telephoto**

SENSOR/FILM SPEED

Use a **Low** ISO setting

FLASH

Force the flash **On**

1 WEAR THE RIGHT CLOTHES

Brightly colored garments may make the skin appear pale and wan. You should also make sure that the clothing of any one person doesn't dominate the picture. Consider your clothes in advance, and try to keep the tones similar.

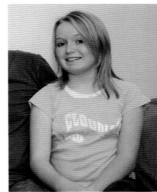
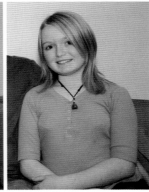

2 PREPARE YOURSELVES

Apply a little face powder—even to male members of your family—otherwise the light from the flash will accentuate any shiny areas. Encourage everyone to comb their hair, if possible.

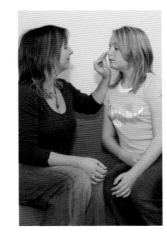

3 GET THE LOCATION READY

If you are going to sit on a sofa, move it away from the wall: this ensures there will be no harsh shadows on the wall directly behind you.

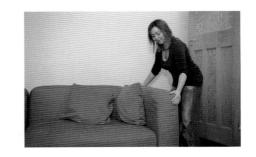

4 USE THE TIMER FEATURE

Set the camera on a tripod, line it up, and arrange the pose, remembering to leave room for yourself to be included. Set the self-timer to give yourself time to occupy the vacant space. Self-timers usually give you a warning a few seconds before the exposure, so you do not have hold frozen grins for long periods of time.

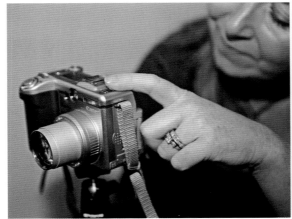
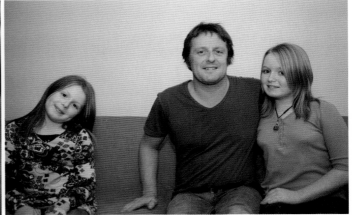

Informal family portraits

If a portrait of a single person is tricky, your problems will be multiplied when you try to create an informal shot of the whole family together doing something they enjoy. One of the keys to success is to make sure every member of the family feels that they contribute something to the image. They should be allowed to choose their own clothes, for example, so that they feel comfortable. Your aim, after all, is to create a relaxed, natural-looking portrait.

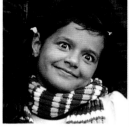 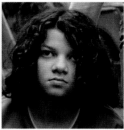 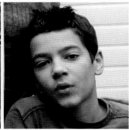

One of the difficulties of taking group portraits is that many shots will include individuals making funny faces, talking, blinking, or looking away from the camera. Check your pictures by enlarging them on the LCD before ending the session.

1 DECIDE ON A LOOK
To avoid losing the children's interest, before you start, experiment with backgrounds and set-ups, using just the parents. Consider where to place the members of the family.

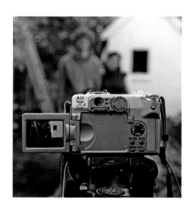

2 CONSIDER LIGHTING
If you are working outdoors, bear in mind that the lighting may change during the time you are setting up. For groups of people, it's easiest to work with even lighting. Avoid having some people in the sun and others in shade, since this is very tricky to get right.

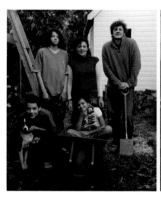 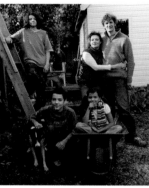

3 POSE AND COMPOSE
With the camera on a tripod it is easy to get your subjects to move while you take the pictures. Keep talking and directing, but carry on shooting. Only review your shots at the end, or you'll miss opportunities.

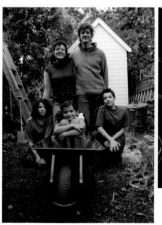 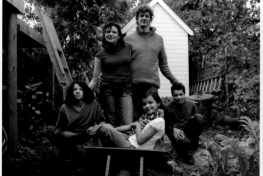 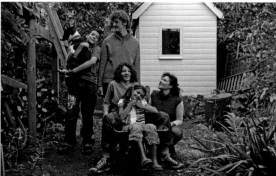

FOR THIS SHOT

I set the zoom to a moderate wide angle to capture the yard and the whole group. I ensured a good depth of field by setting the minimum aperture. Low sensitivity and maximum image size gave good image quality.

CAMERA MODE

Zoom to **Moderate Wide Angle**

LENS SETTING

Set your dial to **Aperture Priority**

SENSOR/FILM SPEED

Use a **Low** ISO setting

FLASH

Force the flash **Off**

4 SET YOUR FOCUS

Symmetrical compositions usually make the most satisfying family portraits, but whatever composition you opt for, focus on the central person of the group.

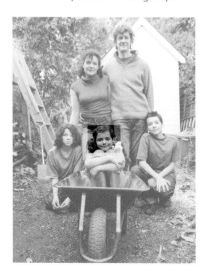

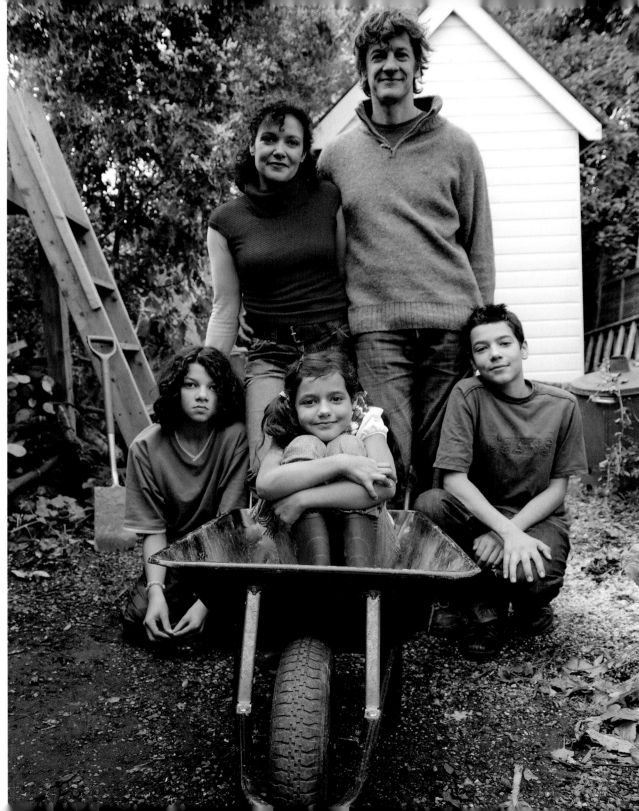

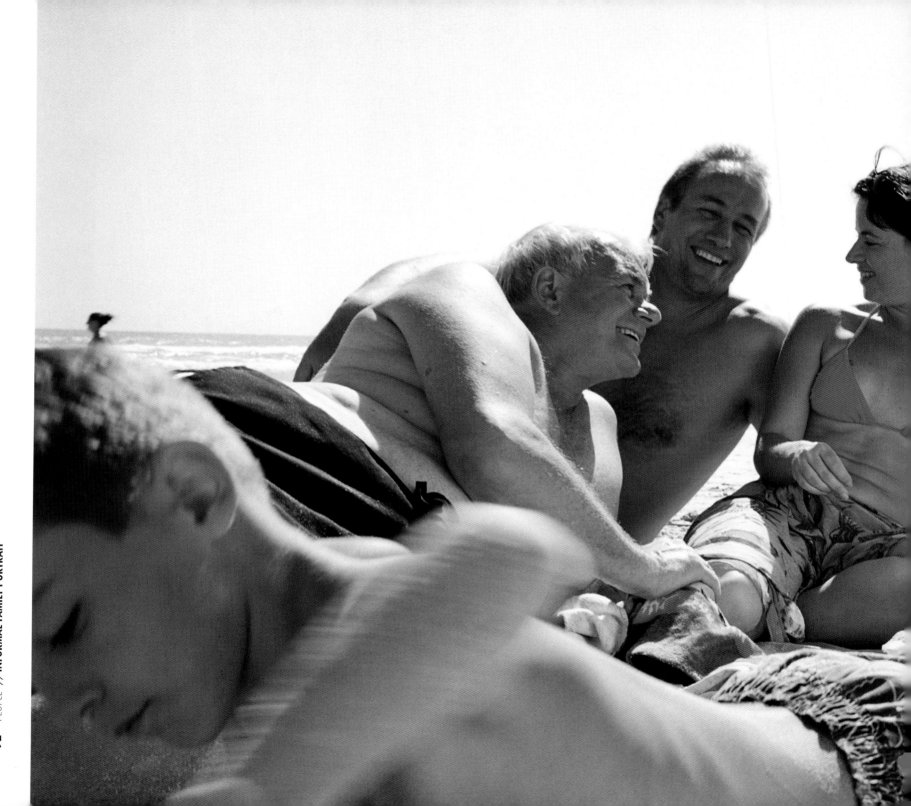

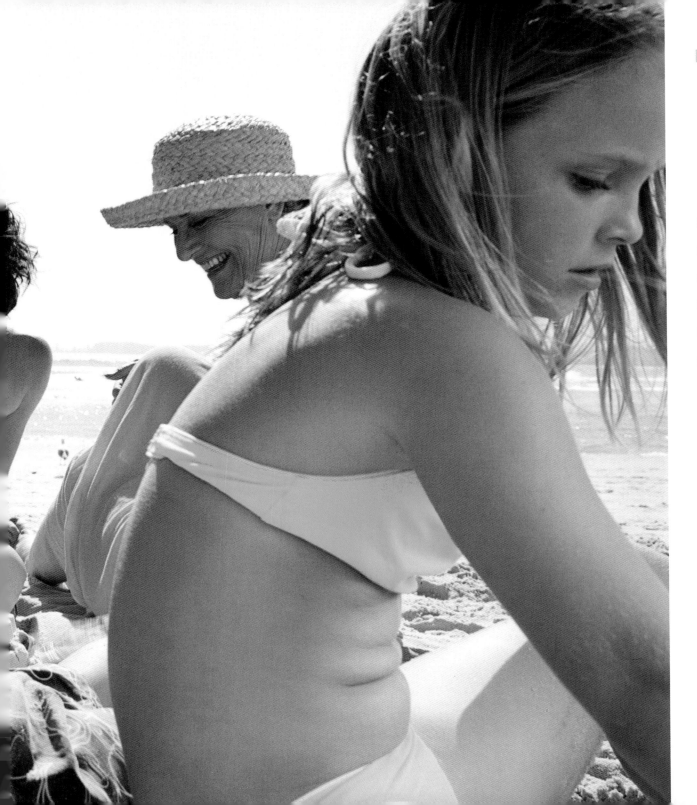

ON THE BEACH

All too often, family vacation pictures look stilted or forced because they have been posed. On the other hand, an unposed picture may be too chaotic to compose well. The secret is to look out for candid but interesting arrangements of people.

1 Keep your zoom at a wide setting and your camera on stand-by.

2 On brilliantly sunny days, use fill-in flash to help bring light into shadows.

3 Don't be afraid to crop in and lose parts of some of the subjects. Not everyone has to be on the same plane.

Formal portraiture

The call for formal portraits is as strong now as it was in the early years of photography, yet few non-professionals ever try their hand in this area. This is a pity, because portraiture is a highly rewarding field. The best portraits are those that reveal something about the sitter. Start by asking family or close friends to sit for you: the rapport you already have will help them overcome any reluctance at being thrust into the limelight and help you capture aspects of their personality.

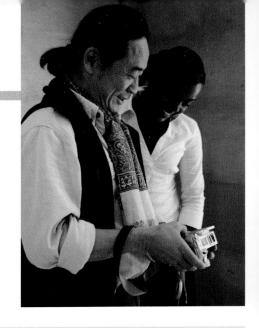

1 RELAX YOUR SUBJECT
Involve your subject in what you're doing from the outset. You can usually get them to relax and to trust you by taking a few informal shots and showing them how good they look. That will give them the confidence to go through a more formal shoot.

2 SCOUT LOCATIONS
Walk around with the sitter, identifying the best spot for the shoot: you'll need good light and an interesting background that is not too loud or busy. Try out a few different places to see what works best.

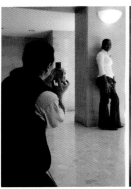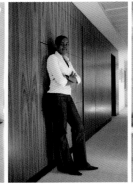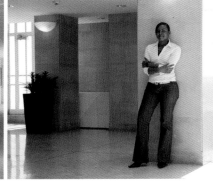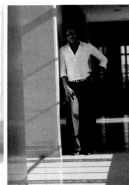

3 INSTRUCT YOUR SUBJECT
Encourage the subject to sit or stand straight while still looking natural. Once you begin taking pictures, keep giving instructions, but don't hold a conversation, since that can be too distracting. Think about the subject's position in the frame, and try different zoom settings from various distances.

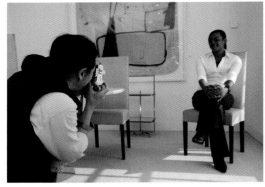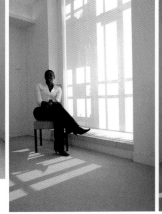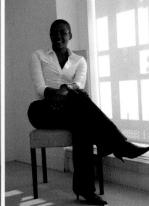

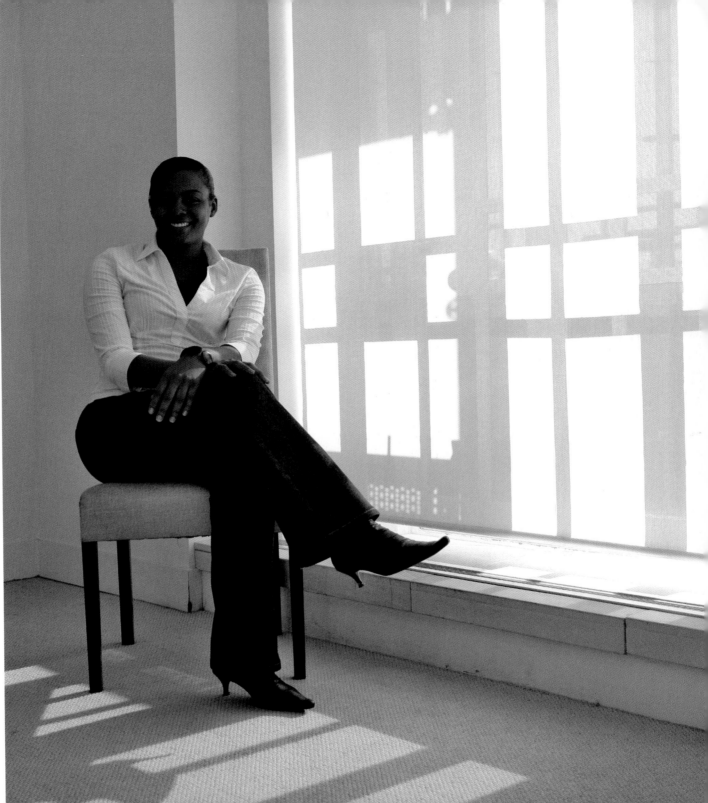

 FOR THIS SHOT
I set the zoom to medium, with a low sensitivity and large file size for the best quality. I compensated exposure to ensure the bright areas were correct.

CAMERA MODE

Set your dial to **Portrait mode**

LENS SETTING

Zoom to **Medium**

SENSOR/FILM SPEED

 Use a **Low** ISO setting

FLASH

Force the flash **Off**

4 INTRODUCE SMALL CHANGES
If you're happy with your exposure settings, fire a sequence. Ask your sitter to make small adjustments to her pose and expression.

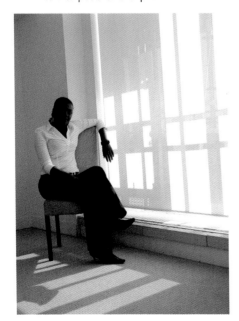

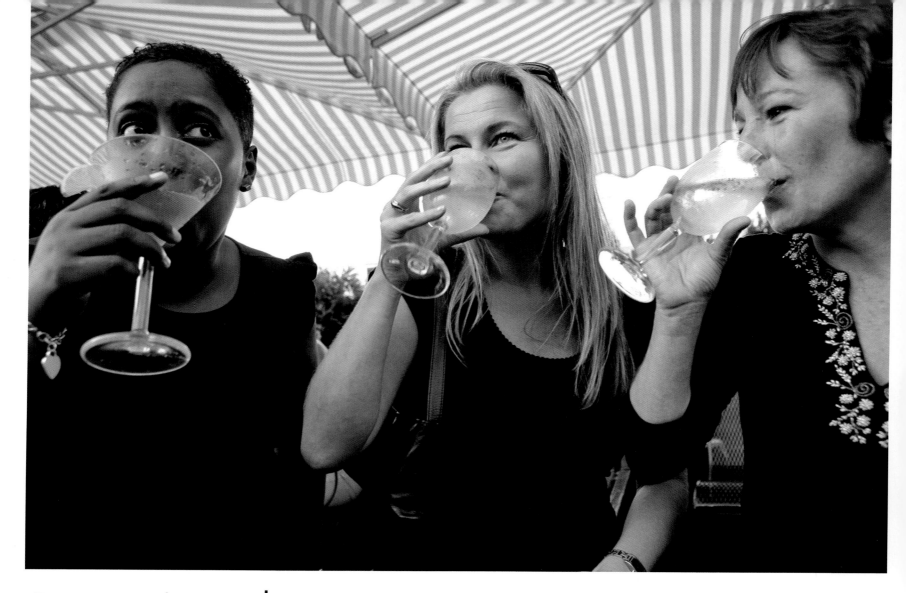

Capturing the party spirit

The jovial atmosphere of a party is an easy subject to photograph: most participants are likely to be enjoying the company of friends, relaxed, and ready with a smile. If you wish to elevate the party snapshot to something with an element of surprise, humor, or style about it, you need to take yourself out of the party, if only for a short time, and become an objective observer. You will then be able to concentrate on catching unposed, revealing gestures.

FOR THIS SHOT

I selected the sports mode and a high ISO, then forced the flash off to preserve the scene's natural light. I used a wide zoom from a low viewpoint to catch the overhead parasol patterns, which contrasted with the dark clothing.

CAMERA MODE

Set your dial to **Sports mode**

LENS SETTING

Zoom to **Wide Angle**

SENSOR/FILM SPEED

Use a **High** ISO setting

FLASH

Force the flash **Off**

ALTERNATIVE VIEWPOINT

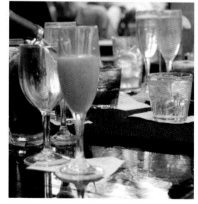

While at a party, keep your eyes open for potential photographic subjects other than just the people present. A big element of most parties is the number of drinks consumed: pictures made at the bar—such as abstract close-ups of glasses holding different-colored drinks—are visually arresting, as well as providing a comment on the party.

1 FIND A VANTAGE POINT

In order to capture the crowds gathered together at a party, you need to take yourself above the scene. A general view with the zoom at wide angle and camera held above the head gets everyone in, and gives a sense of the occasion.

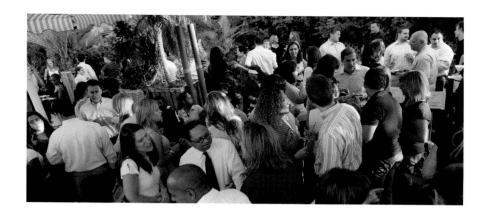

2 FOCUS ON A SMALLER GROUP

Find a small group of friends and engage with them. Show them the photographs you have taken so far and get them involved—they will be more willing to cooperate in future shots.

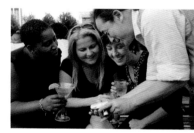

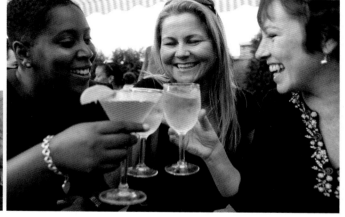

3 WORK WITH YOUR SUBJECTS

Once you have the group's cooperation, you can try different viewpoints, perspectives, and framing— from mid-length wide to extreme close-ups. At the same time, they will be relaxing and getting into the fun of it all. That is when the photographs will start to work for you.

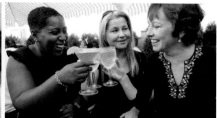
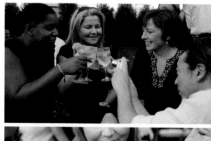
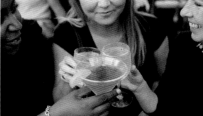
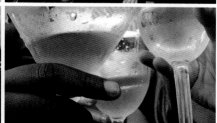

Nude study

The human body in all its rich variety—different shapes, colors, and ages—is a wonderful subject for photography, and one that anyone can handle. The secret lies in working with people you trust and who trust you. You may be surprised at how easy it is to find a subject, especially if you reassure them that the shots will be tasteful and discreet. Don't feel constrained by techniques: the subject is inherently beautiful, and approaches to it are varied.

When color is removed from images of the body, the result is more abstract, almost objectified. Try setting your camera to black and white, or change the image to monochrome on a computer later. If you are shooting in color and are dissatisfied with the way skin tones appear in your image, turning the picture into a black-and-white portrait might help.

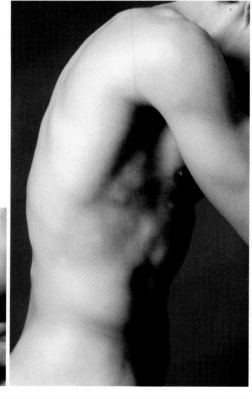
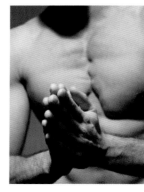

AVOID BUSY BACKGROUNDS
Start by using plain backgrounds, since these show off the body best. Once you have more experience, you can experiment with the complicated visual language of busy backgrounds.

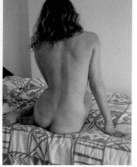

DIRECT YOUR SITTER
Ask your model to assume simple, natural poses. In nude studies, big gestures easily look unnaturally exaggerated.

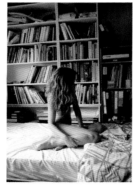
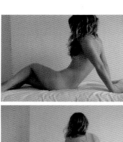
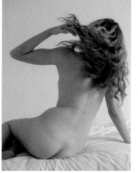

INTRODUCE PROPS
Props—hats, shawls, and other accessories—may help your model to relax by giving her something to handle.

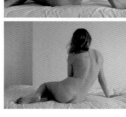
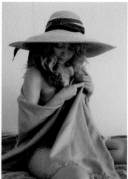
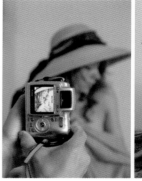

FOR THIS SHOT

I zoomed in with a long focal length setting from a medium distance, with no flash, for a tight composition and to lose the background. I set all the quality settings at maximum, including a low ISO.

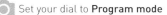

CAMERA MODE

 Set your dial to **Program mode**

LENS SETTING

Zoom to **Medium Telephoto**

SENSOR/FILM SPEED

Use a **Low** ISO setting

FLASH

Force the flash **Off**

4 CONSIDER ZOOM AND CROPS

Ask your model to move smoothly and steadily, as if in a dance. Then try different zoom settings to show more or less of the body.

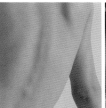 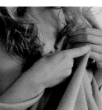

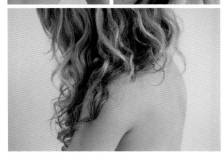

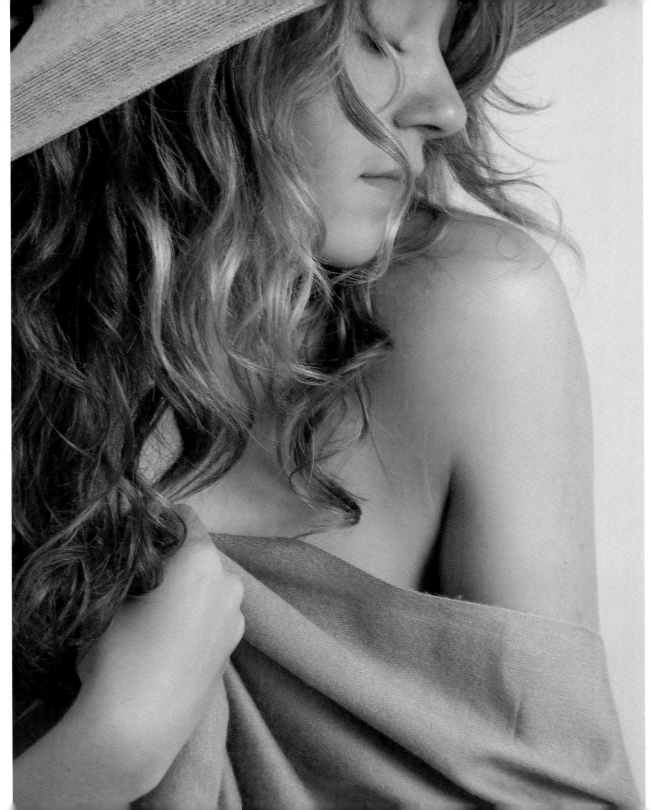

Character-driven portraits

Some people's faces are so full of character, they beg to be photographed. The key to informal portraits is to understand that sitters are likely to be nervous or self-conscious. This can result in awkward, tense poses, or in a tendency to play up to the camera. Get your sitter to relax. For a close-up portrait, instead of standing close to them, set a long focal length. An alternative approach is to use a wider focal length and step back a little to show the sitter within their environment.

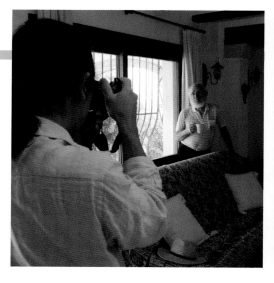

GET THE LIGHT RIGHT
Start by placing your sitter in good light – for example, next to a window that is not in direct sunlight. This light source is not too harsh and allows shadows to define features. Move closer to the sitter as they grow more relaxed.

RELAX THE SITTER
Your sitter will be more relaxed if they have something to do with their hands, such as holding a drink or a tool of their trade, rather than trying to strike a pose. Keep chatting and taking photographs the whole time.

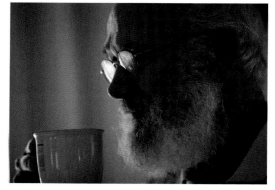

SHARE THE RESULTS
Show your sitter some of your shots so they can tell you what they like and can see what you are trying to achieve. This can be helpful for both of you.

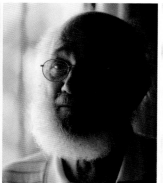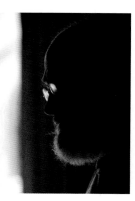

KEEP SHOOTING
Take lots of pictures to help the sitter grow more confident in front of the camera, and to catch the elusive expression that best encapsulates their character. Be aware that small adjustments of position will affect the lighting.

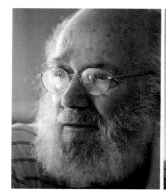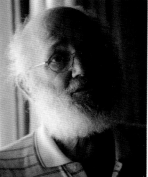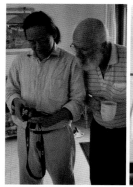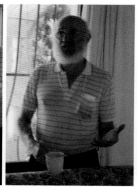

FOR THIS SHOT

I zoomed in from a distance of about 6 ft (2 m) to give a comfortable perspective to the subject. I used the highest quality setting and aperture priority to set the maximum aperture to ensure reduced depth of field.

 CAMERA MODE

 Set your dial to **Portrait mode**

LENS SETTING

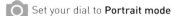 Zoom to **Medium Telephoto**

SENSOR/FILM SPEED

Use a **Medium** to **High** ISO setting

FLASH

Force the flash **Off**

FOCUS ON THE EYE

Make sure that the closest eye is sharply in focus. The rest of the image can be slightly unsharp and still be acceptable.

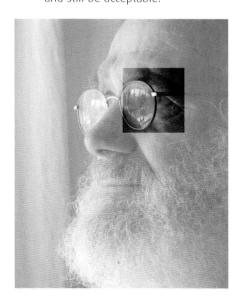

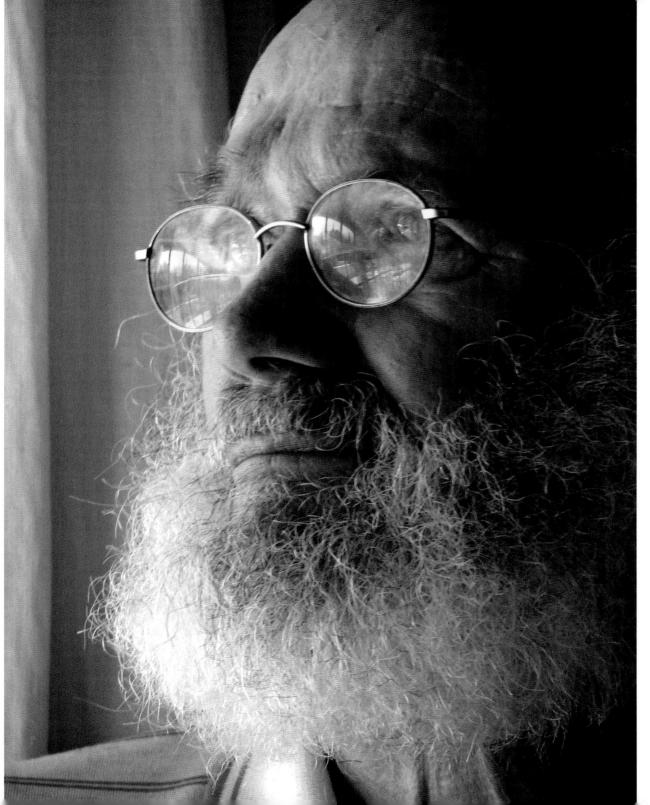

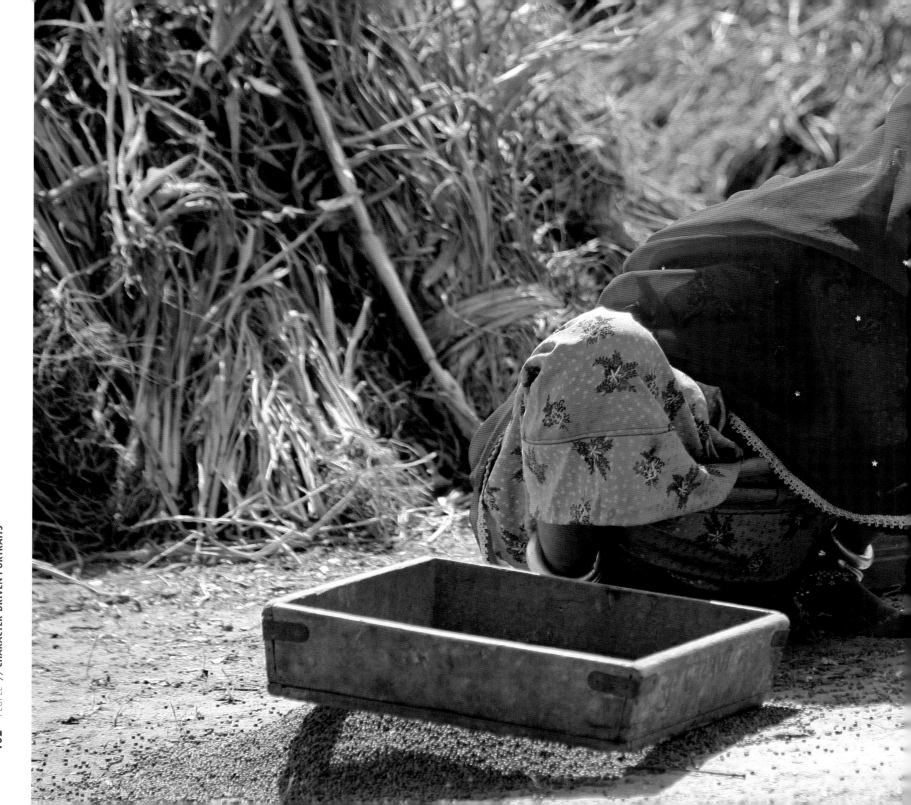

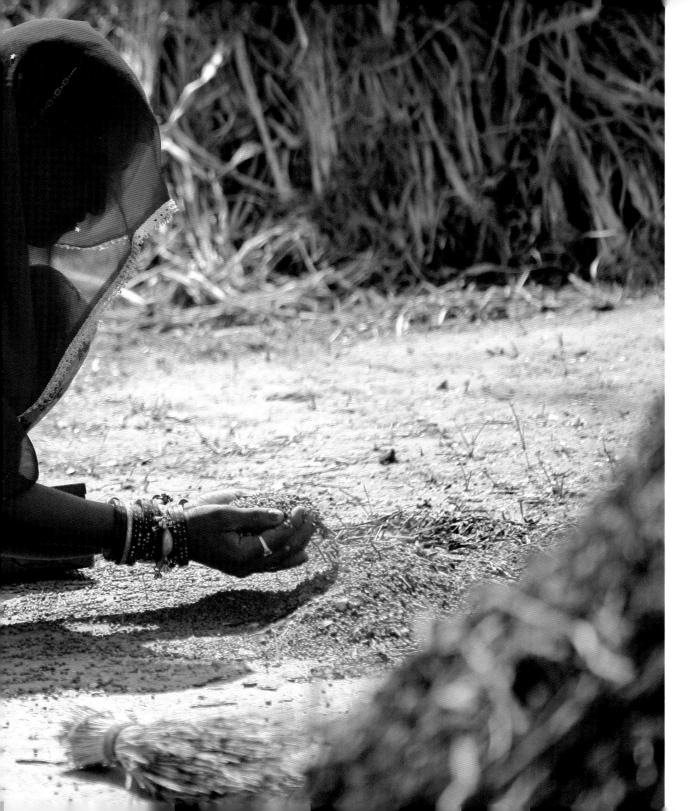

SUNNY RURAL SCENE

Brilliantly sunny days pose a challenge, because it is not easy for the camera to judge the right exposure. For this working scene in Rajasthan, India, I positioned myself with the sun to one side to catch both lit and shadowed parts of the subject.

1 Watch and wait for a telling moment before you release the shutter.

2 Zoom into the scene to reduce the amount of information in direct sunlight.

3 Expose for the colors that matter the most – in this case, those of the woman's clothes.

4 To bring out the colors, such as the vivid red of the scarf, position yourself so that the light shines directly on them.

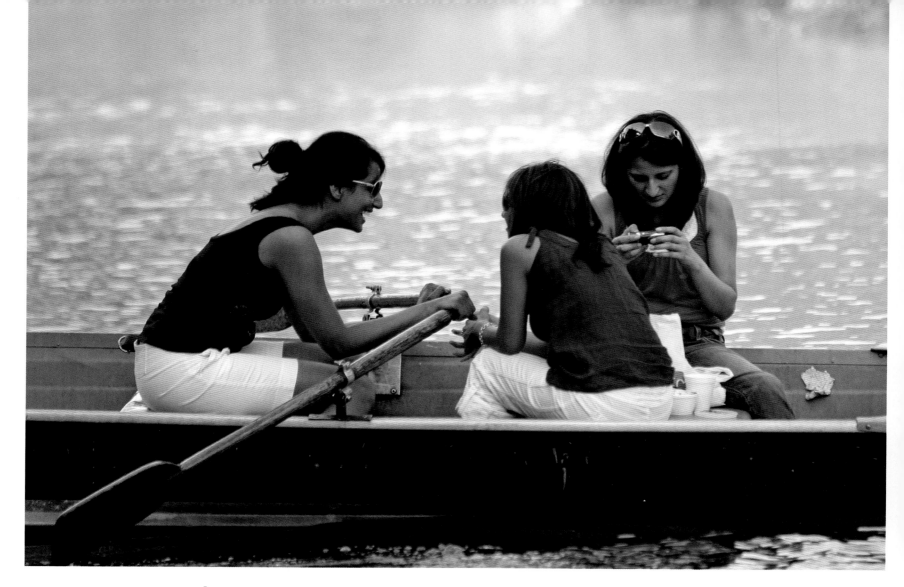

Unposed portraiture

Parks are a rich arena for photography, especially those that include lakes or rivers. As well as the scenery, you can take pictures of local wildlife, and people. The boating lake, with its constantly changing array of faces, is a rewarding place to capture informal shots of people enjoying themselves. A long-lens zoom setting ensures you can photograph people from the shore without making them feel self-conscious about being in your picture.

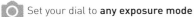
OBSERVE THE SCENE

There will be a lot going on all around you, so take the time to absorb the scene and to notice the subjects that seem to have most promise. Here, there were lots of groups of people rowing on the lake, chatting, laughing, and having fun.

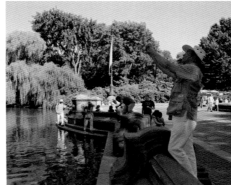

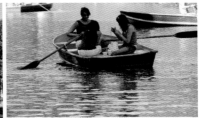

TAKE LOTS OF PICTURES

As you record life on the lake, you will find certain subjects attract your attention more than others. It may be their looks, their boating prowess, or the colors of their clothes. Take different shots of them. You do not have to make a definitive shot at the first try.

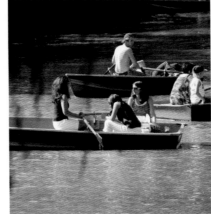

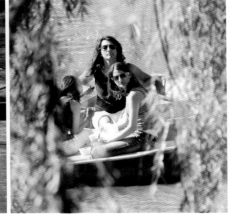

BLOCK BRIGHT LIGHT

If the sun is shining very brightly, position yourself in shade. Subjects taken in diffused light will give you better colors. If your camera has no viewfinder and only an LCD screen, shade it with a hand to improve the clarity of the image.

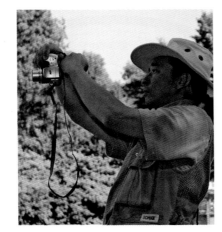

CATCH THE MOMENT

If your favorite subject in the scene is in a good position, do not hesitate to get your shot. Take pictures in quick succession to ensure you catch the right moment.

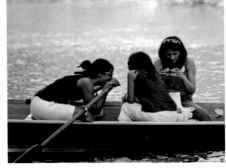

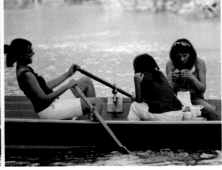

People

We point cameras at the faces of friends, family, and acquaintances more than at any other subject. A person's character is usually all that is needed to make a photograph striking or memorable. But the addition of another element – such as a balanced moment of emotion and composition, or simply a revelation of the sitter's personality – will lift your people photography to another level.

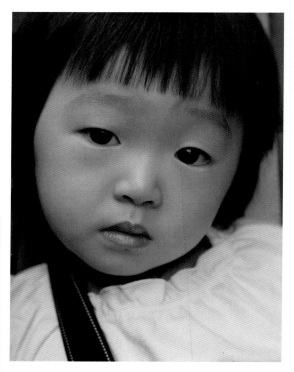

FACE TO FACE
Children are often shy around cameras, but also intrigued by what you are doing: just be sure to make and keep eye contact with them through the shoot.

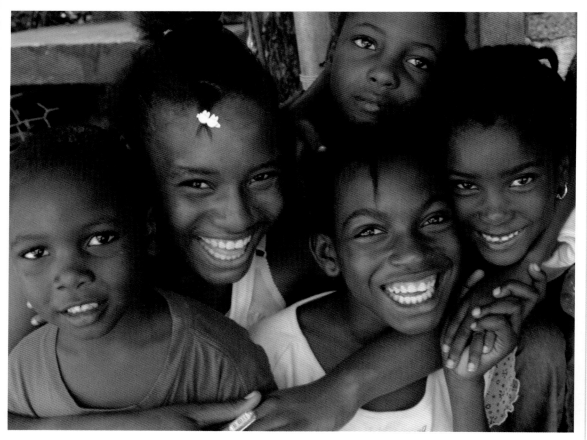

FAMILY GROUP
If you can turn a picture of the family into an enjoyable session full of love and laughter, the photograph will create itself for you.

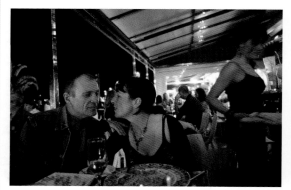

ADDING CONTEXT
What could have been a simple shot of a couple dining looks like a documentary picture thanks to inclusion of the waitress and the restaurant environment.

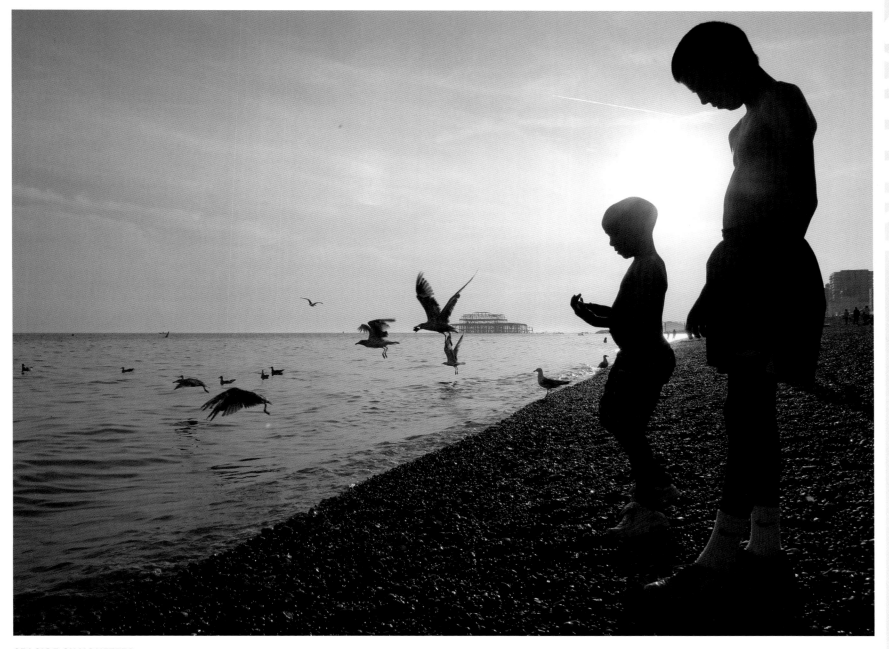

SEASIDE SILHOUETTES
You don't need to show the subject's face to create an effective portrait. Here, I exposed for the sky, rendering the boys as silhouettes.

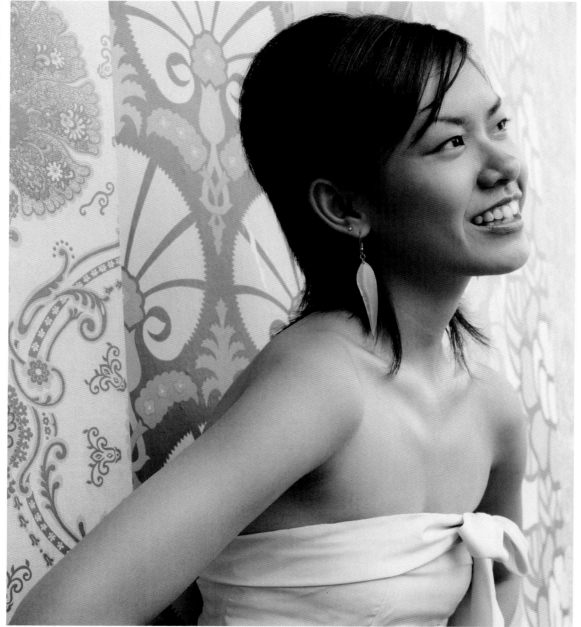

APPROPRIATE BACKGROUND
Normally you would avoid strongly patterned backgrounds for a portrait, but if the colors are right, your portrait may benefit from them.

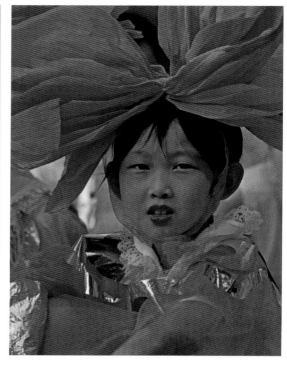

NATURAL FRAME
The mass of pink material forms an effective frame for this girl's face. A frame is important because the light is very soft, reducing the face's defining features.

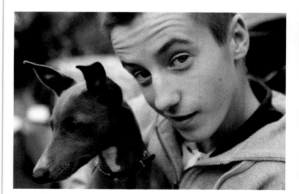

REVEALING CHARACTER
Try showing a person's character indirectly. This can be done through their possessions, the way they dress, or even their choice of pet.

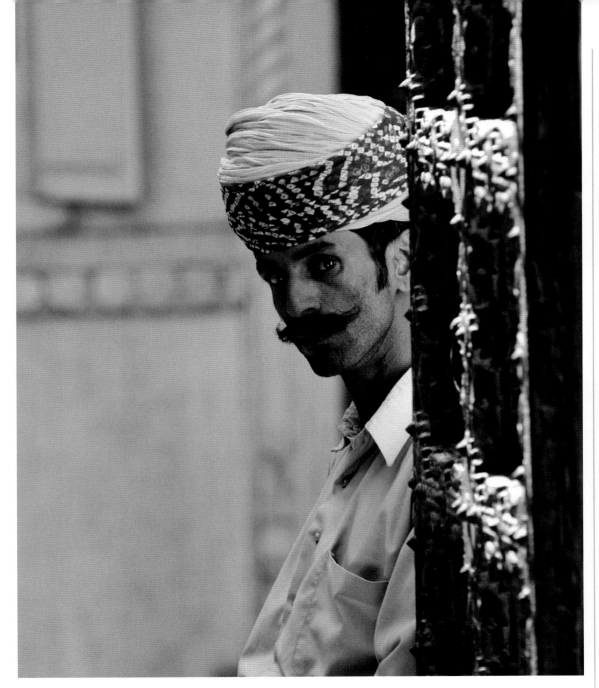

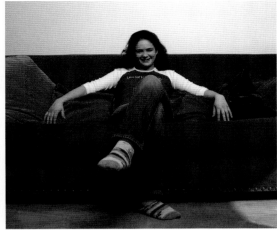

INFORMAL POSE

You can turn a striking formal portrait with strong symmetry and composition into an informal shot with the addition of a broad smile and a relaxed pose.

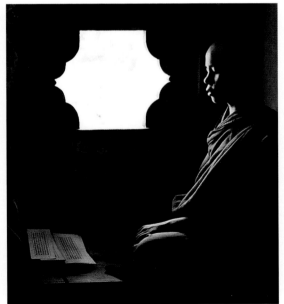

DISTANT PORTRAIT

If people don't know you well, they may be more comfortable if you take their portrait from a distance, using a telephoto setting.

DRAMATIC LIGHT

Don't be afraid to experiment with lighting. Here, the very strong light from the window shapes the face beautifully. Expose to allow shadows to be very dark.

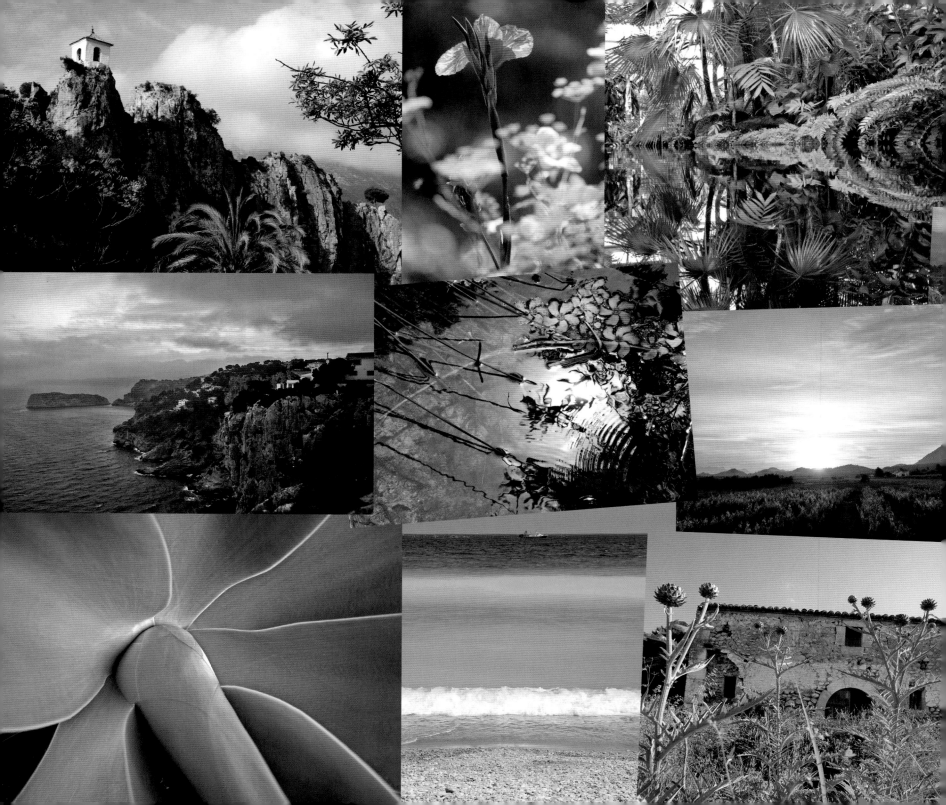

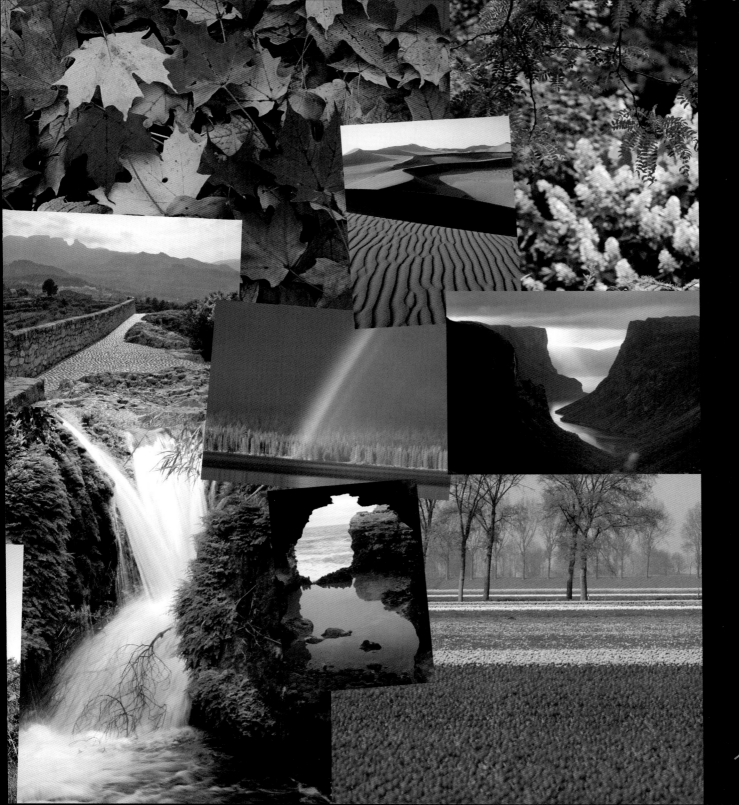

Landscapes
and nature

12345678

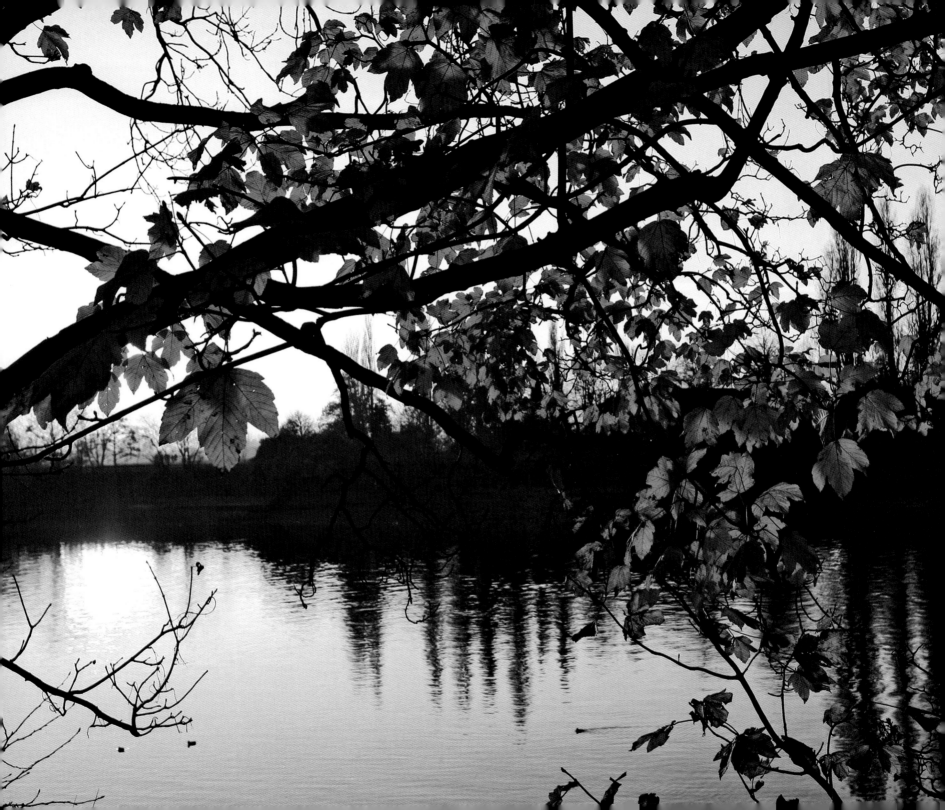

Landscapes and nature can be combined with the latest photographic technology in a wonderfully symbiotic way. Through your images, you can celebrate the many faces of the planet, its plant life, light, and seasonal changes. At the same time, your images may help strike a blow against the forces that threaten the environment. Your enjoyment of the natural world—and your photography of it—calls for a partnership of technique and vision. You will learn how to find the best viewpoints and compositions, blend shadow with light, synchronize the release of the shutter with the peak of the action when photographing natural phenomena, and work in both dim conditions and bright sunlight.

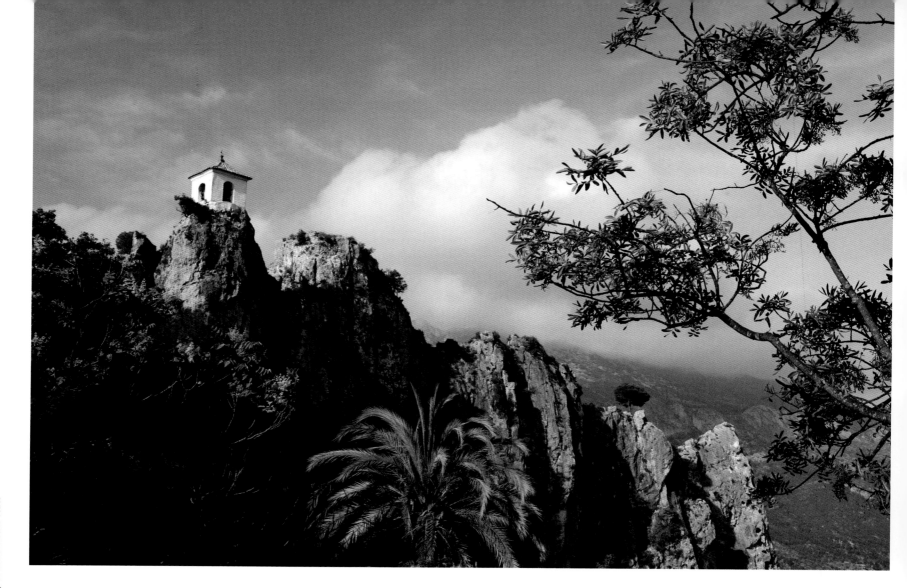

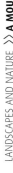
A mountain view

Sometimes, once you have climbed to a well-known vantage point with great views, you might wonder how a single picture can encapsulate the experience of the scene. The choice of what to photograph can be almost overwhelming. In such circumstances, the trick is to put your camera away, walk around, and just absorb the place for a while. The picture that will capture the place for you is the view that gives you the strongest feelings.

FOR THIS SHOT

I set a moderate wide-angle. I found a safe vantage point above the path and, by leaning to the left, I "moved" the tree to the right. Then I waited for lovely light to complete the shot.

CAMERA MODE

Set your dial to **Landscape mode**

LENS SETTING

Zoom to **Medium** to **Wide Angle**

SENSOR/FILM SPEED

Use a **Low** ISO setting

FLASH

Force the flash **Off**

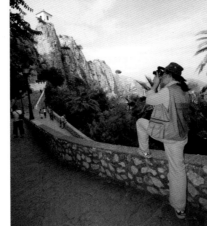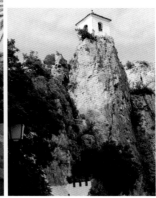

1 EXPLORE VIEWPOINTS

Mountain locations offer many viewpoints, and often your first shot will be the most obvious. This is fine as a starting point, but do go on to try different compositions and focal lengths.

2 INCORPORATE FOREGROUND INTEREST

A contrast between elements in the foreground and any distant ones helps to convey a sense of space and place. But choose with care. A foreground element can very easily become the dominant part of the picture, and that may not be your desired effect.

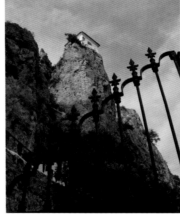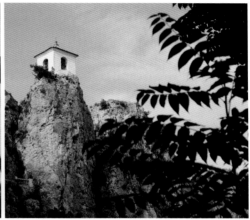

3 FRAME THE SHOT

A lot of mountainside and a lot of sky result in a lot of composition options. Myriad focal-length choices provide even greater possibilities. Aim for a balance of the elements, and look for a framing feature, such as a tree. Wait for the light to bring out the features of the rocky landscape.

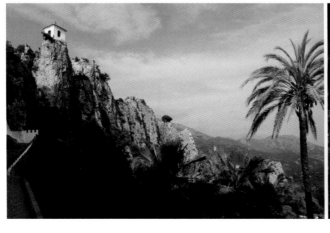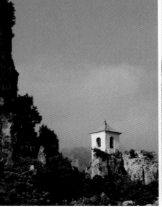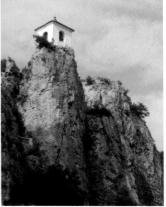

Gardens in bloom

A well-maintained garden in full bloom is a joyous sight and a photographer's dream, offering a wealth of photogenic areas. The hardest part of capturing the beauty conferred on a garden by the summer months is deciding what not to photograph. There is a wide range of gardens, both public and private, that you can explore, and they require different approaches to convey their character. Try out various views, too, from extreme close-ups to long perspective shots.

1 EXPLORE DIFFERENT ANGLES
LCD screens, especially those that flip out and rotate, allow you to hold digital cameras low or high while enabling you to see the composition of your pictures.

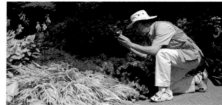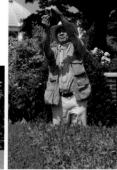

2 SHOOT FROM ABOVE
A formal garden is best shot from above. This vantage position allows you to capture the geometry of the planting. It is not always necessary to capture a wide view; narrower images can show neat symmetries.

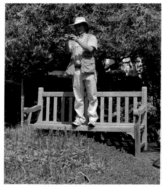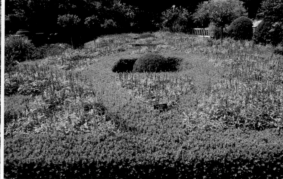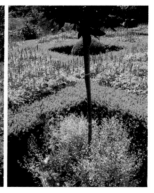

3 GET DOWN AND LOW
With their contrasting shapes and tones, rambling gardens present their own challenges to the photographer. Using a longer lens setting and shooting from a low angle can help you create a semblance of order.

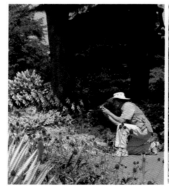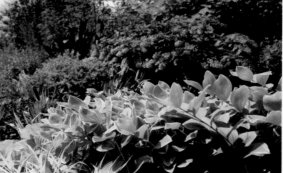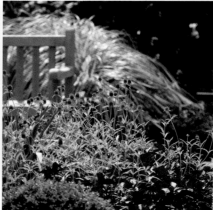

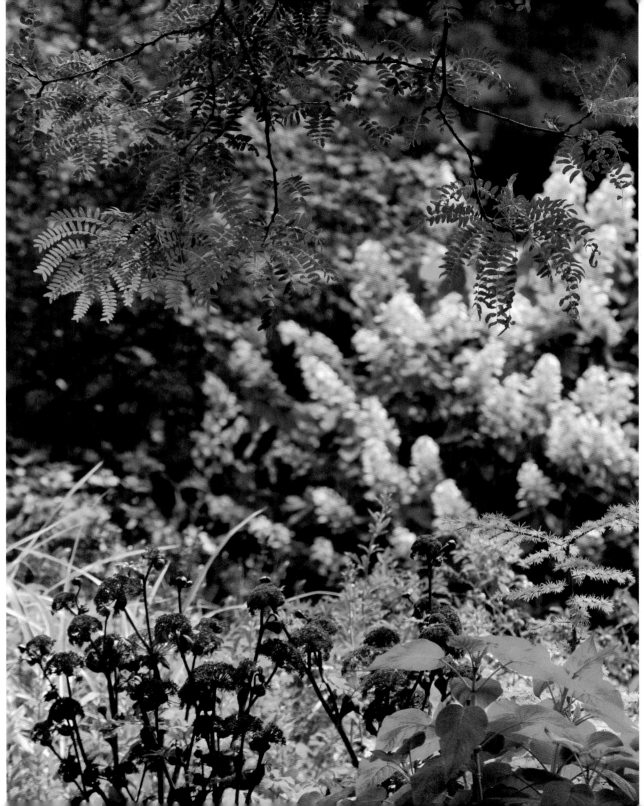

FOR THIS SHOT

I set the zoom to maximum telephoto and selected a low sensitivity to minimize the depth of field. The whole effect of the image is dependent on leaving the background sufficiently blurred.

CAMERA MODE

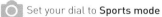 Set your dial to **Sports mode**

LENS SETTING

Zoom to **Maximum Telephoto**

SENSOR/FILM SPEED

Use a **Low** ISO setting

FLASH

Force the flash **Off**

4 SELECT YOUR DEPTH OF FIELD

Using a very long lens on a small part of the garden has the effect of bringing one plane of plants into sharp focus, while everything around it remains nicely blurred.

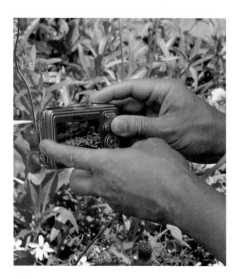

Flowers in close-up

For such reliably beautiful subjects for photography, flowers are incredibly difficult to shoot well. Although they may stay in one place for you, and they are full of color and delightful shapes, there is one major drawback. To make the most of them, you have to move in close, and that is where your problems start. Inaccuracies in focusing are increased, any movement during exposure is magnified, and depth of field is very limited.

 USE A TRIPOD
The best aid to flower photography is a tripod. This keeps the camera still enough to enable as long exposures as possible for maximum depth of field. Make sure you choose days without a breath of wind, though, since the flowers must be still, too.

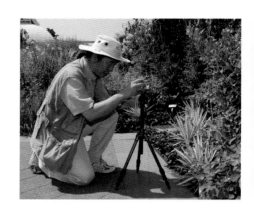

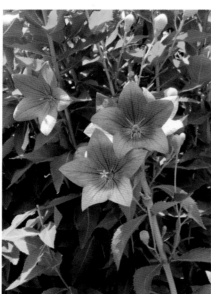

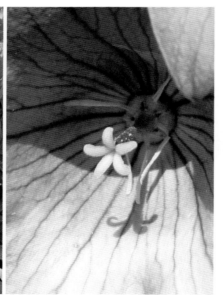

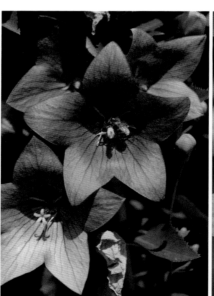

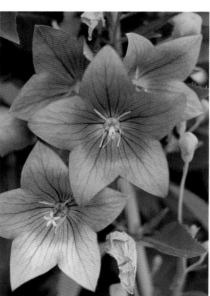

CHOOSE YOUR COMPOSITION
Look for blossoms that have a good shape and are grouped together. This will help you build a strong composition. You can then either shoot the entire group, together with the leaves, or opt for a bee's-eye view of the plant from really close up.

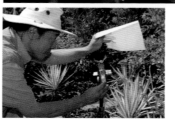

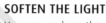 **SOFTEN THE LIGHT**
You can reduce the unflattering effects of hard light by using fill-in flash. Alternatively, hold up a sheet of paper to soften the light falling on the plants or to reflect light from below.

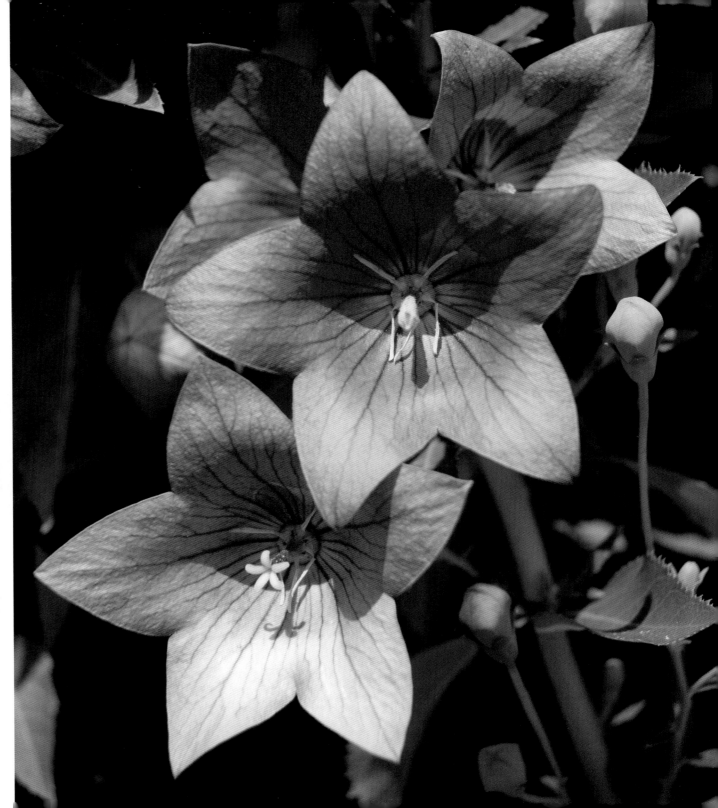

FOR THIS SHOT

I selected the macro, or close-up, mode and angled a sheet of paper to reflect light into the flower. I used the flower mode or aperture-priority exposure with minimum aperture to obtain the greatest possible depth of field.

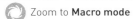

CAMERA MODE

Set your dial to **Flower mode**

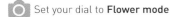

LENS SETTING

Zoom to **Macro mode**

SENSOR/FILM SPEED

Use a **Low** to **Medium** ISO setting

FLASH

Force the flash to **Automatic**

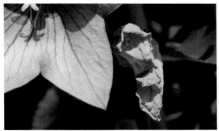

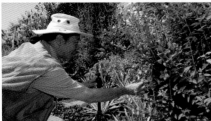

TIDY UP

If you are obsessive about such things, remove any dead blossoms or twigs that get in the way. However, you may prefer the natural look to the aseptic.

Flowers and foliage

The enchanting beauty of plant forms, particularly flowers, has been the object of admiration and artistic effort since the dawn of art itself. Photography enables anyone to record the graphic diversity of plant life with an ease unmatched by other art forms. Take your photography one step further by showing the plants so they are identifiable, while at the same time creating a picture that can stand by itself as a strong image.

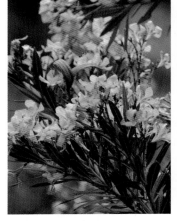

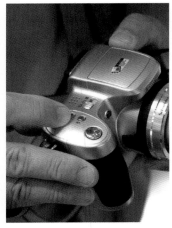

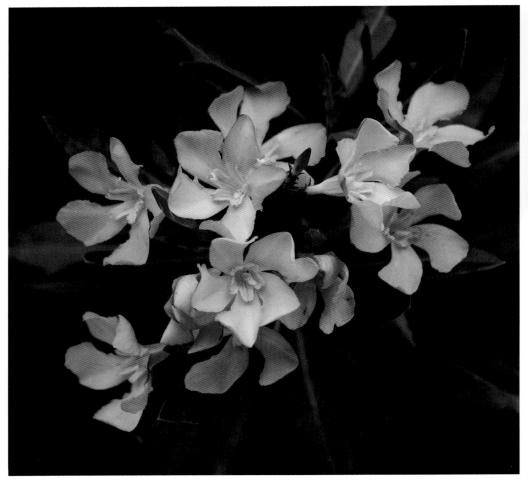

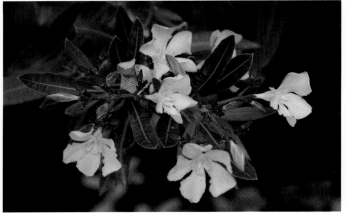

ENHANCING COLORS

At first glance, these flowers seem like an easy subject. However, it soon becomes apparent that the masses of blooms put too much information into the picture. The solution is to isolate a choice bunch against a clean background that enhances their color.

1 Take the exposure from the flowers, and keep the background dark.

2 Use a long focal length setting to help isolate the blossoms and blur the background.

3 Only use flash if it is really dark, otherwise it might spoil the natural lighting.

ADDING INTEREST

Blossoms are spectacular in themselves, but the simple addition of an insect can bring the picture to life.

1 Use flash in full sunlight to help freeze rapid motion and control shadows.

2 Set a long zoom and get as close as you are able to focus for the largest magnification.

3 Focus on a flower and wait for an insect to land on it.

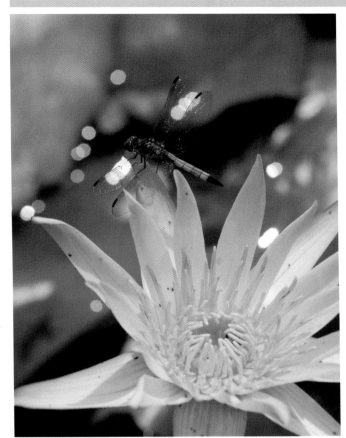

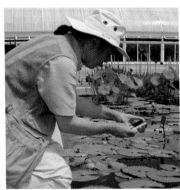

BACKLIT LEAF

Very large leaves, such as those of the taro plant, are often best photographed lit from behind to show their structure.

1 Use a wide-angle setting on the zoom and get as close to the leaf as possible.

2 For a striking shot, focus on a symmetrically arranged detail, rather than a mass of leaves.

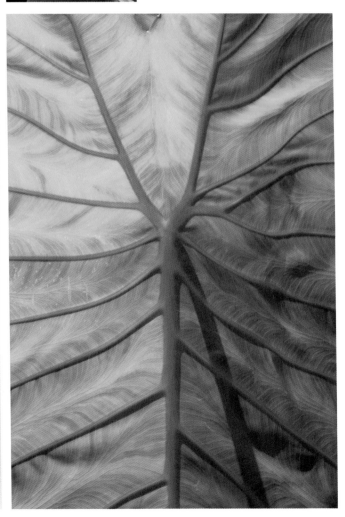

FOCUS ON RAINDROPS

Water droplets hanging from leaves and flowers add a special sparkle and an extra visual layer to pictures of plant forms.

1 For the most appealing image, position yourself so that the drops catch the light.

2 Set the zoom to a long focal length and maximum aperture to blur the background.

3 Compose very carefully: minuscule changes in position can make or break the image.

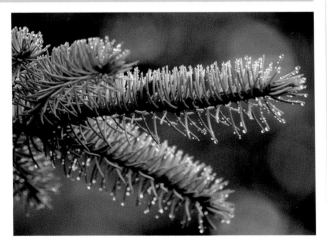

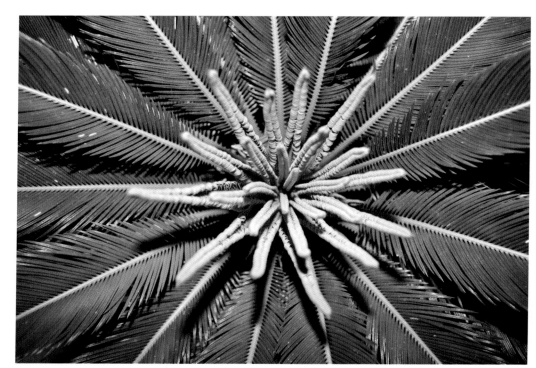

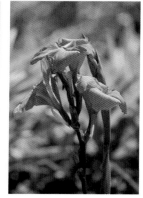

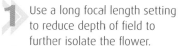

To make the most of brightly colored flowers, look for dark backgrounds that will help isolate both shape and color.

1 Use a long focal length setting to reduce depth of field to further isolate the flower.

2 Expose for the brightest parts to leave the shadowed areas dark in contrast.

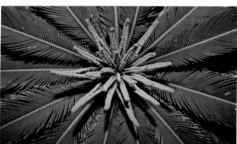

MONOCHROME ABSTRACT

Strong symmetrical plants are ideal candidates for an abstract shot in black and white. To create the most impact, keep the composition simple.

1 Try different lighting: in this instance, direct flash helped to create strong contrasts and clean lines.

2 Hold the camera square on to the plant pattern to make it as abstract and evenly sharp as possible.

3 Set to black-and-white mode if available. If not, capture the image in color, and change it on your computer later.

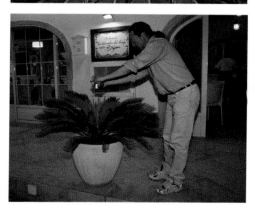

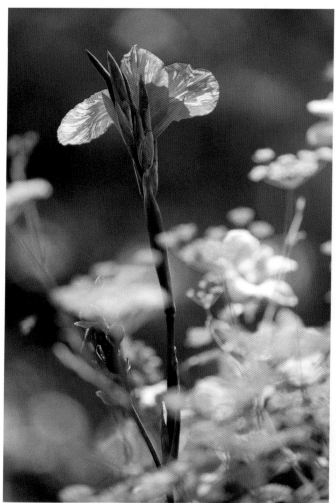

BUSY COMPOSITION

Pictures of plants do not have to show everything clear and sharp. The natural world offers a lively jumble of forms, textures, and shapes, so try to capture that random feeling.

> 1 Push the camera right into the mass of leaves and flowers using the close-up setting.

> 2 Turn the flash off, since it will produce unsuitably hard lighting.

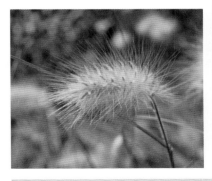

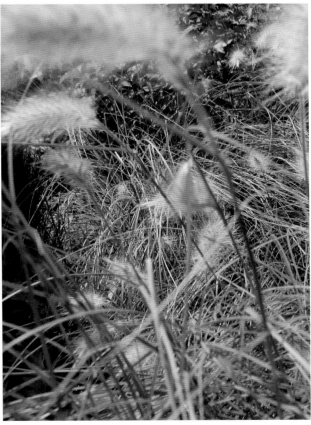

EXTREME CLOSE-UP

The closer you get to plants, they more they reveal to you. However, depth of field drops greatly, so it is hard to get everything looking sharp. Use the highest sensitivity setting available.

> 1 Use the macro, or close-up, mode, as well as a wide-angle zoom setting.

> 2 Try to line up the main features so they are square to the camera, to make the most of depth of field.

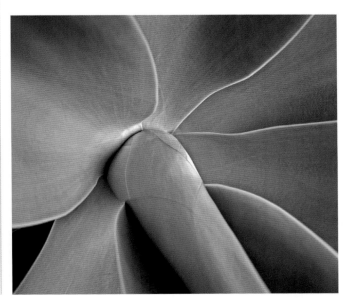

LIFT THE SHADOWS

Use a mirror or a white sheet of paper on the shadow side of the plant (but not in the shadow) to bounce fill-in light. The picture on the far left was taken looking into the mirror, since the flowers were pointing down.

> 1 To help bring out the colors in the darker areas of the flower, create extra light with mirrors or paper.

> 2 If you wish to reflect hard light, use mirrors; white paper or cloth reflects soft light into the shadows.

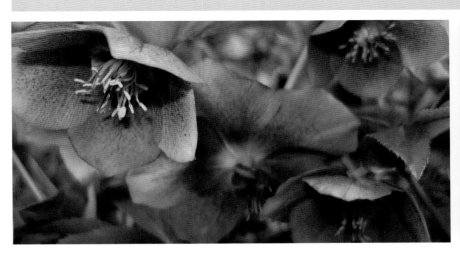

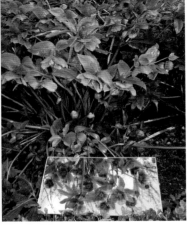

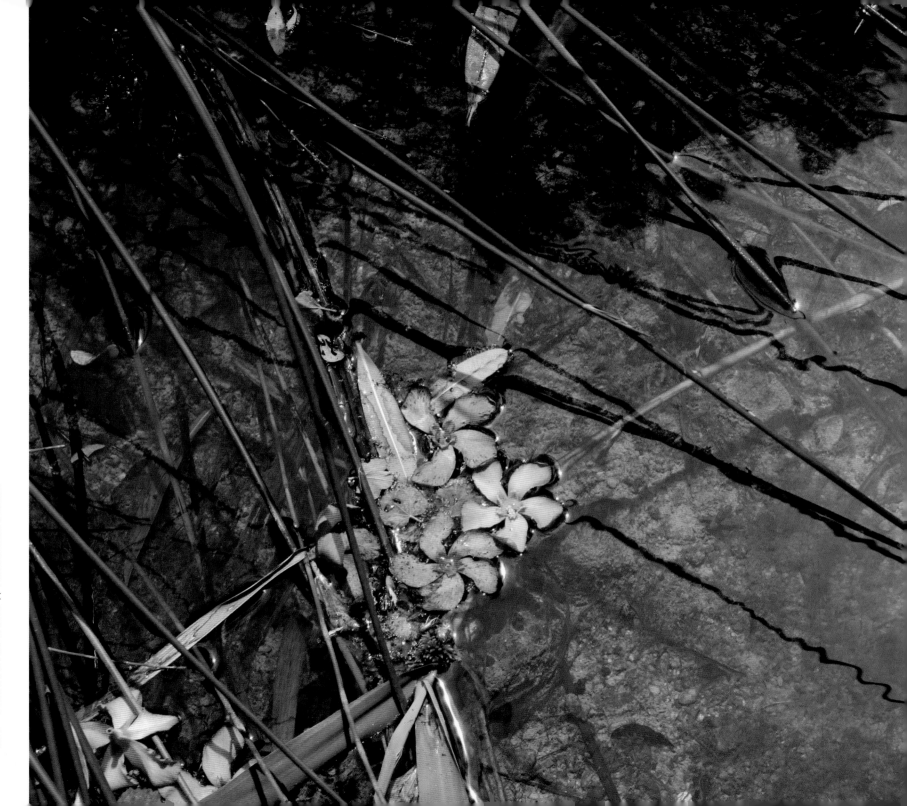

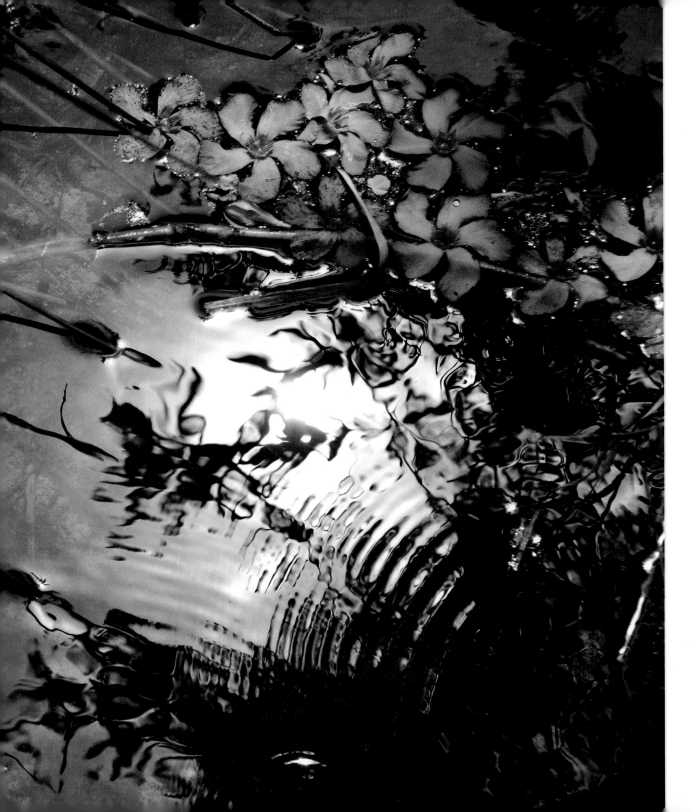

PETALS AND REFLECTIONS

Some petals and twigs floating in water might not seem obviously attractive at first glance. The key to an image such as this is to position yourself so that the sun is reflected in the water: this brings a vital brilliance into the ripples.

1 Measure the exposure from the important tones – in this case, those of the petals.

2 Hold the camera as square to the water as possible to keep everything sharp.

3 Don't remove twigs or dead leaves, even if they seem to be in the way. They add to the chanced-upon look of the shot.

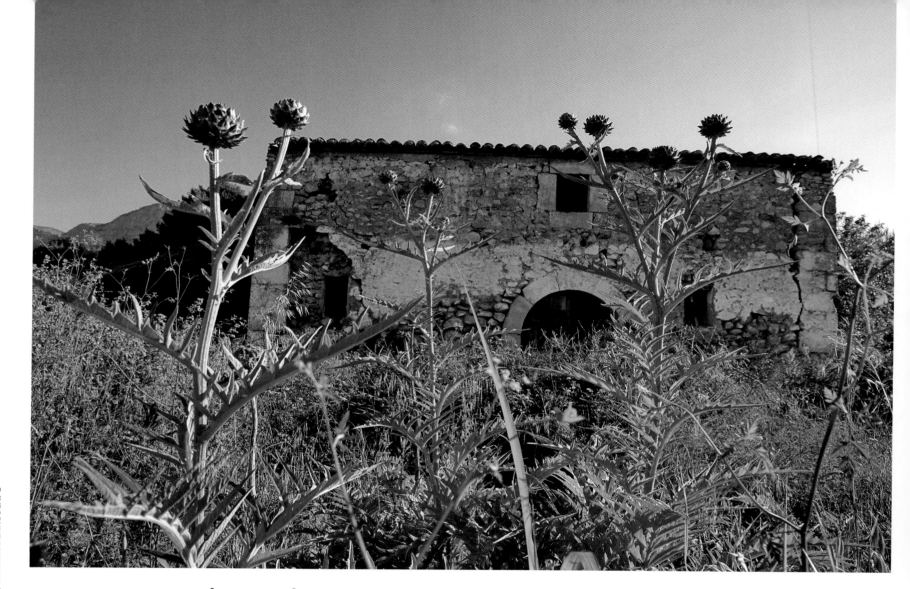

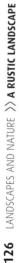

A rustic landscape

As well as a variety of wonderful natural landscapes, sometimes rural locations also yield buildings that perfectly compliment their environment. Tumbledown buildings offer several views, depending on how you shoot them, the time of day, and the quality of the light. This farmhouse could look dismal in the rain, and ominous in moonlight. However, in spite of the poor state of repair and the overgrown garden, in bright sunshine it seems full of charm.

SAFETY FIRST

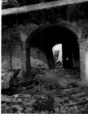
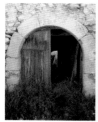
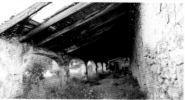

Always make sure that you are not trespassing when exploring a ruined building. Also, if there is any danger of falling debris, protect your head with a hard hat. Seek advice from a builder or architect if you can; if in doubt, keep out.

EXPLORE VIEWPOINTS

Photograph the building's different aspects while walking around it, adjusting camera settings as needed. If one side is shaded, you may need to return at another time of day, when the sun has moved around.

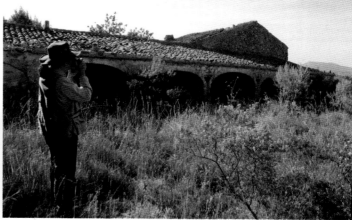

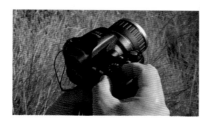

WORK WITH THE LIGHT

If the light is flat, textures will not show up, and you will lose the sense of space, as in the shot on the right. The combination of light and shade in the picture on the far right provides a better sense of shape, scale, and character.

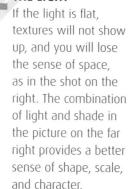
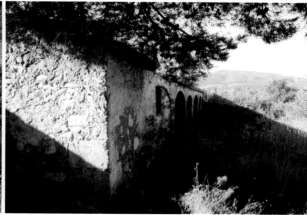

USE THE FOREGROUND

Emphasize some foreground elements by choosing a low viewpoint. Use a wide-angle setting and small aperture to maximize depth of field and keep everything sharp.

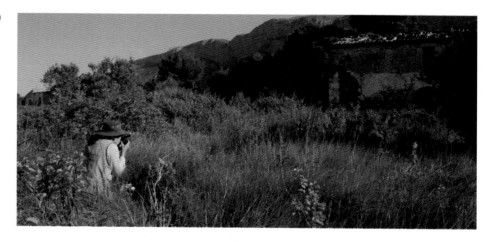

Panoramic views

When faced with a stunning vista, it is natural that you should want to capture as much of it as possible. Digital photography has made it easy to create superb panoramic images. First, take a few shots side by side, panning the camera to take in the whole scene; then "stitch" the images together on a computer. Your panorama can be as modest as two views side by side, or as wide as a 360-degree shot. The wider the view, the more dramatic the visual effect.

1 FIND A SUITABLE SCENE
Any scene so wide that you must turn your head to take it all in is a good candidate for a panorama. It helps if the lighting is even and not changing quickly, and it is also easier to join the pictures if there are no straight lines running across the image.

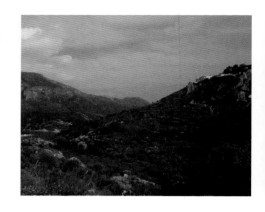

2 ADJUST CAMERA SETTINGS
Set the exposure mode to manual and adjust it for the correct exposure. Set your zoom to 35mm or equivalent; this is the widest setting on the majority of point-and-shoot cameras.

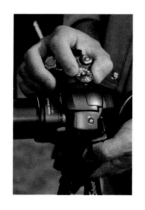

3 USE A TRIPOD
Although not absolutely necessary, you will obtain sharper images and cleaner panoramas if you use a tripod. The tripod also helps ensure the camera is held level throughout the process.

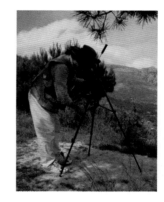

4 ORIENT THE CAMERA
For best results and to reduce distortion, set your camera vertically on the tripod. This will mean taking more pictures to create a panorama, but it will be worth the effort. If it is possible on your model, the camera should rotate above the center of the tripod.

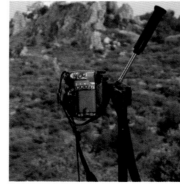
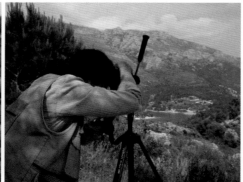

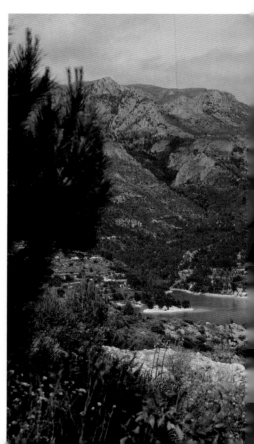

⟫ FOR THIS SHOT

I set a wide zoom, small image size, and low ISO to achieve good quality. I also used manual metering so that the exposure levels would not change from one shot to the next.

CAMERA MODE

Set your dial to **Manual**

LENS SETTING

Zoom to **Wide Angle**

SENSOR/FILM SPEED

Use a **Low** ISO setting

FLASH

Force the flash **Off**

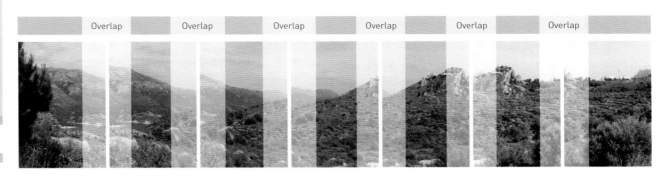

STITCH THE PHOTOGRAPHS

Plan for at least a 30 percent overlap between shots. The panoramic mode on some cameras will help you to do this. Once you have the images on your computer, you can join them "by hand" or use panoramic software.

The overlap enables you or the software to line up one image after another – the greater the overlap, the better the quality of the blend. Be aware, though, that even with small images, the resulting file can be large.

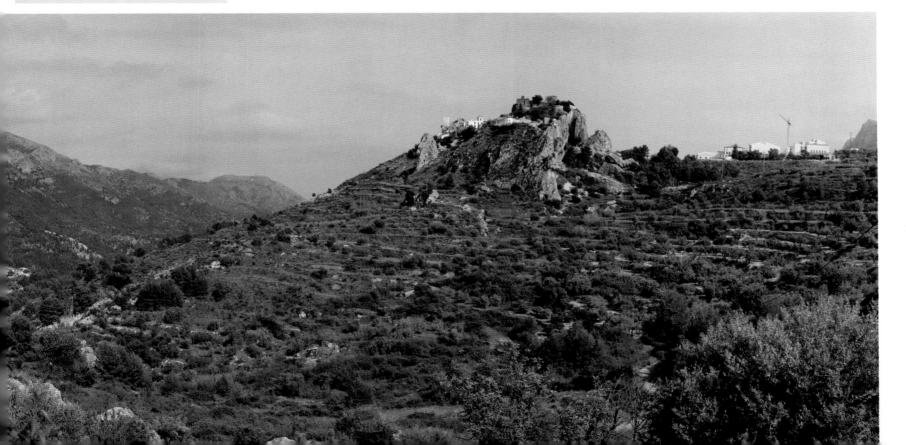

Landscapes in black and white

Photographing landscapes in black and white separates our experience of the scene from our statement about it. It gives us added mastery over the subject. Not only do we select a certain view, we can also choose how it looks. Black-and-white images draw attention to the forms and abstract qualities of the scene, bringing picture composition, rather than subject, to the fore. Different light available at different times of day will also affect the end result.

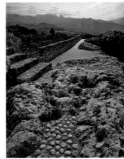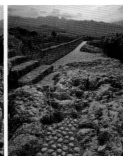

Sepia tone   **Gold tone**

1 EXPLORE POSSIBILITIES

Almost any black-and-white landscape picture will be as effective as its color version. However, some scenes contain elements that work especially well. The textures of an old city wall or terraced hills, for example, may offer promise that other views do not.

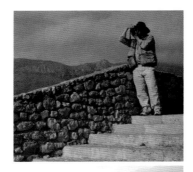

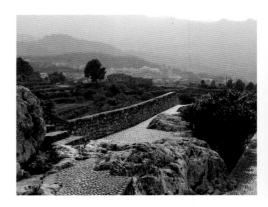

2 LOOK FOR LIGHT AND LINES

Identify strong lines that take the eye through the view, and find the angle in which the lighting helps bring out any shapes and textures. Use your LCD screen to help with composition.

3 EXAMINE THE SCENE

Make a few small shifts in your position—move side to side or get higher or go lower—to find the best view. Take your time exploring and looking closely at your subject: that is all part of the enjoyment of photography.

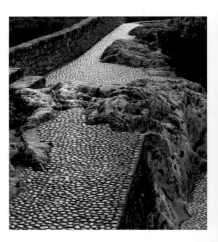

▶▶ FOR THIS SHOT

With the zoom set to its widest and the aperture to minimum, I focused on the middle distance—not to the background—for maximum depth of field. Finally, I set the camera to black-and-white mode.

CAMERA MODE

 Set your dial to **Aperture Priority**

LENS SETTING

Zoom to **Wide Angle**

SENSOR/FILM SPEED

Use a **Low to Medium** ISO setting

FLASH

Force the flash **Off**

4 CONVEY A SENSE OF SPACE

The final image combines a variety of scale and texture, as well as a sense of tone and space. Converting the image to black and white emphasizes all these elements.

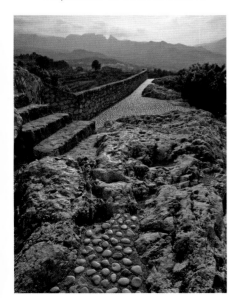

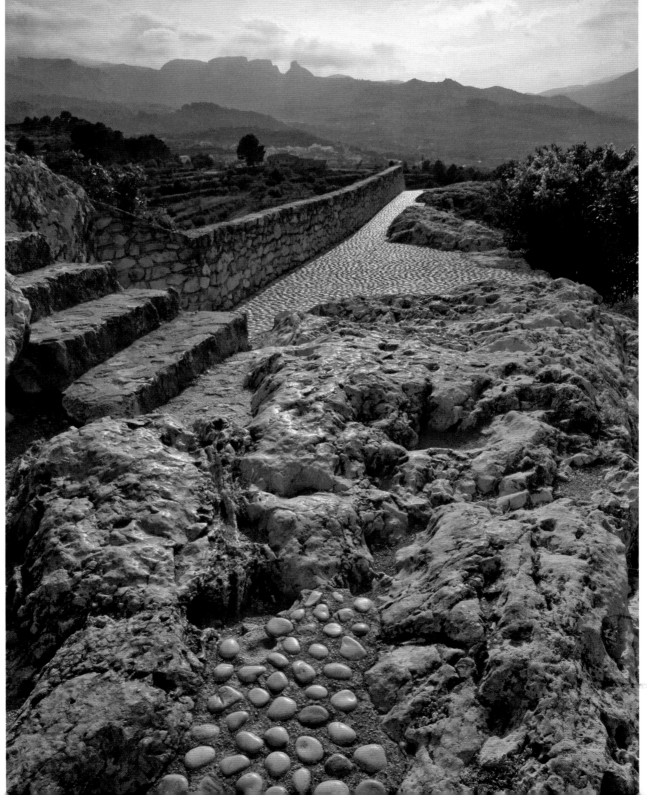

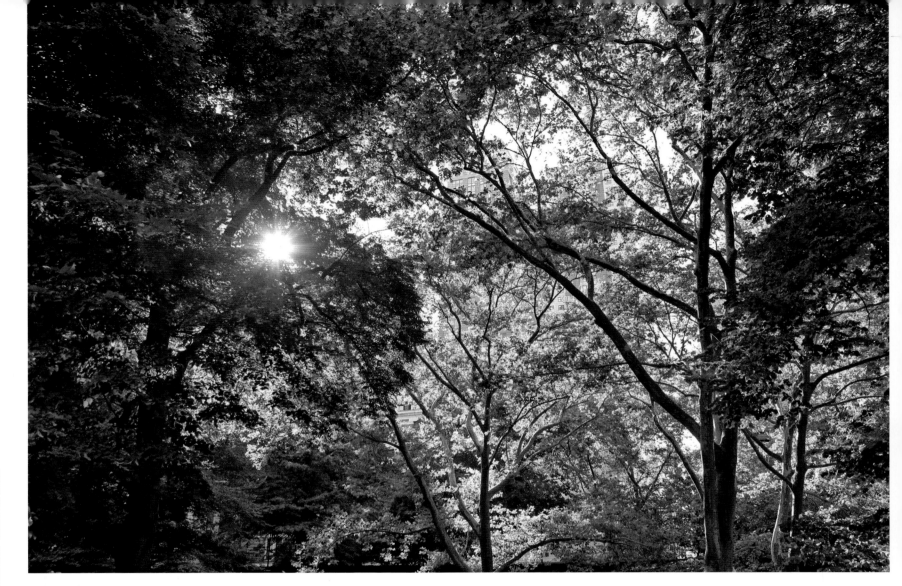

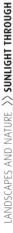

Sunlight through trees

An attempt at capturing sunshine streaming through the leaves of trees presents a series of challenges. First, there is the amount of fine detail that you want to record; then you have to deal with the wide range of light, from the brightest direct sun to the dark tones of the shadowed leaves. Finally, you want to obtain colors that accurately reflect all the delicate variations of green. This is a balancing act that only becomes perfect with practice.

FOR THIS SHOT

I took a picture, reviewed it and had to increase exposure because auto-exposure compensated for the sunlight, thus under exposing. I used a moderate wide-angle lens setting on the zoom, with low sensitivity for good quality.

CAMERA MODE

Set your dial to **any automatic mode**

LENS SETTING

Zoom to **Wide Angle**

SENSOR/FILM SPEED

Use a **Low** ISO setting

FLASH

Force the flash **Off**

1 CONSIDER THE LIGHT

Try to see this scene as the camera does, not as you do with your eyes. A single setting must suit the whole scene, so you will need to find a compromise between the settings needed for the bright areas and those needed for the dark parts.

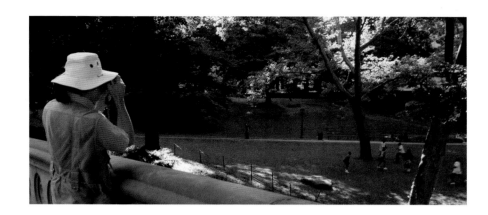

2 WORK WITH THE SUNLIGHT

In this shot, the most striking leaves are those that are lit by the sun while lying in front of darker areas, an effect known as "dark field illumination." Try to compose a shot that makes the most of this lighting effect.

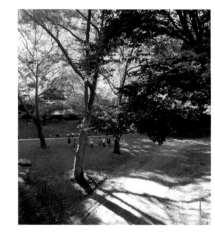

3 VARY YOUR SETTINGS

Since the view is relatively static, you can take the time to review your shots, and set less or more exposure for the best-looking results.

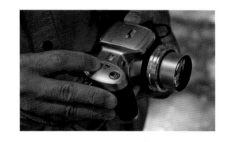

4 CHOOSE YOUR LOOK

There is no single correct exposure, since the right one depends on whether you want to achieve a dramatic look or one that suggests a hazily idyllic summer's day. The scene's huge dynamic range from bright to dark makes a compromise difficult.

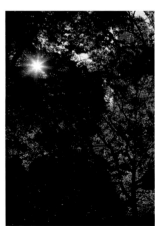
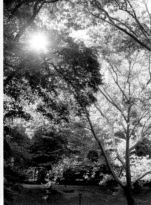

5 ZOOM IN ON THE LEAVES

A strong zoom into the scene neatly finds the middle ground between very bright and very dark. This composition focuses only on the back-lit leaves, so it fails to suggest a sense of place and context.

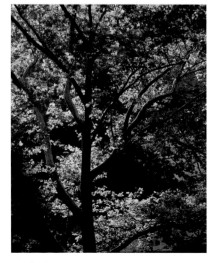

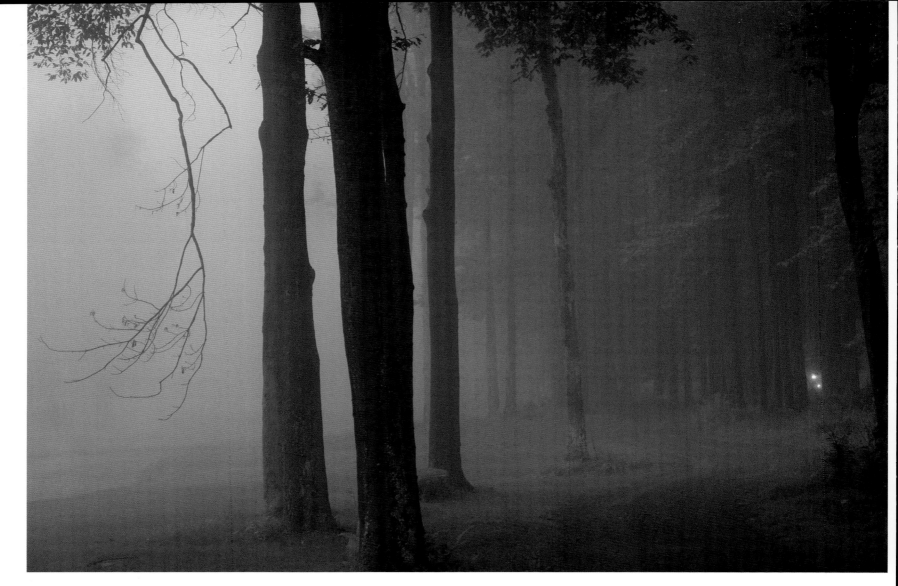

Misty woodlands

Although it might be more tempting to stay indoors on a foggy day than to brave the inclement weather in search of pictures, you will find that your efforts will be rewarded with beautifully atmospheric results. Fog and mist accentuate aerial perspective, so that small distances between nearby objects are pictorially exaggerated. This gives you pictures that are instantly different from the norm. The trick is to find subjects and compositions that exploit that illusion.

FOR THIS SHOT

I chose the landscape mode and set the zoom to normal and a medium sensitivity. The key in this shot was in waiting for the passing car. I pressed the shutter just at the moment the lights appeared between the trees.

CAMERA MODE

 Set your dial to **Landscape mode**

LENS SETTING

 Zoom to **Normal**

SENSOR/FILM SPEED

 Use a **Low** to **Medium** ISO setting

FLASH

Force the flash **Off**

1 SCOUT THE LOCATION

The gently meandering path next to a golf course is crucial to this composition. It takes the eye on a walk through the picture, creating a sense of mystery. In the fog, however, the path disappears before going too far into the trees.

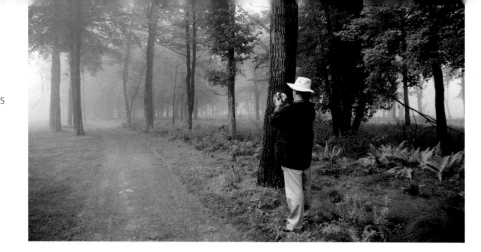

2 TRY DIFFERENT EFFECTS

Another salutary feature of fog is that it drains color away from everything, presenting you with a ready-made pastel palette. The lack of vibrant colors in the landscape means you can experiment with delightful subtleties of tone and contrast.

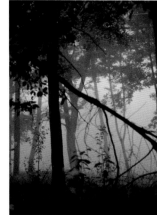
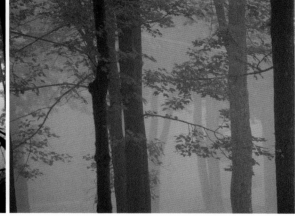

3 USE BRACKETING

Achieving the correct exposure in foggy conditions is critical – you have only a narrow range of brightness to work with, so an error can affect the entire image. Bracketing the shots – that is, taking a series of correct, over-, and underexposed shots – will ensure you have plenty of images to choose from.

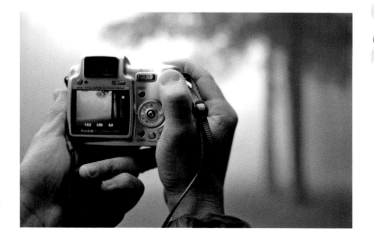

4 ADD HUMAN INTEREST

You might decide to include some subtle hints of human presence or civilization in your picture. As well as giving a sense of scale to the image, this golf cart, with its indistinct outline, highlights the denseness of the fog.

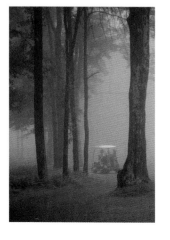

Seasons and weather

Today's compact and lightweight cameras make it possible to follow the seasons photographically with hardly any effort, documenting the effects of the weather on the environment around you. Your camera can be your companion irrespective of the weather conditions. Just be sure to look after it properly: when it rains, keep the camera dry; in cold weather, keep it warm in your pocket until you are ready to use it.

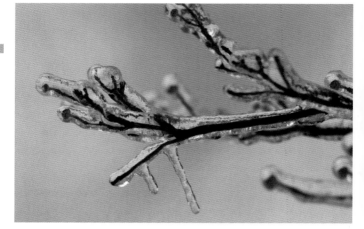

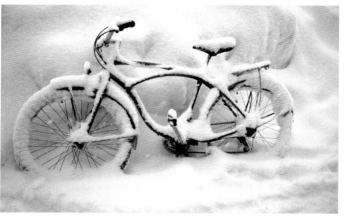

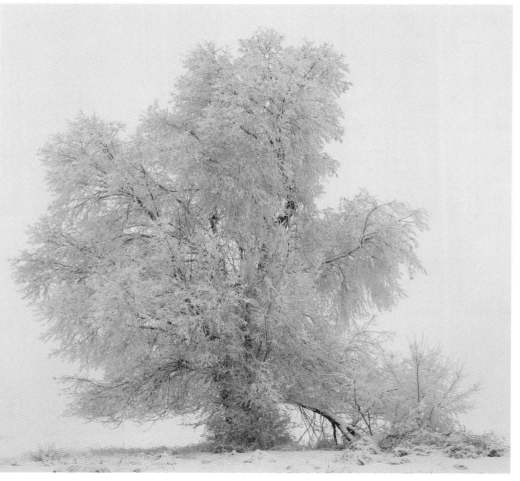

SNOW AND ICE

A blanket of snow and ice transforms the landscape into a white expanse, and gives even the most mundane objects a magical appeal.

1 Take pictures of snow scenes on both dull and sunny days, since both provide good light.

2 You may need to increase exposure to keep whites snowy white.

3 Use the highest quality available to capture the detail of fine textures.

CAPTURING RAINBOWS

One of the most entrancing weather effects is the rainbow, which is caused by water droplets acting as prisms. Rainbows are tricky to capture because their intensity is variable and their position changes rapidly.

1 Look out for rainbows after a shower: they appear in front of you when your back is to the sun.

2 For a different composition, capture part, rather than the whole, of the rainbow with a long zoom setting.

3 Against a dark sky, the colors are intensified. But even a less brilliant rainbow adds magic to a scene.

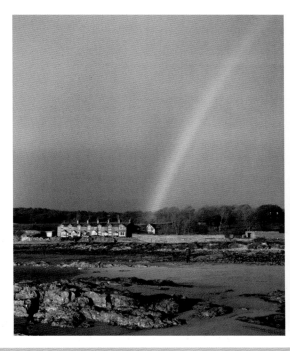

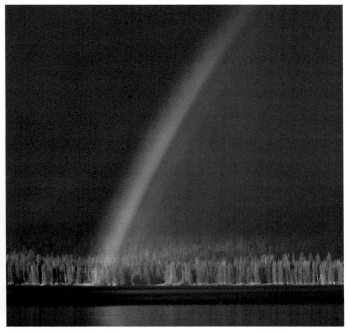

RAINY SCENE

Colors look more intense to the camera than they do to you, which means successful results even on dark, rainy days. If in doubt, shoot anyway: you are likely to be pleasantly surprised.

1 Shoot through a window – this will enable you to show the raindrops clearly.

2 Set a high sensitivity and raise color saturation and contrast in the camera.

3 Use the zoom at a wide setting to benefit from its larger maximum aperture.

SEASONAL CHANGES

The effects of the changing seasons on a favorite view, even just from a window, make an attractive and fascinating series of images. You can frame each shot the same way, or vary the composition as needed.

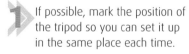 If possible, mark the position of the tripod so you can set it up in the same place each time.

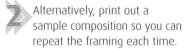 Alternatively, print out a sample composition so you can repeat the framing each time.

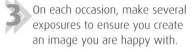 On each occasion, make several exposures to ensure you create an image you are happy with.

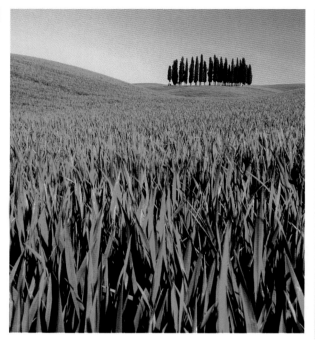

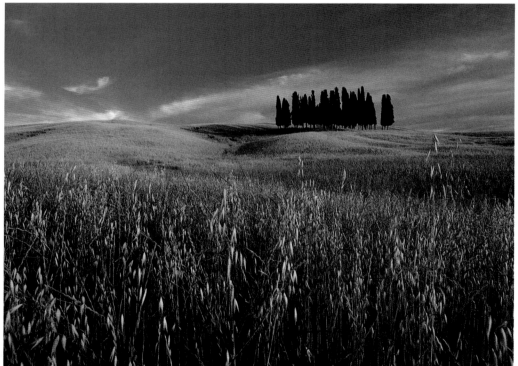

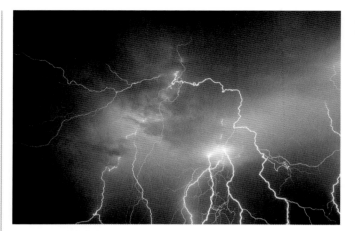

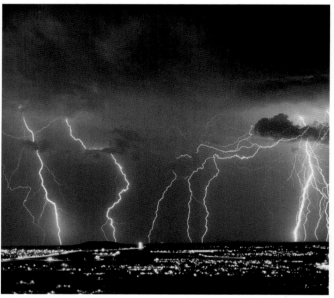

LIGHTNING STRIKES

It is easier to take studies of lightning in areas where thunderstorms are seasonally predictable. Just listen to weather forecasts, and arrive at vantage points in good time. If you chance upon an electrical storm, you will have to react quickly to get the shot.

Shoot from a safe, sheltered environment, such as inside a building.

Use a tripod, and click the shutter as soon as you see any lightning flash.

Set a long shutter time (several seconds) to catch multiple flashes.

FALL COLORS

The warm brilliance of fall colors in temperate climates is a delightful subject for photographers.

 Take broad views of the colors to place them in context.

 Frame contrasts between stark tree forms and the vibrant colors.

3 Try holding the camera level over fallen leaves to create a mosaic effect.

4 Experiment with different exposure settings to adjust color rendering.

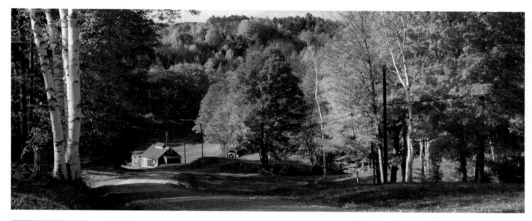

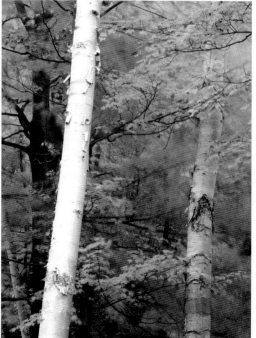

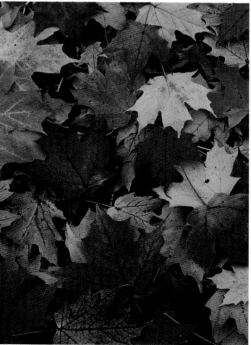

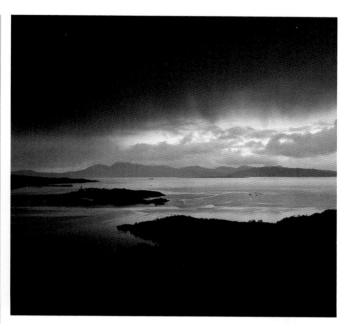

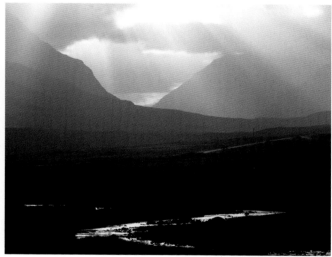

STORMY WEATHER

The light conditions that accompany stormy weather – not only during the storm itself, but also before and after – are often wonderfully atmospheric and photogenic.

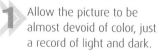 Allow the picture to be almost devoid of color, just a record of light and dark.

2 Make exposures as the conditions change to capture a whole sequence.

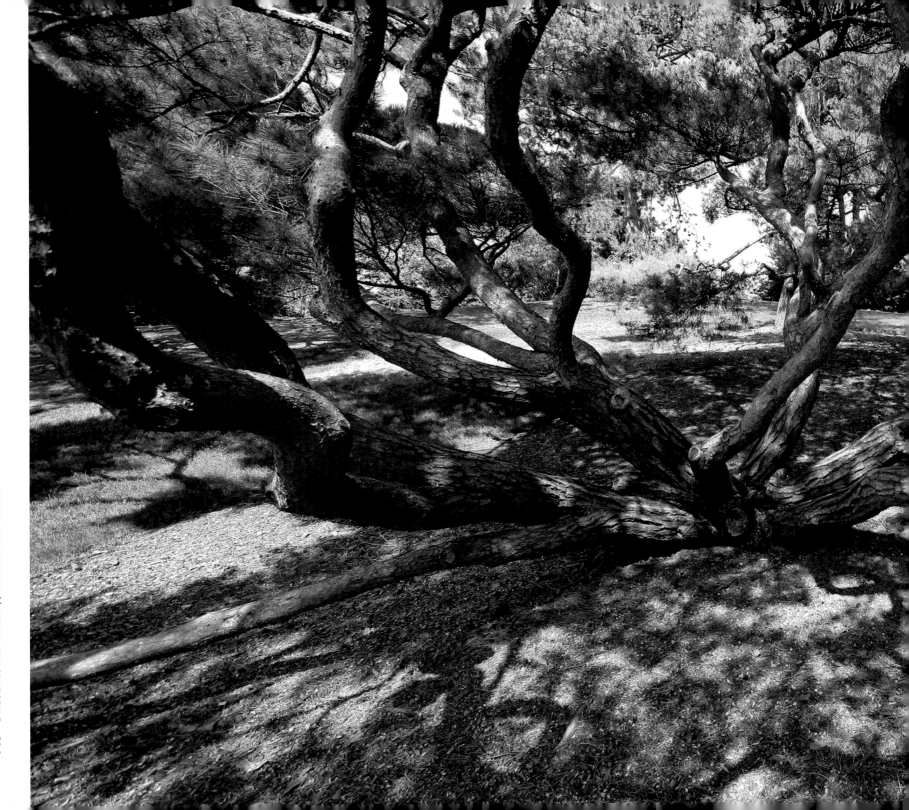

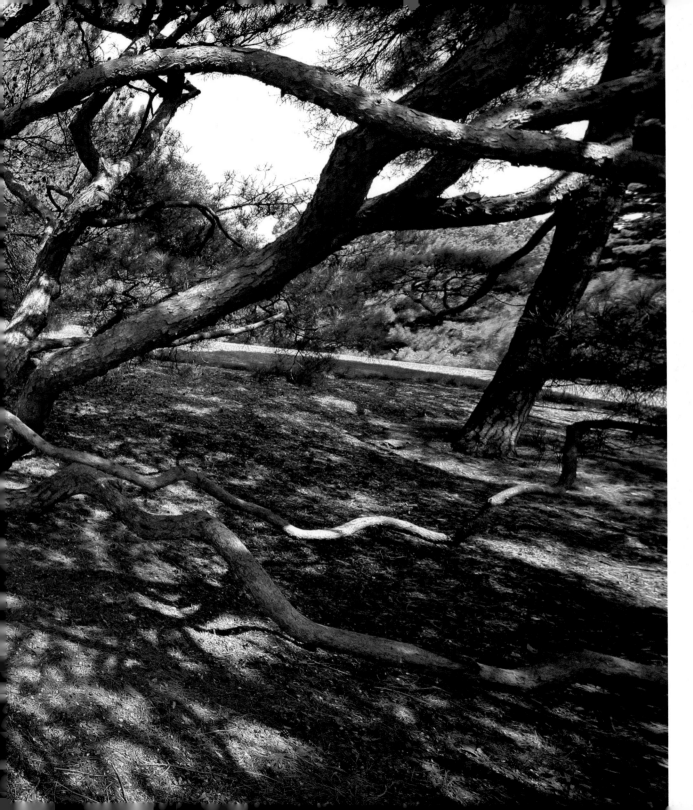

SUNSHINE AND SHADOWS

The spreading branches of this conifer demand to be photographed with a wide-angle lens. If your camera can't take all of the subject in one shot, try a panorama of two or three pictures taken side by side, and stitch them together on a computer later.

1 If possible, use a lens with an extreme wide angle to highlight the breadth of the tree.

2 Use the highest-quality settings available in order to capture as much detail as possible.

3 Set the camera to landscape mode or minimum aperture for the greatest depth of field.

4 Include a person in the background if you wish to impart a sense of scale.

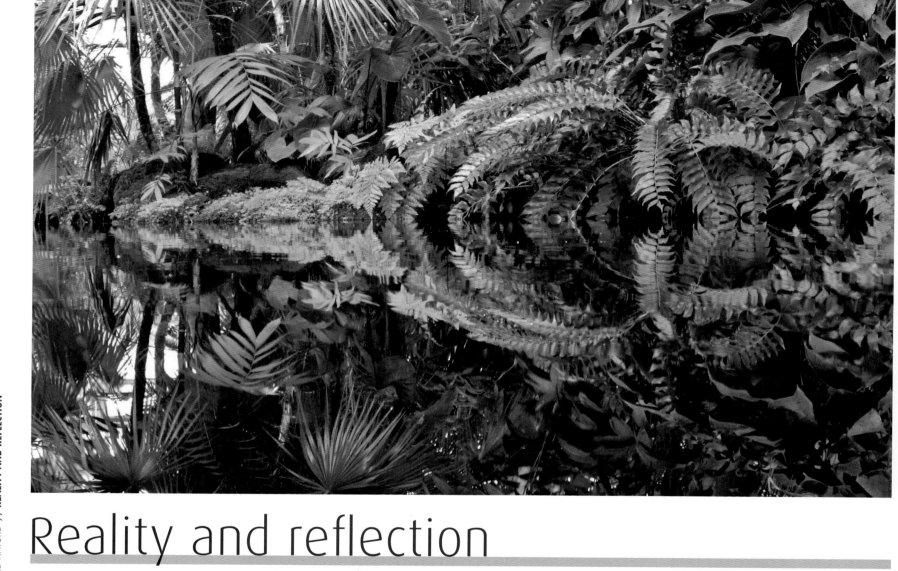

Reality and reflection

A visual phenomenon with an affinity for the camera, reflections provide a wealth of photographic opportunities. The particular way in which a camera sees the world – that is, constrained in a frame, and limited in depth of field – works well with the upside-down, inside-out world of the reflection. Let the image take the lead. Some of the most expressive examples of reflections are observed on still water, where they produce striking symmetrical effects.

FOR THIS SHOT

The wide-angle setting allowed me to get as much in frame as possible. I set a high ISO because of the low light levels and held the camera as still as possible because a tripod was not practical. Flash helped light the deep shadows.

CAMERA MODE

 Set your dial to **Landscape mode**

LENS SETTING

Zoom to **Wide Angle**

SENSOR/FILM SPEED

Use a **High** ISO setting

FLASH

Force the flash **On** if needed

1 STUDY REFLECTIONS

Investigate the way in which the reflection changes its shape as you change your position – both from side to side and up and down.

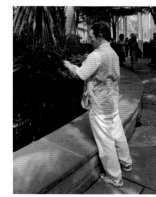

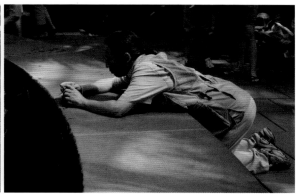

2 SELECT YOUR SETTINGS

Use the widest-angle setting on your camera, and supplement this with a wide-angle attachment, if possible. You might need to use flash to fill in any shaded areas.

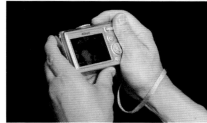

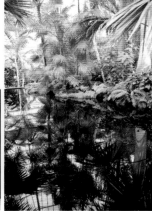

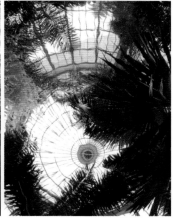

3 MOVE IN CLOSE

Often, the best view of a reflection can be found right down at water level, because it is along the water line that you can get an almost fully symmetrical view. Try turning your camera to bring the lens closer to the water, taking care not to get it wet. Treat the subject like a landscape, using maximum depth of field.

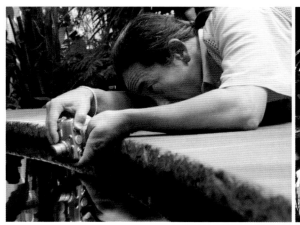

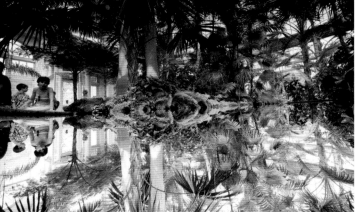

Colors of the seashore

You don't need to be vacationing on a paradise island to create a stunning beach shot. This pebbly beach, though pleasant enough, was not immediately inspiring, but with careful framing and some patience, it offered many rewarding opportunities. The key is to keep a careful eye on the light and water. The conditions that bring together a color in the sea with good light, wave conditions, and sky may come and go within minutes, or even seconds.

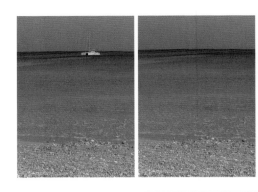

1 TRY DIFFERENT VIEWS
Explore different ways of looking at the beach. Views from near the ground offer close-ups of textures and collapse the foreground, while higher views allow you choice of emphasis: foreground or background. Watch the waves, and discover how different types react with light.

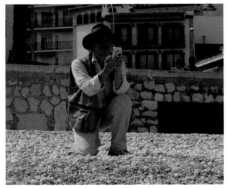
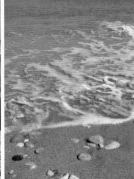
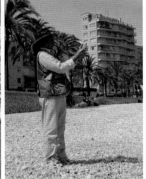
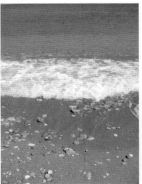

2 SET THE SCENE
If you wish the scene to look pristine, remove any detritus that might blight the shot – such as discarded bottles or other litter. Different story can be told by leaving them in place, so it may be interesting to try shots both with and without.

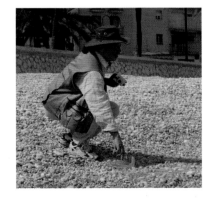

3 GIVE A SENSE OF SCALE
Any view that focuses on one element to the exclusion of all others offers little contrast. But once contrast is introduced, there must be enough of it to give a good indication of scale and context. This shot is nearly there, but the addition of the white foam lifts the entire image.

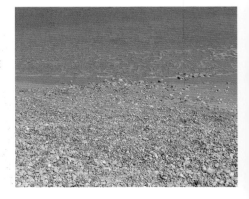

FOR THIS SHOT

I waited until there was an ideal combination of light in the water and gentle waves. The trawler being chased by seagulls gives a sense of distance without disturbing the abstraction of colors.

CAMERA MODE

Set your dial to **Program Mode**

LENS SETTING

Zoom to **Long Focal Length**

SENSOR/FILM SPEED

Use a **Low** ISO setting

FLASH

Force the flash **Off**

CHECK THE IMAGES

In very bright conditions, it will be difficult to see your LCD screen. Make use of any available shade to review your images.

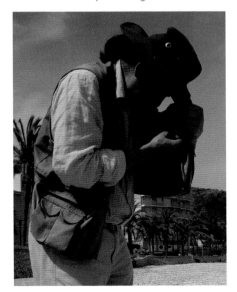

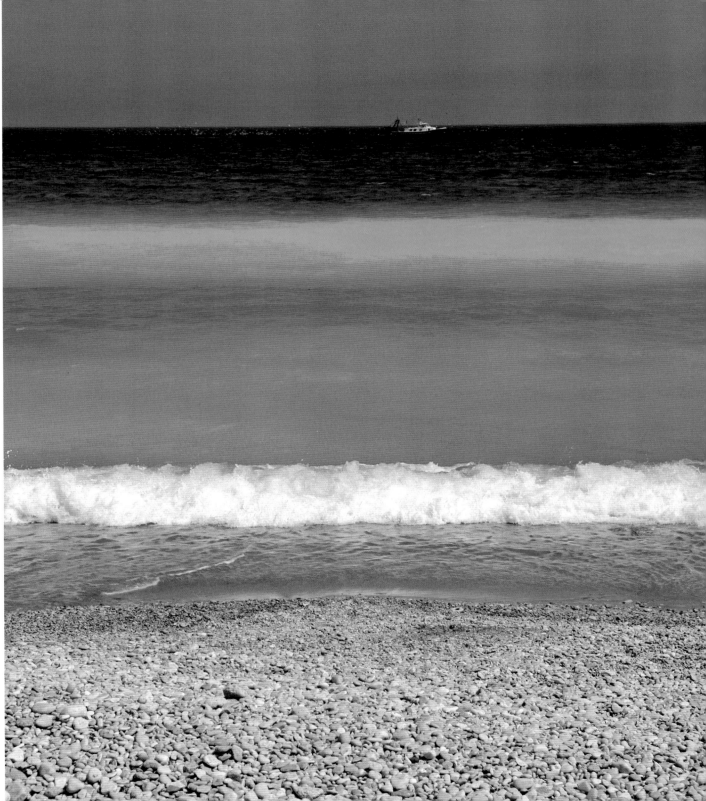

Crashing waves

We have all seen the dramatic effects of a rough seas crashing onto rocks. But often, by the time we get the camera out, all is calm again. However, waves come in cycles, and if you wait a while, you will be able to anticipate the next big swell. In that time you can choose your position, set up the camera, and prepare for the moment. Even then, it will take a few attempts to catch the waves at the peak of their action.

1 SCOUT THE LOCATION
Most coastlines have areas of lively wave activity, but a great spot is not just one where the waves crash wildly – it is one where the background will show up the splashes of water, and where the rocks also offer interesting or attractive shapes.

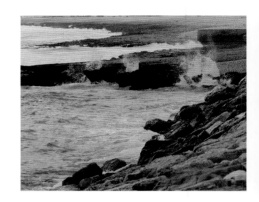

2 SET THE CAMERA
If possible, set all camera functions to manual. The shutter time should be short, so select shutter priority or sports mode with a high sensitivity. On an overcast day or in low light, use the flash to help freeze the movement of the spray.

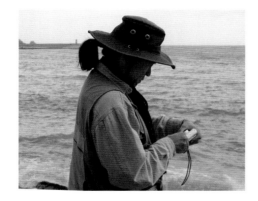

3 PROTECT YOURSELF
Position yourself out of danger. On some coastlines, exceptionally large waves can suddenly rise up and soak you, so stay at a safe distance. Use a long zoom setting to capture the action without being too close to it.

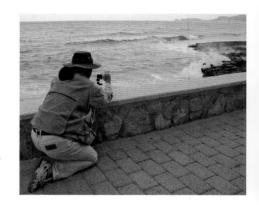

4 USE A SUPPORT
If you want to wait comfortably with the camera aimed at the right spot, use a tripod. Once it is set up, all you have to do is relax and watch the sea, then just steady the tripod while you release the shutter. You could even use a remote control for added stability.

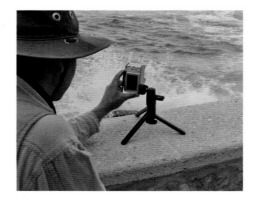

5 KEEP SHOOTING
Take as many pictures as you can, and try slightly different framings, zoom settings, and orientations. One of them is sure to give you the perfect picture.

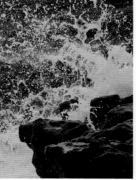

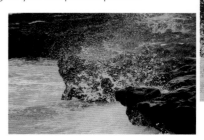

⟫ FOR THIS SHOT

I pulled back the zoom to take in a wider view – fortunately, since the spray of water reached quite high. By setting a very short shutter time, I was able to catch the water droplets sharp and frozen in mid-air.

CAMERA MODE

 Set your dial to **Sports mode**

LENS SETTING

 Zoom to **Medium** to **Wide Angle**

SENSOR/FILM SPEED

 Use a **High** ISO setting

FLASH

Force the flash **Off**

6 GET THE TIMING RIGHT

Make sure you release the shutter just before the peak of action, so you don't miss the splash and spray of water droplets.

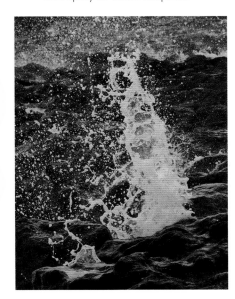

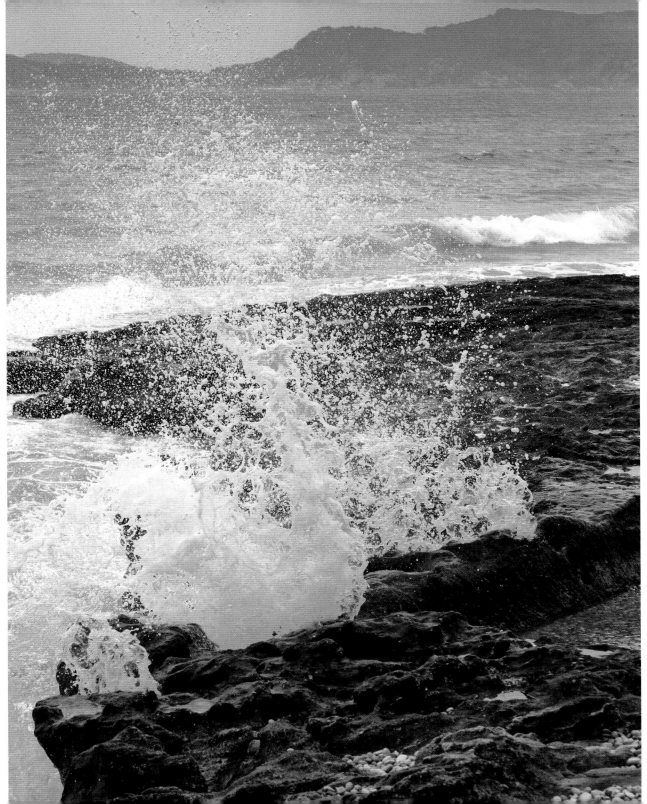

Fast-flowing water

Despite their universal beauty, waterfalls are incredibly difficult to photograph well. Even professionals have trouble with them. The reason for this is that the lighting is often tricky, since it combines deep shadows with bright areas, which even include dazzling snow-white waters. In addition, access to the best vantage points can be challenging, if not downright dangerous. The secrets are to take your time to understand the environment, to wait for good light, and to realize that less of the scene can be more.

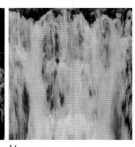
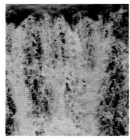
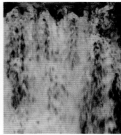

¹/₂₅₀ **sec**   ¹/₁₂₅ **sec**   ¹/₆₀ **sec**

You can obtain sharp images of moving water with short shutter times, but the results look static. A much longer exposure gives a milky effect. Try different settings and check the LCD screen to see which effect you prefer.

EXPLORE THE AREA
The harder you work, the more secrets a landscape will reveal to you. Explore slowly, carefully, and safely. A position that is not promising at first may be perfect once the sun has moved a little.

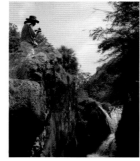
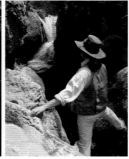

SET UP THE TRIPOD
A tripod is almost essential for waterfalls, since you'll set a small aperture for maximum sharpness. In the shade of overhanging rocks, light is likely to be low, so you will need a long shutter time.

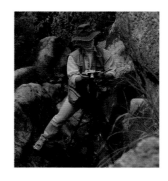

CHOOSE YOUR FORMAT
Dramatic scenery can work well in either portrait or landscape formats. Each has its own advantages, so be sure to try both.

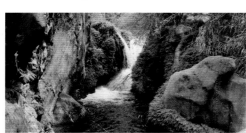
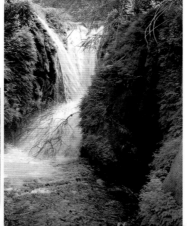

SET THE CAMERA
Experiment with various shutter settings. The best setting will depend on the flow of water at your location and the effect you wish to obtain.

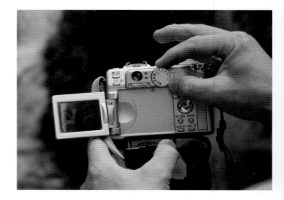

FOR THIS SHOT

 I used a normal focal length for this scene, to take in some of the surroundings but keep the falls as the main subject. With a shutter time of $^1/_{60}$ sec, I was able to catch some water droplets without making the flow too static.

CAMERA MODE

 Set your dial to **Landscape mode**

LENS SETTING

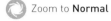 Zoom to **Normal**

SENSOR/FILM SPEED

 Use a **Medium** to **High** ISO setting

FLASH

 Force the flash **Off**

VARY THE COMPOSITION

 To help you gain experience and confidence in your composition, try different framings and zoom settings in your shots.

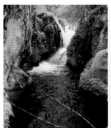 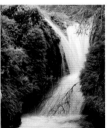

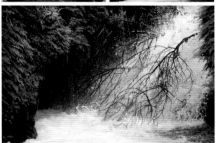

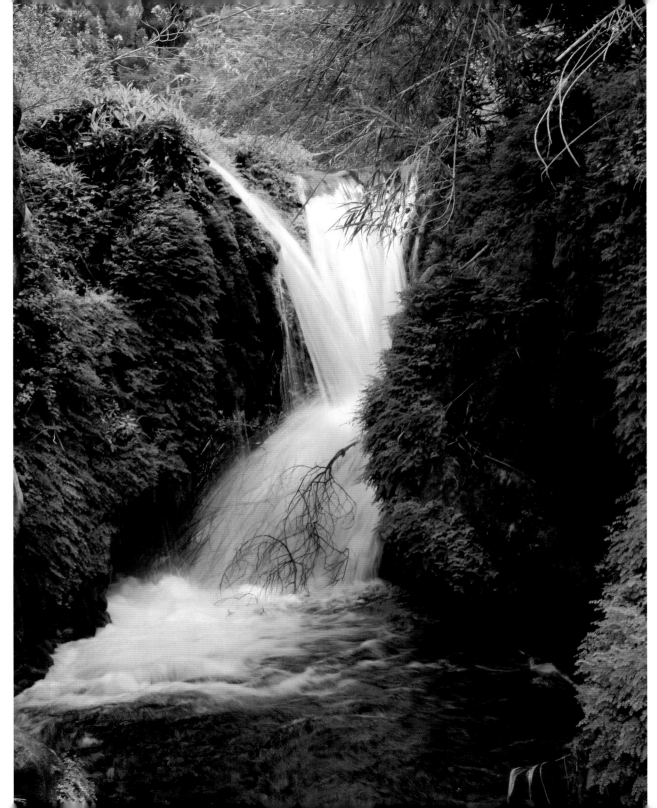

FAST-FLOWING WATER >> LANDSCAPES AND NATURE   149

A tranquil scene

The most important consideration when photographing a peaceful, idyllic rural location, such as a quiet riverside, is how to convey the atmosphere of the scene. The picture has to carry, in tones and colors, what is experienced in sounds, scents, and space, too. Try using gradients of tone to lead the eye through the picture; this will help simulate the experience of space. Use color to suggest movement, and visual clues to suggest sounds.

1 **SELECT A LOCATION**
The route that led you to your chosen spot is unlikely to be the most photogenic, so explore a little to find the best position.

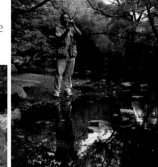
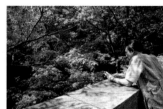

2 **CONSIDER THE FORMAT**
The natural, landscape format may be the most obvious choice, but it is not necessarily always the best. A portrait shape can be used to highlight the vertical nature of the scene.

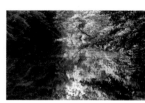
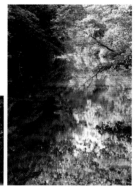

3 **EXPLORE REFLECTIONS**
When the air is still and water quiet, reflections can play a big part in a landscape. Don't focus too much on the reflection, however; you may lose the feel of the overall scene.

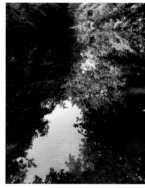
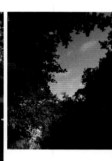

4 **INCLUDE FOREGROUND INTEREST**
A key method of conveying a sense of space and distance is to position yourself low down and include objects in the foreground. Too much emphasis on the foreground loses the context, though, so experiment until you get the balance just right.

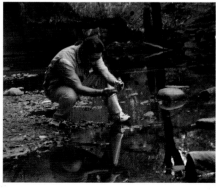
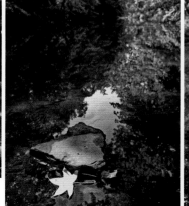
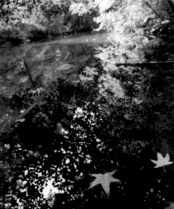

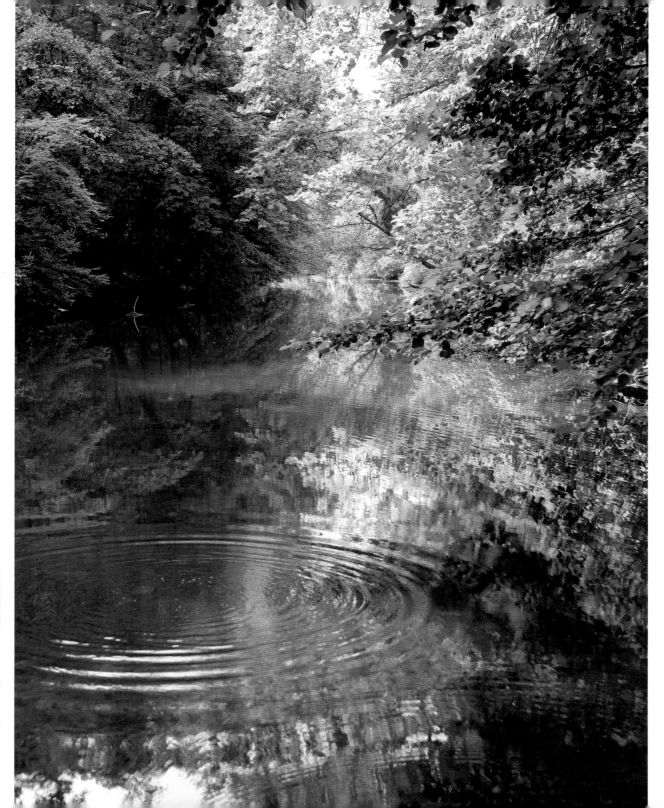

 FOR THIS SHOT

With the zoom set to a moderately wide angle, I selected the landscape mode for an extensive depth of field. For good image quality, I chose a large image size and medium sensitivity.

CAMERA MODE

 Set your dial to **Landscape mode**

LENS SETTING

Zoom to **Wide Angle**

SENSOR/FILM SPEED

Use a **Low** ISO setting

FLASH

Force the flash **Off**

5 ADD MOVEMENT

To create a sense of dynamism and movement within the scene, try tossing a pebble into the water. The ripples add an extra dimension and are suggestive of sound.

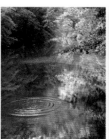
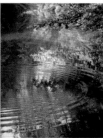
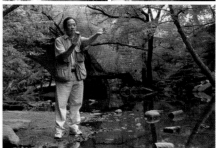

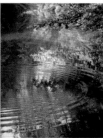

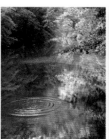

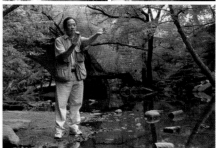

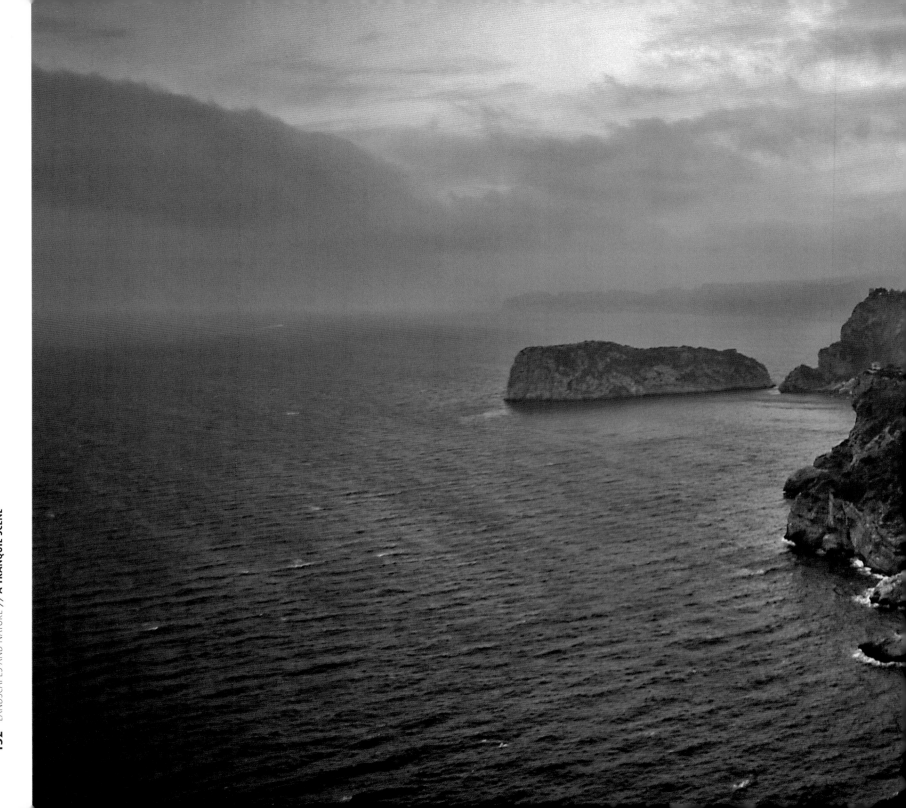

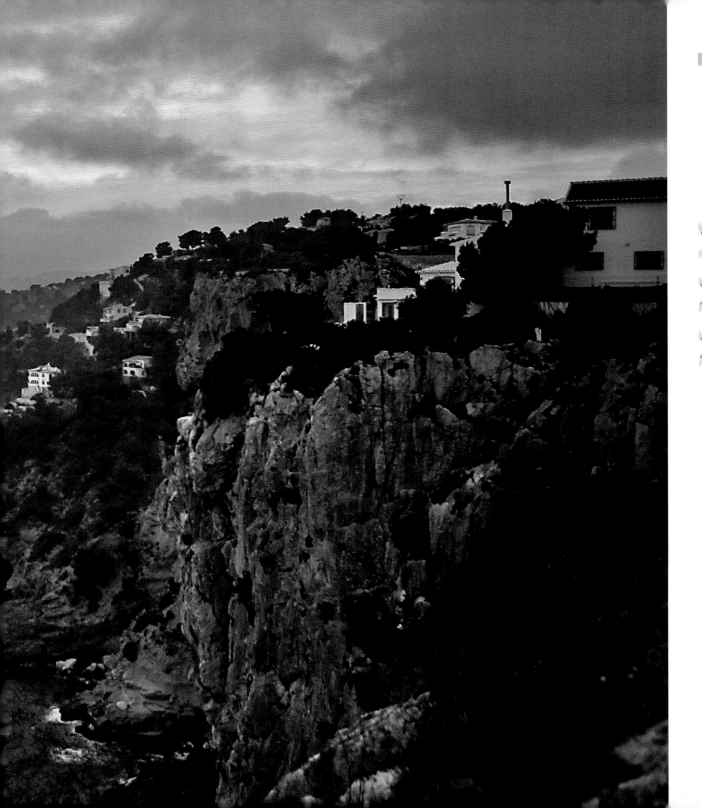
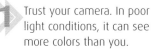

A photograph can conceal a great deal: this tranquil-looking sunset belies the near-gale-force winds blowing at the time of the shoot. Don't be put off by the weather, unless it could endanger you. Find shelter, lean against something for support, and get the picture.

1 Trust your camera. In poor light conditions, it can see more colors than you.

2 Use a high ISO setting in dim light, but be aware that the image quality might be affected.

3 If necessary, you can intensify and increase the contrast of colors using image software at a later stage.

A TRANQUIL SCENE >> LANDSCAPES AND NATURE **153**

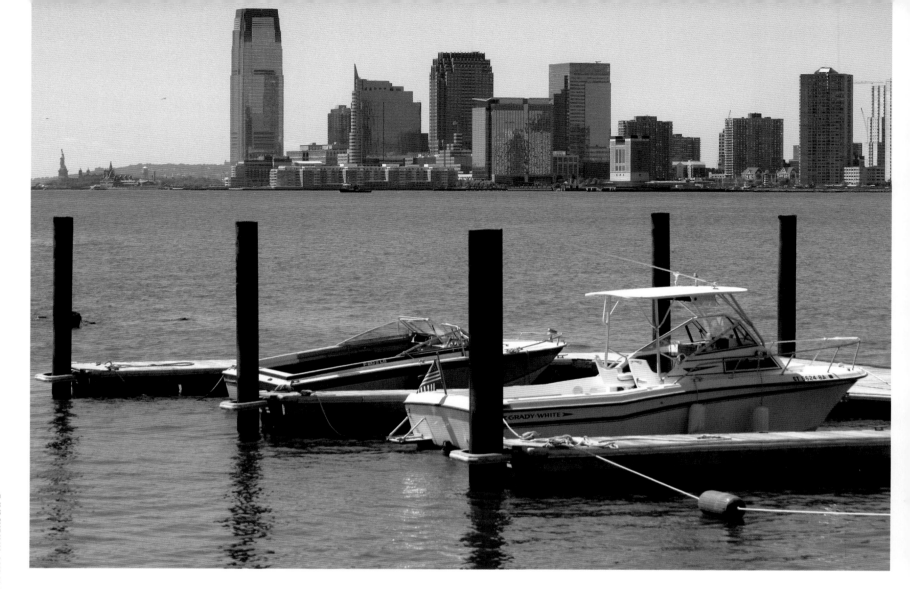

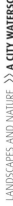

A city waterscape

154

The beauty of photography is that you can set off to make one kind of picture, yet return with something completely different. The intention on this occasion was to find pictures at a marina. At first sight it was not very promising: no one was around, the day was fiercely sunny, and the posts for the boats were unsightly. But a careful exploration revealed a pattern between the posts and the skyscrapers in the distance. There is always something worth photographing.

FOR THIS SHOT

Using a very moderate telephoto setting, I positioned myself carefully, lining up the mooring posts with the landmarks in the distance. A medium ISO setting allowed for minimum aperture, giving maximum depth of field.

CAMERA MODE

 Set your dial to **Landscape mode**

LENS SETTING

 Zoom to **Medium Telephoto**

SENSOR/FILM SPEED

Use a **Medium** ISO setting

FLASH

 Force the flash **Off**

1 LOOK AROUND

Examine your location closely. Walk around while actively searching for viewpoints. Be open to all possibilities, and your eye is sure to be caught by a pattern or an interesting combination of elements.

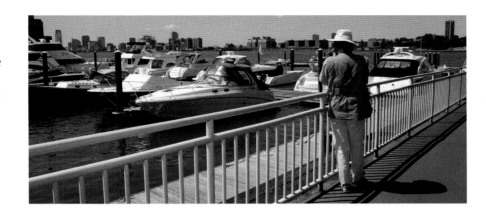

2 EXPERIMENT WITH FORMAT AND VIEWPOINT

Try out different focal-length settings, as well as different viewpoints and formats. Review the results as you go along to see if there are any interesting patterns emerging.

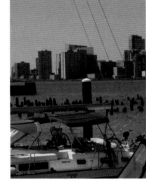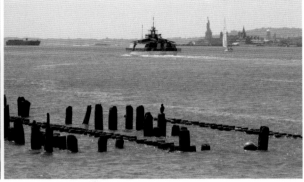

3 REDUCE FLARE

Many point-and-shoot cameras are inadequately protected against strong light coming from in front of the camera. This problem is made worse when you're dealing with sun flare from water. Use your hand to cast a shadow over the lens; this will provide it with some shade. In the film world, this is called a "French flag."

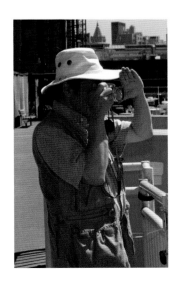

4 TRY DIFFERENT COMPOSITIONS

You may find yourself repeatedly returning to a certain subject, as if subconsciously drawn to it. In this case, it was the posts in the water. Work this subject to the full, extracting all you can from it. Make it a mini-project until you have one image that surpasses the others.

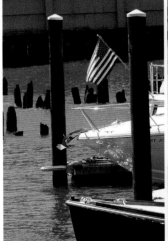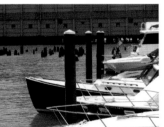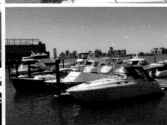

The colors of sunset

Everyone loves to watch a glorious sunset, but photographs of this spectacle are often underwhelming. Technically, sunsets are challenging subjects; their great range from light to dark makes it easy to lose details in the foreground. However, there are a few tricks that will help you to produce stunning sunset photographs. Start by filling the image with interesting elements in the sky and on the ground. Then balance the exposure so that you capture both.

1 ARRIVE EARLY
The balance of light between sky and ground shifts subtly but quite rapidly towards sunset. There is only a short window when these two are perfectly balanced, so you need to get into position in good time to ensure you capture this moment.

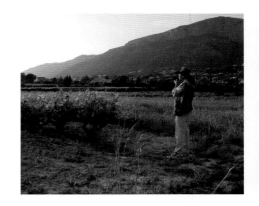

2 CHOOSE YOUR SETTINGS
Use the best-quality setting the camera can offer, and select low sensitivity so that the skies are smooth-toned.

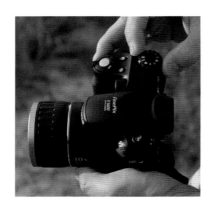

3 PROTECT YOUR SIGHT
Take care not to look directly at the sun, and don't leave the lens uncapped and pointed at the sun: the light could damage the shutter. While the sun is high, holding a hand above the lens can help reduce flare.

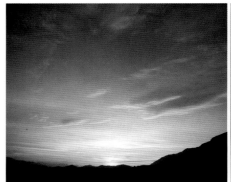
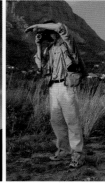

4 TURN AROUND
Take the time to look behind you, too: the sky and landscape opposite the sunset will be bathed in beautiful light and deserving of a photograph. This area will not present the same contrast problems as the sunset.

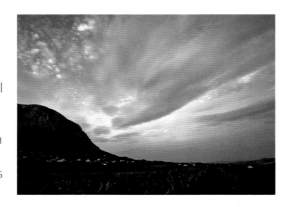

5 CHOOSE WHETHER TO ZOOM OR NOT
The colors in the sky at sunset typically span from warm yellows to deep blues. These will be taken in on a wide view, but a zoomed-in view may be more dramatic, concentrating on the sun.

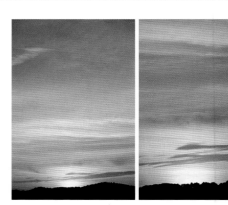

FOR THIS SHOT

The sun was very low, but some rays still reached the vines in the foreground. I set the zoom to wide angle and selected the landscape mode to help ensure a generous depth of field. The vertical format takes in a large expanse of sky.

CAMERA MODE

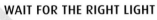 Set your dial to **Landscape mode**

LENS SETTING

Zoom to **Wide Angle**

SENSOR/FILM SPEED

Use a **Low** ISO setting

FLASH

Force the flash **Off**

WAIT FOR THE RIGHT LIGHT

When the sun is as low as possible, you can balance light in the sky with light on the foreground. Most people opt for the landscape format when shooting a sunset, but don't limit yourself to this.

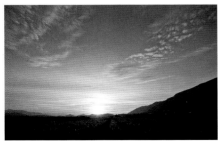

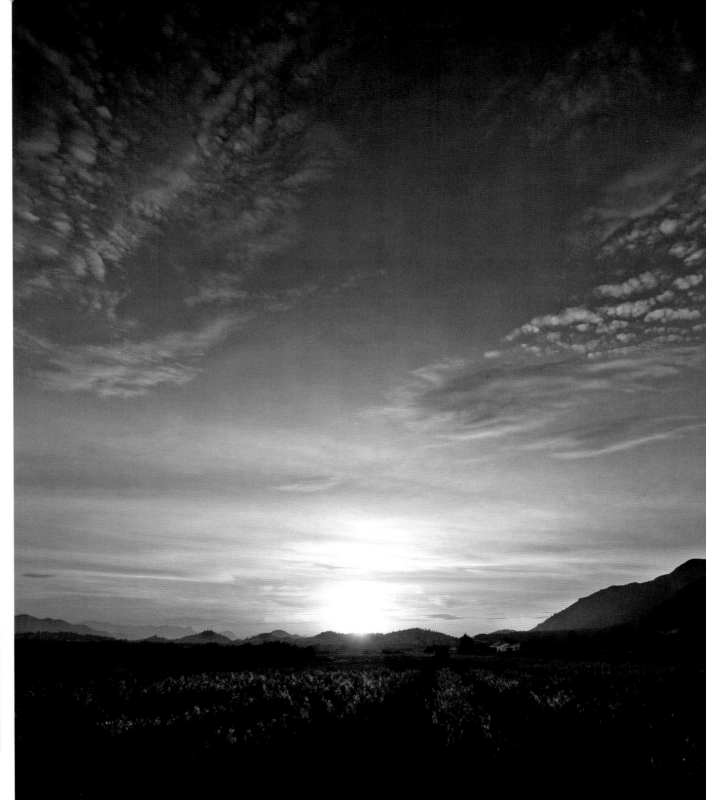

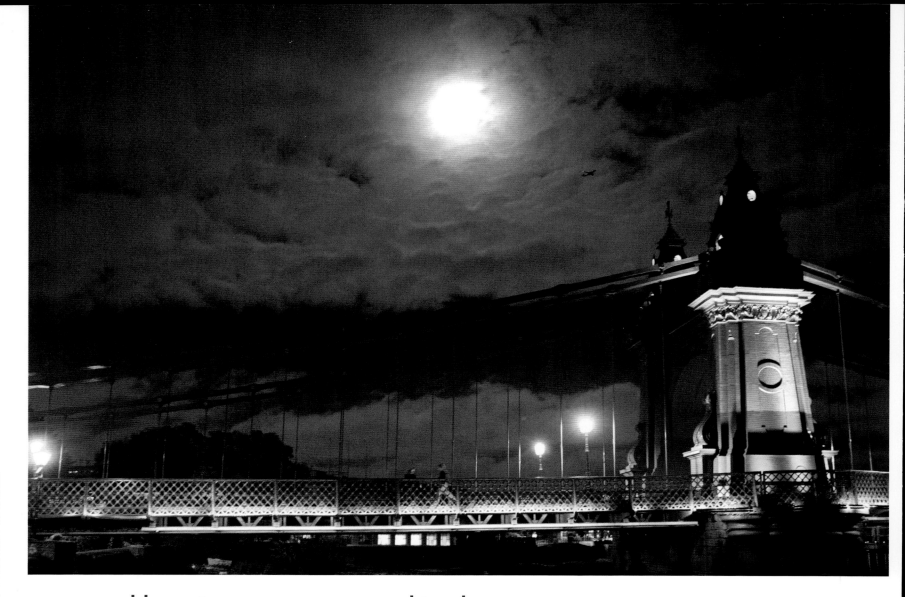

An alluring moonlight

The moon is a most fascinating subject for photography, but it is also a very tricky one. One key point to bear in mind is that when the moon is close to the horizon, it looks much larger to the eye than it does to the camera. Even when high in the sky, the moon appears larger than it really is because it is so bright. That brightness can be overpowering in a night-sky picture in which everything else is dark. One solution to this problem is to shoot on a cloudy night.

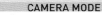

FOR THIS SHOT

I set a focal length of normal to wide angle, selected a high sensitivity, and used a tripod for sharpness. I then waited for clouds to pass in front of the full moon to enlarge the visible disc of light.

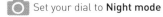

CAMERA MODE

Set your dial to **Night mode**

LENS SETTING

Zoom to **Normal** to **Wide Angle**

SENSOR/FILM SPEED

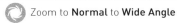

Use a **High** ISO setting

FLASH

Force the flash **Off**

ZOOM TO THE MOON

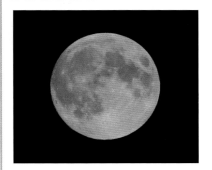

Even with your zoom set to maximum, the moon may still appear too small in the frame. Take the picture with the moon in the center, then enlarge it later with image-manipulation software on your computer. Alternatively, if your camera has a digital zoom, you could use that for the same effect.

1 USE A TRIPOD

Set the camera on a tripod to ensure the sharpest results. The added advantage of a tripod is that you don't have to hold the camera in position while you wait for a good cloud or a change in the moon's position.

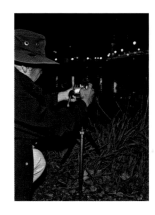

2 SET THE SENSITIVITY

Don't go any higher than is necessary when setting the sensitivity. The higher you go, the more likely it is that your images will be noisy, with a grainy look (as here), uneven colors, and possibly lines evident. Using a tripod, you can afford to reduce the sensitivity a little.

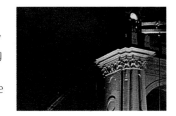

3 CHECK YOUR IMAGES

Review any pictures to check the exposure and the sensitivity. The camera will probably overexpose, resulting in an image that looks brightly lit, as on the far right. Dial in exposure compensation to reduce the exposure to achieve the look on the near right. Notice how small the moon appears in these shots, both taken with a wide-angle zoom setting.

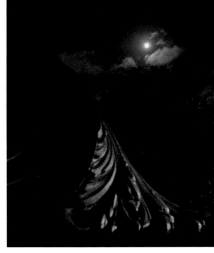
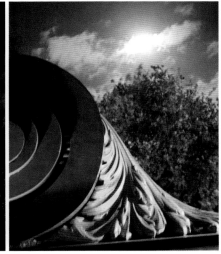

4 FRAME THE SHOT

Use foreground elements to create extra visual interest and to frame the moon. If the moon is too small in the image, wait for a cloud to pass in front. This will brighten the sky around the moon and make it seem much larger.

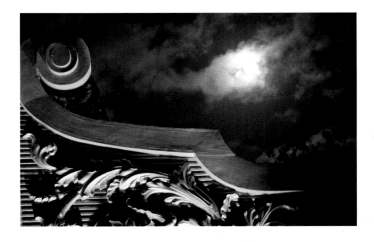

Cloud formations

One of the most rewarding photographic subjects is not only completely free, but you need only to look up in the sky to find it. Great cloud formations are always worth photographing. Clouds change constantly, often assuming wonderful shapes and textures, carrying gorgeous colors, and interacting with the landscape. Seize the moment. You can create a fabulous picture of clouds even in the uninspiring surroundings of an urban parking lot.

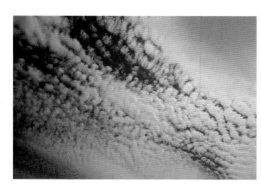

 KEEP WATCHING THE SKY
Clouds can change shape and position very quickly, so you may have only minutes while an optimum shape or pattern is held. Keep an eye out for any changes, and watch for shifts of light on the ground – that is a sign of changes in the sky.

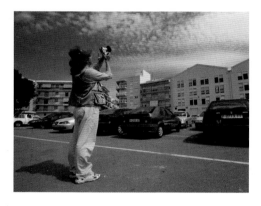

FIND A VIEWPOINT
Walk around and, if possible, look for an additional subject for your image. These surroundings may appear unattractive, but with careful framing you can leave unsightly elements out of your composition.

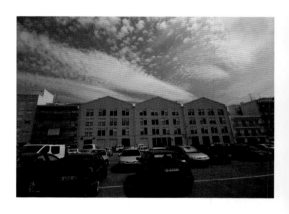

 USE A WIDER ANGLE
The majority of cloud formations will benefit from a very wide-angle view. If possible use a wide-angle attachment to increase the view to that of a 28mm or 24mm lens, or wider.

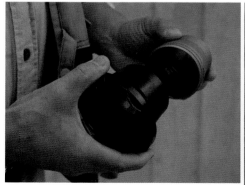

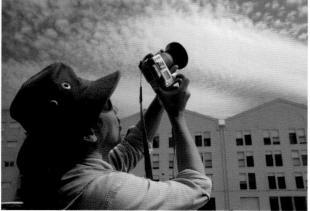

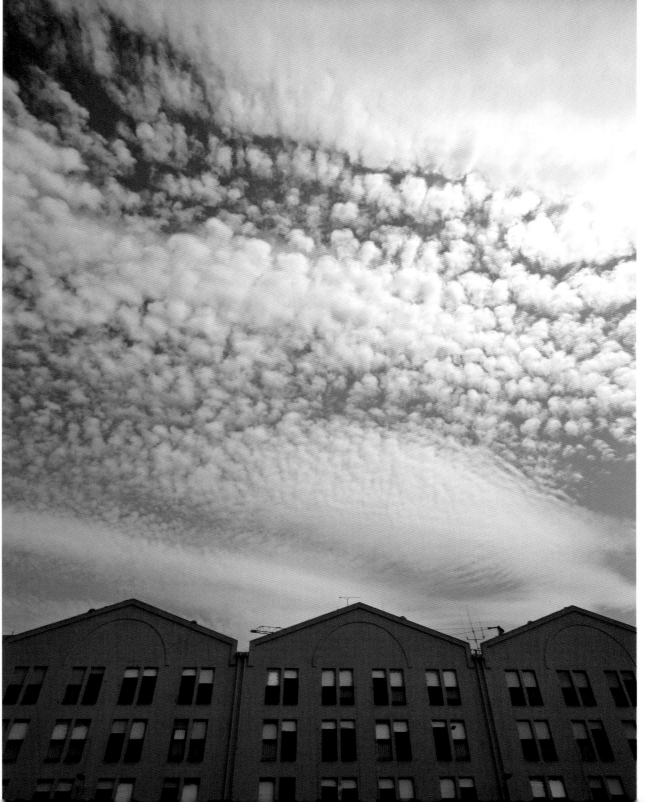

FOR THIS SHOT

I used the widest-angle setting, supplemented with a wide-angle attachment. I waited for the best cloud arrangement and lighting, then I set the camera to the highest quality to capture all the subtle tones and details.

CAMERA MODE

Set your dial to **Landscape mode**

LENS SETTING

Zoom to **Wide Angle**

SENSOR/FILM SPEED

Use a **Low** ISO setting

FLASH

Force the flash **Off**

GET THE TIMING RIGHT

Beware of lens flare and never look directly into the sun. The best results are achieved when clouds partially obscure the sun or when the sun is at the edge of a cloud.

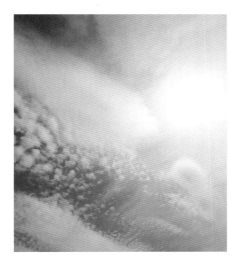

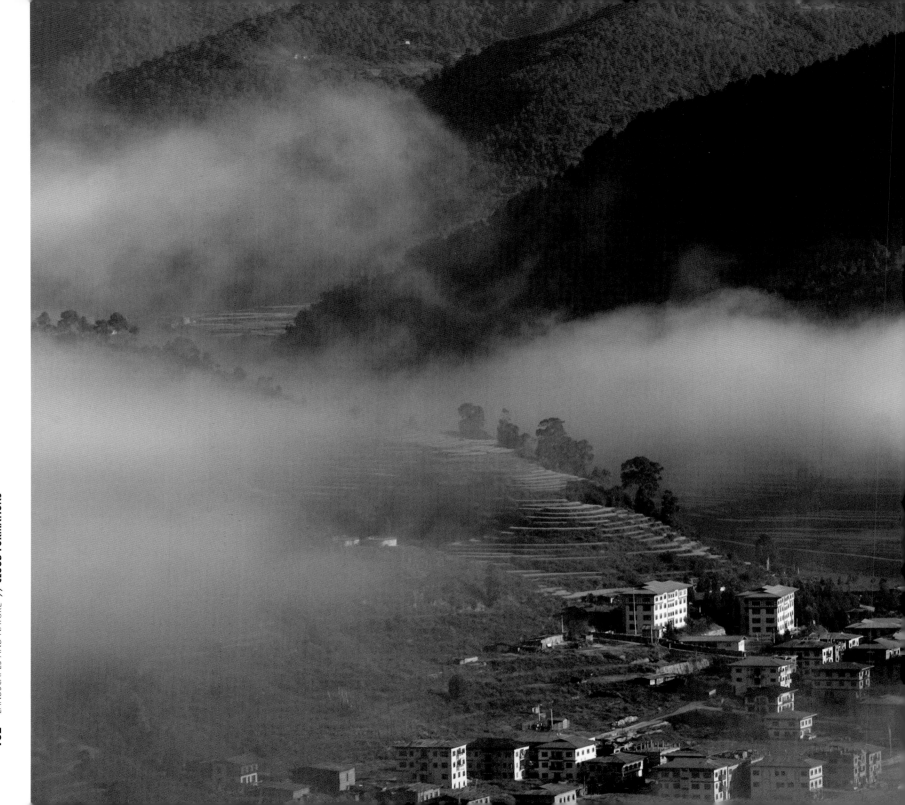

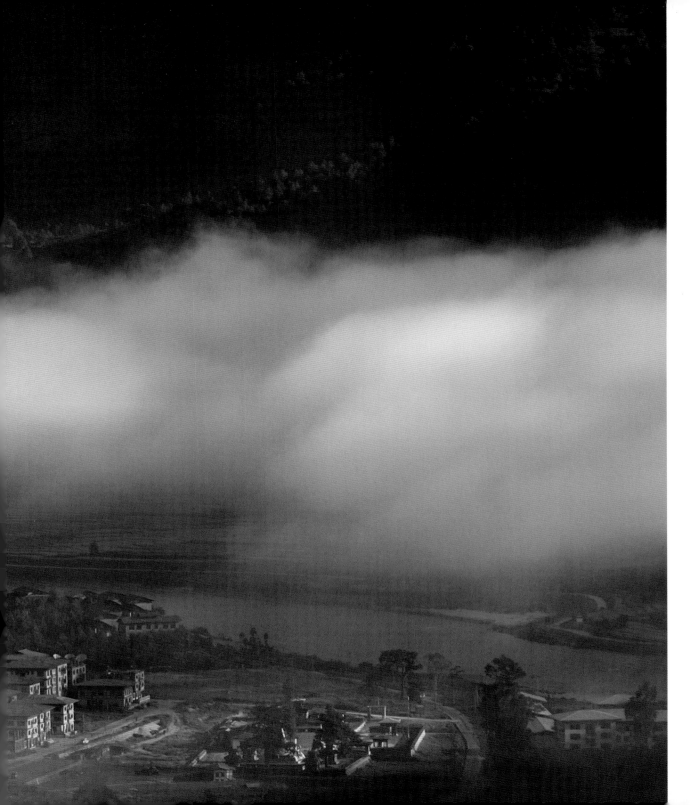

LOW CLOUDS

I took this shot early in the morning. The composition benefited from the beautiful early light of day, which was still low in the sky, but I was also fortunate in witnessing and capturing the spectacle of these low clouds rising from hills.

1 Choose your vantage point the previous day, working out where the sun will rise.

2 Make sure you strike the right balance of light and misty cloud before taking your photograph.

3 Select the highest quality settings, because you will want to capture all the subtle tones.

Landscapes and nature

Any attempt to capture an awe-inspiring landscape or a breathtaking view in a photograph is likely to fail. The magnificence of nature can't be contained in a picture. What you can do, however, is to compose a picture so that people looking at it are led on a journey that mimics your visual experience. Your picture can compress the scene into a few concise visual statements.

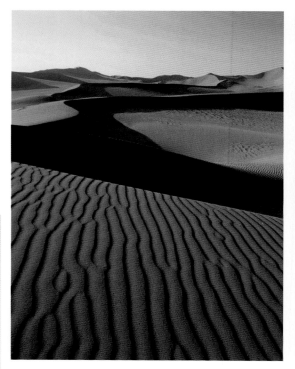

PARALLEL LINES
Use the parallel lines in the desert sand to lead from the foreground to the distant horizon, where different textures delight the eye.

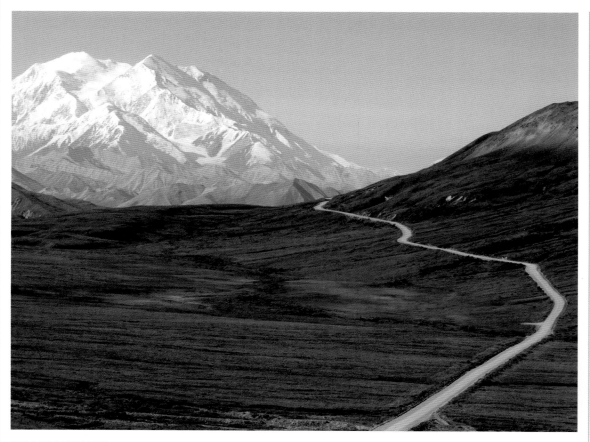

LEADING THE EYE
A road winding through the picture is an effective and natural way to take the eye through the image toward the mountain in the distance.

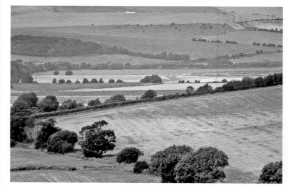

AERIAL PERSPECTIVE
Notice the way in which colors become paler as the distance increases. This is another effective way to imply a sense of depth in the picture.

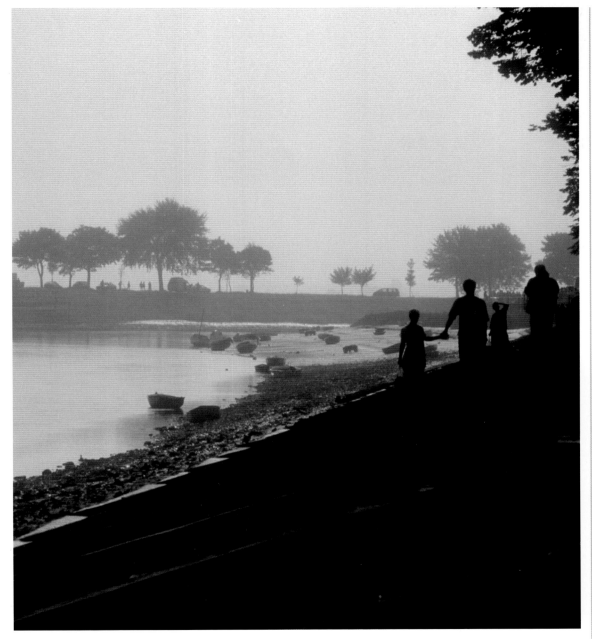

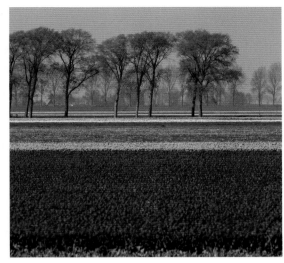

COLOR COMPOSITION
Give a spatial vivacity to a composition by distorting the sense of distance. In this picture, this effect is achieved by the distinctive bands of color.

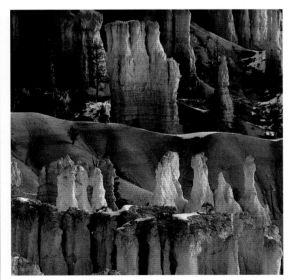

TWO-TONE SCENERY
You can use tonal values to create different planes within an image. Allow foreground subjects to darken to silhouette to create a sense of nearness.

ABSTRACT COMPRESSION
You don't always need a wide angle for landscapes. Use a long telephoto view to compress large rock formations into an abstract pattern.

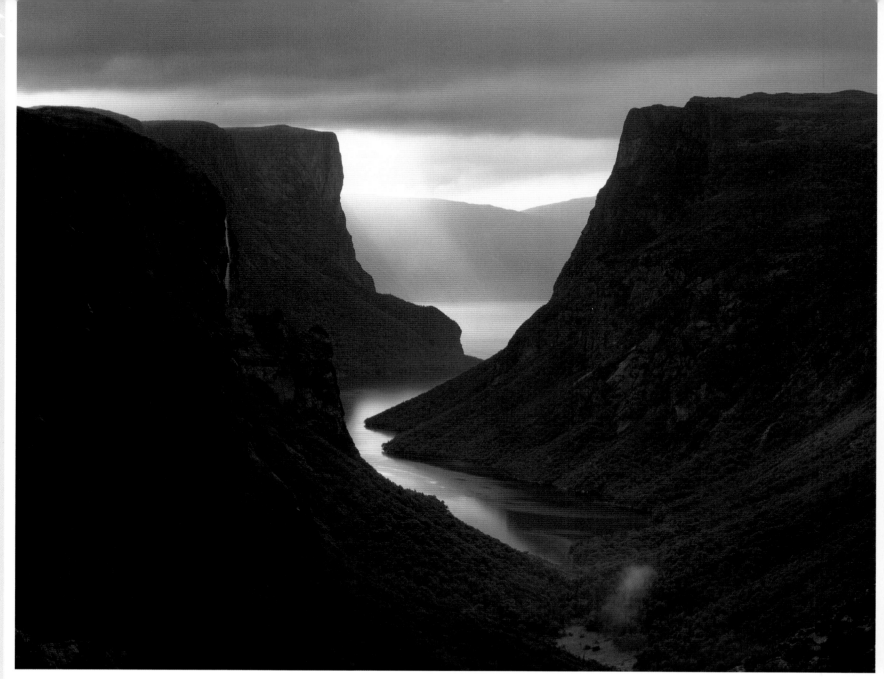

CATCHING THE CLOUDBURST

In order to capture a fabulous moment such as this, you either have to be very lucky, or must return to the same spot again and again until everything is perfect. The silvery trail of the river leads the eye up to the lake, where it joins the cloudburst, lighting up the darkness in this dramatic composition.

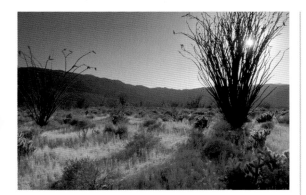

GRADIENT SKY

One way to even out very bright skies is to place a gradient filter – dark at one end, and fading to clear at the other – in front of the lens.

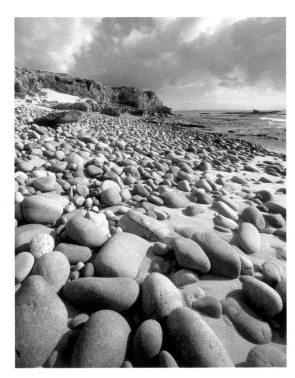

ROCKY FOREGROUND

To suggest a sense of rapidly receding space, give your composition a busy and interesting foreground. These large stones hint at the dynamism of the scene.

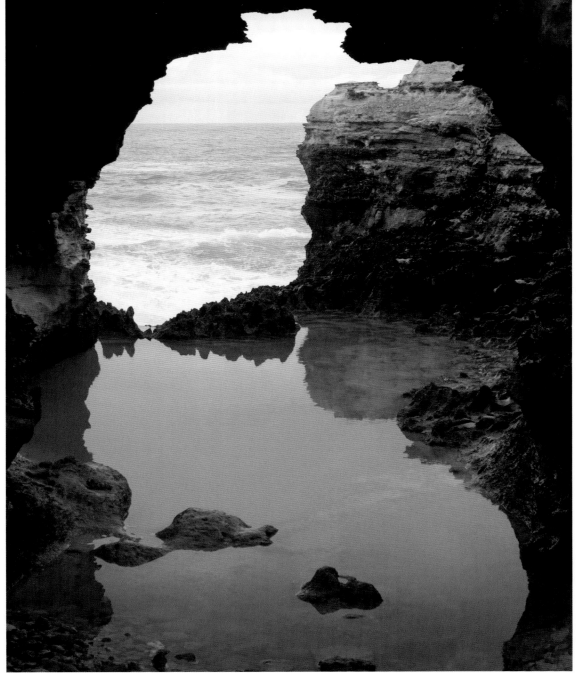

ARCH FRAME

The arch is a natural framing device and a powerful compositional tool that concentrates the viewer's gaze into the scene within it.

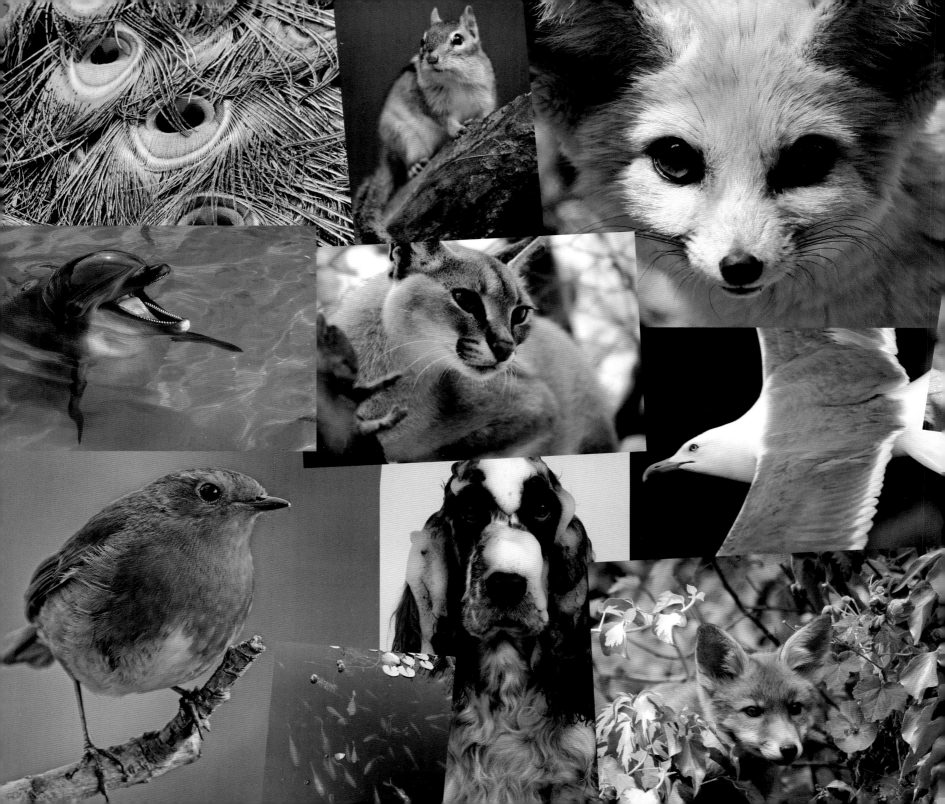

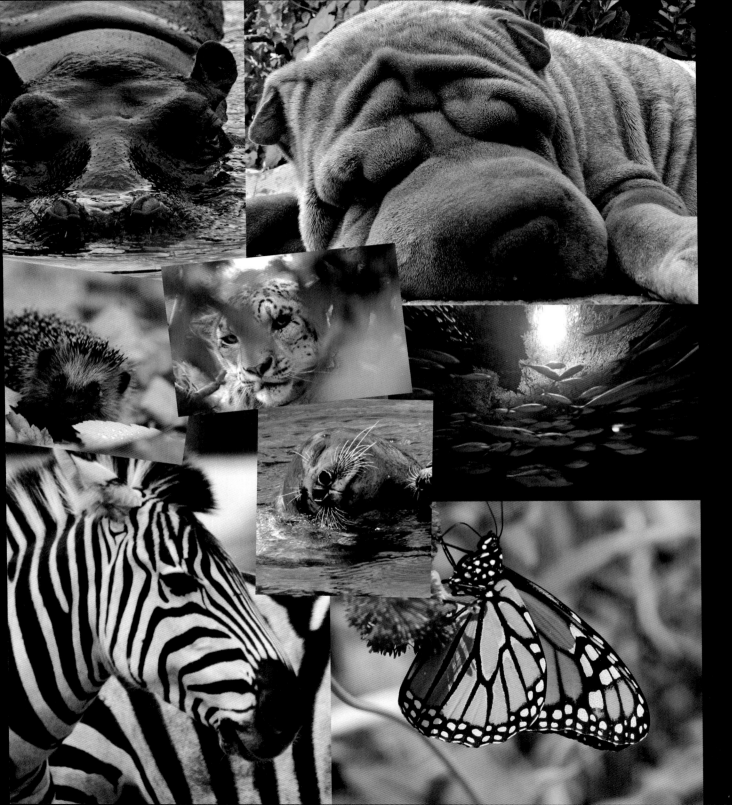

Animals

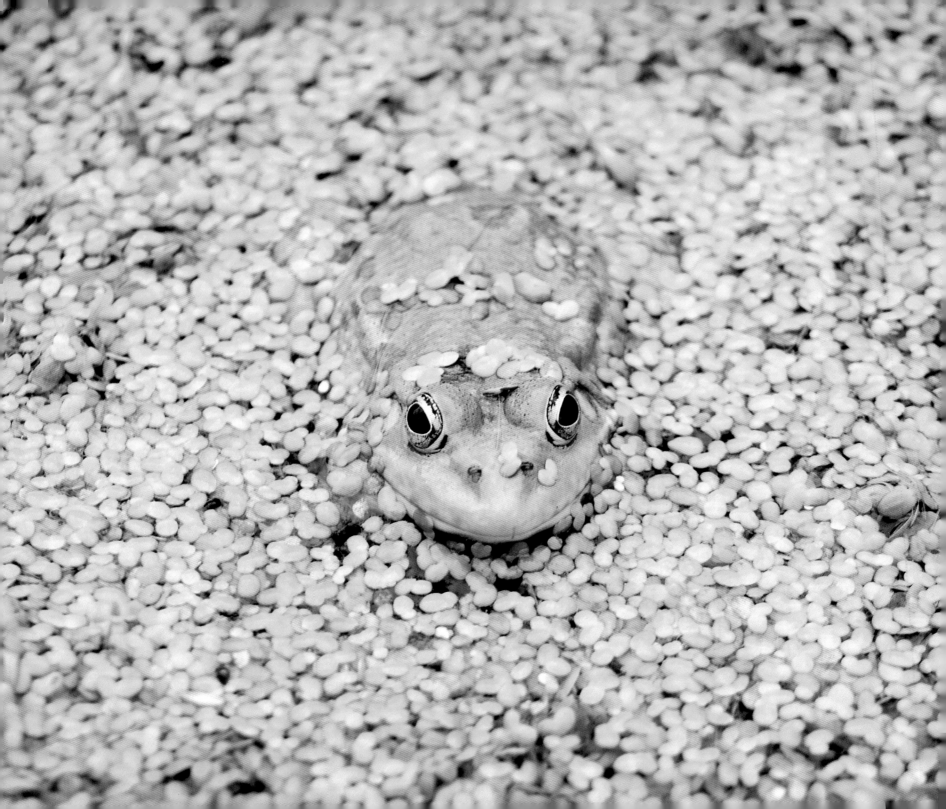

Animals offer photographers an exciting arena, the doors of which have only recently been thrown open to all photographers thanks to stunning technical and optical advances. For example, many modern digital cameras offer an optical reach that can be used to magnify distant animals; such a tool was once too costly for anyone other than professional photographers. In addition, modern zoos and aquaria strive to create authentic-looking environments for their animals. You need only add the other key ingredients, such as knowledge of your chosen animal's habitat and behavior, plus a good supply of patience, which is usually necessary to fit in around the animal's patterns of activity.

Posed pet portraits

In spite of the undeniable wisdom of the old adage "Never work with children and animals," these remain arguably the two favorite subjects for photography. The best way to approach a portrait of your pet depends on the animal's character and which of its qualities you wish to capture. An action shot of your dog jumping for a ball or chasing a stick is dynamic and exciting, but a formal pose brings an almost-human air to the portrait.

The alternative to photographing your pet outdoors is to work indoors. Cover the floor with white cardboard and hang white sheets to create a plain backdrop. Use a long lens setting to minimize the need for a background. Work with light from a large window, or rely on your camera's flash. Using electronic flash will enable you to capture the sharpest images of your pet.

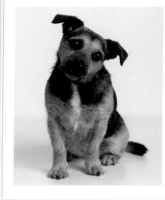
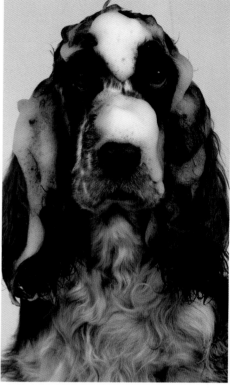

1 SET THE EXPOSURE

If your pet's fur is very dark or nearly white, you may need to adjust exposure from normal to ensure it is accurately captured. Take some test shots before the session, and check by zooming into the image on the LCD screen.

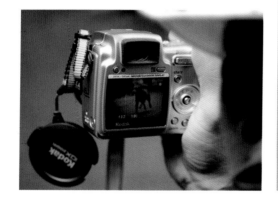

2 CREATE A FUN SHOOT

A static pose doesn't have to be a dull one. Offer the dog a treat, such as a biscuit, or allow it to run, jump, and play freely. Getting the dog to have fun will bring a sparkle to its eye that might otherwise be missing.

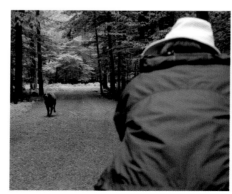
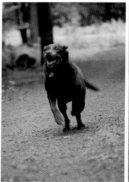
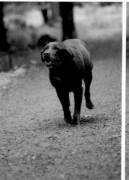
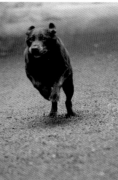

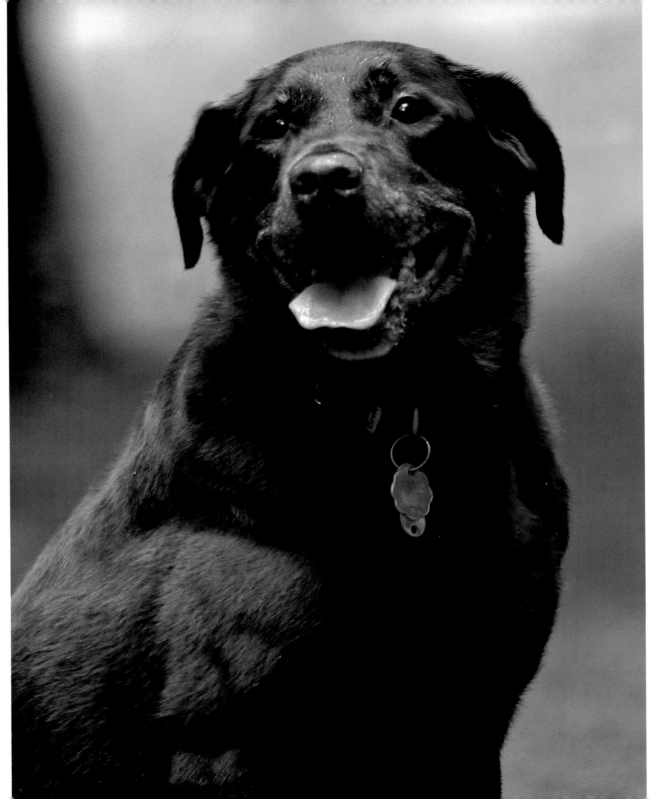

 FOR THIS SHOT
In choosing to zoom in from a distance, I was unable to achieve sharpness on both the long snout and the eyes, so I concentrated on the eyes. With a high sensitivity, I worked at maximum aperture for the shortest exposure times.

CAMERA MODE

 Set your dial to **Sports mode**

LENS SETTING

Zoom to **Maximum Telephoto**

SENSOR/FILM SPEED

Use a **High** ISO setting

FLASH

Force the flash **Off**

3 SEIZE CALM MOMENTS
Take the picture when the dog is relaxed and settled. It is easier to get the whole animal sharp and in focus if you opt for a full-length portrait.

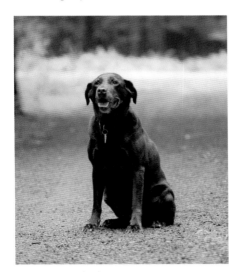

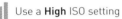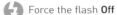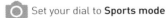

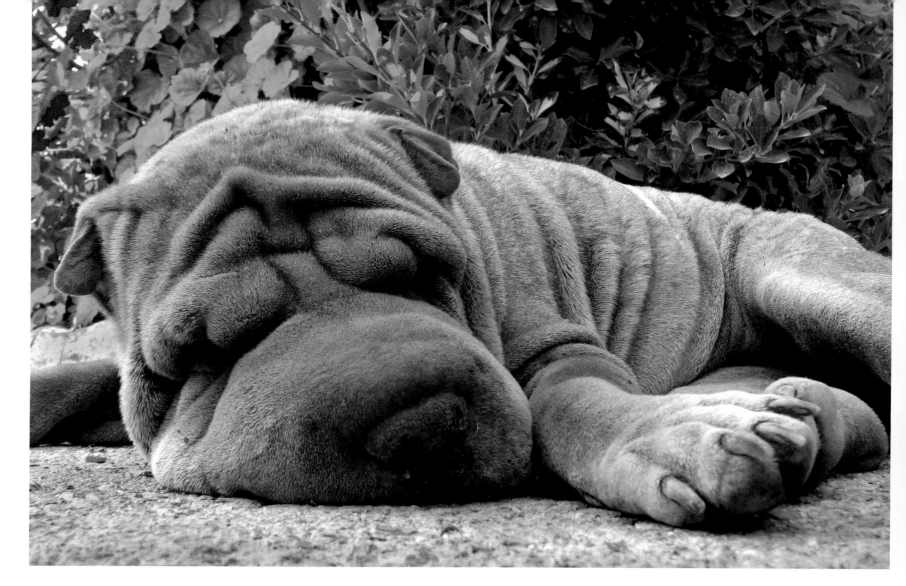

Fun pet portraits

One challenge of photographing pets lies in capturing their character in an appropriate way. This wrinkled old Shar Pei was portrayed from a worm's-eye view to emphasize his face, big paws, and relaxed pose. Photographically the task is simply to get close and wide, and to ensure you focus on the right part of the animal. Cameras with flip-out LCD screens are advantageous for low viewpoints, since you can monitor the image without having to lie on the ground.

FOR THIS SHOT

A worm's-eye view with the camera set to wide-angle and placed on the ground gave me an amusing, intimate viewpoint. I opted for maximum depth of field, since the subject was static and the camera stabilized by the ground.

CAMERA MODE

Set your dial to **Minimum Aperture**

LENS SETTING

Zoom to **Wide Macro**

SENSOR/FILM SPEED

Use a **Low** to **Medium** ISO setting

FLASH

Force the flash **Off**

---

1 LET SLEEPING DOGS LIE

Always think safety first. If you do not know the animal, check with its owners that it is friendly and will not react badly, especially if it has been woken up from sleep.

2 SELECT SETTINGS

Set the camera to macro or close-up mode, and use a wide angle. Turn off the flash. If you have one, flip out the LCD screen so you can see the image while the camera is at ground level.

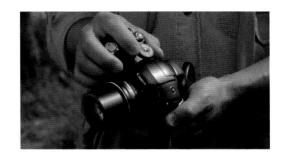

3 USE THE RIGHT LIGHTING

To make sure the delicate and subtle textures of fur register, you must work in subdued lighting. The open shade under a bush is ideal. Move slowly and quietly to avoid startling the dog.

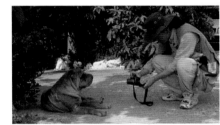

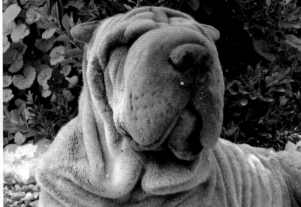

FILLING THE FRAME

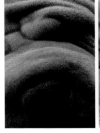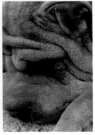

The textures of animal's fur and features can comfortably fill the frame with subtle colors and lights. However, if you venture too close with your camera, you are in danger of losing the identity of the animal. Try to find a suitable balance between detail and context.

4 USE FOCUS LOCK

Don't focus on the nearest part of the animal: you want to capture the face rather than the feet. It doesn't matter—indeed, it might be better—if not all of the animal is in focus. Point the camera at the area you wish to keep sharp, press the shutter halfway to obtain and lock focus, then reframe for the shot.

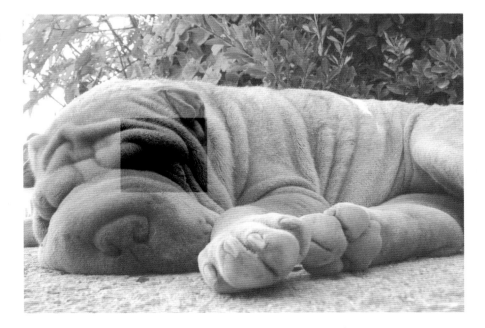

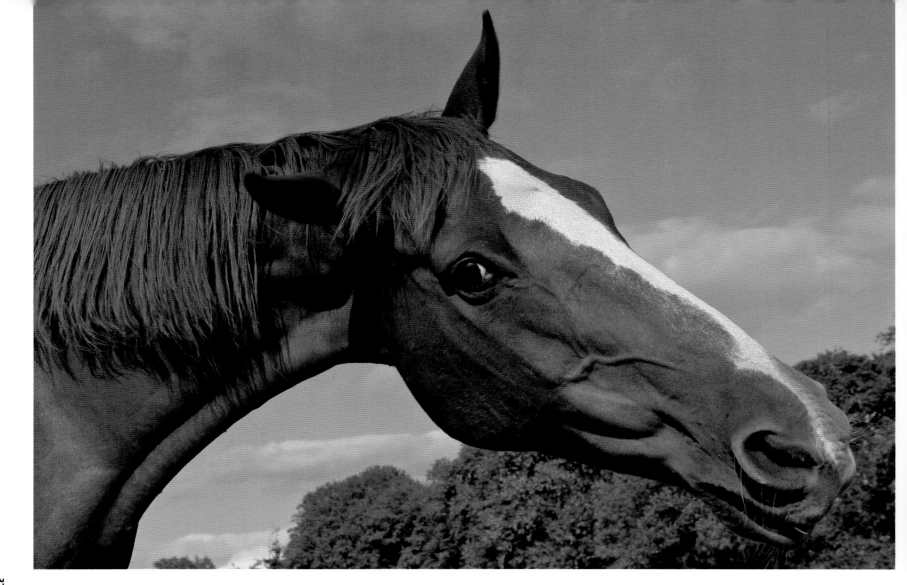

Equine elegance

With their beauty of form, variety of movement, and diversity of mood, horses are extremely rewarding to photograph, irrespective of the weather or lighting conditions. As with all animal subjects, the more you understand about horses, the easier it is to photograph them. Horses have their own well-defined personalities, which can be by turns shy, frisky, friendly, or aloof. Try to ensure that your pictures capture their individuality.

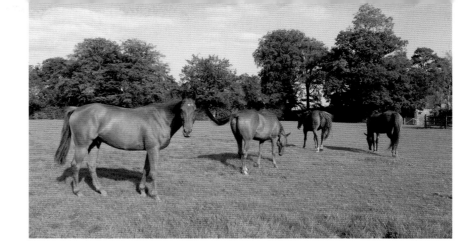

FOR THIS SHOT

I selected the sports mode and set the zoom to normal focal length, so as neither to exaggerate the perspective nor to compress the space. I forced the flash off, and since it was a bright, sunny day, I selected a low sensitivity.

CAMERA MODE

Set your dial to **Sports mode**

LENS SETTING

Zoom to **Normal**

SENSOR/FILM SPEED

Use a **Low** ISO setting

FLASH

Force the flash **Off**

1 TRY DIFFERENT COMPOSITIONS

Experiment with different types of shot. In this instance, there is little activity and no mystery to the atmosphere. A portrait of one individual horse makes a stronger shot than an undynamic group picture.

2 AVOID DISTORTION

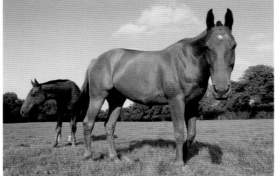

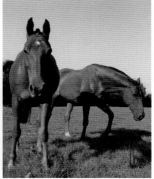

Encourage horses to come closer by offering them a treat. Avoid shooting from close up with a wide-angle setting when the horse is facing you, since this can distort the image, making the head appear unnaturally large, as in the picture on the near right.

3 SET TO SPORTS MODE

Before the scene starts to arrange itself into a suitable composition for the camera, select the settings you need—such as sports mode for action. You can check exposure with a shot of any part of the animal.

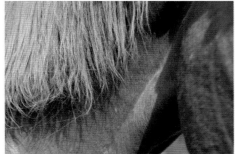

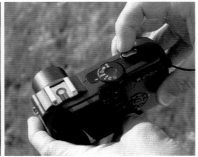

4 TRY DIFFERENT VIEWPOINTS

A horse's head is very long, which makes capturing its entire extent in sharp focus extremely difficult to do. It is usually easier and more photogenic to show the horse in profile rather than than face-on.

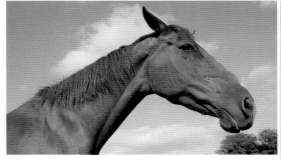

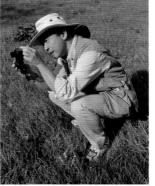

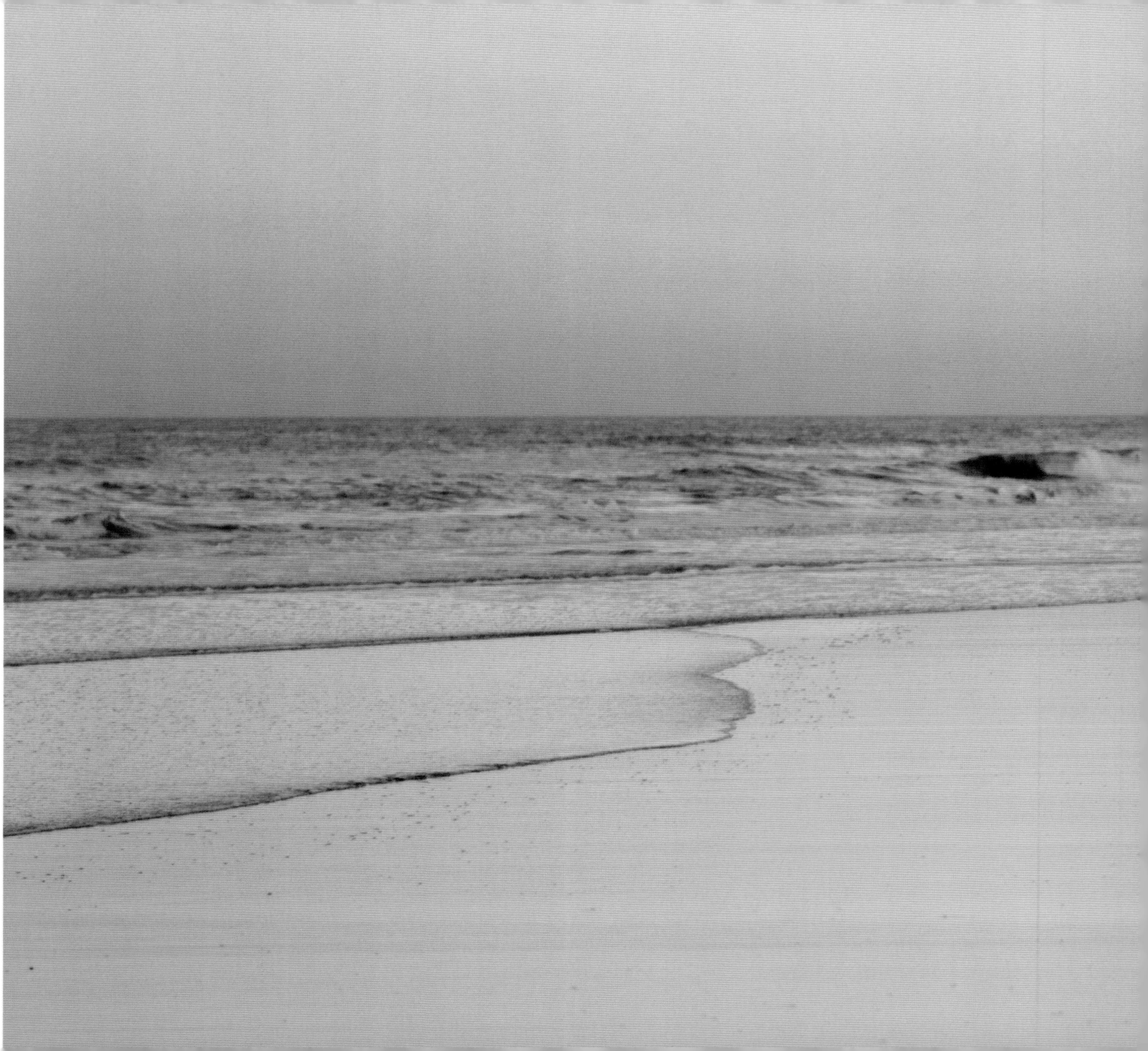

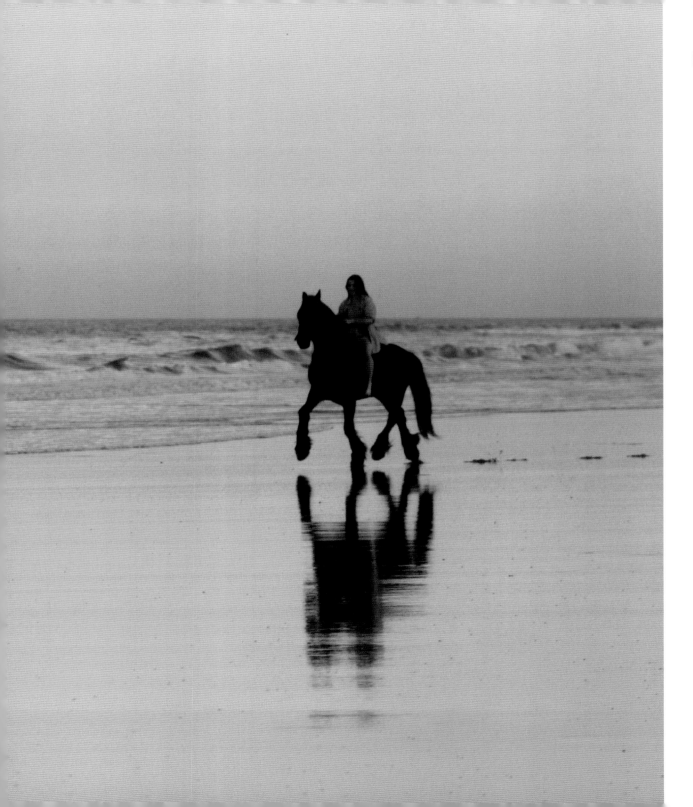

SUNSET RIDE

The image of a rider on a horse strongly symbolizes man working with nature and a sense of individual destiny. Such an evocative image is surprisingly easy to photograph: you need only a wide open space within which to set off the subject.

1 Include a large amount of space in the picture to give a sense of freedom and liberation.

2 Compose the image so that your subjects move into the space available in the image.

3 For best rendition of large areas of smooth tone, use the highest quality settings.

Birds in flight

The graceful flight of birds soaring on thermals is a visual treat and an inviting subject for photography. It is also very demanding. Birds are usually far away; they tend to move very quickly; and the light may be against you. However, if you can find a clifftop position that is safe, the prospects are good. Set your camera to its longest focal length, select the sports mode to capture action, and then keep shooting for as long as you can.

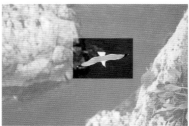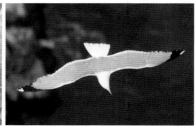

If you find that the birds appear rather small in the viewfinder, you can move to the longest setting on your zoom. This may call up the digital zoom function, which enlarges the central portion, but this process impairs image quality.

1 STAY SAFE
Try to find a vantage point that brings you relatively close to the seagulls soaring around the cliffs. Make sure you are safe and don't lean too far to obtain any shot. Set the autofocus mode to follow or servo focus.

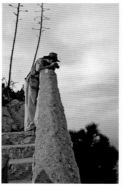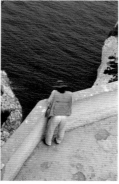

2 BEWARE AUTOFOCUS
The camera should continually focus as you follow the bird. If you find autofocus unreliable, you can focus on a spot that the birds frequent, and shoot as they fly by.

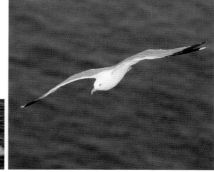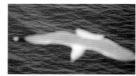

3 CHART BEHAVIOR
Watch the birds to establish whether they have a favorite spot for landing or taking off – for example, a cliff where the wind is weaker. Learn the birds' behavior, so that you are better informed and more likely to capture the images you want.

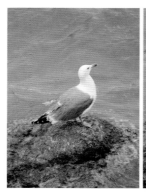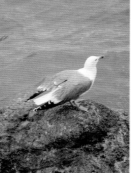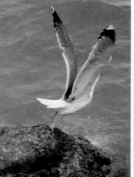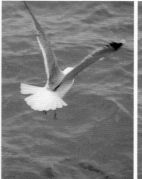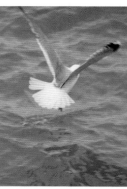

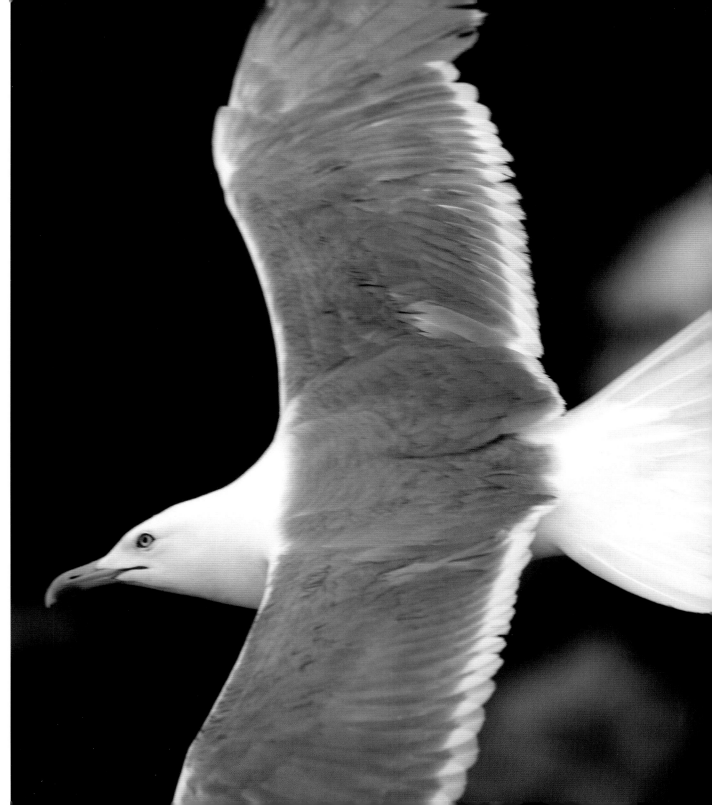

 FOR THIS SHOT

I followed the gull as it passed and released the shutter. This helped keep the bird sharply focused. I used a short shutter time, high sensitivity, and set the longest focal length. Then I took lots of pictures at every opportunity.

CAMERA MODE

Set your dial to **Sports mode**

LENS SETTING

Zoom to **Maximum Telephoto**

SENSOR/FILM SPEED

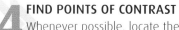 Use a **High** ISO setting

FLASH

Force the flash **Off**

4 FIND POINTS OF CONTRAST

Whenever possible, locate the bird against a neutral background so that its shape shows up clearly. The sea is ideal for this. You can make it look nearly black by setting the exposure for the bird.

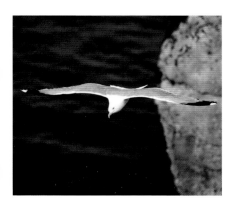

Exotic birds in close-up

Within the animal world, birds are among the most colorful subjects. Zoos provide unique photographic opportunities, especially for those who can't afford to stalk wild birds for weeks at a time to obtain portraits in the wild. As with many photography projects, proper preparation is at least half the process. A close-up portrait of any wild animal, captive or otherwise, starts with observing its habits and trying to predict its movements and behavior.

 ATTRACT THE SUBJECT
If you are allowed to offer the birds some to acclimatize them to your presence. Taking pictures as you do this will get them used to the sounds of the camera. You will often find that one of the birds is more daring than the others, so that is the one to court.

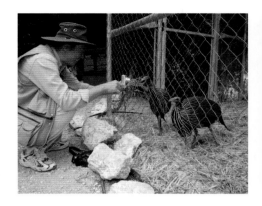

WORK THROUGH THE FENCE
One advantage of simple digital cameras is that the lens is small enough to poke through fencing, but only do this if it is safe.

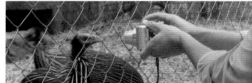

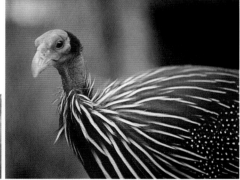

KEEP SHOOTING
Angle the camera to avoid any telltale signs of the cage, and take pictures all the time. Birds move so quickly and unpredictably that if you see what you want to photograph, you will have already missed the picture.

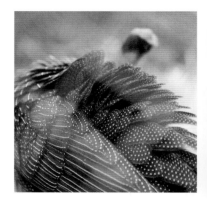

TAKE CLOSE-UP SHOTS
If the bird obligingly comes beak-to-lens to investigate you and the camera, keep clicking away. You may have to change modes—from close-up to normal focusing distances, and back again—as the bird moves around the enclosure.

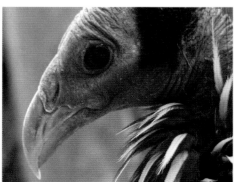
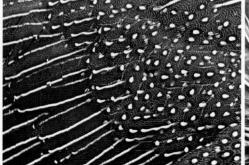
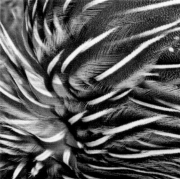

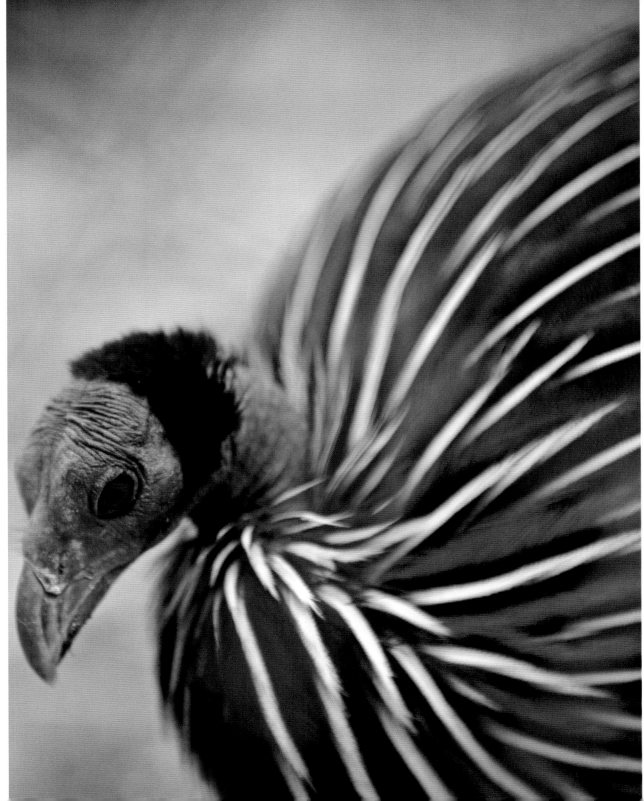

FOR THIS SHOT

A telephoto setting kept the bird in frame, while moving with the bird helped blur the fence. I chose the sports mode to ensure the shortest shutter times and to freeze movement. This was aided by a medium to high sensitivity setting.

CAMERA MODE

Set your dial to **Sports mode**

LENS SETTING

Zoom to **fill the frame**

SENSOR/FILM SPEED

Use a **Medium** to **High** ISO setting

FLASH

Force the flash **On** if needed

5 BEWARE OF FLASH

Flash can produce strange effects if the bird is extremely close to the lens. Only use it if the zoo or park permits it.

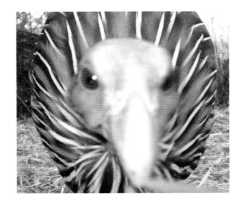

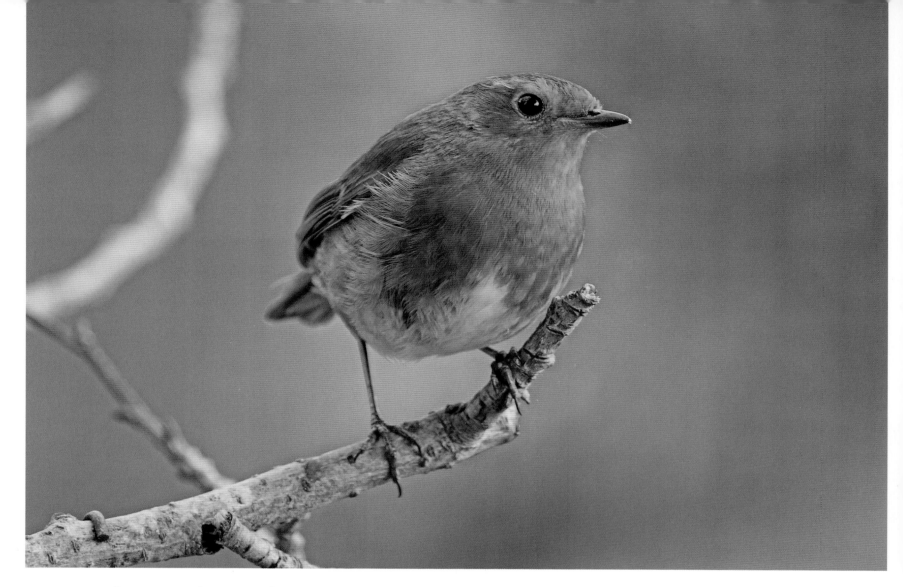

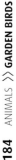
Garden birds

Garden birds are among the most accessible wildlife for photographers, because it is relatively easy to attract them close enough to capture a highly detailed study. Simply invest in a bird feeder, and wait for the local bird community to find out that your garden is worth a visit. Watch them and learn their routines – for example, seed-eating birds tend to feed early in the morning and late in the afternoon – so you can be ready with your camera at the right time.

1 ATTRACT THE BIRDS

Set up birdbaths and tables, and hang bird feeders in your garden. Place them in spots where they have a pleasant background from your vantage point.

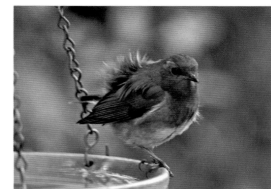

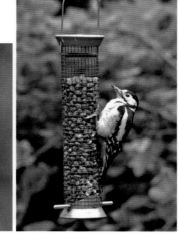

2 CLEAN YOUR WINDOWS

If you decide to use the house as your hide, you will be taking photographs through the windows. Make sure they are clean.

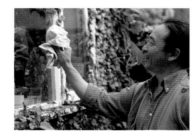

3 HAVE PATIENCE

Get into position and wait with your camera trained on the spot where you expect the birds to land, so you can be ready when they arrive. If possible, use a tripod and a remote shutter release; otherwise, hold the camera steady by resting your elbows on the windowsill or your fingers against the window.

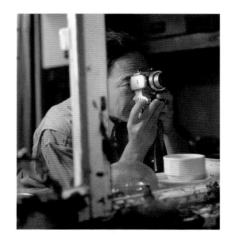

4 KEEP SHOOTING

Don't wait for an attractive composition before releasing the shutter: by the time the shutter runs, the birds could have flown out of the picture. Simply keep taking as many pictures as you can for as long as you can. You can crop your images to focus on the best elements at a later stage.

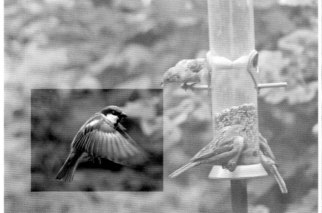

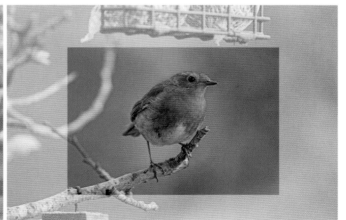

Wildlife close to home

Photographing local wildlife can be every bit as challenging as taking pictures of animals in game reserves or safari parks. Persevere, however, since this type of photography offers excellent practice for the budding wildlife photographer, enabling you to observe the animals and their behavior at close quarters, experiment with different compositions, and learn to wait patiently for the right shot.

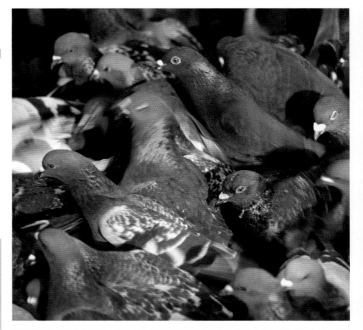

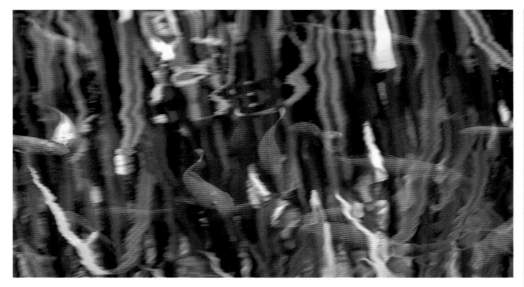

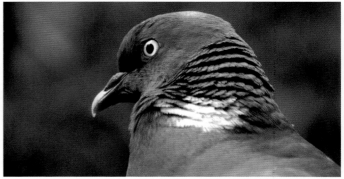

COLOR CONTRAST

Goldfish in ponds are a rewarding subject because their bright colors contrast strongly with the dark waters. By using different effects you can create various types of images, including vibrant near-abstract shots.

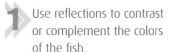 Use reflections to contrast or complement the colors of the fish.

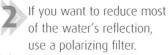 If you want to reduce most of the water's reflection, use a polarizing filter.

If the water is dark, expose for a lighter area, or the fish will be overexposed.

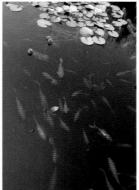

FRAMING OPTIONS

Large gatherings of birds may result in pulsating, dynamic patterns; press the shutter button repeatedly so as to have a range of shots. Alternatively, you can try singling out individual birds.

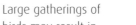 For large groups, crop in very close to create an almost abstract pattern.

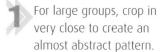 For individual portraits, emphasize the outline of the bird and its feathers.

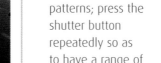 To throw the background out of focus, use the longest focal length setting.

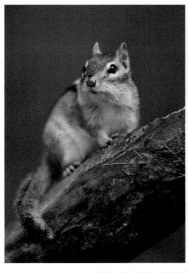

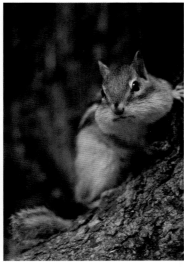

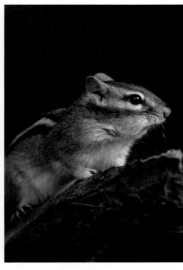

CAPTURING QUICK MOVEMENT

Small, lively animals are easier to photograph if you have help – for example, someone offering food to attract them and keep them close.

1 Focus on a spot and wait for the animal to return to it rather than chase after it.

2 If your zoom does not magnify the animal enough, take the picture anyway; you can enlarge it at a later stage.

3 Flash may startle the animal, and it will slow down the camera. Use short exposure and shutter times to capture sharp images.

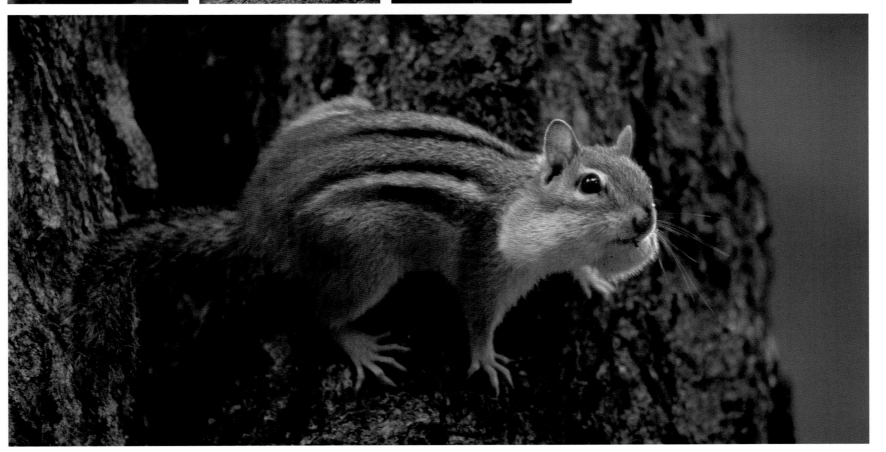

COMPOSITIONAL LEVELS

If you are lucky enough to have a garden, you can encourage creatures to visit by providing food and shelter. As the animals become used to your presence, they will be less nervous around you and more likely to ignore you and the camera.

1 Take a plastic sheet with you so you can lie right down on the ground if the composition demands it.

2 Support your camera on a small table tripod, which combines good stability with maneuverability.

3 Add interest to your photography by creating a series of pictures in different contexts, not just one shot.

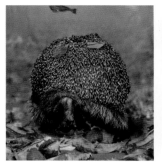

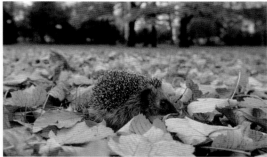

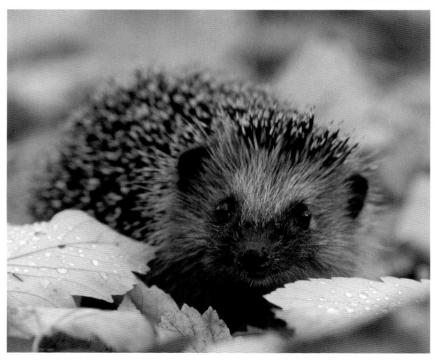

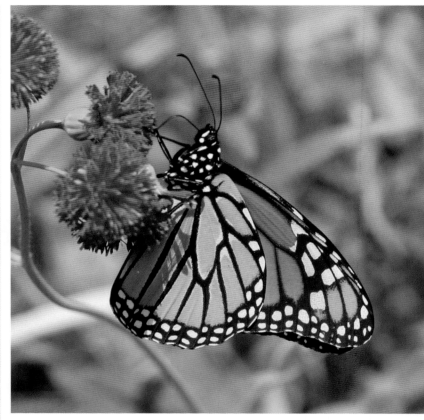

INSECT CLOSE-UPS

The key to getting good close-up shots of insects such as butterflies is to keep your distance and zoom in to avoid disturbing them.

1 A butterfly will settle on the same flower several times, so focus on that spot and wait for it to return.

2 If you need to get closer to the butterfly, move only the camera rather than your entire body.

3 You might want to use flash to help freeze movement and enhance the colors.

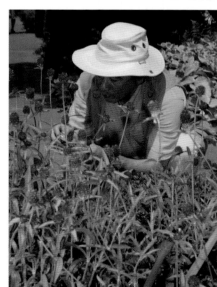

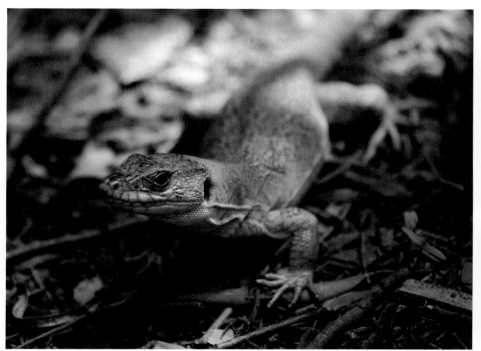

The best time to photograph cold-blooded animals such as reptiles is in the cool of the morning or evening, when they are least frisky and their movements are slower.

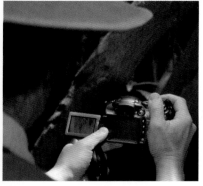

1 If possible, have a helper encourage the animal to move toward you, but avoid causing any distress.

2 Set the camera to close-up mode with the zoom at a long setting, and focus on the eyes, if possible.

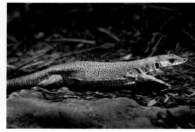

3 Avoid using the flash – it is unkind to the animal, and the resulting image will look unnatural.

MOVEMENT IN WATER

Waterfowl make superb subjects for photography. This is partly because they don't move as quickly on water as they do on land or in flight; but also because water offers a neutral, yet constantly changing, background.

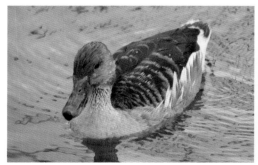

1 Use short exposure to freeze the bird's movement and the ripples in the water.

2 Experiment with compositions, from a close-up of the bird's head to its entire body.

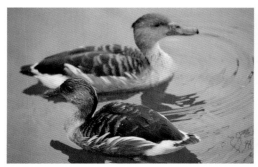

3 Try panning with the camera to follow the bird's movement during exposure.

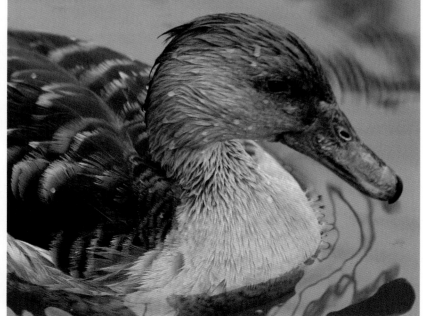

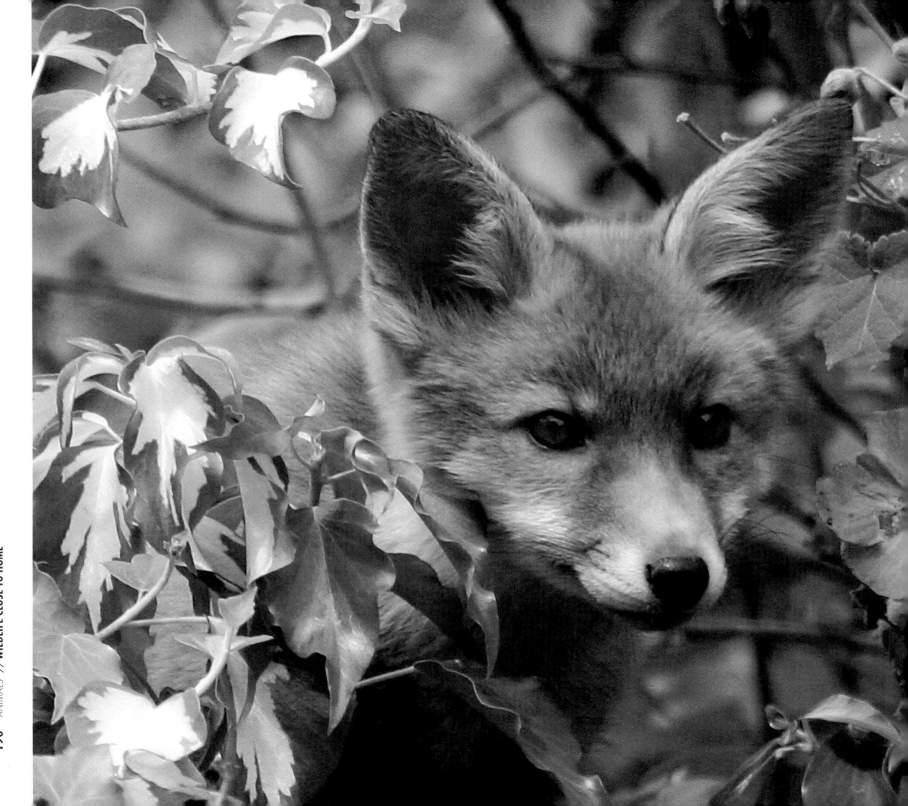

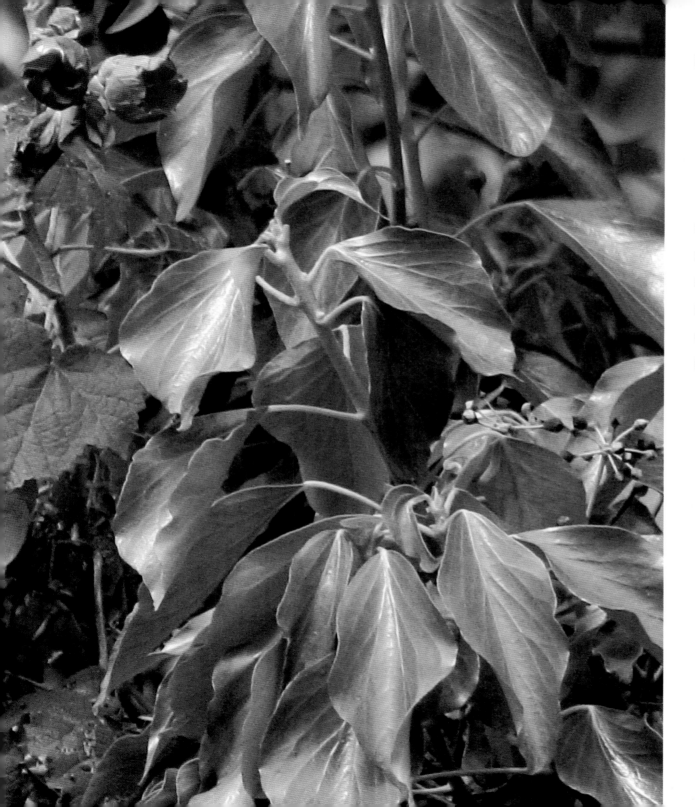

URBAN FOX

Even in urban environments it is possible to find wildlife to photograph. Indeed, some animals, such as foxes, are more common in city gardens than in the countryside. You need to know their ways and habits to photograph them; then, you have to lie in wait.

1 Wild animals are creatures of habit, so learn where they go and at which time of the day.

2 You may have to wait for hours on end, so set your camera on a tripod.

3 Use a long lens setting or set the camera close to where you expect the animal to appear.

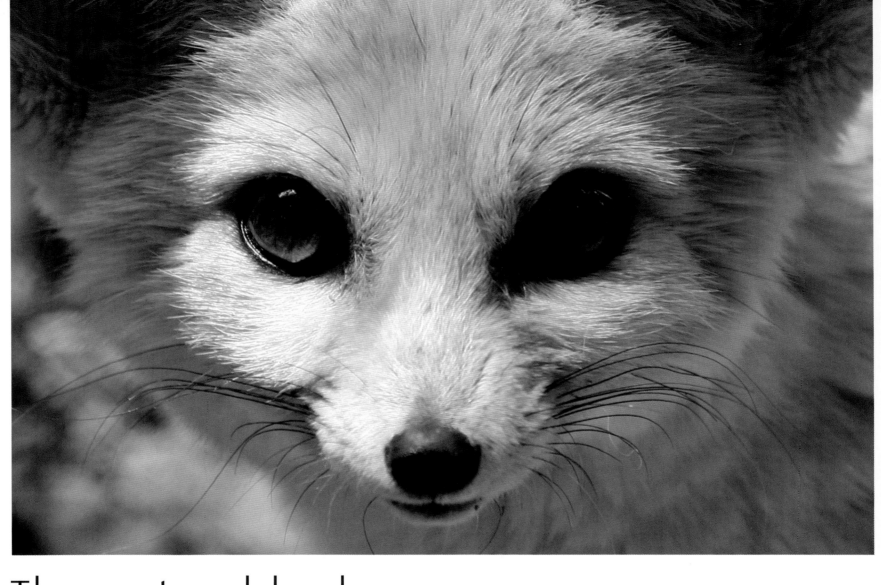

The natural look

Thanks to the incredible quality of modern zoom lenses, you can take animal pictures that even professional photographers would be proud of. You can achieve the wildlife look even when the animal is in captivity. Through careful planning and sensitive positioning of your camera, it is possible to make bars and cages disappear entirely. The animals shown here had been rescued from private owners who were unable to care for them properly.

RESPECT THE CAGES

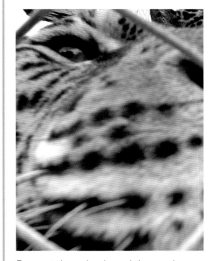

Respect the animals and the need for cages, and obey all relevant rules. Many animals can move much faster than humans, so keep your distance, and never put your fingers through the bars of a cage for any reason.

1 TREAD LIGHTLY

In many animal-rescue centers, it is possible to approach close to the animals, which are often accustomed to humans. Nonetheless, be as quiet as possible and avoid sudden movements so as not to startle them.

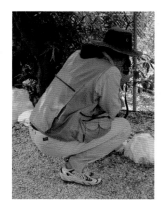

2 BE PATIENT

You may have to wait some time for the animal to look your way, so keep your camera ready at your eye.

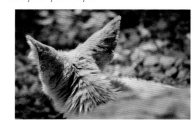

3 LOSE THE CAGE

Use the longest zoom possible and move as close to the fence as you can. Set the lens aperture to the largest to minimize depth of field; this, in turn helps to throw the wires of the cage out of focus as they disappear.

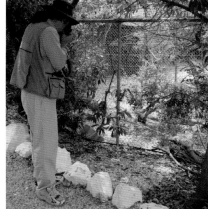
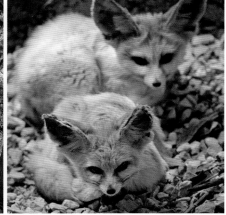

4 CROP IN ON THE EYES

A huge amount of expression is carried in the eyes, so try cropping into this area to create a final composition. For an extreme crop such as this to be successful, select the highest quality setting on the camera when shooting.

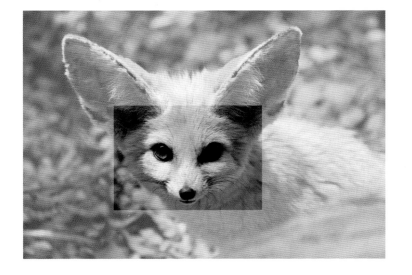

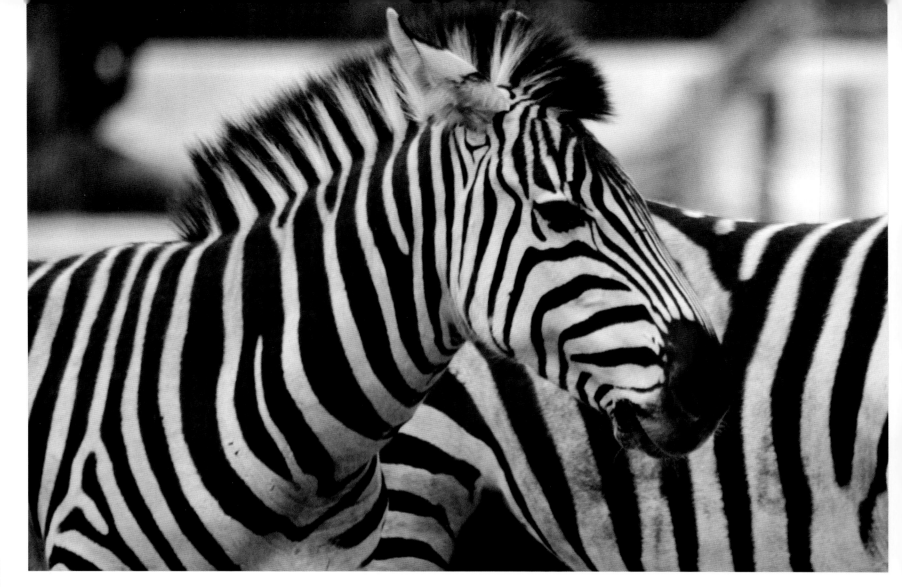

Wildlife from a car

The closest many of us ever get to big-game animals is at the safari park. You drive through the park slowly, you have to photograph with the car windows up, and you are not allowed to stop. To ensure successful photography under these trying conditions, you need to take some simple precautions. The key to satisfying images is to keep an eye on the background. Try to make it as unobtrusive as possible, so as not to distract from the animals.

FOR THIS SHOT

I zoomed in all the way to get as close to the animals as possible, but the shot still showed too much. I made a severe crop to emphasize the patterns, and also to help reduce the impact of the fence in the background.

CAMERA MODE

📷 Set your dial to **Sports mode**

LENS SETTING

◎ Zoom to **Maximum Telephoto**

SENSOR/FILM SPEED

📶 Use a **Medium** to **High** ISO setting

FLASH

⚡ Force the flash **Off**

1 PREPARE THE CAR

If they are not already spotlessly clean, wash all the windows of your car, both inside and out. That will enable you to photograph through any of them as the situation demands. If your car has tinted windows, try to use a different car.

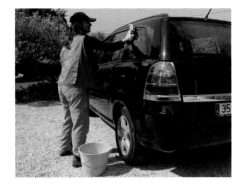

2 REMOVE OBSTACLES

Work out in advance how to remove other elements that might block your view, such as headrests. Once you know how to do it, you can do so just before entering the safari park.

3 CHOOSE CAMERA SETTINGS

Set your camera to short exposure times to catch action, and also because you may have to shoot while the car is moving.

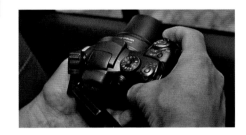

4 STEADY YOURSELF

Hold the camera as close to the car window as you can, to minimize reflections, but do not touch the glass with the camera, as the vibrations will blur your pictures. Instead, press a finger against the window to support the camera. This will help you absorb car vibrations.

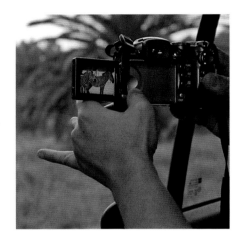

5 SEIZE YOUR OPPORTUNITIES

Photograph as quickly as you can, because you have only one chance. Very few shots will be perfect, but you can improve the best ones after the trip with cropping or other manipulation.

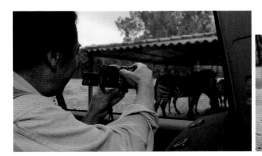

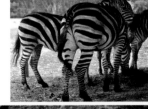

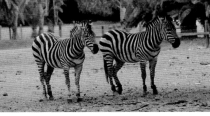

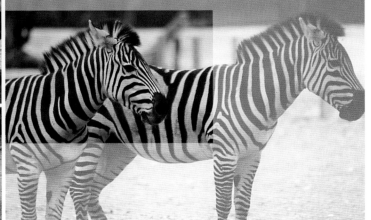

Around the animal park

An animal or safari park offers a wealth of marvelous photographic opportunities. The pictures you take will also give you and anyone else who sees them the chance to appreciate the beauty of the animals and all that they represent. Be sure to take lots of memory for the camera (you don't want to be forced to delete pictures to make space for more shots while in the middle of a tour). Take spare batteries, too.

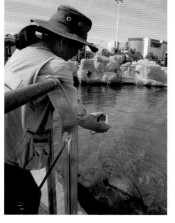

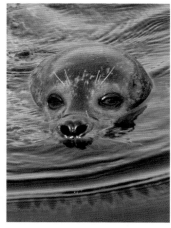

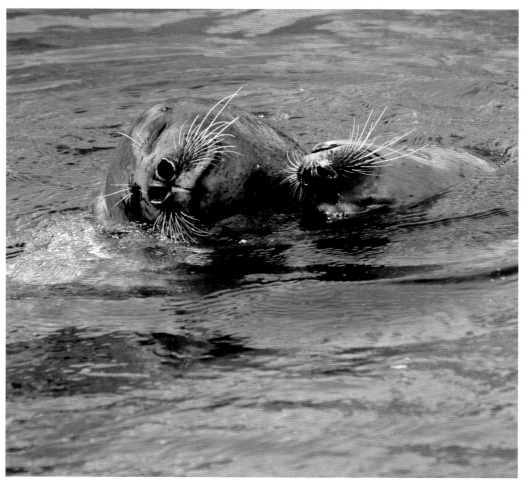

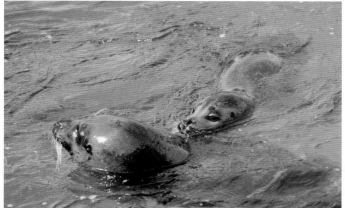

ANIMALS IN WATER

These seals were quite active and excited because it was coming up to feeding time. I looked around to find a position where the water had the most colorful reflections; then I simply waited for the right moment.

1 Learn about the animal's routine to be sure to see them out and about.

2 Use a short exposure time to capture sharp images of movement.

3 Set your zoom to a medium length and allow the action to come into frame without zooming back and forth.

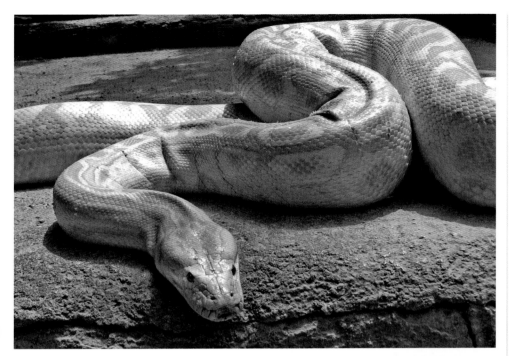

IRIDESCENT CLOSE-UP

A peacock's beautifully colorful plumage cries out to be photographed. This is one of the rare occasions when taking pictures of animals that calls for the use of the flash.

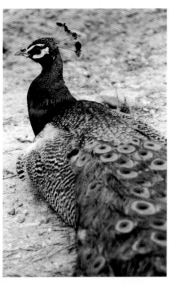

1 Use a high-quality setting to capture all the fine detail and subtle colors.

2 If possible hold the camera level over the bird's feathers.

3 Zoom in and use the flash to capture the sheen of the colorful feathers.

NOSE-TO-LENS PORTRAIT

If the animal handler says it's safe, get as close to the animal as focus will allow, and take a close-up portrait. It may require a little courage, but the results will be worthwhile.

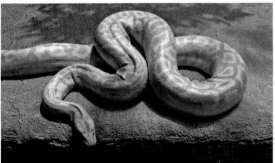

1 Move slowly and deliberately so as not to intimidate the animal.

2 Force the flash off, or it might startle the animal into a defensive reaction.

3 Use a wide-angle setting to give a dramatic perspective from close-up.

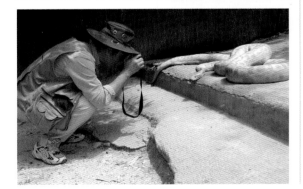

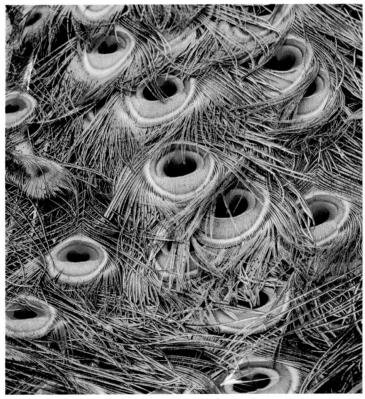

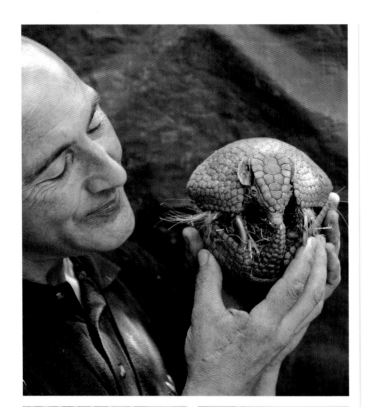

CAPTURING CHARACTER

Some animals, such as the hippopotamus, tend to be active only around feeding time. This means that you have a small window of a few minutes to catch a dynamic, characterful portrait, so be prepared.

1 Observe the animal carefully to help you predict their movements.

2 Set a long telephoto for the most impressive close-up portraits.

3 Position yourself so that you enjoy good lighting when the animal appears.

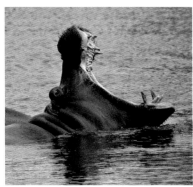

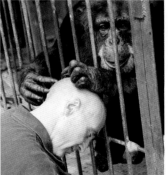

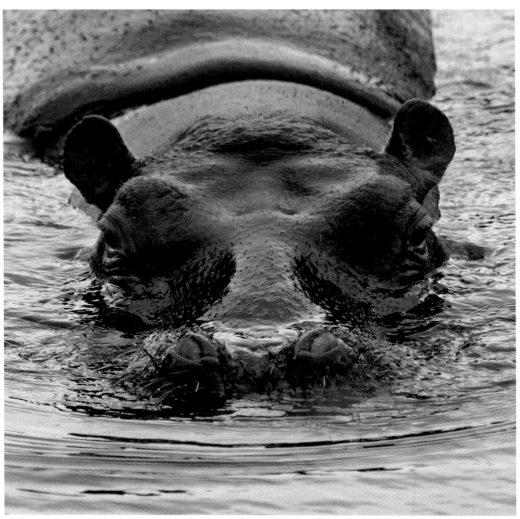

PLAYFUL INTERACTION

Guided visits are excellent opportunities for taking photographs that illustrate the relationship between keepers and animals.

1 Use a normal focal length zoom setting for the most natural perspective.

2 Don't be tempted to use flash, even in low light. Instead, set high sensitivity.

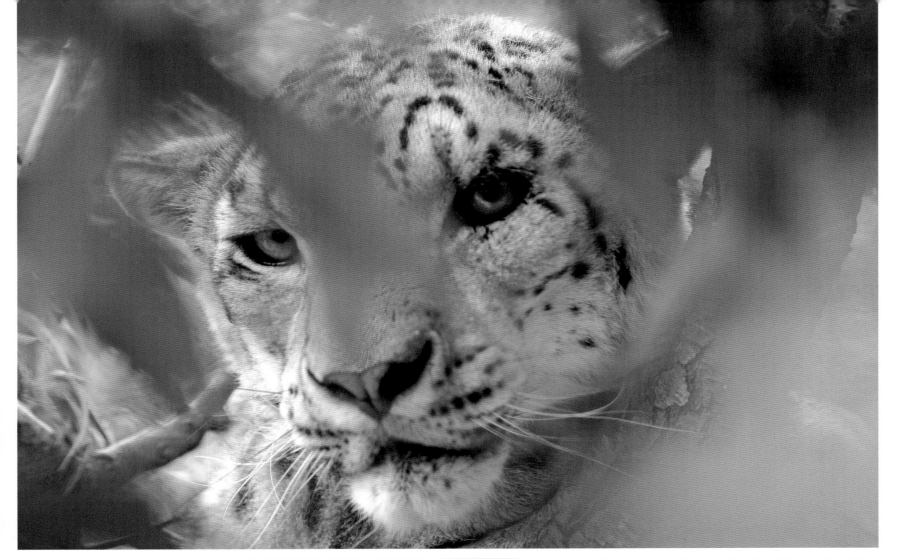

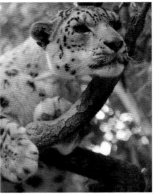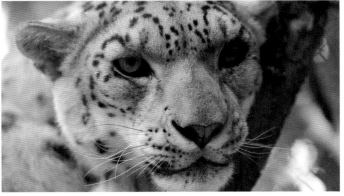

WILDLIFE CLOSE-UP

Many animal portraits, like those of humans, show the face without any obstruction. In the wild, animals spend a lot of time hiding in vegetation. The most natural-looking images are those that give a sense of being taken in the wild.

1 Move very slowly and quietly to avoid alarming the animal.

2 Use the longest telephoto zoom setting to fill the frame with the face.

3 To help throw the foreground foliage into blur, combine the long zoom with focus on the eyes.

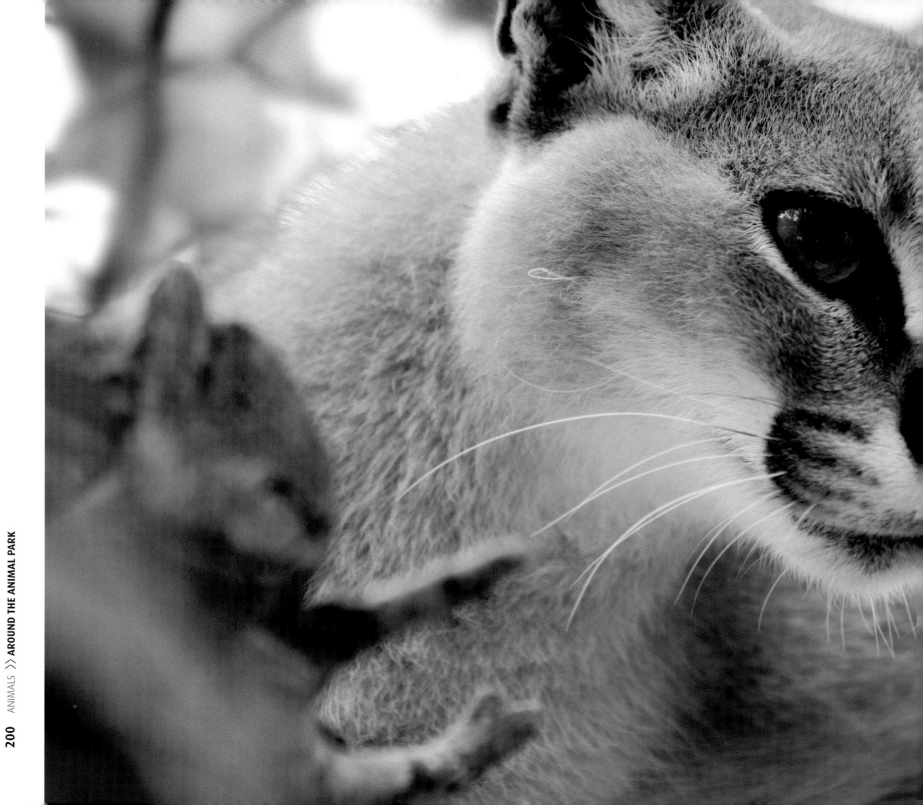

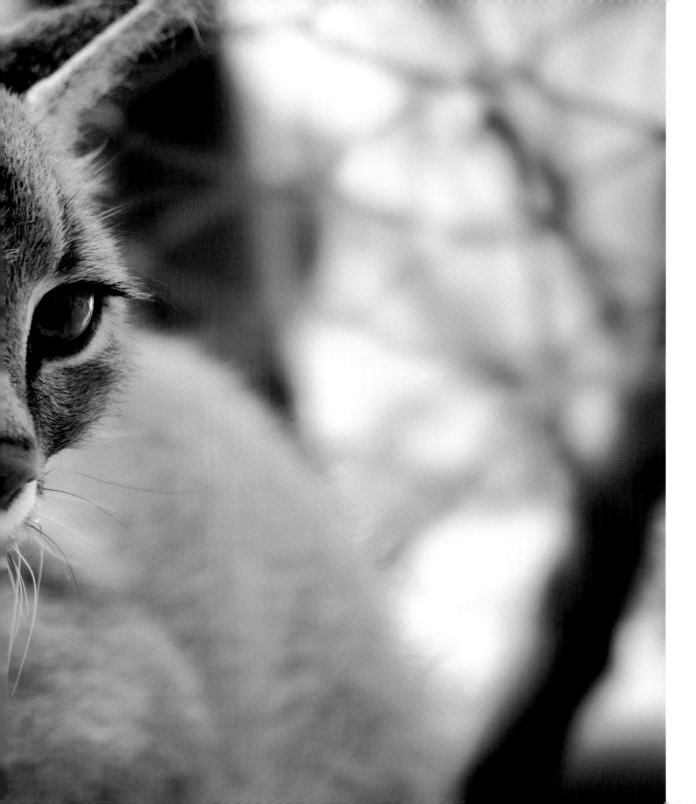

BIG CAT PORTRAIT

The best portrait subjects are those who are totally themselves, and few can match the self-possession of big cats. A patient wait – camera at the ready and closely observing the animal – is usually rewarded with stunning pictures.

1 Spend some time observing the animal's behavior, and allow it to get used to your presence.

2 When photographing wildlife from a distance, use the longest focal length setting available.

3 Hold the camera steadily, preferably on a tripod, or use a support such as a fence.

4 Always keep the focus on the animal's eyes. If these are sharp, it will not matter so much if other areas are soft.

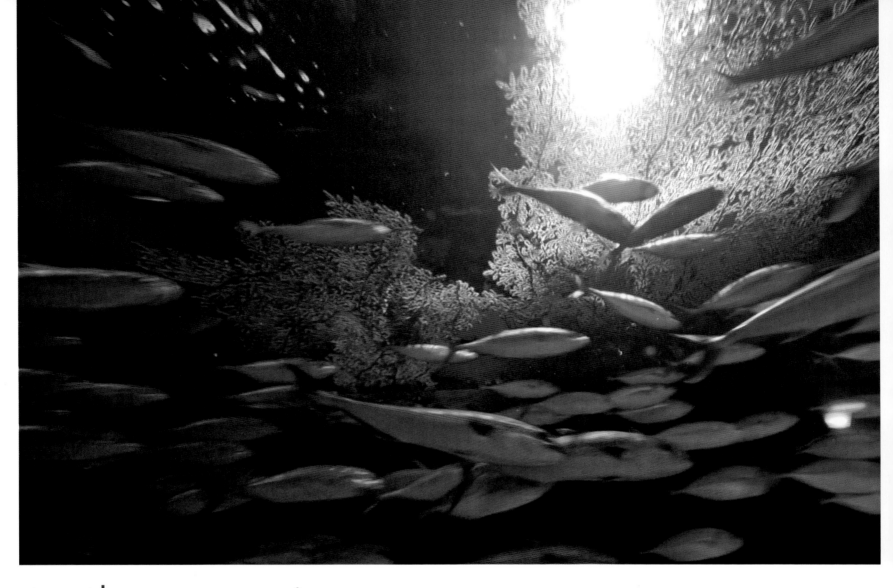

At the aquarium

The easiest way to photograph underwater life is by walking through glass-covered tunnels in a large aquarium. This is a thrilling experience because you are almost inside the scene, with the fish swimming around and above you.

In this kind of environment, the light levels are very low, so you will need to set the highest sensitivity on your camera, and you must turn off the flash: it could blind the fish.

FOR THIS SHOT

The first thing I did was switch off the flash. Then I set the camera for action and low light. The overall color balance came out blue-green, due to the water and glass.

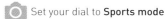

CAMERA MODE
Set your dial to **Sports mode**

LENS SETTING
Zoom to **Wide** to **Normal**

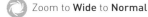

SENSOR/FILM SPEED
Use a **High** ISO setting

FLASH
Force the flash **Off**

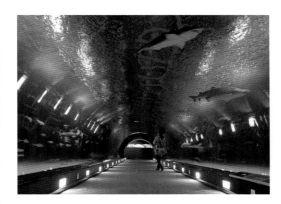

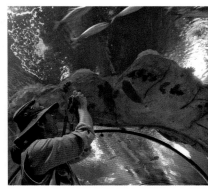

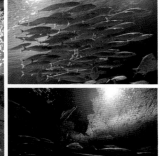

PREPARE THE SHOT
Walk around the aquarium and check for the positions with the best lighting. Set your camera to sports mode and the highest sensitivity (800 ISO or higher) if you want to get the sharpest images possible.

THINK LIKE A SHARK
Notice where the fish swim and try to work out their favorite routes, as well as spots they return to repeatedly. Position yourself so that the fish will pass an attractive background and interesting light. That way, you will be ready for them as they come around.

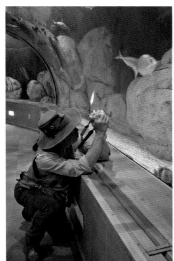

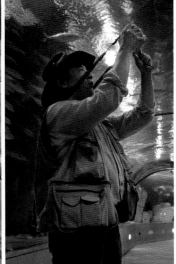

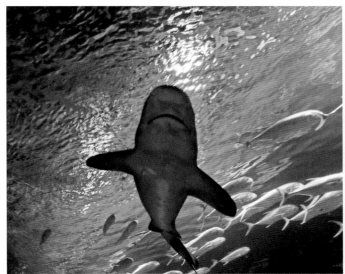

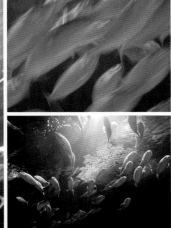

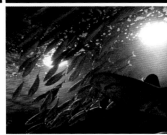

STEADY YOURSELF
Tripods may not be permitted, so lean on any available surface or hold the camera strap taut if you are standing. Avoid zooming too far: this is likely to make the lens slower, and then it will be more difficult to catch the action.

CAPTURING MOVEMENT
Consider whether to try for group shots or pictures of individuals. Experiment with longer exposures to evoke movement through blur, and work with patterns of light and shade to give a sense of the swirling movements.

Movement underwater

It is a tremendous privilege to be able to get close to wild animals, even if they are held in captivity. Of course, it is easy to grab a few quick shots of these creatures and then hurry on to the next attraction, but by taking a little more care and effort, you will capture a far more rewarding picture. Next time you visit an aquarium or zoo, really take the time to observe the animals. Some may even enjoy engaging with you.

COLOUR ADJUSTMENT

The depth of the water and the thick glass of the aquarium combined may give a strong green color cast to all your images. You can try to correct this in camera using the white-balance feature, or adjust it later using image-manipulation software. Of course, you can leave it, too, keeping it closer to what you saw.

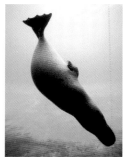
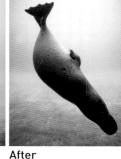

Before   **After**

1 MAKE FRIENDS
Some animals enjoy human contact, so instead of treating them as passive things, try interacting with them.

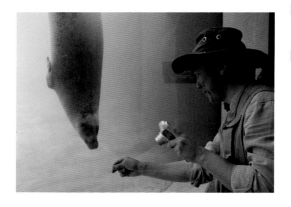

2 CONSIDER THE COMPOSITION
Try a wide variety of shots. You could consider including other people in the picture, or get up close to the animal for a portrait. Make absolutely sure that your flash is switched off first.

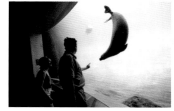
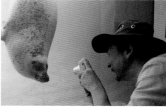

3 OBSERVE AND SHOOT
Follow the animals as they swim around. The more you watch their movements, the better you might be able to anticipate a good picture. As soon as you think the animal is about to assume an interesting position, release the shutter so you don't miss the shot.

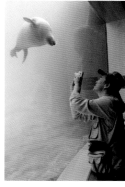
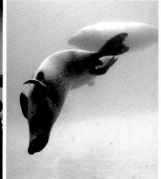
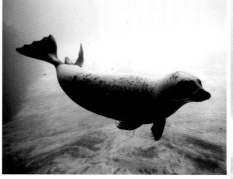
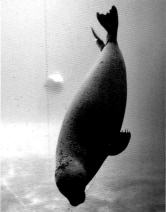

FOR THIS SHOT

First I turned off the flash. I set a high sensitivity to compensate for the low light, and set the zoom to wide angle for maximum aperture. The sports-mode setting helped ensure the shortest exposures, so freezing any movement.

CAMERA MODE

 Set your dial to **Sports mode**

LENS SETTING

 Zoom to **Wide Angle**

SENSOR/FILM SPEED

 Use a **High** ISO setting

FLASH

Force the flash **Off**

4 MAKE EYE CONTACT

Spend some time in front of the enclosure, so the animal gets used to your presence. To create the most engaging shot possible, make eye contact.

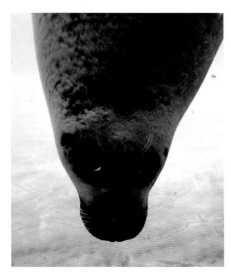

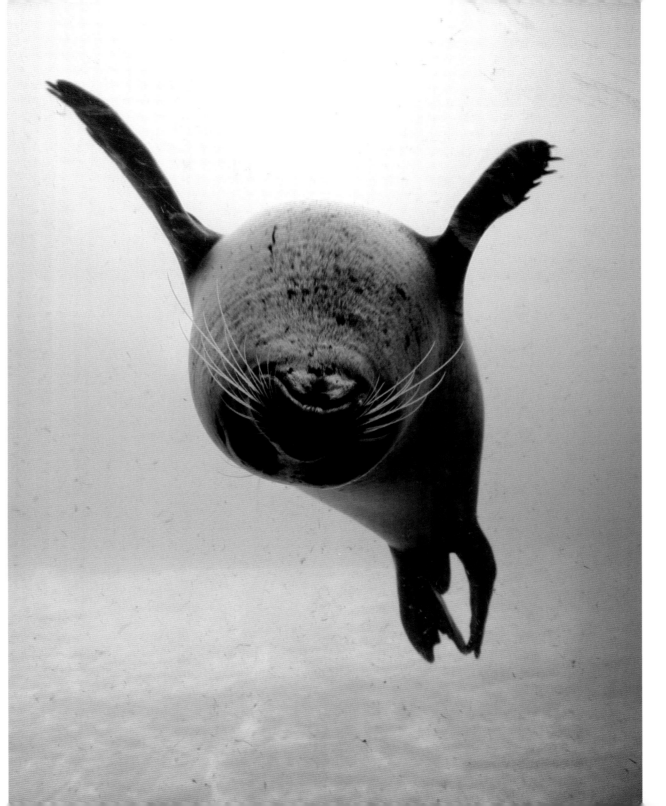

Animals

The key to photographing any animal successfully – whether wild, domestic, or in captivity – is patience. In the wild, in particular, you may need to track an animal's habits over a period of time in order to photograph it at all. Even when visiting a zoo, observing and waiting for a few minutes for the best shot in the right light will be handsomely rewarded.

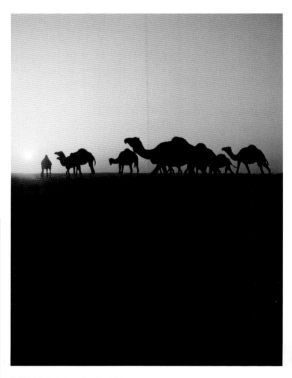

DESERT SILHOUETTES
The camel is as recognizable by its outline as it is in close-up. For an atmospheric silhouette such as this, photograph early or late in the day.

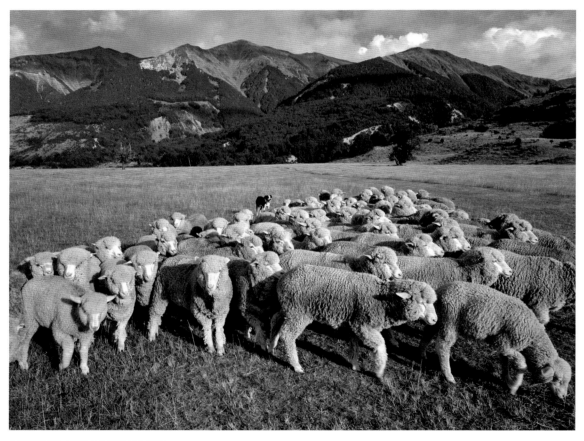

ANIMALS AND LANDSCAPES
Sheep are closely linked to the landscape they inhabit. Try showing them grouped in an interesting way, rather than scattered across the hillsides.

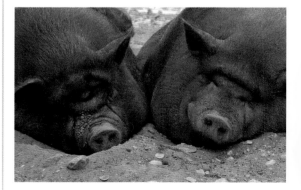

GROUND LEVEL
For more intimate views of ground-loving animals, position yourself down low. Digital cameras make it easy to photograph from awkward perspectives.

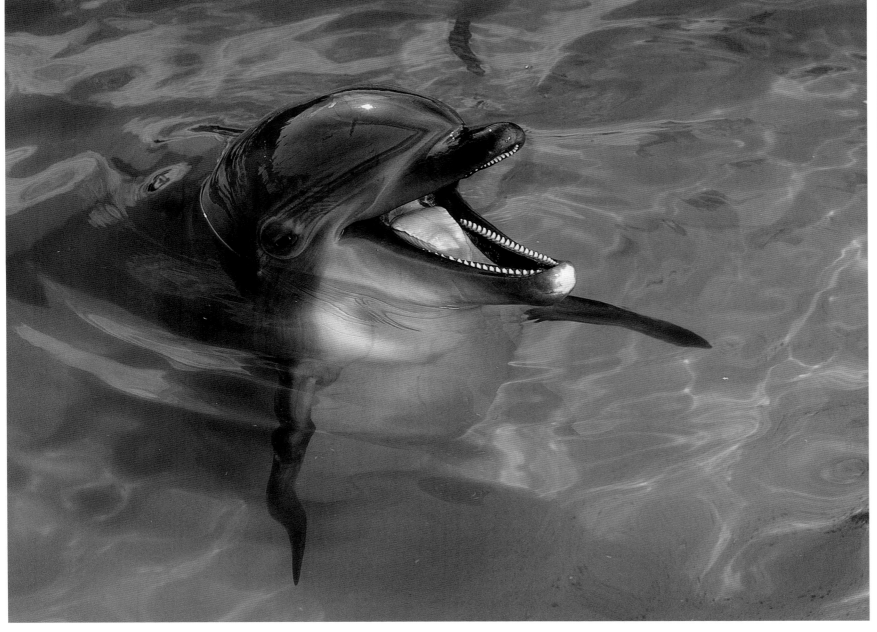

RIGHT PLACE, RIGHT TIME

When taking pictures of performing animals, such as this dolphin, it is essential to get a ringside seat. Not only will the light be better, but being closer will also prove highly beneficial when you are trying to take action shots. Good-quality close-up views like this one would be impossible from a distance.

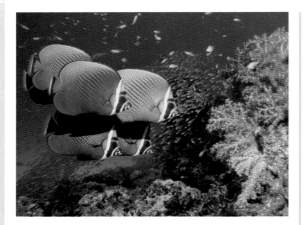

UNDERWATER PHOTOGRAPHY

Take advantage of the fact that many digital cameras now offer waterproof housings for depths to about 16ft (5m), and explore the underwater world.

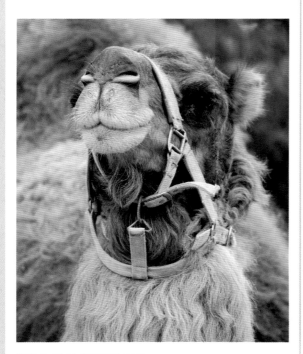

HEAD AND SHOULDERS

Use a long zoom setting to isolate an animal's head, then incorporate its body as the background to create a harmonious color composition.

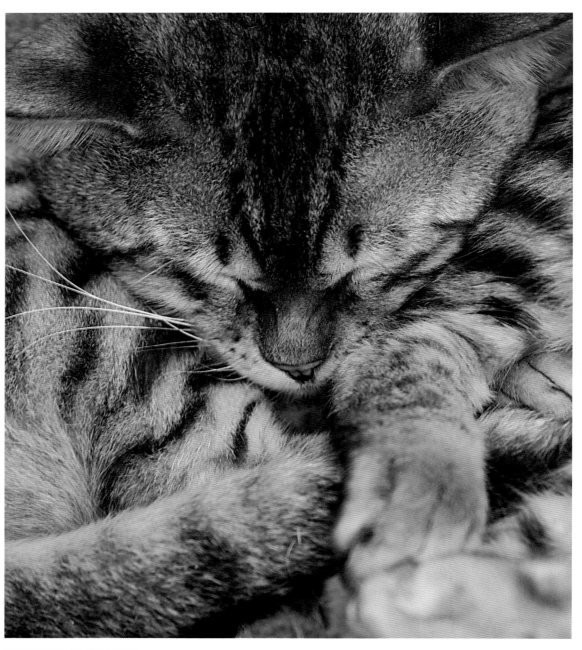

DECEPTIVE FAMILIARITY

Crop tight on your subject and remove context to create interesting images. In this picture, the limbs of the sleeping cat look anatomically wrong. The reality, though, is that this is a bundle of several cats, but that information has been withheld. The pattern of stripes in the cats' fur adds visual appeal.

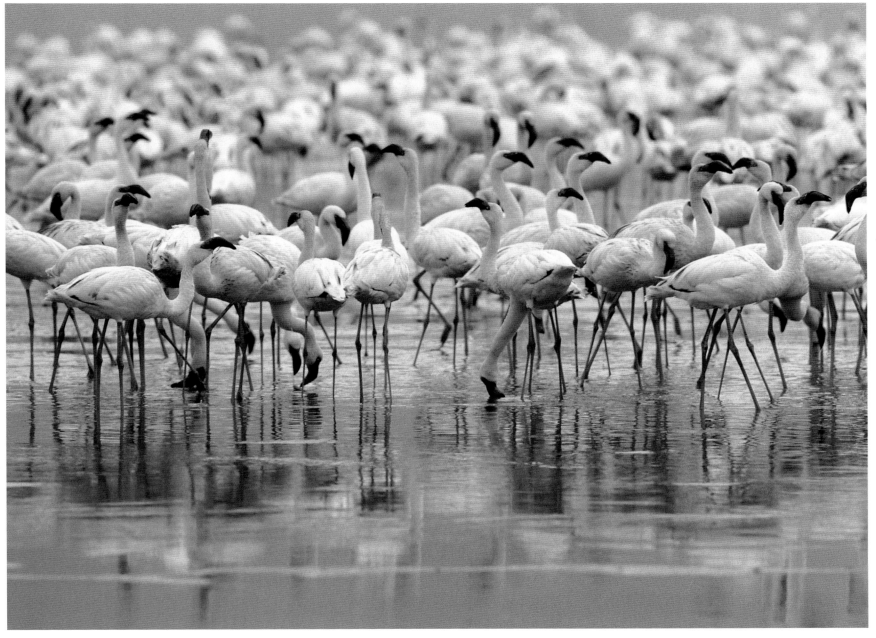

SUPER-ZOOM ADVANTAGE

It can be very difficult to get close to large groups of shy animals, such as these flamingos. If that is the case, you will need to use a digital camera with a super-zoom – longer than 300mm. This composition benefits from a shallow depth of field, which blurs all but the middle ground, creating the focus of the shot.

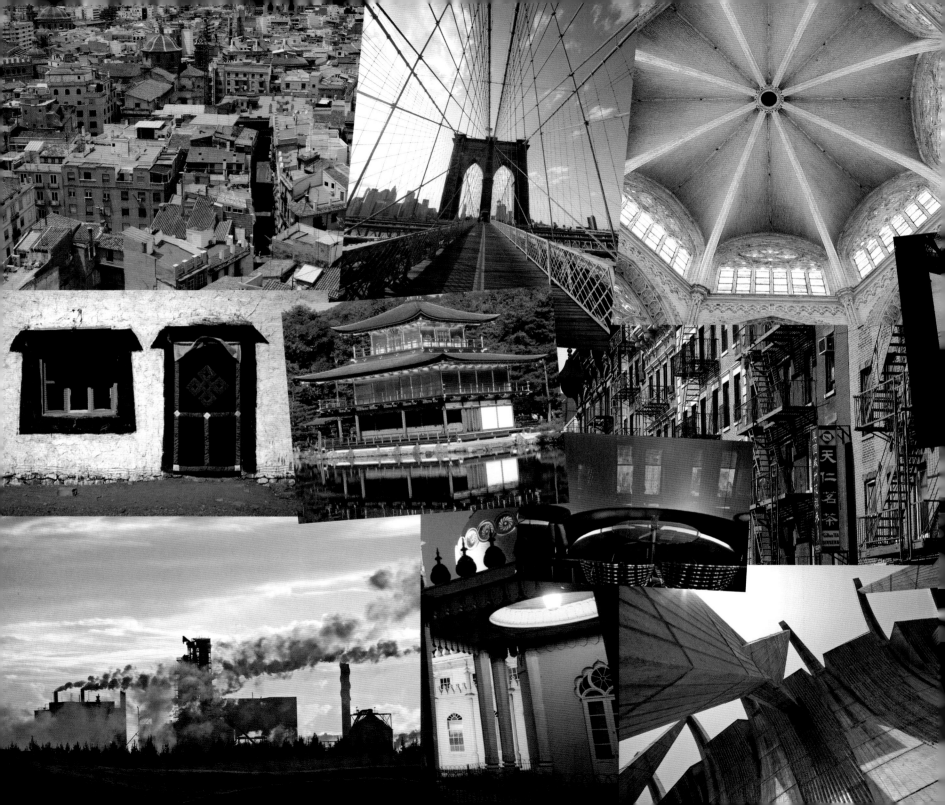

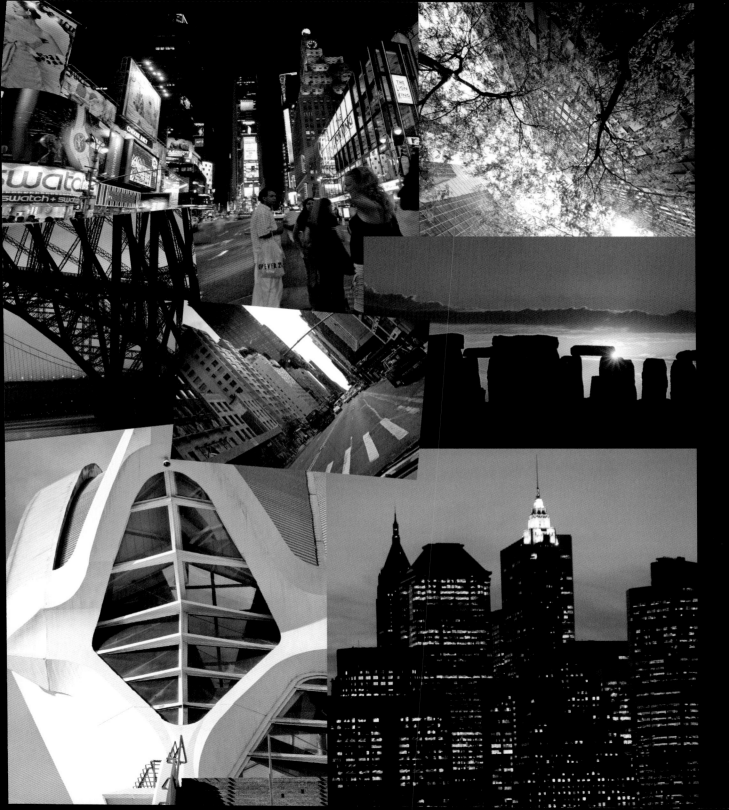

Architecture

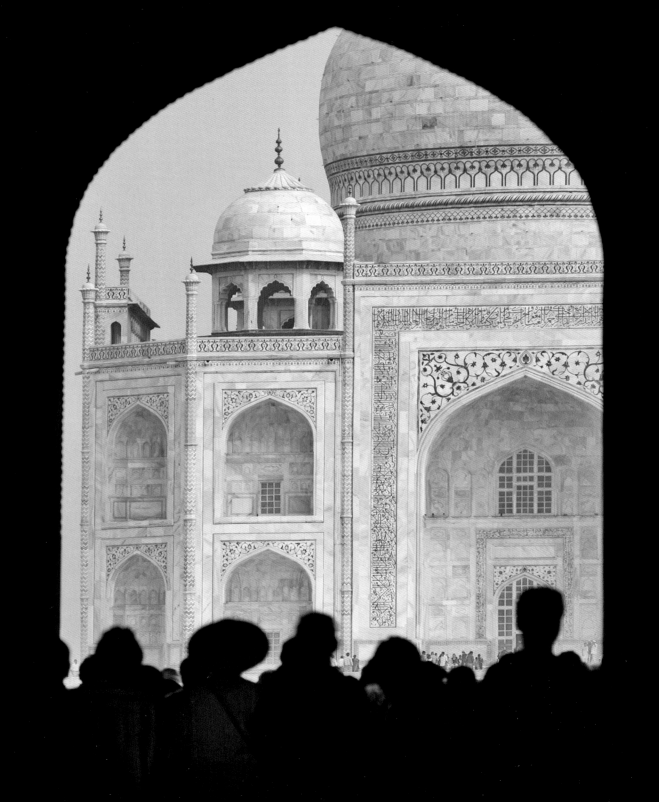

Architecture offers an enormous advantage over almost any other field of photography: your subject will stay in one place, and will do so not only from day to day but from decade to decade. It is, therefore, easy to locate the subject, and if at first you do not get it right, you can return in the sure knowledge that it will be there tomorrow. But this does not mean that the photography of buildings is easy. To create something fresh, you need to consider light and viewpoint just as much as you consider the building. You will learn that the more a subject offers itself to you, the harder you'll have to work to marry lighting and form accurately, and the more care you will need to take over composition.

Focusing on details

The outside of many beautiful buildings can be difficult to shoot due to the hordes of tourists milling around. In such cases, take the opportunity to concentrate on the details. Many architectural details were designed to be looked up to, to enspire awe; however, a photograph taken from the same position does not have the same effect. The key is to find a perspective that works for photography, even though it may not be that intended by the architect.

1 CONSIDER THE LIGHTING

Wander around the building, looking for interesting details. Since many tall buildings are in deep shade for part of the day, you may have to wait for the right lighting conditions, especially since tripods can be a nuisance in crowded areas.

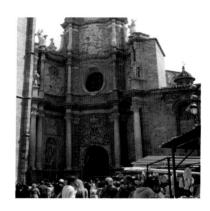

CONVERGING PARALLELS

CONVERGING PARALLELS

You can make a virtue of necessity when you have to take pictures close up to a tall building. If possible, use a wide-angle lens for a large field of view, and tilt the camera to an extreme angle. The result is a strong convergence of parallel lines. Compositions that have some symmetry often work better than those without.

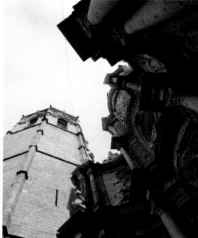

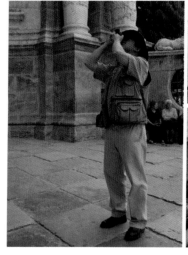

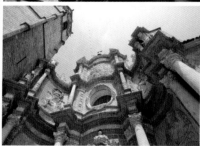

2 CONSIDER THE END RESULT

It is natural to start by taking pictures from a position close to the building, but in so doing you will find yourself looking up the noses of any sculptures, and losing the sense of the soaring structure. Find a position a little further away, and use a longer zoom setting to evoke a sense that you are hovering in front of the details.

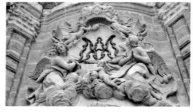

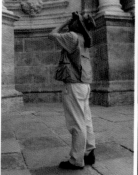

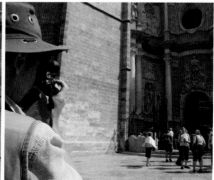

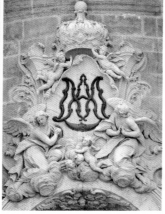

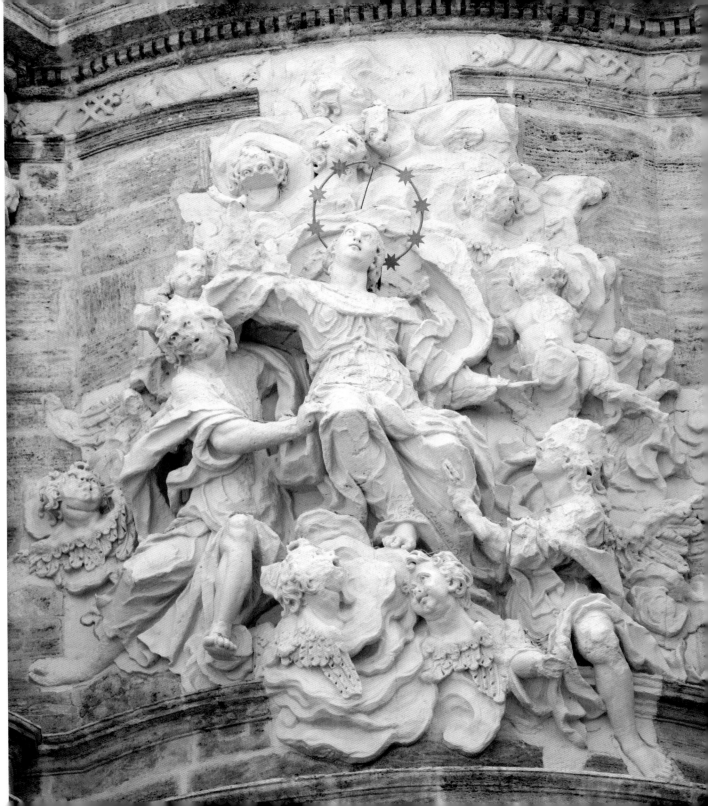

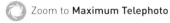
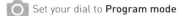
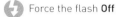

3 FIND THE BEST ANGLE

A shot from underneath can render sculptural details as a confusing jumble. By moving further away you can improve the look, as well as the lighting.

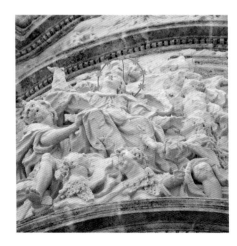

Form and space

Often featuring intriguing spatial effects, modern architecture is a fascinating photographic subject. The challenge lies in being able to do justice to the wealth of opportunities available, and to take advantage of the architect's vision to create great images of your own. When you first encounter an architectural complex, a natural reaction is to go for the wide-angle setting to capture as much of the scene as possible. But beauty is often in the detail.

At twilight, buildings are no longer lit by a single large light source. Instead, there are numerous small sources that illuminate only small areas. Such lighting design is a delight to the eye. Since much of the character of the scene depends on contrasts between the warm color cast and the blue sky, switch your camera to night mode to avoid correcting warm colors to a neutral white.

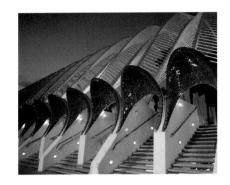

1 EXPLORE THE LOCATION
Some places provide endless inspiration, while others make you work harder to find strong compositions. It may be that you need simply to try to understand what the architect had intended, so walk around and take it all in.

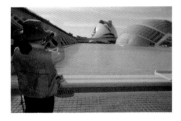

2 EXPLOIT THE ELEMENTS
When you find a feature or an area that you like, mine it to the full. Try different viewpoints and different zoom settings, and cover the entire area comprehensively. This way you will not regret missing a shot later.

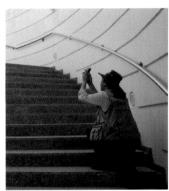
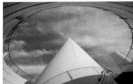
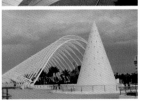

3 LOOK FOR PATTERNS
Most modern buildings offer much to admire. The challenge is to use the one-dimensional medium of photography to portray a complex three-dimensional subject. Look for rhythmic patterns and recurring shapes and forms that characterize the structure.

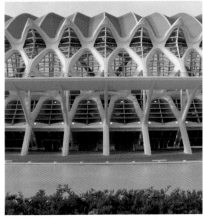
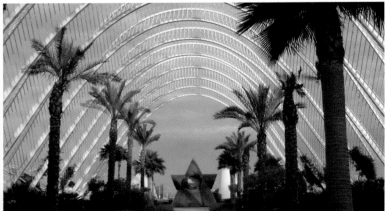

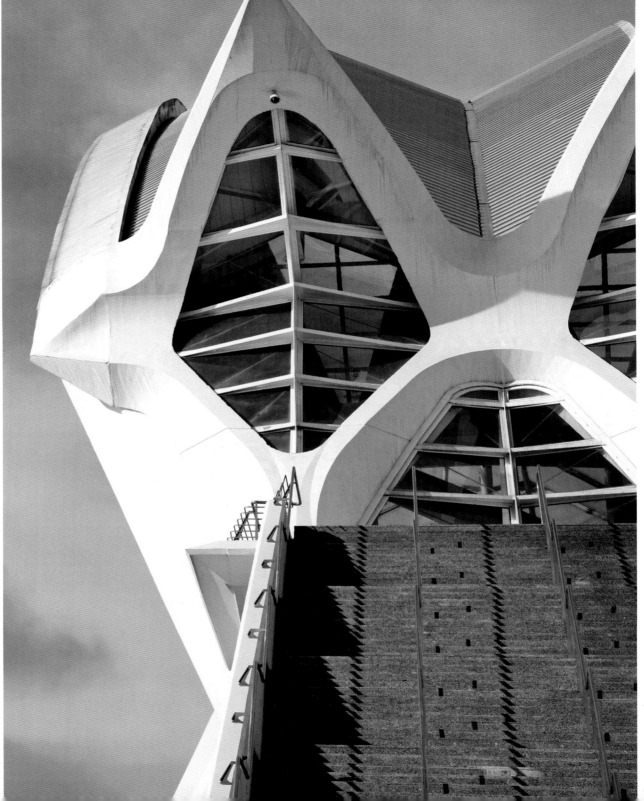

I used the telephoto setting to bring out contrasts in texture and the rhythms visible throughout the image. With high-quality settings, I obtained clear lines and details, as well as smoothness in the sky and white areas.

CAMERA MODE

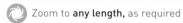 Set your dial to **Landscape mode**

LENS SETTING

Zoom to **any length,** as required

SENSOR/FILM SPEED

 Use a **Low** to **Medium** ISO setting

FLASH

Force the flash **Off**

CREATE A VISUAL THEME

A set of images linked by a particular theme – stairways, for example – is often more effective than a single shot.

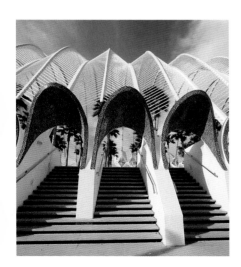

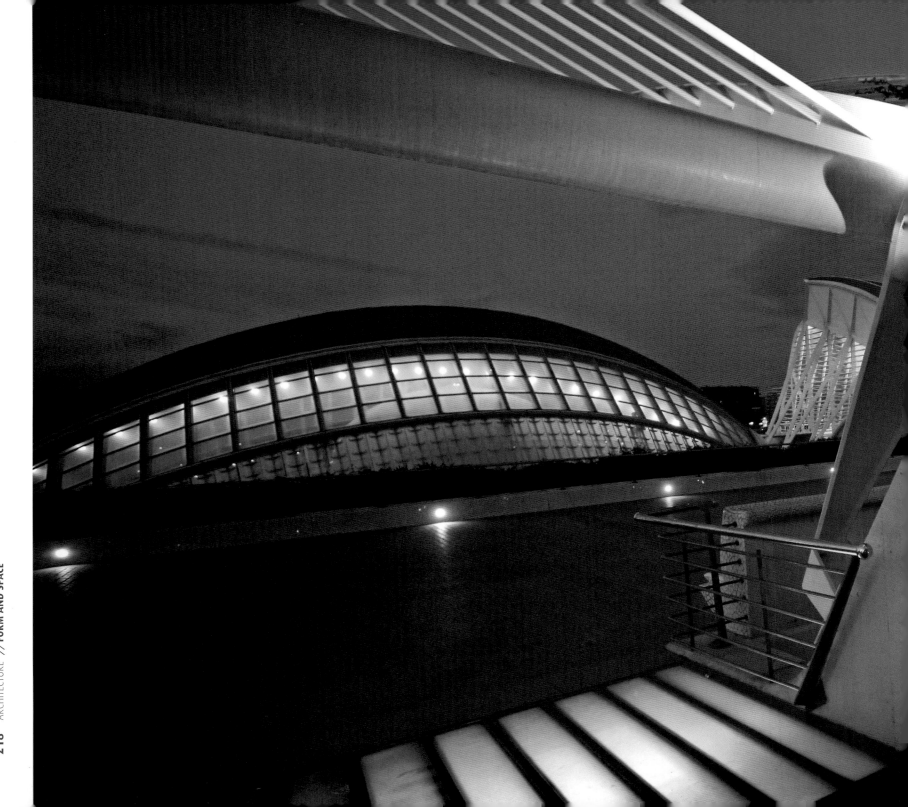

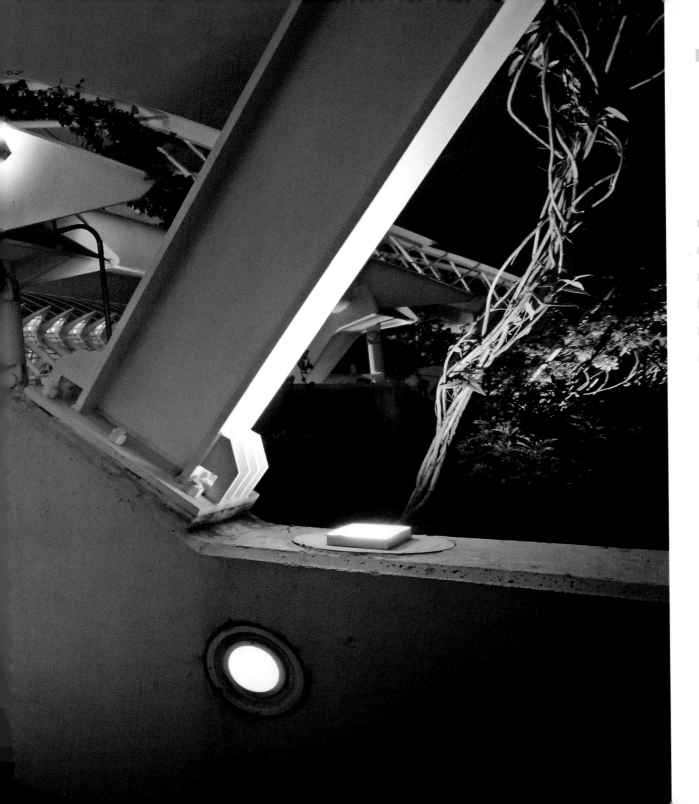

COLOR OF LIGHT

Photography, more than any other form of artistic expression, has opened our eyes to the variety and richness of colors at night. Not only is the camera attuned to colors in low light, but it can even capture tonal subtleties that escape normal vision.

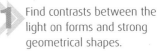 Find contrasts between the light on forms and strong geometrical shapes.

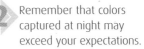 Remember that colors captured at night may exceed your expectations.

Use a tripod so you can set a low ISO for the best image quality and sharpness.

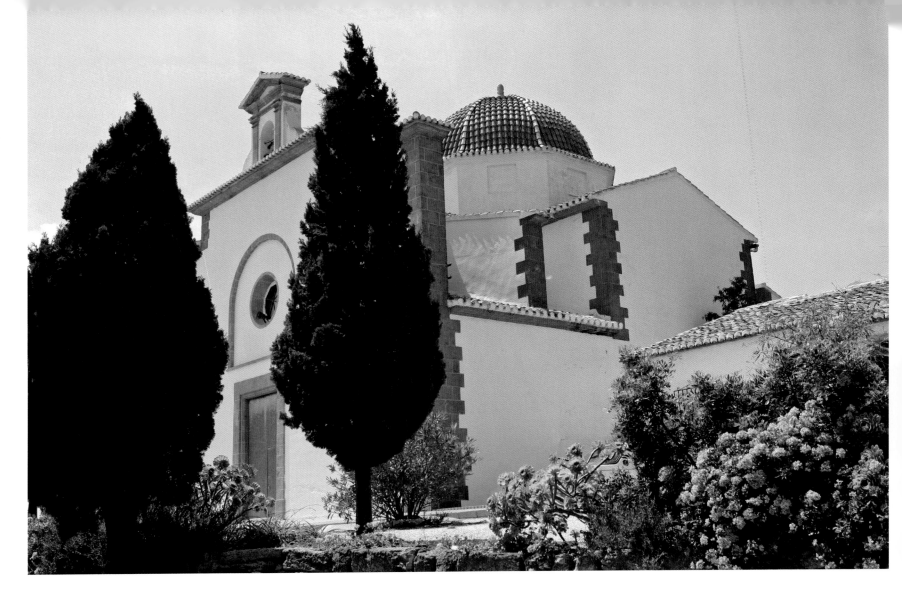

The postcard look

This pretty, blue-domed church bathed in sunlight is an utterly photogenic prospect. However, as is often the case with handsome or iconic buildings, the best viewpoint is also the one that reveals crowds of tourists, street signs, or other unsightly elements. In this case, there were cars visible from every angle. Fortunately, there was plenty of greenery too. With a little cunning, it is usually possible to find a position that shows off the building while concealing any eyesores.

FOR THIS SHOT

I achieved the best quality overall by using a moderately wide-angle zoom, the highest-quality image setting, and a low ISO. To ensure the greatest depth of field, I selected the landscape exposure mode.

CAMERA MODE

Set your dial to **Landscape mode**

LENS SETTING

Zoom to **Wide Angle**

SENSOR/FILM SPEED

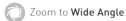 Use a **Low** ISO setting

FLASH

Force the flash **Off**

POLARIZING FILTERS

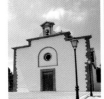 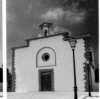

Without filter   **With filter**

If the sun is more or less behind you when taking the picture, you can use a polarizing filter. This is a lens accessory that darkens the blue of the sky. It is a dramatic effect that cannot be imitated accurately with image manipulation. Polarizing filters can be used even with most point-and-shoot cameras.

1 CONSIDER VIEWPOINTS

Take time to explore the building from different angles. Here, a view with the sun to the back would give the brightest whites and the bluest skies, but that was not the best view of the church. The shadow side was very attractive, but cars could be seen and the trees obscured the building too much.

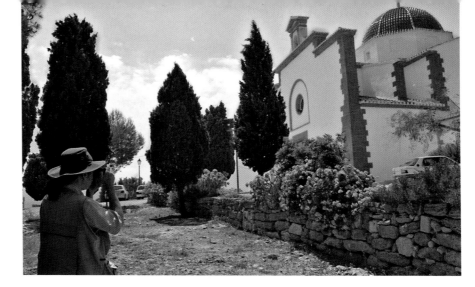

2 EXPERIMENT WITH ZOOM

It is possible to zoom in on details to get past any distractions. However, the sense of the whole and the identity of the building are lost: the details could belong to any Mediterranean edifice.

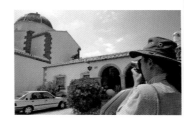 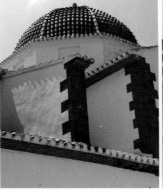 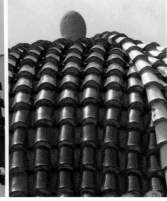

3 TRY VARIOUS FORMATS

A portrait format can be the answer to removing unsightly distractions. However, a wider landscape shot suits this subject better and gives a picture-postcard look. The composition can be refined further. For example, crouching down was an effective way to hide the cars behind the bushes.

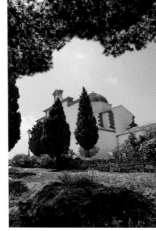 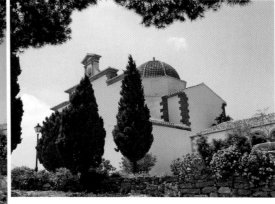

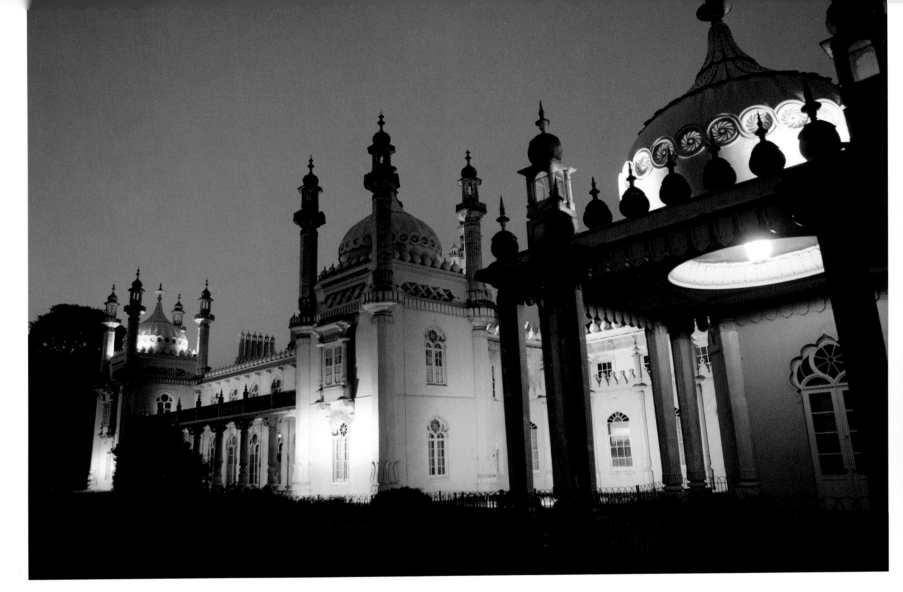

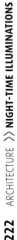
Night-time illuminations

If you thought that stunning pictures where the sky is a deep shade of blue and the building's features are beautifully lit were the exclusive domain of professional photographers, think again. There is a simple secret to obtaining eye-catching pictures: start photographing at dusk. At that time of day, the sky still retains some light, but it also begins to be tinged with darkness. The rich blue hue nicely balances the lights on the building.

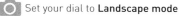

FOR THIS SHOT

With the lens set to the widest angle, I selected a high ISO, and landscape mode for a balance between good depth of field and a medium-long exposure time. I turned off the flash and used a tripod for the sharpest results.

CAMERA MODE

 Set your dial to **Landscape mode**

LENS SETTING

Zoom to **Wide Angle**

SENSOR/FILM SPEED

Use a **High** ISO setting

FLASH

Force the flash **Off**

BE EARLY

Arrive on location with enough time to set up, then shoot through the twilight of early evening and into the night. The weather and brightness of the lights on the building both affect the ideal shooting time, with different conditions producing different results.

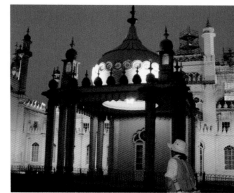
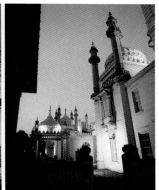

CHECK YOUR PROGRESS

A tripod makes shooting much easier. The available light will change rapidly, so this is a situation when you need to check the images as you work. Try different exposures to find the best settings.

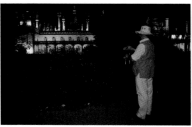
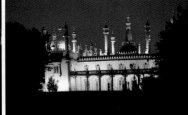
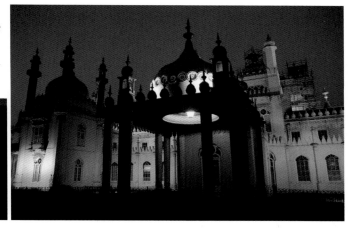

ADD HUMAN INTEREST

Make positive use of any passersby: even if only as silhouettes, they can add to your image by giving it a human dimension. However, because your exposures will be very long, the people might be blurred.

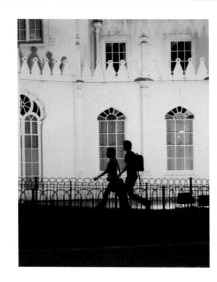

TRY VARIOUS ANGLES

You might choose to keep the camera level when shooting, as in the picture on the right. However, for a more dynamic take, aim the lens upward: this makes parallel lines such as the columns appear to converge, as in the main picture opposite, giving the impression that the building is leaning back.

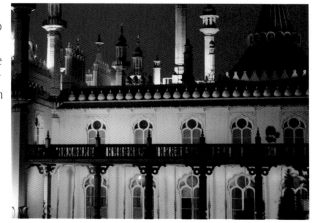

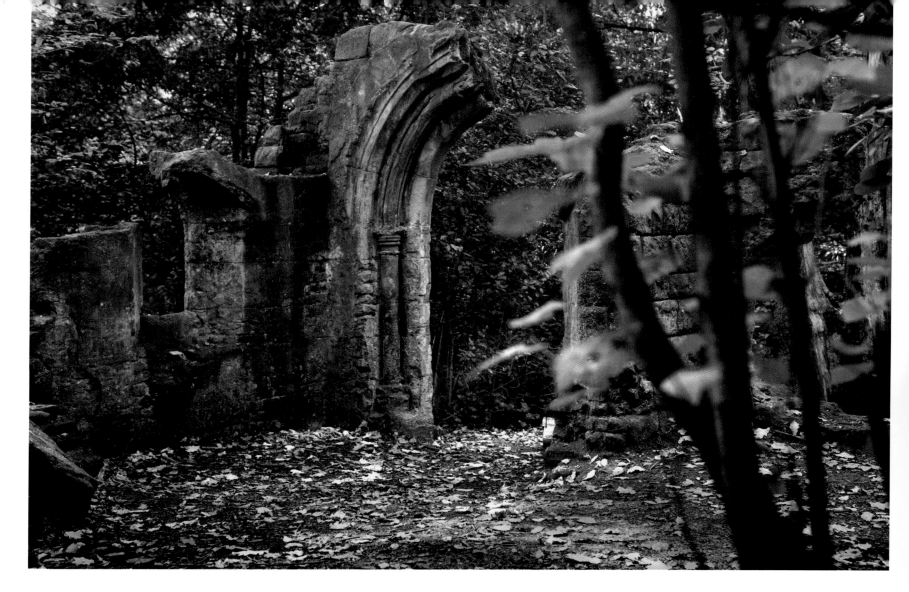

Romantic ruins

From the earliest days of picture-making, photographers have gravitated toward buildings, initially because they stood still, suiting the very long exposure times that were once needed to make a picture. Of particular interest were the ruins of ancient buildings; this was largely for their romantic associations with the past. But even in the age of color photography, black-and-white pictures are still very effective in bringing character to a ruin.

With the camera on a tripod, I set a medium telephoto zoom, highest image quality, and a low ISO setting, with the flash off. I made the exposure using the self-timer to avoid camera shake.

CAMERA MODE

Set your dial to **Landscape mode**

LENS SETTING

Zoom to **Medium Telephoto**

SENSOR/FILM SPEED

Use a **Low** ISO setting

FLASH

Force the flash **Off**

MOOD WITH COLOR

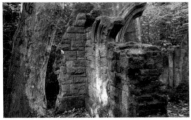

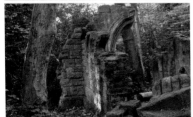

If the ruins are largely monochrome, you might choose to work in color. You can vary the mood by changing the white balance: try different settings on the camera – tungsten, sunny, fluorescent, and so on.

1 GET STEADY

If the area is shaded by trees, or if there's not much natural light, you are better off using a tripod. If you are resting it on a bed of leaves or on soft ground, make sure the tripod is stable by pushing it in a little.

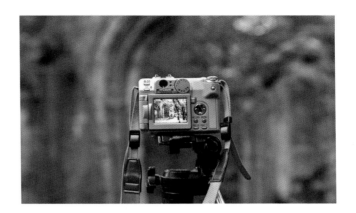

2 EXPLORE THE LOCATION

Look for areas of the ruins that show up dramatically against the surroundings, and use broken arches and windows as framing devices. You can also look for signs of nature reclaiming the space. Work with the available light, examining the way light and shadow fall.

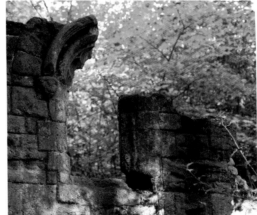

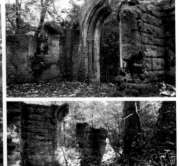

3 SELECT A VIEW

The result of your explorations will be a favorite perspective, one that conveys mood and works as a photographic composition. Trees and foliage in the foreground can convey a sense of chance discovery. You may want to focus past them, allowing them to blur, to create depth.

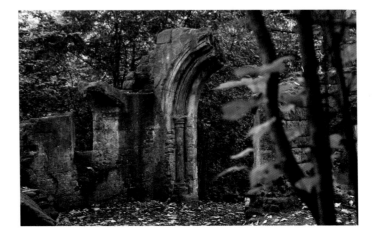

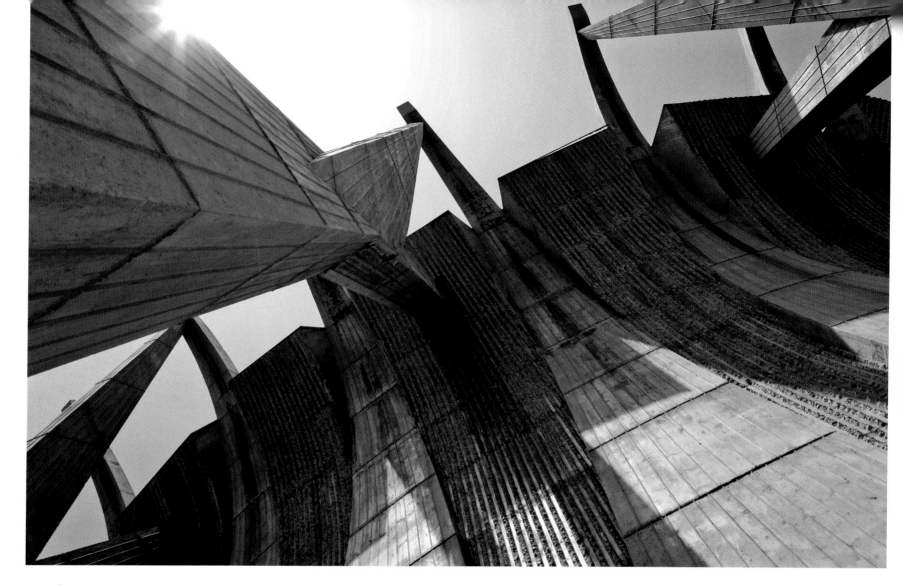

Abstract views

Many examples of modern architecture offer a visual treat, especially those that utilize massive forms with an almost tangible exuberance and energy. Photographically, such buildings are a gift, but the question remains how to capture the qualities inherent to a building in one image that says it all. In the example above, the spirit of the building is encapsulated in the interplay of hard with soft, of wavelike curves with stiff, straight lines.

FOR THIS SHOT

Wide-angle views are the easiest to compose, but for details, a normal focal length is fine. I used a high-quality setting to capture the textures. I also made sure the lens was clean in case the sun was going to be in shot.

CAMERA MODE

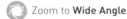 Set your dial to **Program mode**

LENS SETTING

Zoom to **Wide Angle**

SENSOR/FILM SPEED

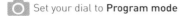 Use a **Low** to **Medium** ISO setting

FLASH

Force the flash **Off**

OVERCOME AWKWARD LOCATIONS

It is often impossible to photograph a building in its entirety because you cannot stand far enough back without coming across obstructions or putting yourself at risk in a traffic-heavy street. Instead, move close to the building and explore it in detail. The widest-angle zoom setting will help capture a sense of space.

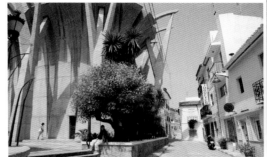
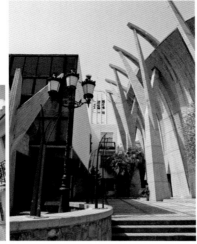

SHOOT SKYWARD

The soaring lines of a tall building encourage you to look upward. For the widest possible field of view, try crouching to get as far away as possible from the upper structure. Taking an abstract approach frees you to hold the camera at any angle.

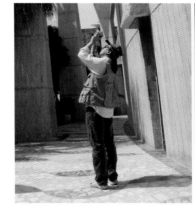
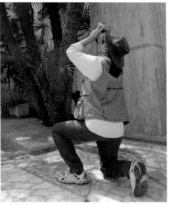

TAKE MANY SHOTS

On a sunny day, you can work with the sun to exploit the flare, or you can avoid it altogether. Try different shots to ensure you have a good selection from which to make your final choice. The most abstract image is the one with least sense of scale.

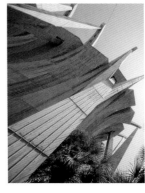
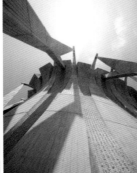
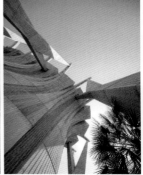
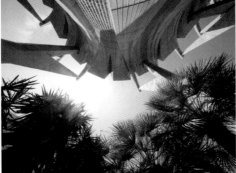

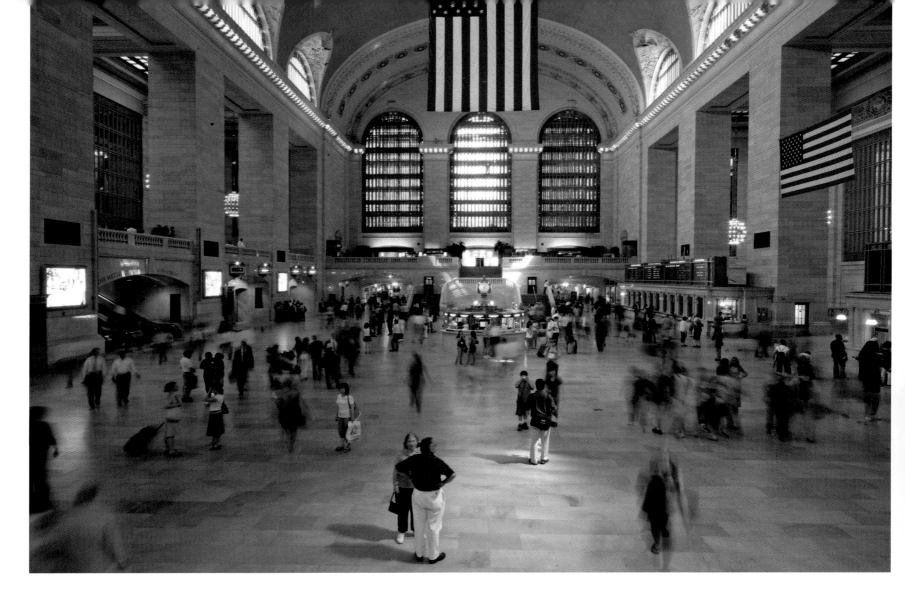

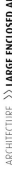
Large enclosed areas

As daunting a task as it might seem to take a picture of a monumentally large interior, there are ways to make it easier. Indeed, architects themselves design and build in such a way that you are automatically led to the best vantage point. Once you stand at that point, the building's lines all come together to create a beautiful composition. Timing and patience will provide the extra elements needed to capture the character of the space

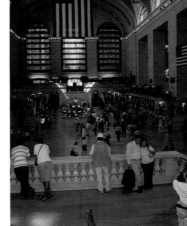

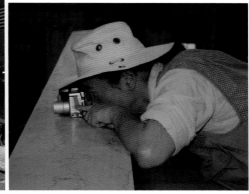

FOR THIS SHOT

With the zoom set to wide angle, I held the camera level so that the verticals were straight and parallel. I used a medium to high sensitivity and set a long shutter time – about 1 second – making sure the camera was well supported.

CAMERA MODE

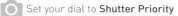

Set your dial to **Shutter Priority**

LENS SETTING

Zoom to **Wide Angle**

SENSOR/FILM SPEED

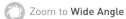

Use a **Medium** to **High** ISO setting

FLASH

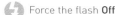

Force the flash **Off**

A DIFFERENT APPROACH

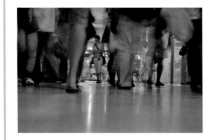

For an unusual perspective, try something completely different. Here, I placed the camera on the polished floor to capture a sense of the great human traffic that moves through the building. From the floor position, half of the field of view picks up the reflections of lights and passersby.

1 FIND A VANTAGE POINT

Explore the building and look for a position that offers you the best view. From this vantage point you will be able to observe the people and the space unobstructed. In busy locations, try to avoid using a tripod by resting the camera on a balustrade or ledge.

2 USE THE LIGHT

In a dimly lit interior, you might experience problems with underexposure. It would be natural to increase sensitivity to make the most of the light, but that would lead to a short exposure, and the motion blur of the people would be lost. Instead, use the ISO setting that gives a shutter time of about 1 second to capture a good amount of light and movement.

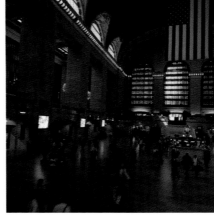
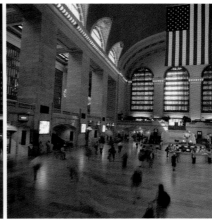

3 FOLLOW THE BUILDING'S LINES

In a strongly symmetrical space, it is usually best to follow the architect's lead and aim for symmetry, rather than take an off-center shot that doesn't do justice to the building's lines.

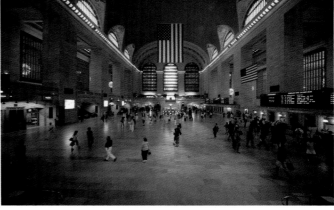
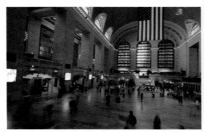

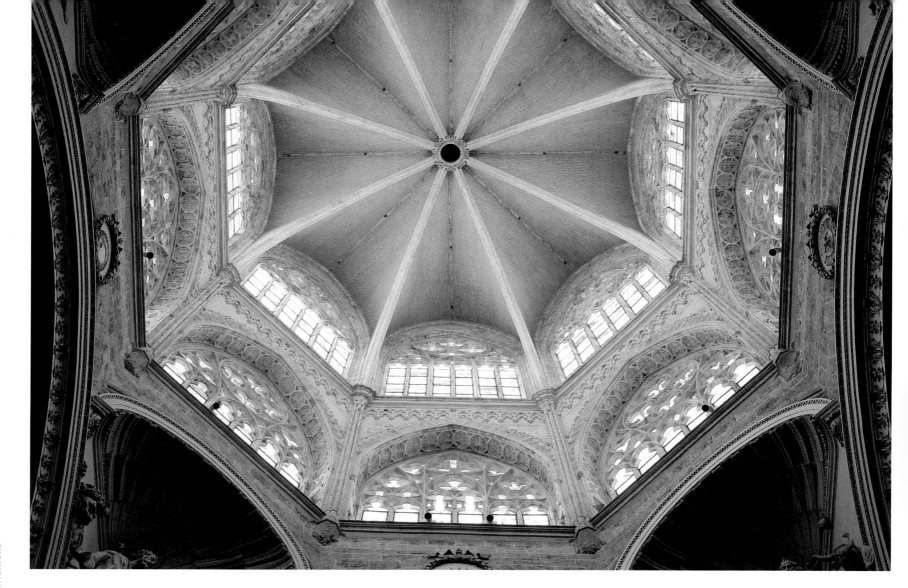

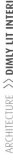
Dimly lit interiors

Places of worship such as cathedrals or mosques usually feature richly ornate and beautiful interiors. These buildings tend to be dimly lit to create an atmosphere of contemplation. Unfortunately, many do not allow tripod photography. The trick to capturing this atmosphere is to understand that your camera can see more colors than you can, and to use your imagination to find alternative places you can rest your camera, such as pews and pillars.

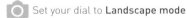

FOR THIS SHOT

To photograph the ceiling, I placed the camera on the floor pointing straight up, with the lens set to wide angle. A high ISO was needed to make the most of the available light. I released the shutter using the timer set to 2 seconds.

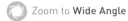

CAMERA MODE

Set your dial to **Landscape mode**

LENS SETTING

Zoom to **Wide Angle**

SENSOR/FILM SPEED

Use a **High** ISO setting

FLASH

Force the flash **Off**

1 TURN OFF THE FLASH

Before you explore the interior, make sure you turn off your camera's flash. This is usually a requirement in such buildings, but even if you were permitted to use it, flash destroys the subtle lighting that gives the space its character.

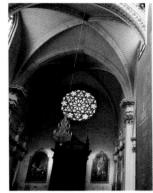
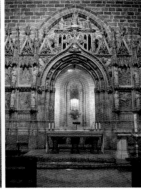
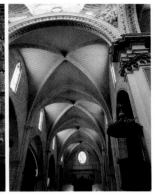

2 USE AVAILABLE SUPPORT

Any accessible firm surface can be turned into an impromptu camera support. Use books or cardboard to fine-tune the angle of the camera tilt. Set the self-timer to release the shutter for the most shake-free shot; just hold the camera while the shutter runs.

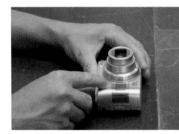

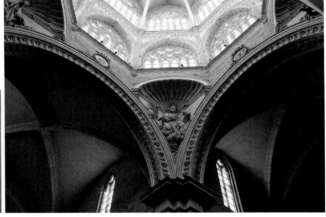

3 BRACKET EXPOSURES

In large interiors there is often a wide range between the darkest areas and the brightest ones (usually the windows). This can make them tricky to photograph. If possible, take exposures that give dark results, as well as light ones, and choose the best later.

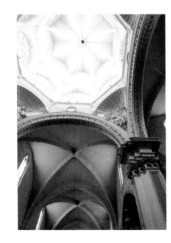

4 GIVE YOURSELF OPTIONS

You may not be able to predict accurately what you are shooting, so move the camera around and take several pictures in each position. You can review on the spot or crop them later.

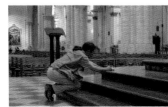

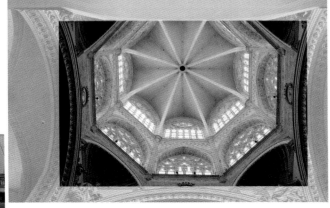

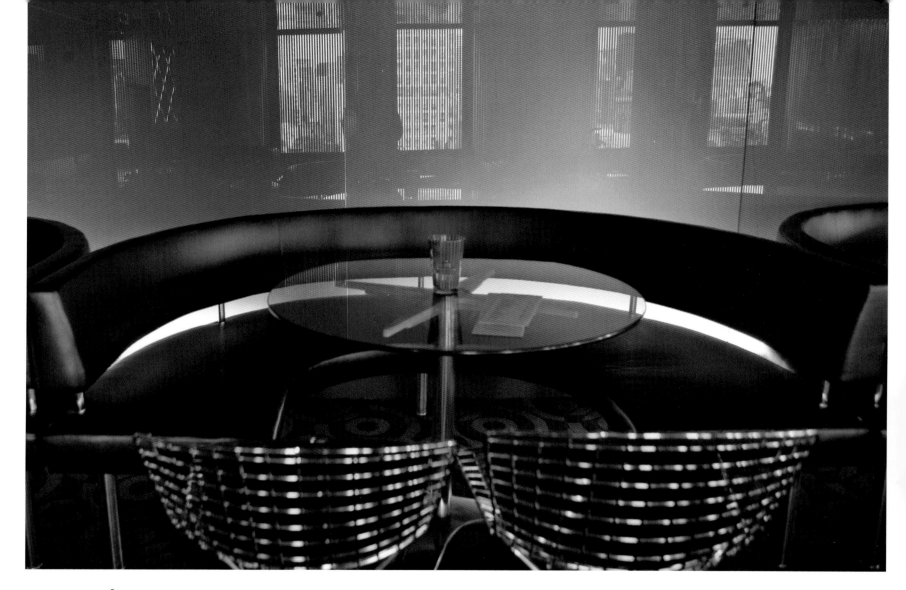

Modern interior spaces

The main driving forces behind much modern interior design are detail, color, and often limited space. Unlike the grandiose vastness of castles and mansions, a modern interior calls for an intimate style of photography. Observe it with the designer's eye: what looks like a stark corner may well reveal itself as an inviting private area. To capture the true spirit of the design, turn off the flash – irrespective of how dark the space is – and work with the available light.

FOR THIS SHOT

I selected aperture priority to obtain maximum depth of field, then set the zoom to wide angle in order to take in the space. I underexposed a little so that the dark bench seats remained dark.

CAMERA MODE
Set your dial to **Aperture Priority**

LENS SETTING
Zoom to **Wide Angle**

SENSOR/FILM SPEED
Use a **High** ISO setting

FLASH
Force the flash **Off**

1 SEEK PERMISSION

Some establishments do not permit any photography inside. Even if the photographs are for your own reference only and not for commercial purposes, be sure to obtain permission before you start taking pictures of a trendy restaurant or bar.

2 LOOK AROUND

Explore the area with a view to finding out the best angle for a picture. Consider colors, light, and shapes. In a varied space such as this, with lots of dark corners, smaller areas will be easier to photograph than a wide view.

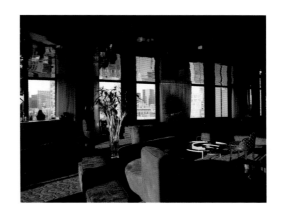

3 CONSIDER LIGHT AND REFLECTIONS

Modern interiors often feature mirrors, so be sure to avoid your own reflection. Sometimes the most attractive views – here, the sunset lighting up the collection of bottles – evoke a feeling rather than reveal much about the design itself.

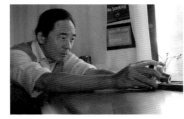

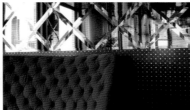

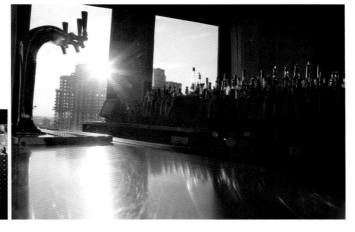

4 FOCUS ON THE DETAILS

Modern designers will give you plenty to interest the eye in terms of details and color contrasts. Experiment with as many abstract or graphic details as you can.

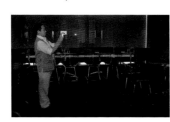

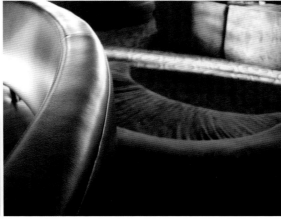

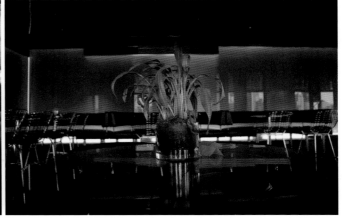

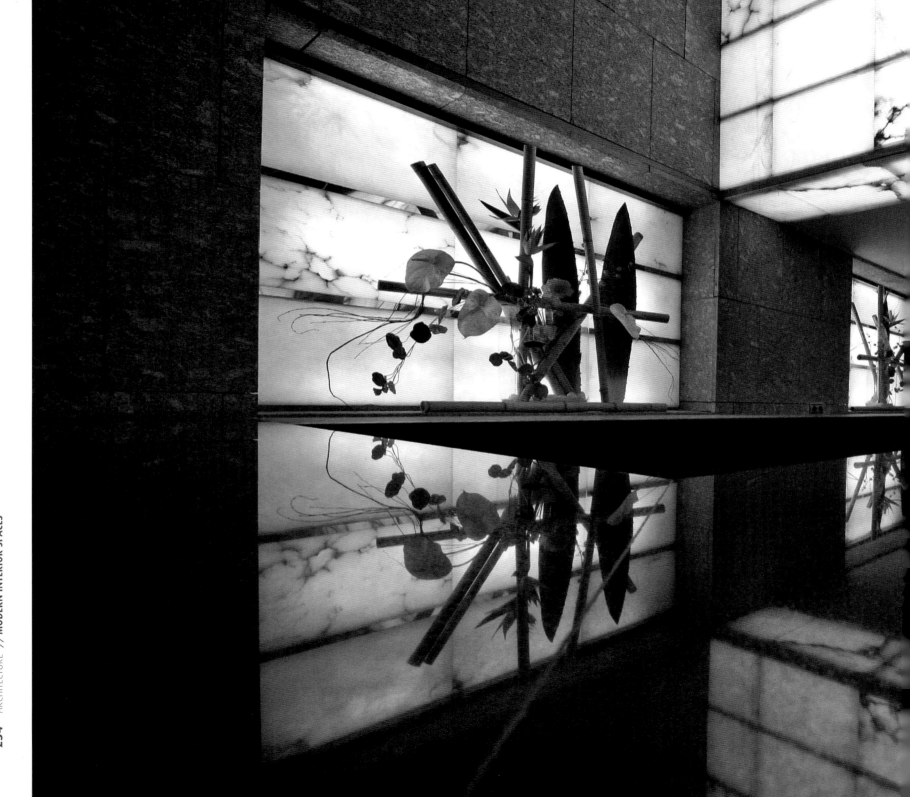

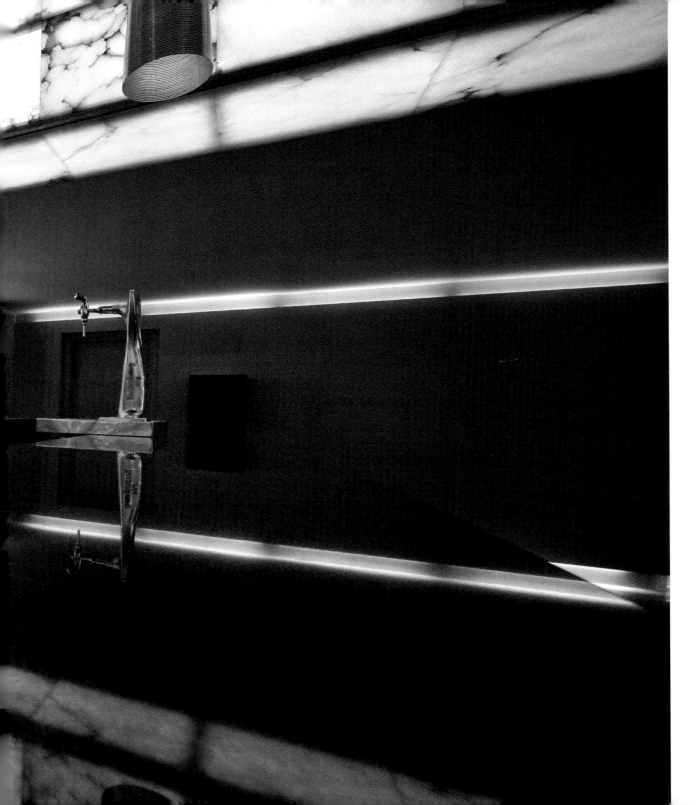

LINES AND LIGHTING

Photography is the natural partner for modern interior design: the camera can probe all the stylistic elements offered by designers. In this shot, the clean lines, lighting, and reflective surfaces of a hotel bar come together to create a striking image.

1 Seek reflections. The key theme of many modern interiors is a shiny, polished look.

2 When shooting in dim light, turn off the flash, or it will ruin any subtle lighting effects.

3 Use wide-angle settings for both context and extensive depth of field.

4 If the colors are not wholly accurate in your shot, correct them later with image software.

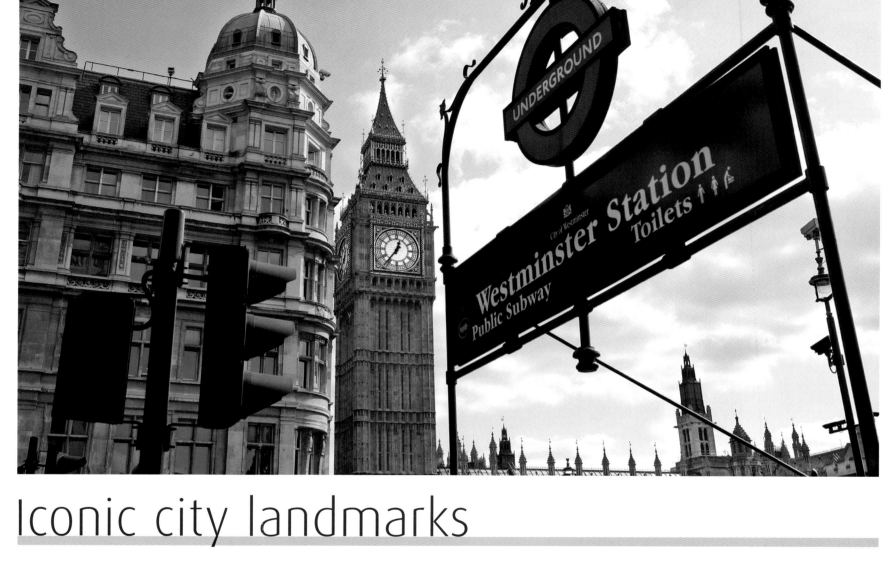

Iconic city landmarks

Important architectural landmarks present quite a challenge to the photographer. Although they are eminently photogenic, iconic buildings are such well-known sights that it is very hard to look at them from a different, unusual perspective.

As a result, out of sheer familiarity, we tend to photograph them from the same position as everyone else. However, it is surprising how much variety you can come up with after exploring a location and keeping your eyes open.

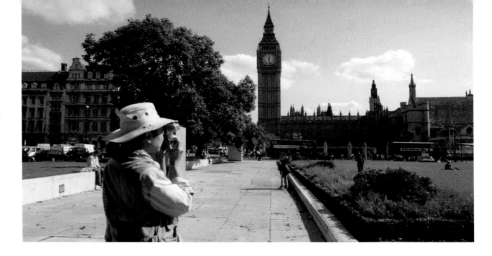

FOR THIS SHOT

I selected auto-exposure with a wide-angle zoom setting supplemented by wide-angle attachment to tuck the tower of Big Ben between street furniture and buildings.

CAMERA MODE

Set your dial to **Landscape mode**

LENS SETTING

Zoom to **widest possible**

SENSOR/FILM SPEED

Use a **Low** ISO setting

FLASH

Force the flash **Off**

1 TRY A CONVENTIONAL APPROACH

The reasons behind the familiar views of any city landmark are revealed when you visit the site. There is often a limited number of uninterrupted views, so most shots are taken from what seems to be the best spot.

2 IDENTIFY PROBLEMS

It is natural to try to get close to your subject, but this gives rise to a number of issues. First, it is difficult to shoot a tall building without making it appear to lean back. Second, shooting toward a bright sky causes exposure problems.

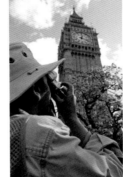 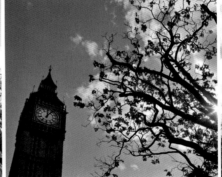 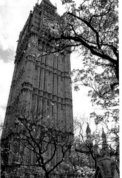

3 INCLUDE OTHER ICONS

Avoid taking obvious pictures, as well as the problems of close shots, by moving some distance away. This may also enable you to include other city icons – in this case, transport signs, red buses, and traditional telephone boxes. Look for a composition that brings an element of surprise or informality.

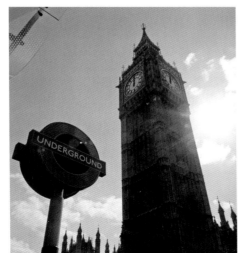 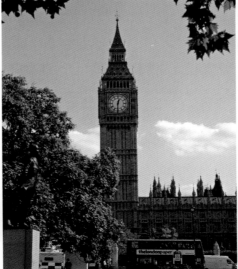 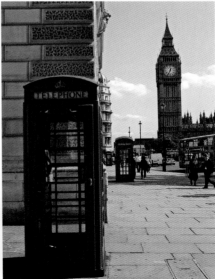

World landmarks

The world is so thoroughly photographed that it is almost impossible to make a wholly original photograph of any of the great landmarks and monuments. But you should still strive to create images that are more interesting than the ordinary snap, which usually captures only the most obvious view in a cursory way. The key is to work with the available light and to take the time to appreciate the landmark's visual character.

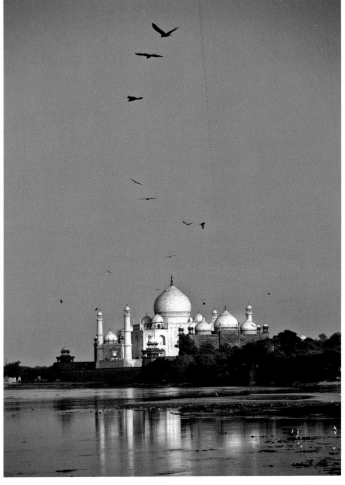

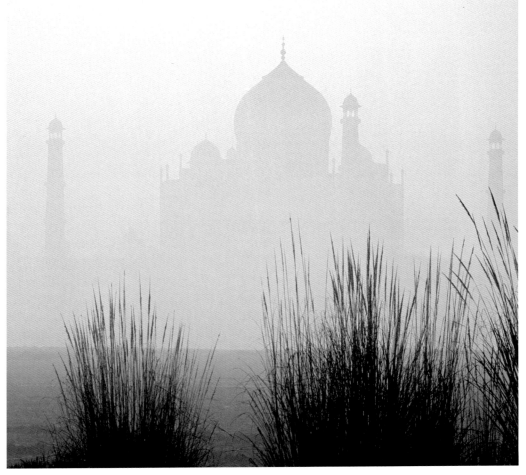

CHANGING LIGHT

One of the glories of the Taj Mahal in Agra, India, is that it is breathtakingly beautiful in any light. The marble reflects any bright light, and its outlines are eloquent even in fog.

1 Photograph from all angles, not just the main approach to the landmark.

2 Select the largest picture-size settings to ensure the finest-quality images.

3 To capture the scene's delicate light, select optimum image quality.

TIGHT CROP

Many monuments, such as the Statue of Liberty, are extremely difficult to access. That being so, start shooting as soon as it comes into view.

1 Rather than standing close and looking up, which would cause distortion, shoot from further away and zoom in.

2 Use a long zoom to crop in on the key features and to highlight the texture of the surface.

3 Shoot from different angles to find a telling outline and to make use of the negative space around the statue.

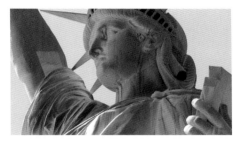

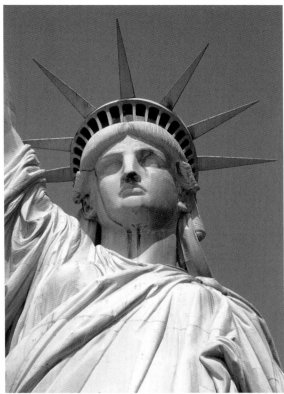

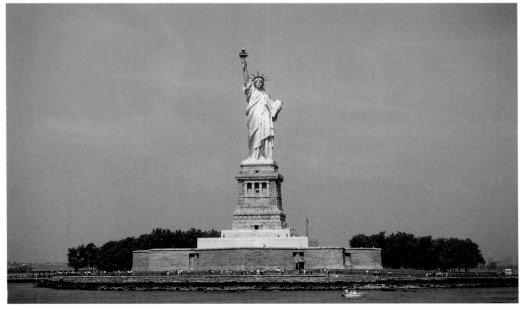

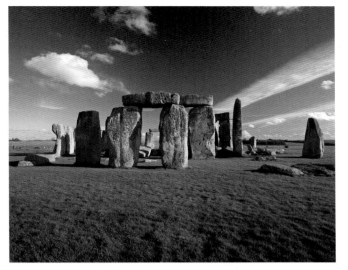

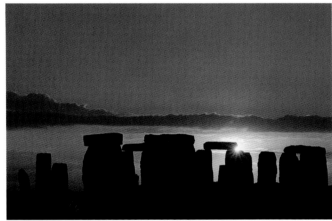

EVOCATIVE COMPOSITIONS

It is a luxury to be able to visit a landmark at different times of the day. If you do, it is worthwhile comparing the effects of different lighting and color on the same scene. These two views of Stonehenge, England, evoke completely different feelings.

1 Shoot in broad daylight to capture vibrant colors, strong shadows, and clouds.

2 Create a more atmospheric image composition by shooting a silhouette of the landmark at sunset.

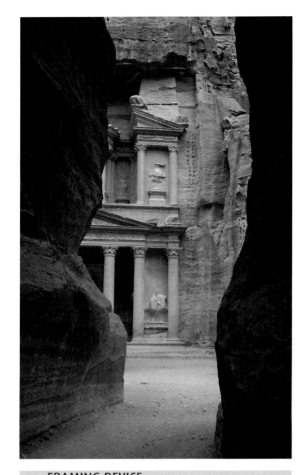

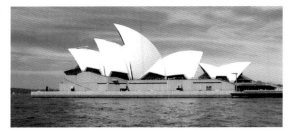

DISTINCTIVE SHAPES

Buildings with strong, unusual shapes—such as the Sydney Opera House—can dominate the landscape for miles around. Take advantage of that, and photograph from different distances and angles.

1 Make full use of your zoom—irrespective of the distance. Use both wide and long from both far and near.

2 Try photographing in black and white: gray tones are effective at highlighting shapes and geometrical forms.

3 You do not have to get all of the building into a shot: a portion can be just as revealing as an overall view.

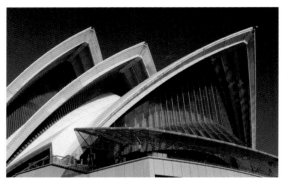

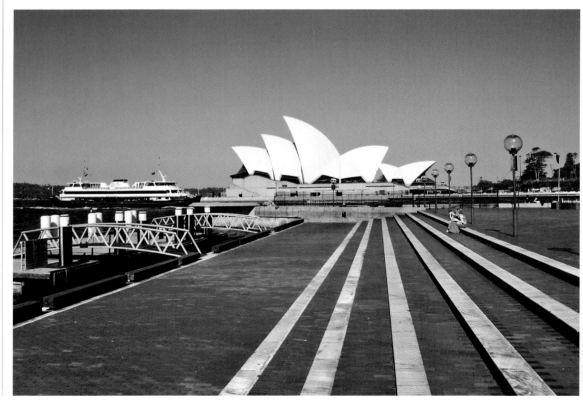

FRAMING DEVICE

This view of Petra, Jordan, works particularly well thanks to the framing device created by the walls of the ravine, which open out to reveal the astonishing carving.

1 Experiment with both portrait and landscape formats. Each will emphasize different features of the landmark.

2 Use maximum depth of field if you wish to keep both the frame and the main subject as sharp as possible.

3 Expose for the main subject, otherwise the dark periphery may cause the camera to miscalculate the correct exposure.

SUNSET PYRAMIDS

If the sun is too fierce during the day, you might have to work at dawn and dusk, when the light will be softer, with a warm, appealing glow.

1 Concentrate on capturing the subtle colors of the sky, and allow the pyramids to fall into silhouette.

2 Try photographing your subject from different angles and with different lens settings—it does not necessarily have to fill the frame in every shot.

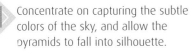

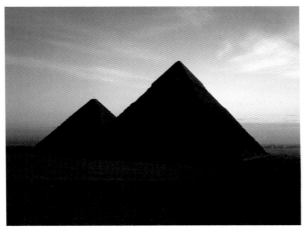

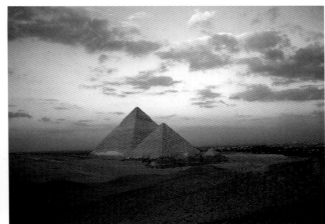

ENHANCING TEXTURES

There is a romance about ancient ruins, such as the Temple of Poseidon in Athens, that is always photogenic. You can enhance the appearance of old white stone or marble by contrasting it with deep blue skies.

1 Try to keep the camera level to minimize the effect of converging verticals.

2 Use a polarizing filter of the type recommended for your camera.

3 Use a long exposure to maximize depth of field for overall sharpness.

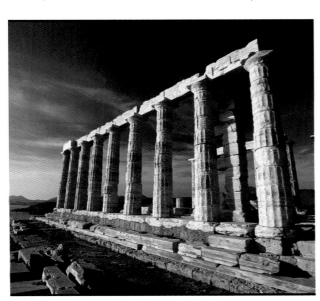

TWILIGHT BALANCE

The magic hour for photographing urban landmarks such as the Eiffel Tower is twilight, when the sky darkens and artificial lights come on.

1 Try different exposure settings to see which gives the best results for color and tone.

2 Use a tripod if possible, to avoid having to set a high sensitivity in compensation for the low light.

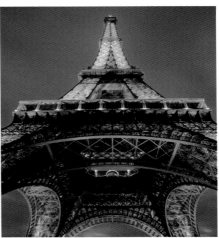

Radiant stained glass

Many original stained-glass windows in cathedrals and other places of worship were first made when glass was a precious commodity, as a statement about wealth—both financial and spiritual. Designed as they were to dazzle and inspire awe, they naturally draw the photographer to them. In order to render the colors accurately, you will need to expose for the light in the windows, while ignoring the darkness surrounding them.

1 STEADY THE CAMERA
The interiors of cathedrals are usually dimly lit. You may not be permitted to use a tripod, but there are many pews, chairs, and pillars you can lean on to steady the camera.

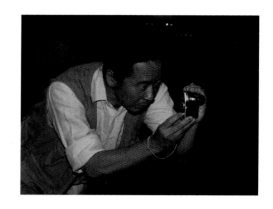

2 GET THE RIGHT EXPOSURE
Strike a balance between under- and overexposing. Bringing out shadow detail in the stonework will bleach out the colors in the window. It is usually best to expose for the window.

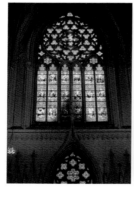
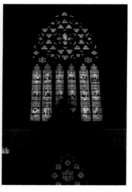

3 MAKE YOUR SETTINGS
Flash photography is usually forbidden in places of worship, but it will probably be useless to your picture, anyway, so switch flash off. Setting a medium sensitivity will help you capture details of pattern and color in the window.

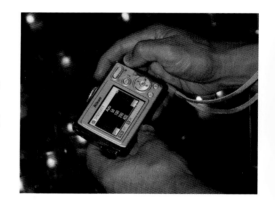

4 TRY DIFFERENT APPROACHES
A dramatic view looking up from underneath the window exploits converging parallels as a visual device. If you don't want this effect, try capturing details within the windows, or use a wide-angle view to capture something of the soaring, inspiring spaces.

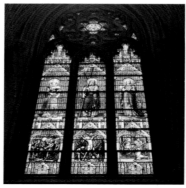
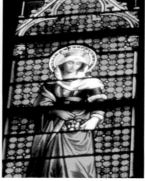
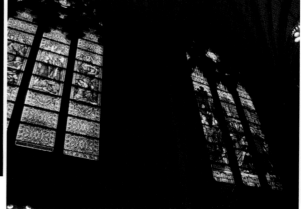

FOR THIS SHOT
Shooting from the opposite side of the cathedral, I chose the longest zoom setting to fill the frame, reducing the need to tilt upwards too much. I set medium sensitivity to balance an acceptable exposure time with quality.

CAMERA MODE

 Set your dial to **Auto-exposure mode**

LENS SETTING

Zoom to **Maximum Telephoto**

SENSOR/FILM SPEED

Use a **Medium** ISO setting

FLASH

Force the flash **Off**

5 GIVE A SENSE OF PLACE
Put the window into context, and explore the effects of varying the visual balance between the window and the interior space.

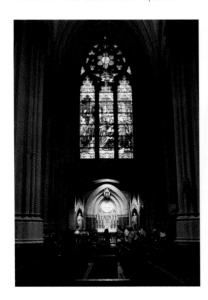

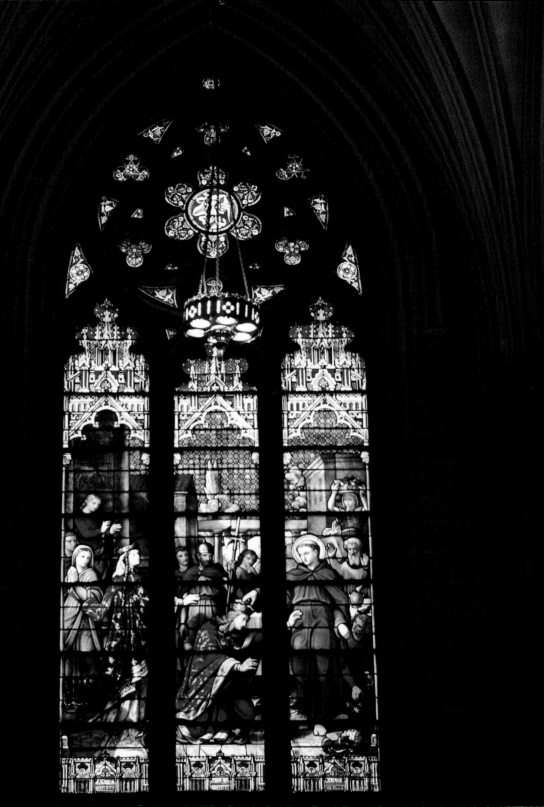

City fountains

Fountains in town squares are designed to be the center of attention, a focus of activity, and an artistic showpiece. One of the basic decisions a photographer must make is whether to focus on the subject itself – the fountain – or on the life around it, trying to place the fountain in its context. The simplest approach is to concentrate on the fountain as an architectural entity: the details of the statuary and the water jets are more than enough to delight the eye.

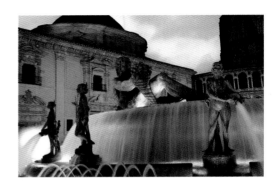

1 OBSERVE WATER TEXTURE

Most fountains provide different kinds of water – from fast jets to light spray. Take a few test shots to determine which is the type of water texture that most appeals to you.

 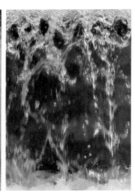

2 PROTECT YOUR CAMERA

The fine mist produced by fountains drifts in the wind, so make sure you are upwind to avoid spray damaging the camera. If the sun is out and you stand with your back to it, you may see a small rainbow.

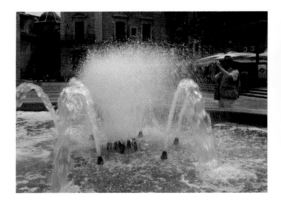

3 CAPTURE CHARACTER

Pigeons and other birds often congregate around fountains, using them as a lookout point and a birdbath. They are part of the character of the fountain, so take some fun shots that reflect this.

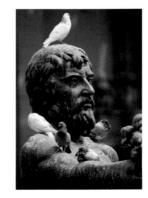

4 INCLUDE CONTEXT

Walk around the fountain, looking for pleasing combinations of water, statuary, and background. Select a wide-angle view to include the surroundings even when your viewpoint is close to the fountain.

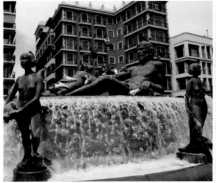 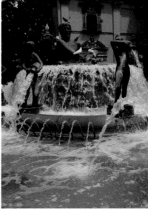

FOR THIS SHOT

I set the zoom to telephoto to throw the background out of focus. A shutter setting of $\frac{1}{320}$ sec captured just the right amount of movement in the water. I also used the flash to fill in shadows.

CAMERA MODE

Set your dial to **Landscape mode**

LENS SETTING

Zoom to **Telephoto** to **Normal**

SENSOR/FILM SPEED

Use a **Medium** to **Low** ISO setting

FLASH

Force the flash **On**

DECIDE ON AN EFFECT

Use long exposures – for example, $\frac{1}{30}$ of a second – to give the water a milky effect, and very short exposures to make the water appear frozen.

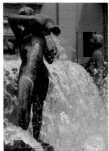
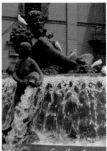
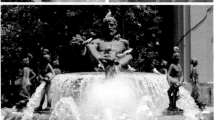

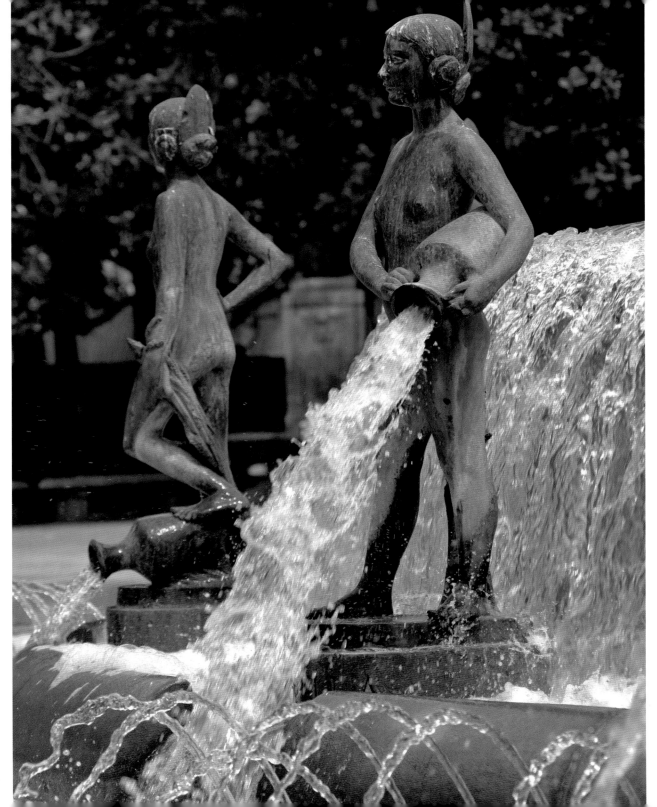

Bridge life

Throughout the world, bridges are the conduits of much of the surrounding life. Whether dating from the Middle Ages or recently unveiled, stone or metal, suspended or cantilever, bridges are full of photographic potential. Start taking pictures of the structure as soon as it comes into view. These studies of the bridge from a distance will help you explore its many characteristics, suggesting ideas and angles for many fine images.

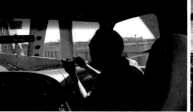
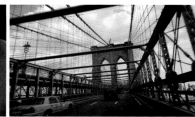

Start photographing the bridge from the moment you first catch sight of it during your approach – even if you are traveling by car. The sequence of pictures may create a narrative that you could use in a travel diary or blog, helping to give a greater sense of context to any pictures you take on the bridge.

1 APPROACH THE BRIDGE

The best way to experience a bridge is on foot. In some countries, bridges are structures of military importance, and photography may be prohibited. Check if you are in any doubt.

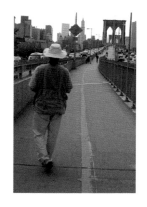

2 THINK CONTEXT

Place the bridge in its context, within its own environment, by showing the city or other backdrop. Exploit details such as girders and cables instead of trying to avoid them. They are not eyesores, but an intrinsic part of the structure.

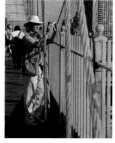
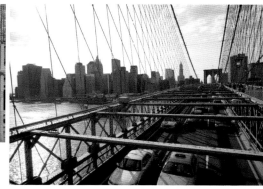

3 SHOW BRIDGE LIFE

Another approach is to show the life that is carried by the bridge. The foot traffic and vehicles that use it contribute as much to the character of the bridge as its construction and location.

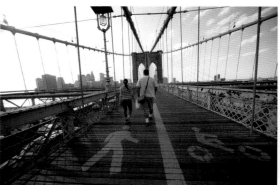
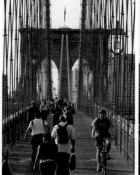
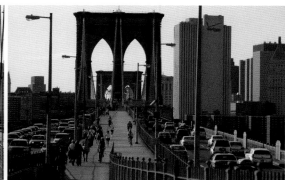

FOR THIS SHOT
I used an almost normal zoom setting, while the landscape mode helped ensure a good depth of field. To avoid making the tower look as though it is leaning back, I tried to keep the camera as level as possible.

CAMERA MODE

 Set your dial to **Landscape mode**

LENS SETTING

Zoom to **Normal** to **Moderately Wide**

SENSOR/FILM SPEED

Use a **Medium** ISO setting

FLASH

Force the flash **Off**

4 CONSIDER THE VIEW
An extreme wide-angle view can be effective but distorts the lines of the bridge. A less wide view is more natural.

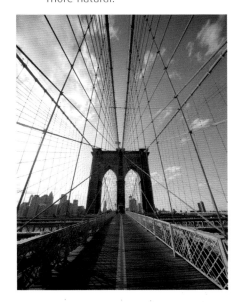

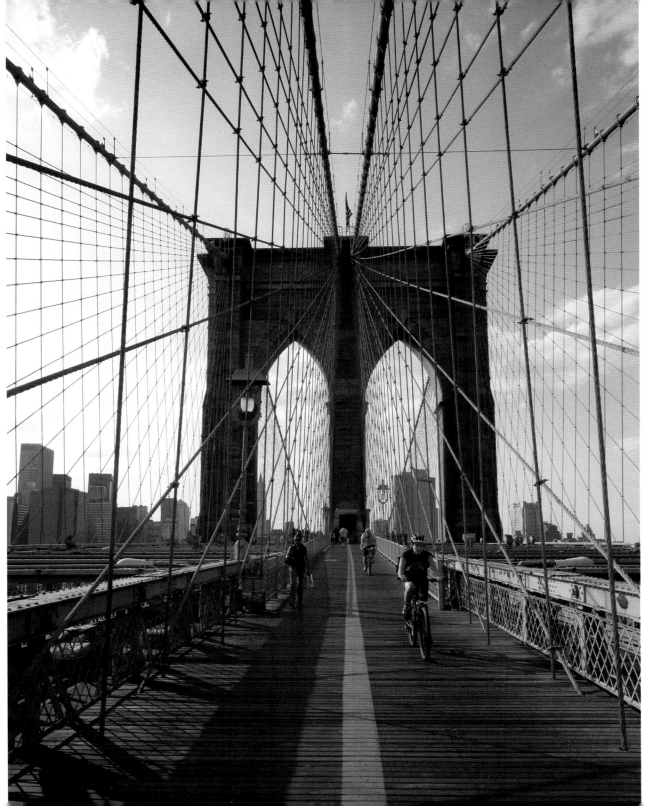

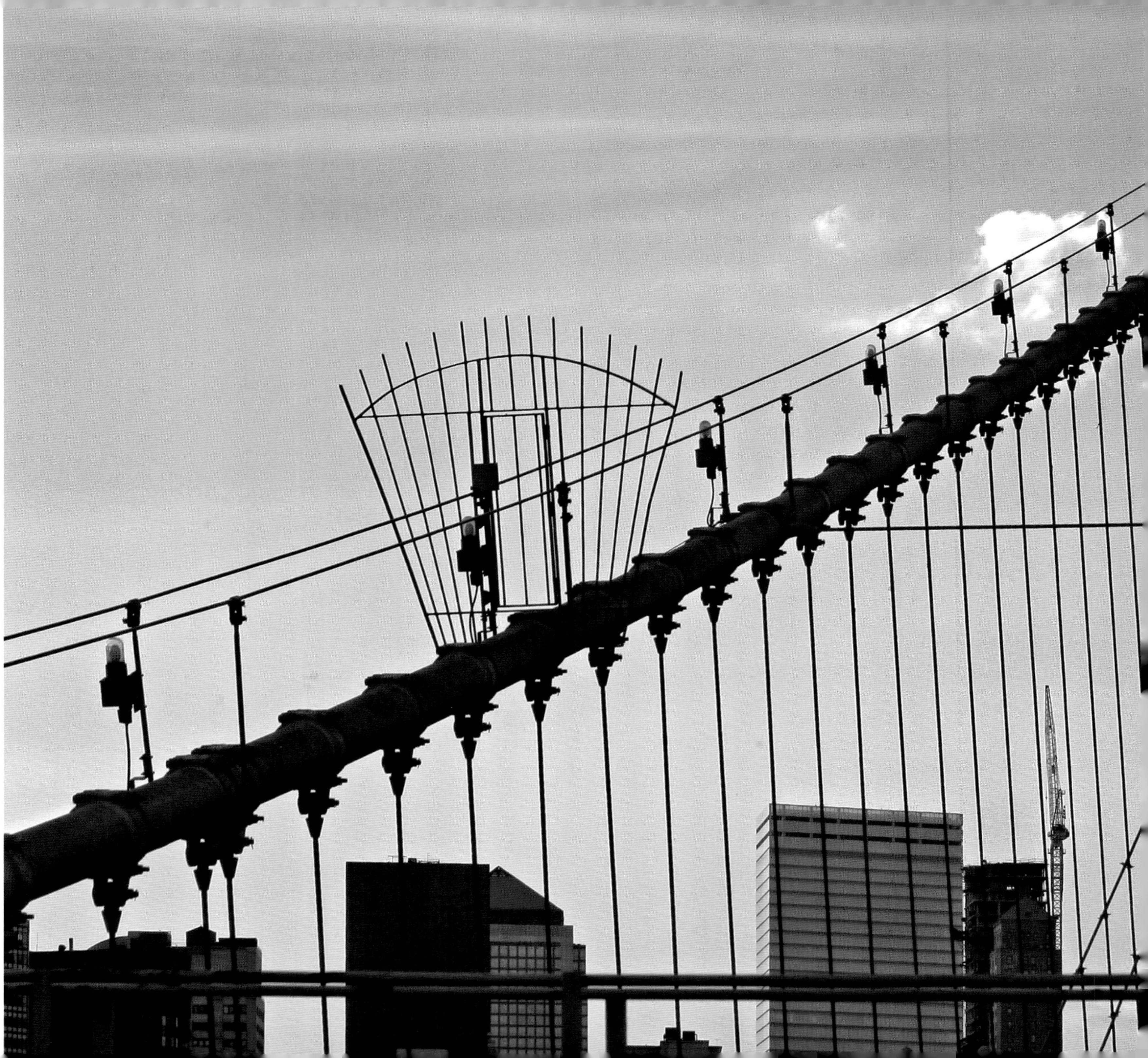

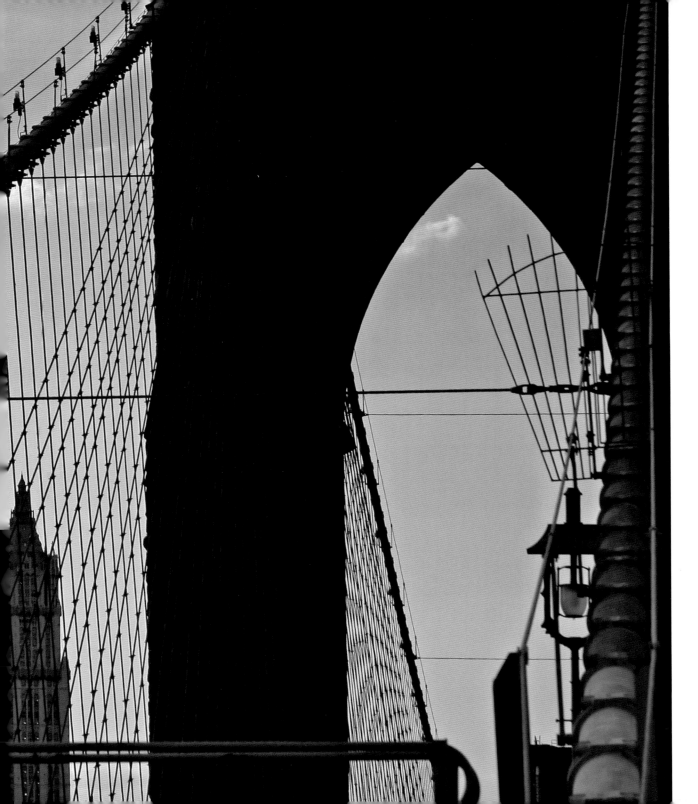

BRIDGE IN SILHOUETTE

In this picture, the struts and cables of New York's Brooklyn Bridge have been used as a framing device for the city skyline beyond. Look out for similar opportunities, which are manifold in modern urban environments.

1. Expose for the sky: this has the effect of making the foreground very dark.

2. If necessary, force a little underexposure for the darkest silhouettes.

3. Use a long zoom setting to cut out unwanted foreground elements and concentrate on graphic shapes and outlines.

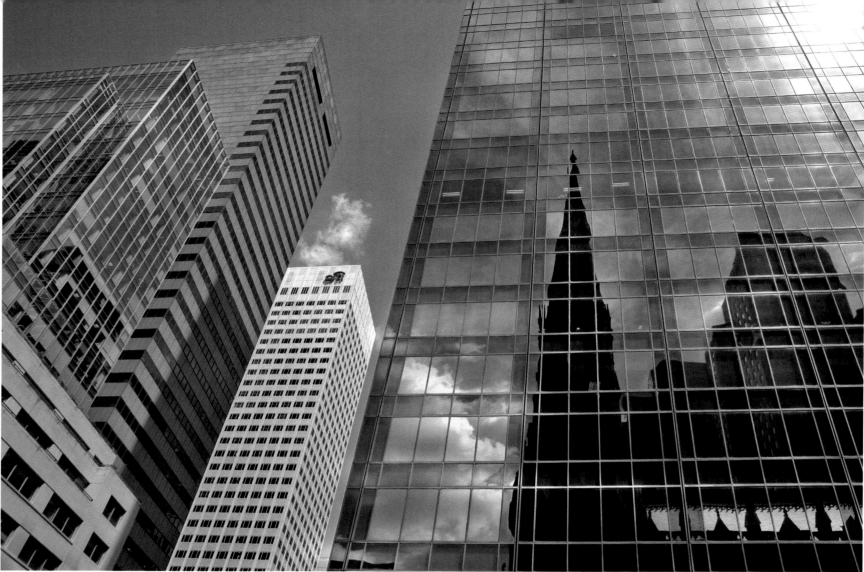

Contrasting old and new

More often than not, cityscapes are dominated by a contrasting variety of architectural styles: Gothic churches rub shoulders with modern office towers, and 19th-century buildings share space with state-of-the-art glass skyscrapers.

This urban juxtaposition can lead to a uniquely photographic endeavor. We look for ways in which viewpoint, color, tone, and composition fuse together to create an image of contrasts and many layers.

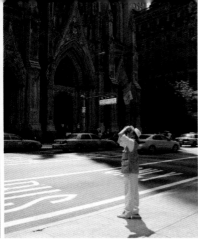
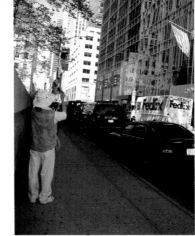

FOR THIS SHOT

With a wide-angle zoom setting, I caught this passing cloud on the gold-covered windows while sunlight was being reflected off the cathedral's roof. I used a low ISO setting and large file size to maximize image quality.

CAMERA MODE
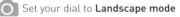
Set your dial to **Landscape mode**

LENS SETTING
Zoom to **Wide Angle**

SENSOR/FILM SPEED
Use a **Low** ISO setting

FLASH
Force the flash **Off**

1 SURVEY THE LOCATION

Walk around the area of interest looking for potential points of view. Be open-minded: from a different angle, a location of apparent little promise may yield the day's best picture.

2 SET THE CAMERA

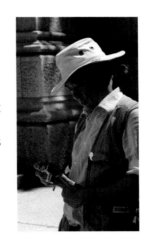

If possible, leave the lens at a fixed setting so you can focus your attention on composition rather than lens controls. In most cases, wide angle is the most versatile setting; this is also, conveniently, the default on most cameras that switch themselves off if they are not used for a few minutes.

3 TRY DIFFERENT ORIENTATIONS

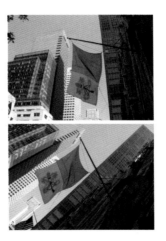

Consider tilting the camera at an unusual angle, either vertical or horizontal. The correct angle to shoot a scene is not always the one that follows the upright, formal orientation, but the one that gives you the best picture.

4 EXPERIMENT WITH VARIOUS COMPOSITIONS

The obvious approach here is to contrast the ornate neo-Gothic spire with the modern glass building. All these pictures have their merits, but they lack something special. Keep shooting until you find a composition that you are happy with.

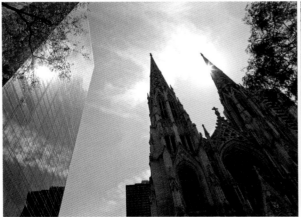
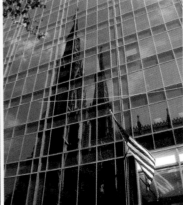
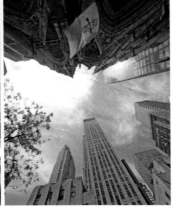

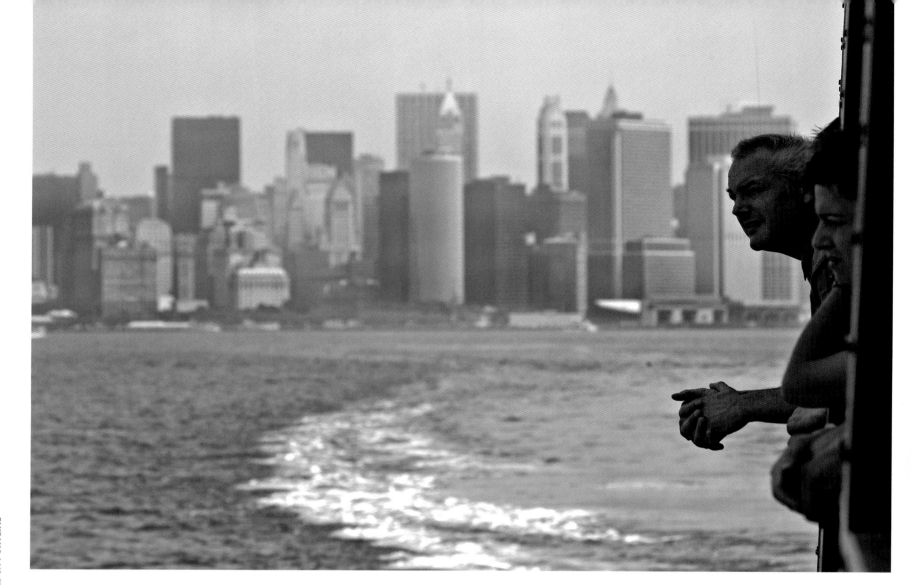

An unusual city skyline

Many great cities are situated on a river or by the sea, so you need simply to cross the water to find an uninterrupted view of the skyline. Unfortunately, however, everyone else will also be drawn to the same vantage point, whether a bridge or the opposite bank. The trick is to use your imagination to find your own personal vision—a different approach to the view. Here, a trip on the Staten Island ferry provided an unusual take on New York City.

FOR THIS SHOT

By leaning out as far as possible, with a long zoom setting, I was able to focus on fellow passengers. I set a high ISO and shutter priority to ensure the images would be sharp, and used a small depth of field to blur the city skyline.

CAMERA MODE

 Set your dial to **Aperture Priority**

LENS SETTING

Zoom to **Maximum Telephoto**

SENSOR/FILM SPEED

 Use a **Medium** ISO setting

FLASH

Force the flash **On**

AN ALTERNATIVE APPROACH

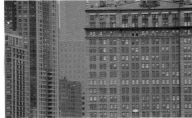

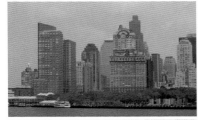

By zooming in and filling the frame with buildings, you can create a usable—if commonplace—city image. An advantage of this type of photograph, is that it can be taken under any lighting conditions.

STAND FIRM

Keep a wide, relaxed stance to absorb any rolling of the ferry. If you lean on the superstructure, you may transmit vibrations to the camera. Use your wrist strap for added safety.

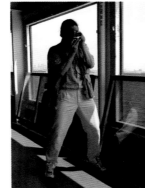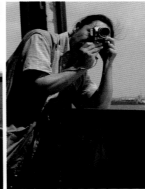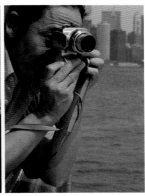

CORRECT IMAGES LATER

It is hard to keep an eye on the horizon when a boat is rolling, even if only slightly. Don't worry about pictures that are not quite straight; you can easily correct them later on a computer. Keep shooting, and don't waste time reviewing as you go along—the scenery changes very quickly.

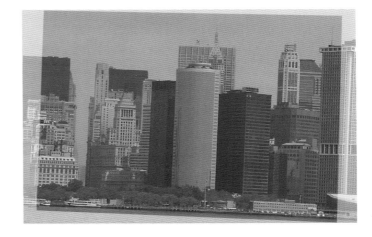

LOOK FOR THE UNUSUAL

Decide whether to include elements such as people or other structures in the picture. If you try to tie all the elements of the moment together, the result will be far richer visually.

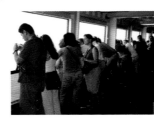

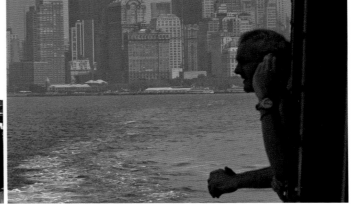

City streets

Filled as they are with local flavor, a city's streets are often as picturesque as the official tourist attractions. They are also a mine of intriguing subjects, such as unusual street art or scenes with a human interest. Keeping your camera at the ready helps to keep your eyes and mind looking and searching. Some locations only need a person or play of light to complete them, so spend a few moments in wait of the perfect shot.

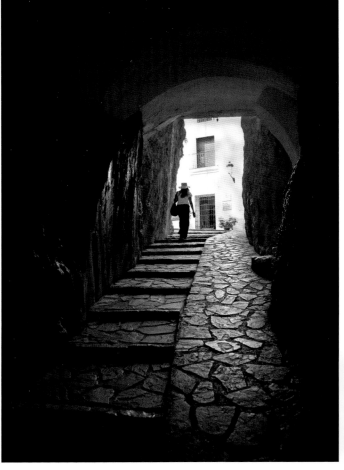

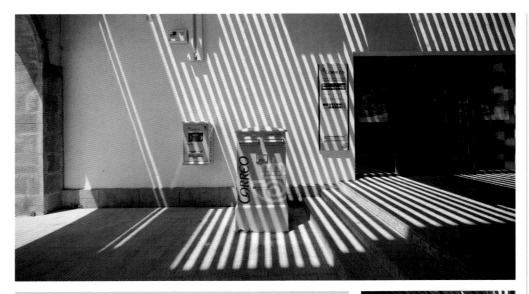

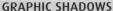

GRAPHIC SHADOWS

You may walk past a location every day without noticing anything unusual or attractive about it. Then one day, a stunning pattern of shadows from the sun might transform it into a strong graphic composition, bringing it to life.

1 Try photographing the scene from several different angles.

2 For the simplest and strongest results, adopt a square-on perspective.

3 Use landscape mode or smallest aperture for maximum depth of field.

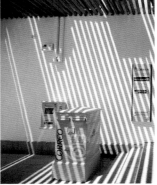

FOCAL POINT

A flight of steps in a sloping alleyway leads the eye up to a bright focal point. However, a figure or some activity is needed to reward the eye for traveling there.

1 Use a wide-angle setting to capture the lead-up to the focal point of the scene.

2 Wait for a figure to complete the scene, but press the shutter button in good time.

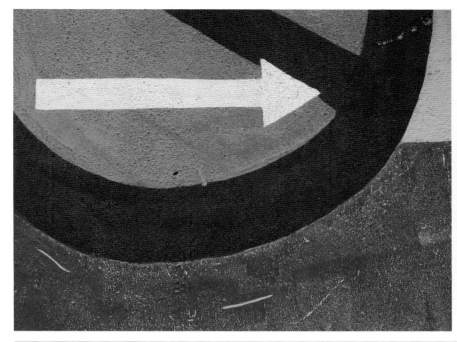

STREET SIGNS

Being designed to attract attention, street and shop signs make eye-catching photographs and interesting additions to scrapbooks. They are visual reminders of the places you've visited.

1 You can use any zoom setting since you are copying flat artwork.

2 Keep your compositions simple, and let the signs speak for themselves.

3 To emphasize the graphic qualities of the signs, frame them up square on to the camera.

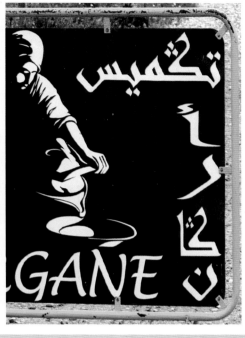

UNUSUAL POINT OF VIEW

Mirrors can offer you many unusual points of view. Those mounted on cars and motorcycles even come with a ready-made frame to help you compose your picture.

1 Measure the exposure from the reflection of the scene; allow the surroundings to be dark.

2 Make your camera focus past the mirror to the image behind. You may need to point it to the scene outside the mirror, and hold the focus point.

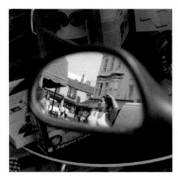

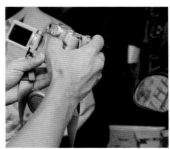

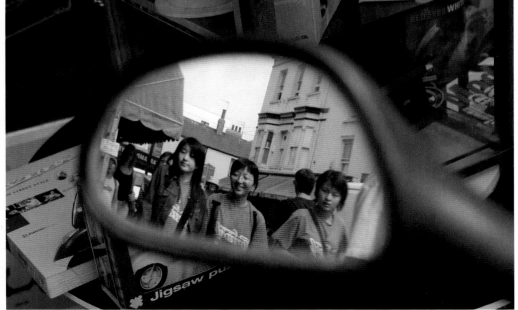

EVERYDAY SIGHTS

When walking around a city, it is possible to photograph almost every step of the way, recording shop fronts, changes in light, signage, graffiti, and much more. While individually, each picture may seem of little significance, as a collection they make a powerful impression.

1 Use a small to medium image size to maximize your memory card's capacity.

2 Photograph from all angles, and try slanting the camera for graphic variety.

3 Record in both landscape and portrait formats to give you greater flexibility with your images later.

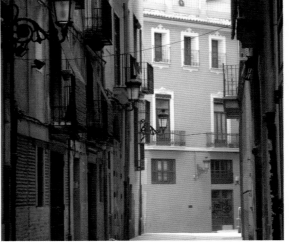

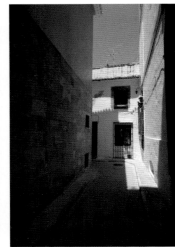

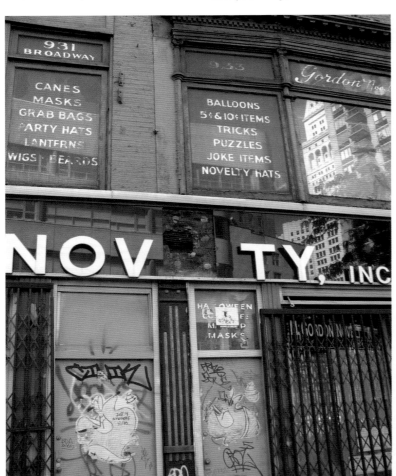

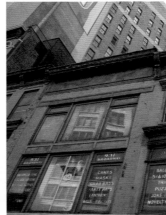

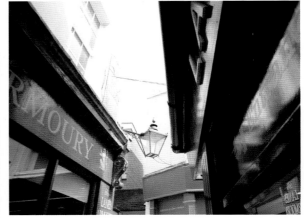

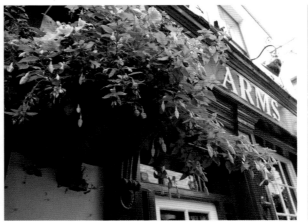

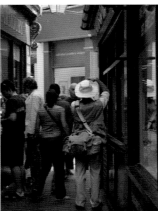

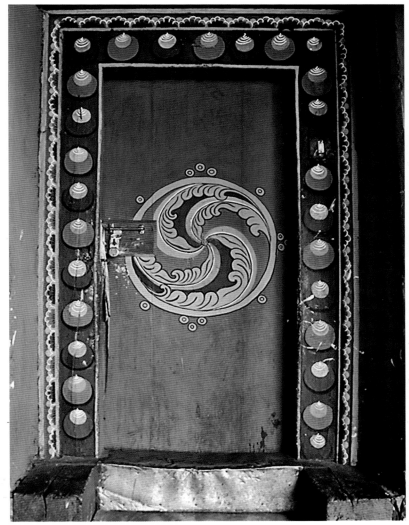

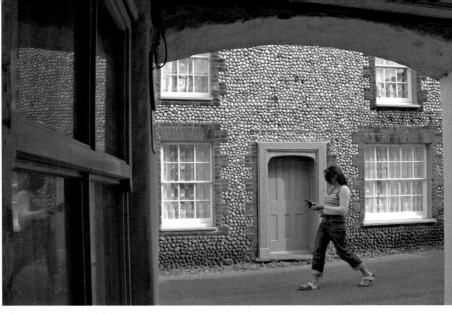

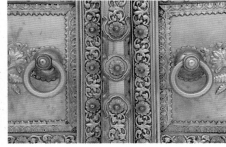

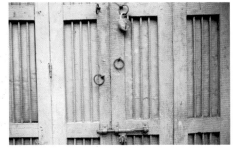

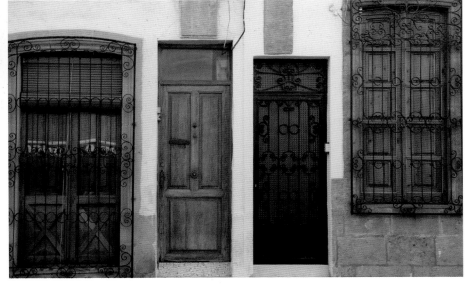

DOORS AND DOORWAYS

One universally recognizable theme for photography is that of doors and doorways. Whether you see them as symbolic or simply decorative, as a collection they have a strong visual impact. For variety, you might include pictures through partially open doors, into the street or passageway beyond.

1 Use a mid-range zoom setting and hold the camera square for the least amount of distortion.

2 Include people walking in the street or through the door to create more visual interest.

3 Take close-up shots of door furniture and other details, to vary the scale of your pictures.

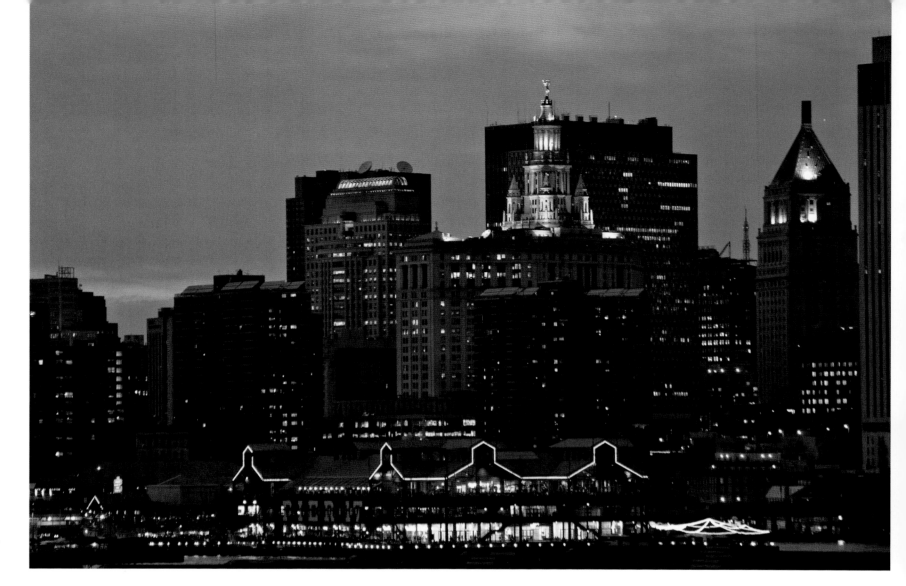

A nocturnal cityscape

One of the key advantages of photographing a city at night is that you can work with just about any kind of weather. You do not need a cloudless sky; you can work in the rain and snow; and you can succeed even in partial fog. This is because you are concentrating on the interplay of masses of dark tones with little spikes of bright color and light, so the usual need for interesting shadows and tonal gradations are redundant. You work purely with light.

FOR THIS SHOT

I used a long zoom to home in on an attractive pattern of lights, while still showing some sky. I deliberately underexposed slightly to ensure shadows remained dark without being fully black, which was how they appeared to the eye.

CAMERA MODE
Set your dial to **any exposure mode**

LENS SETTING
Zoom **as needed**

SENSOR/FILM SPEED
Use a **High** ISO setting

FLASH
Force the flash **Off**

1 START AT TWILIGHT

Set yourself up before it gets too dark. A practical reason for this is so you can see what you're doing, but it is also useful to catch the light as it shifts from too bright to too dark. Find a way to support the camera if you have no tripod.

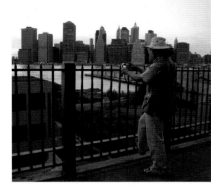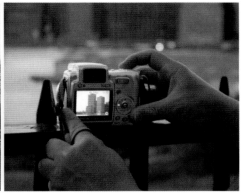

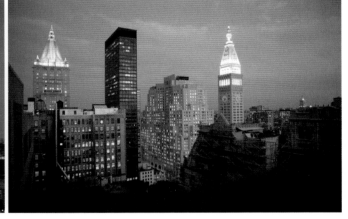

2 LOOK FOR UNIQUE BUILDINGS

Certain cities have buildings by which they can be defined. If you want to produce a picture-postcard night scene as a portrait of the city, try to include those unique elements.

3 EXPERIMENT WITH FORMAT AND ZOOM

During the time that the sun begins to set, experiment with different zoom settings and formats. Make changes in exposure, too. Notice how the same lights appear to be brighter as the night gets darker overall. And remember that the camera will see more colors in the dark than you can.

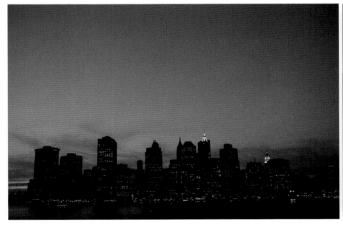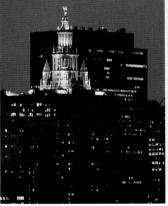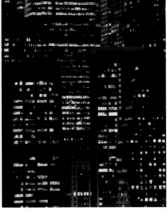

City skyscrapers

Visitors to skyscraper-dominated cities who are unfamiliar with such buildings can be easily identified because they are always looking straight up and not where they are going. Capture this initial visual excitement by looking for strong patterns, preferably with clear symmetry, as well as dramatic lighting and a variety of texture. A wide-angle view will help exaggerate the convergence of parallels to convey a sense of receding space.

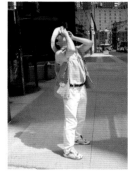
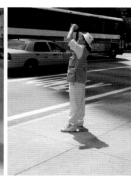

1 MOVE AROUND

You will most likely compose your image almost entirely by moving around at street level. Your instinct may be to move as far back as possible, but the best shots are often taken from right up close to buildings.

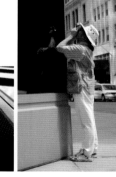

2 INCLUDE VISUAL CLUES

Search for contrasts in shape and scale between elements. Look for architectural or urban features that create interest, such as a sign that gives an indication of where you are.

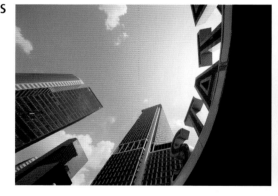

3 USE JUXTAPOSITION

A composition that contrasts hard-edged high-tech buildings with the soft leaves of a street-level tree makes for a captivating image. A wide-angle setting helps keep it all in focus.

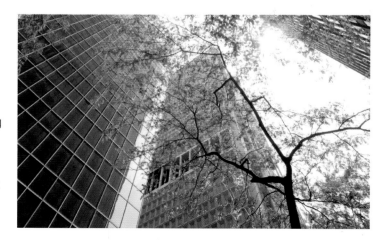

4 BEAT EXPOSURE PROBLEMS

It can be difficult to balance an exposure for the sky – which makes trees very dark – with an exposure for the leaves – which bleaches the blue sky. Try different angles, or return at another time of the day. The solution here was both to change angle and to use flash to light the leaves from below.

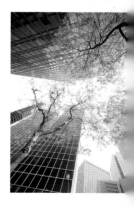

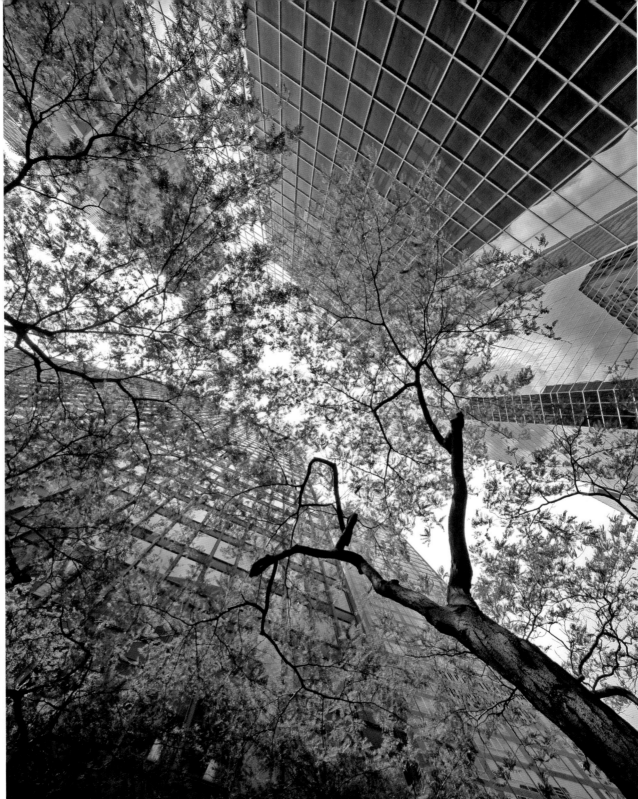

FOR THIS SHOT

I chose the widest-angle zoom and selected the highest quality settings, including low ISO. The flash was forced on to light the leaves, but it wasn't strong enough to illuminate those at the edge of the frame.

CAMERA MODE

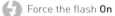

Set your dial to **Landscape mode**

LENS SETTING

Zoom to **Wide Angle**

SENSOR/FILM SPEED

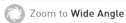

Use a **Low** to **Medium** ISO setting

FLASH

Force the flash **On**

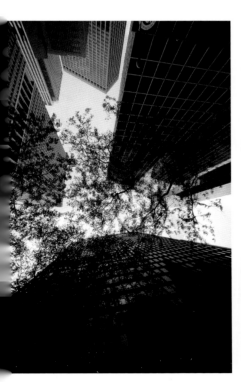

CITY SKYSCRAPERS >> ARCHITECTURE   **261**

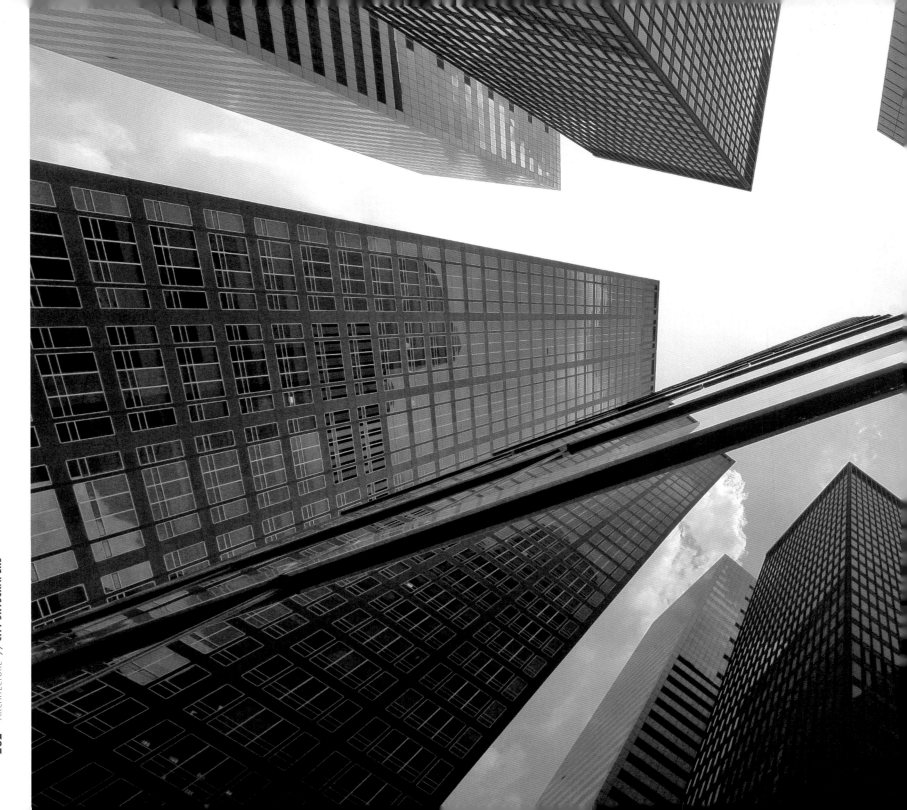

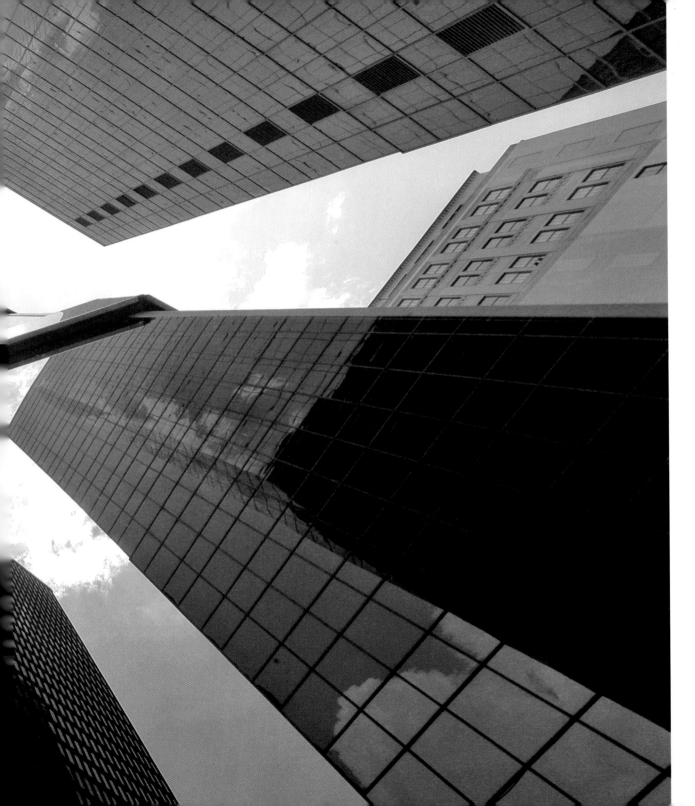

SOARING SKYWARD

Thousands of people pass these buildings in the Wall Street area of New York City every working day, but many are too busy to appreciate the drama of light and form. It only takes a moment to look up and appreciate the symmetry of the reflections.

1 If possible use a wide-angle attachment to achieve the widest possible view.

2 For the greatest depth of reflection in a mirrored surface, stand as close to it as possible.

3 Use maximum quality settings to achieve smooth, clean tones and the best color.

4 Set to aperture priority, with minimum aperture for maximum depth of field.

Reflected city

As photogenic as they are, many buildings suffer from an excess of familiarity. When faced with an iconic skyscraper or a world-famous cathedral, it is easy to rely on hackneyed old viewpoints. However, by looking for unusual views, you will have much more fun. You will also see more than the average photographer, since your search will be purposeful: by looking for a new perspective on what you think you know well, you extend the reach of your photography.

REFLECTING THE CITY

Reflections—whether on a pool of water, a polished surface, or shiny glass— make up a major element of the visual experience of a modern cityscape. Pictures of reflections are most effective when you have maximum depth of field, so strive to get as much of the image as sharp as possible when you compose.

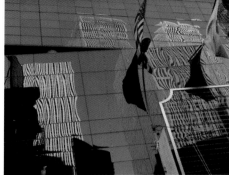

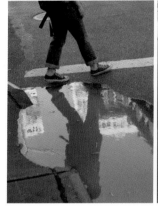

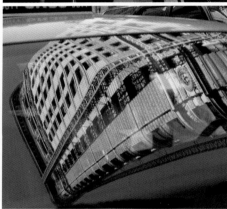

1 SEEK REFLECTIONS

Instead of looking at the buildings themselves, concentrate on reflective surfaces that project back the surrounding architecture, such as the polished bonnet of a car.

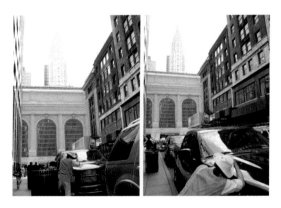

2 VARY THE VIEW

Create interesting distortions and reworkings of the buildings' lines by moving the camera to different angles.

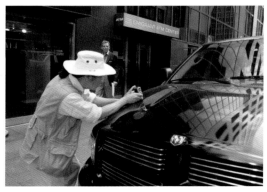

3 FIND A VISUAL PATHWAY

The black surface absorbs a great deal of light, darkening the reflected sky and making it easy to set the right exposure. The curves of the car lead the eye to the building in the background.

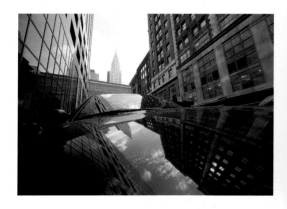

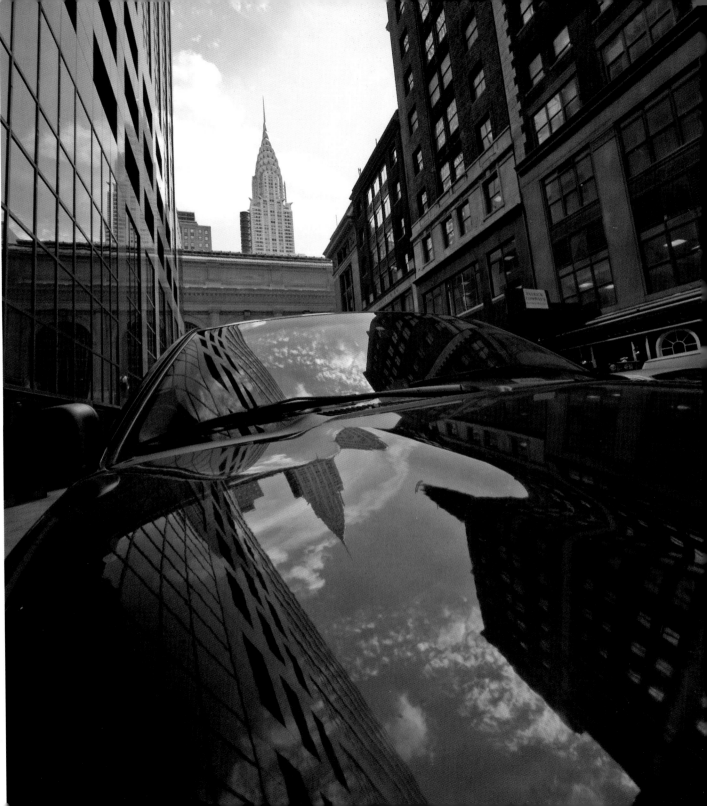

 FOR THIS SHOT
I selected the landscape mode for the greatest depth of field and used the widest lens setting to capture as wide a view as possible. Low sensitivity ensured the best quality, and I used the car for support.

CAMERA MODE
Set your dial to **Landscape mode**

LENS SETTING
Zoom to **Maximum Wide Angle**

SENSOR/FILM SPEED
 Use a **Low** ISO setting

FLASH
Force the flash **Off**

4 TRY DIFFERENT POSITIONS
Even the subtlest changes in position can make a big difference to the final images, so take the time to experiment.

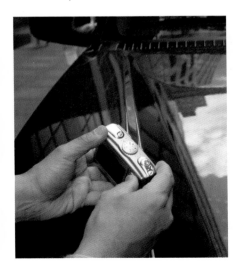

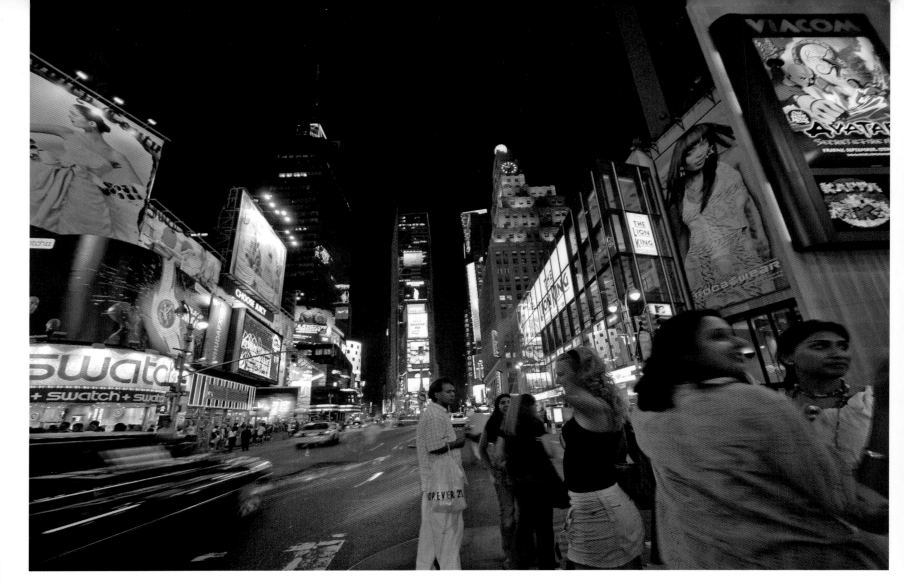

The city by night

The centers of many major cities become spectacular light shows when night falls, with the illumination from billboards and buildings mingling with the lights from passing cars to create a riotous carnival of color. Photographing a scene made up of large swathes of darkness with small areas of intense light requires a good deal of practice, but the best tip for capturing the energy and excitement of a busy night-time city scene is to include human interest in the image.

FOR THIS SHOT

I used a wide-angle attachment to work as much of the scene as possible into the picture. To capture movement blur, I set a high sensitivity and selected shutter priority. I also tried various flash settings until I got it right.

CAMERA MODE

 Set your dial to **Shutter Priority**

LENS SETTING

 Zoom to **Wide Angle**

SENSOR/FILM SPEED

 Use a **High** ISO setting

FLASH

 Force the flash **On** if needed

1 TAKE YOUR TIME

Once darkness falls, light conditions remain unchanged for several hours. This gives you the freedom to look carefully for a place to photograph. Look for locations that combine lively movement of people and traffic with good views of the lights.

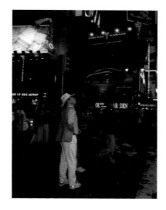

2 EXPLORE THE CAMERA'S SETTINGS

If your camera allows it, set it to night-scene mode; otherwise, turn off the flash and capture the scene at a high sensitivity.

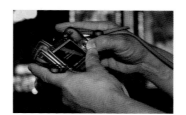

3 CAPTURE MOVEMENT

The downside of long exposures – blur caused by movement – can work in your favor. The light trails of passing cars exude pace and energy, but you will need to use a tripod.

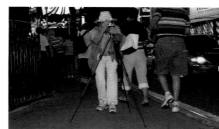

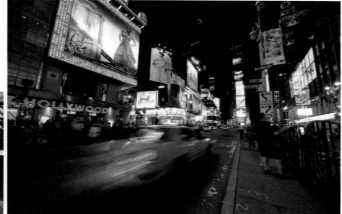

4 FIND REFLECTIONS

The ubiquitous glass of modern design and architecture means that the cityscape will be reflected in myriad window panes. This creates interesting interplays of light that you can include in your shot.

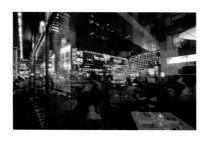

5 USE THE FLASH

Working with a tripod gives you the chance to combine sharp definition with movement blur, especially if you use it in conjunction with the flash. This will freeze any movement in the foreground, while still allowing other movement to blur. Set a long shutter time (about 1/8 of a second) and force the flash on, then experiment with different exposure times.

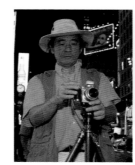

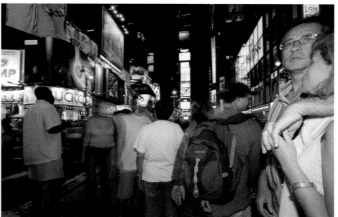

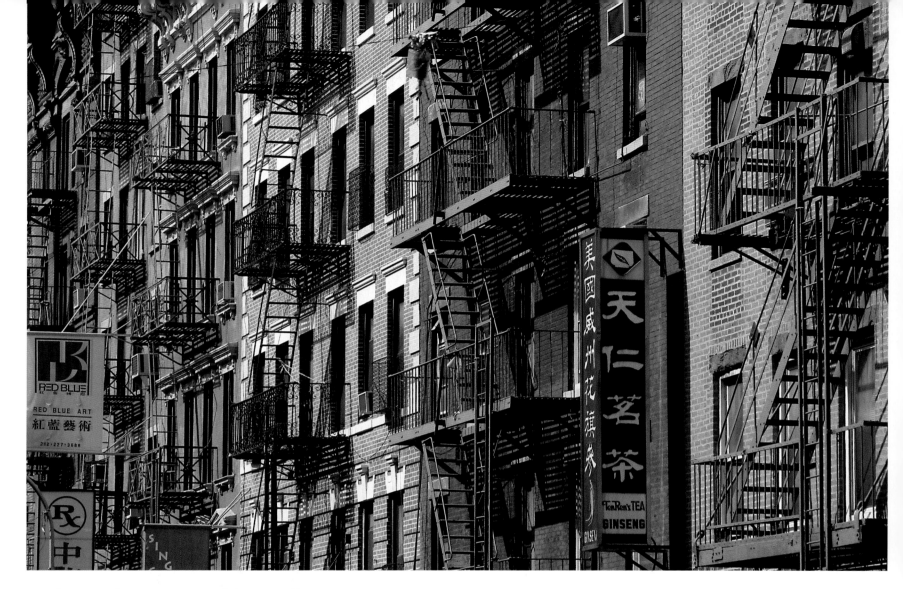

Black-and-white street scene

Colors in a scene – particularly if there is a multitude of different hues – can conceal just as much as they reveal. This is most apparent when the riot of colors in a scene such as this is reduced to a palette of gray tones.

In turn, this reveals patterns of steps, textures of brick, and contrasting calligraphy. It takes practice to "see" in black and white, but once you learn the skill, it can be hard to unlearn, and working in monochrome can become a favorite mode.

FOR THIS SHOT

To avoid tilting the camera up too much – and thereby exaggerating converging parallels – I zoomed the lens all the way, but some cropping was still needed. I chose the landscape mode, but any is fine, and a medium ISO setting.

CAMERA MODE

Set your dial to **any exposure mode**

LENS SETTING

Zoom to **whatever is required**

SENSOR/FILM SPEED

Use a **Medium** ISO setting

FLASH

Force the flash **Off**

LOOK PAST COLORS

This street scene is full of color, but beneath it all are the strong patterns and groupings of lines that work so well in monochrome.

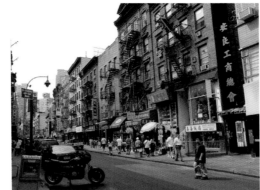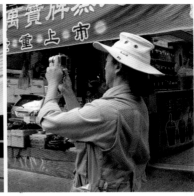

IDENTIFY WHAT WORKS

Experience will guide your choice of which picture makes it in monochrome. Here, the first picture has strong patterns but does benefit from color. The next image relies on color to separate its elements. But the third image would work equally well in black-and-white as it does in color.

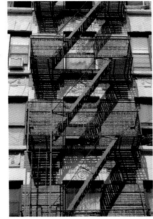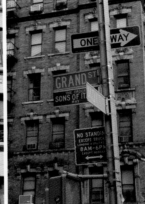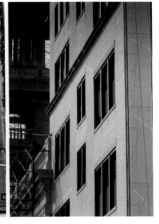

CROP TO MAXIMIZE THE EFFECT

Cropping a picture to eliminate some of its outer margins can be an effective way of tightening up the composition. It is not the same as zooming in. What makes cropping so useful is that you can favor one side of the picture over the other.

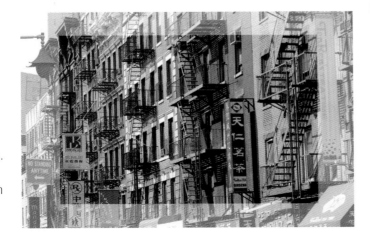

SELECT B&W MODE

Many digital cameras offer a setting that makes the camera act as though it is exposing black-and-white film. If your camera does not have this facility, change the image on your computer or print it in black and white.

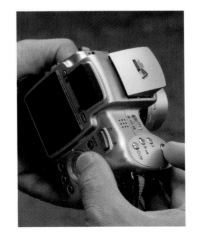

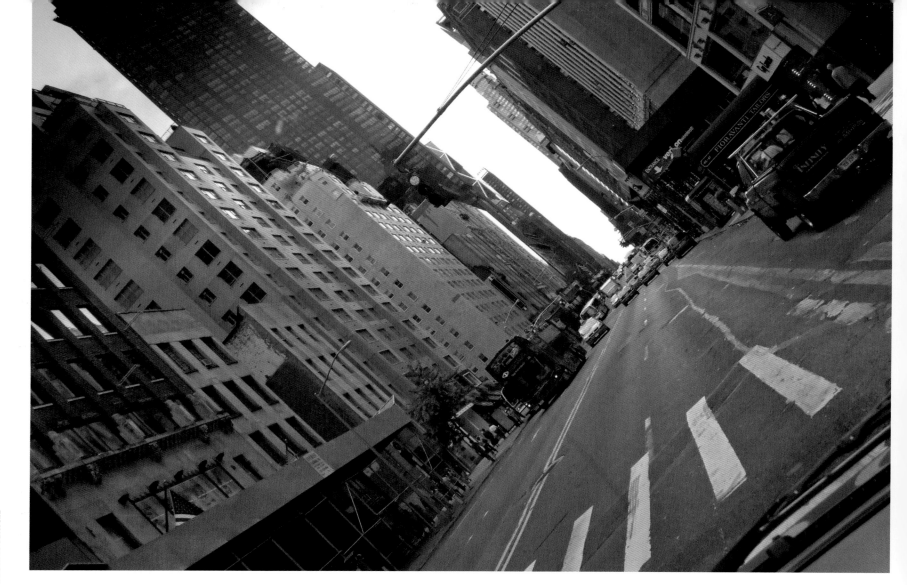

Cityscapes from a vehicle

Most of us spend many hours of our lives traveling in cars. However, not many people realize that this is an ideal position for taking pictures. If you are a passenger, you can look around and enjoy many fine picture-making possibilities. Always keep your camera at hand: photographic opportunities often appear with little notice. As you become more experienced, you will be able to spot them from a distance and be prepared as you approach.

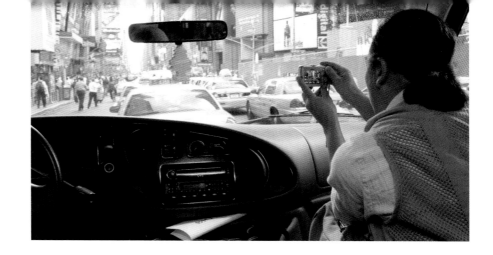

FOR THIS SHOT

Even with the lens zoomed to minimum, the field of view was insufficient, so I tilted the camera to get more of the buildings and road markings in view. To reduce camera shake, I set a high ISO for the briefest exposure.

CAMERA MODE
Set your dial to **Sports mode**

LENS SETTING
Zoom to **Wide Angle**

SENSOR/FILM SPEED
Use a **High** ISO setting

FLASH
Force the flash **Off**

1 MOVE CLOSE TO THE GLASS

For image quality, it is best to keep the lens as close to the glass as possible. But don't put yourself at risk: unbuckle the seatbelt for more freedom of movement only in stationary traffic and if local laws permit.

2 TRY DIFFERENT APPROACHES

Winding down the side window will eliminate the glass between you and your subject. For a different approach, you can also use the body of the car as a useful framing device.

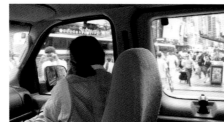

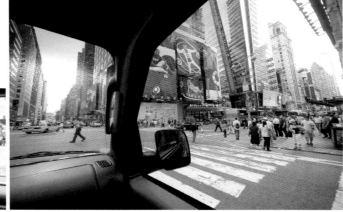

3 SEIZE UNIQUE PHOTO OPPORTUNITIES

Traveling in a vehicle gives you many interesting viewpoints that are not available when walking, especially since many tunnels and some roads are closed to pedestrians. Buses give you a more raised perspective.

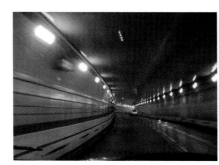

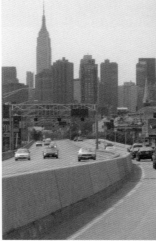

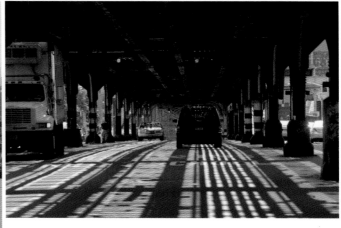

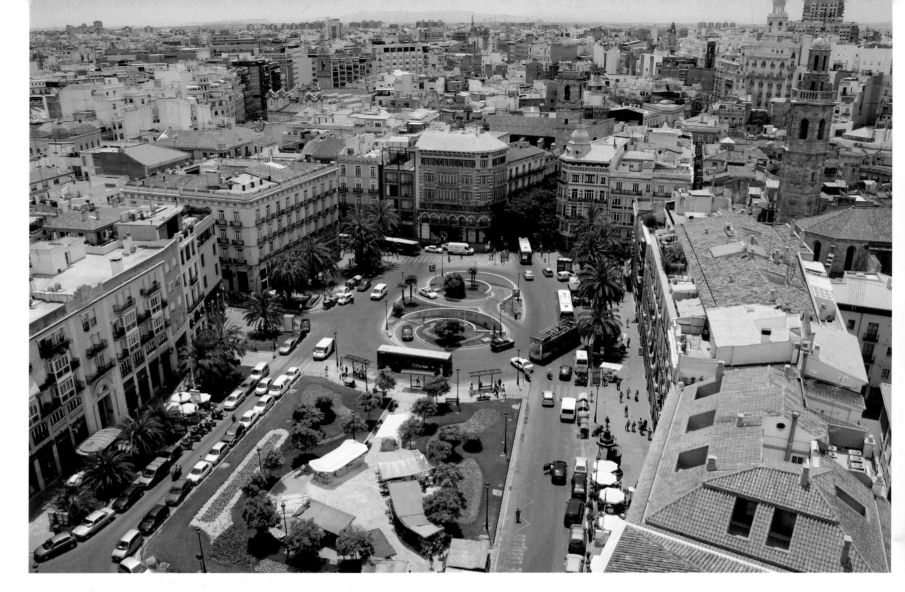

An urban landscape

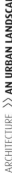

Innovative perspectives are often extreme perspectives, and few are as extreme and effective as views from high elevations. Looking down on street life, rooftops, or fields gives you pictures that are completely different from those that can be obtained at ground level. Because you are more distant than usual, the emphasis should be on composition: lines, patterns, texture, and shape. There is little camera technique needed – just look with your eyes open.

FOR THIS SHOT

By focusing a wide zoom setting at infinity, I created a good depth of field, so everything in view is sharp. I set a low ISO because the lighting was good and I wanted maximum detail. To avoid flare, I shaded the lens.

CAMERA MODE
Set your dial to **Landscape**

LENS SETTING
Zoom to **Wide Angle**

SENSOR/FILM SPEED
Use a **Low** ISO setting

FLASH
Force the flash **Off**

AERIAL PHOTOGRAPHS

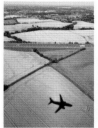 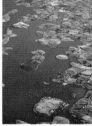

Whenever you take a flight somewhere, try to position yourself in a window seat either in front of the wing or a long way behind. You can then make the most of the delightful opportunities of aerial photography to entertain you during the flight. Use a normal to medium-wide setting with a high ISO setting to catch the sharpest images.

1 PLAY IT SAFE
From viewpoints such as the tops of fortresses or towers, you often have to lean out for your shot. Make sure it is safe to do so, and loop the camera strap around your hand or neck to keep a safe hold on it.

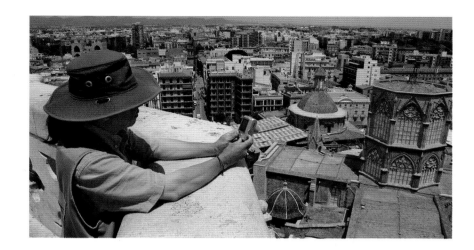

2 SEE THROUGH THE CHAOS
Wide views of rooftops often result in a chaotic image. Look for patterns or lines of streets that will pull the image together. Or zoom in to smaller details, such as abstract patterns of roof tiles or the contrast between windows and brickwork.

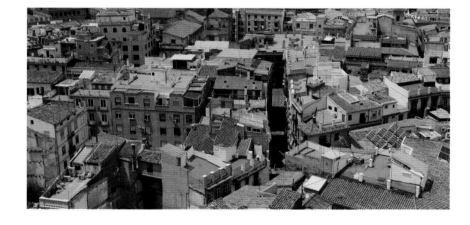

3 FIND THE UNUSUAL
Don't just shoot the expected – look further and deeper. You often have to wait for the right shot, such as these pedestrians in the square finally forming an interesting pattern.

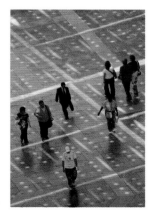

4
Look for buildings that might add structure or direction to your shot. Here, the blue domes in the foreground lead the eye to zigzag toward the distant skyline of the city.

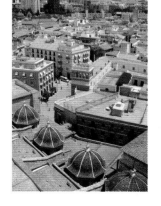

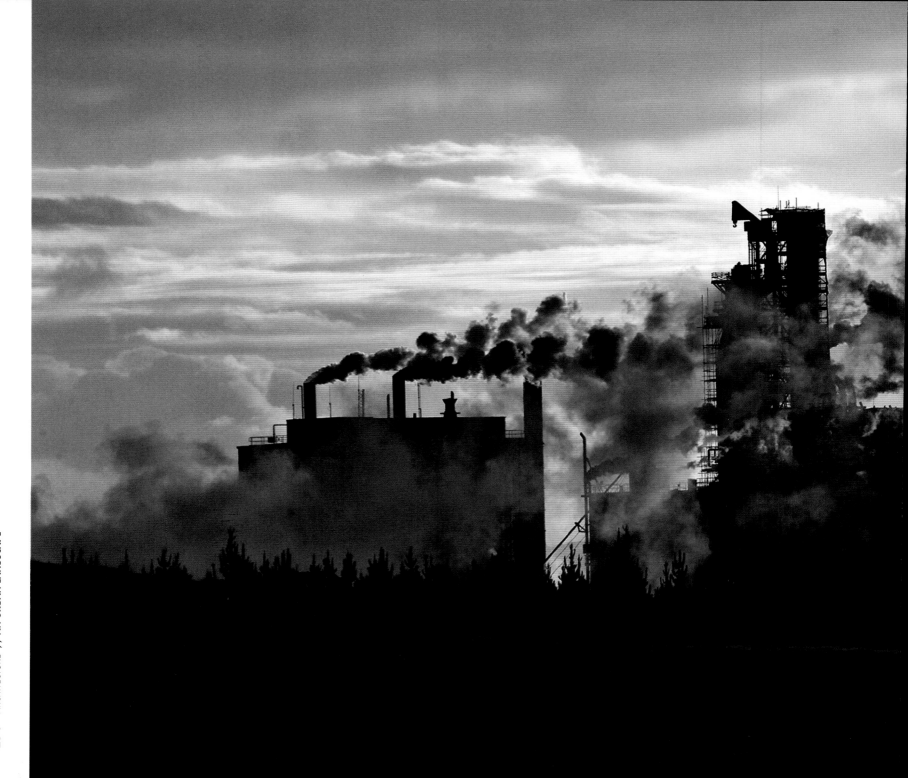

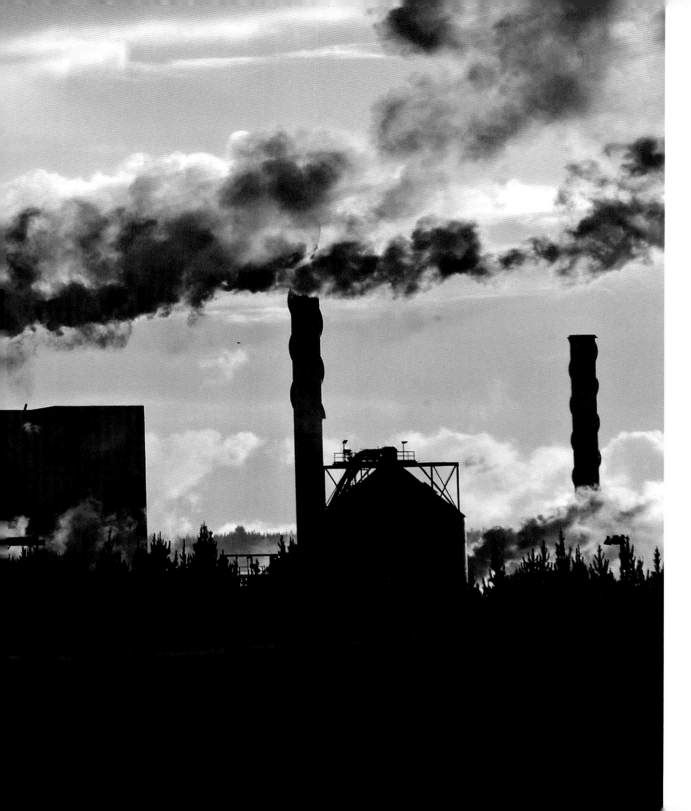

INDUSTRIAL APPEAL

You may travel past an industrial landscape such as this paper mill every day without seeing any photogenic potential in it. However, sun, cloud, and smoke can sometimes conspire to create a stunning composition.

1 Look at familiar scenes and try to imagine what conditions could transform them.

2 Shoot in the low sun of early morning or evening for the best light.

3 It's unlikely that you will be able to get very close, so you may need a long zoom setting.

Architecture

The built environment offers such a wide variety of form, color, and tone that it would be possible for a photographer to specialize in this field and never run out of subjects. Even individual secondary themes – such as textures, vernacular styles, or lighting design – can provide an endless stream of images. Architecture is such a broad subject that you can try out a range of photographic techniques.

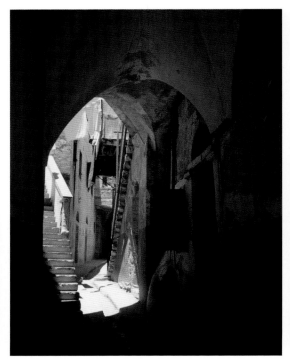

INTERESTING LINKS
Include passageways and other architectural links between various buildings for a fascinating adjunct to the portrayal of the buildings themselves.

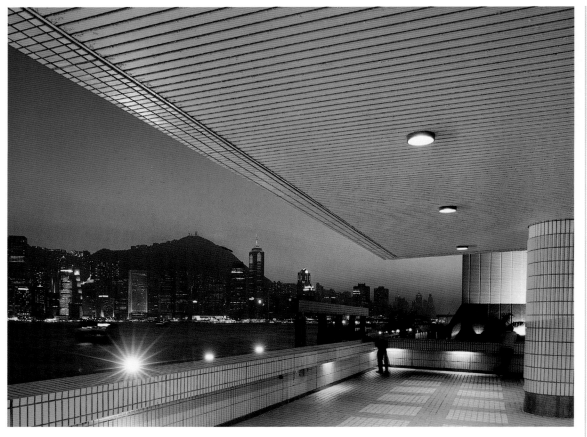

MIXED LIGHTING
The lights of buildings at night often create dramatic combinations of shape and color. Try to make use of the juxtaposition of artificial and natural light.

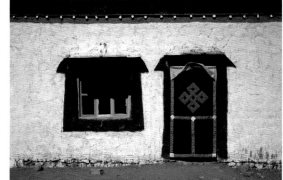

OBJECTIVE FRAMING
Document vernacular styles of decoration with straightforward photography: try to frame up square to the subject.

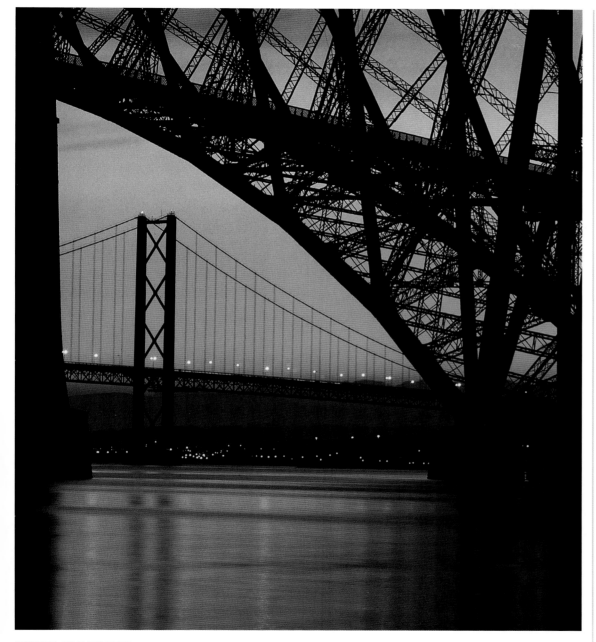

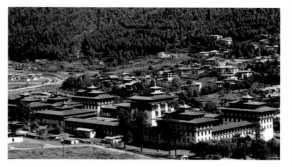

ESTABLISHING CONTEXT

When you travel to major sites, start photographing as soon as you approach, so you have images that place the buildings in their context.

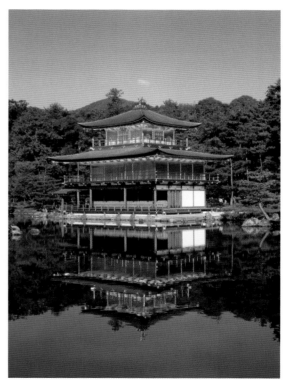

SUNSET SILHOUETTES

Open structures of girders, such as those of bridges or towers, work well against strong, even fields of color. It is not always necessary to show details in shadows.

MIRROR EFFECTS

When photographing buildings near water, frame the image to maximize the symmetrical effect, especially if the water is clear and still.

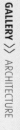

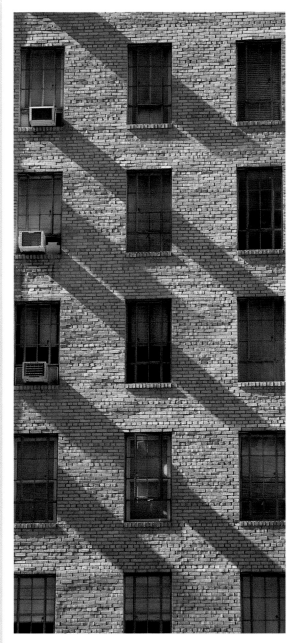

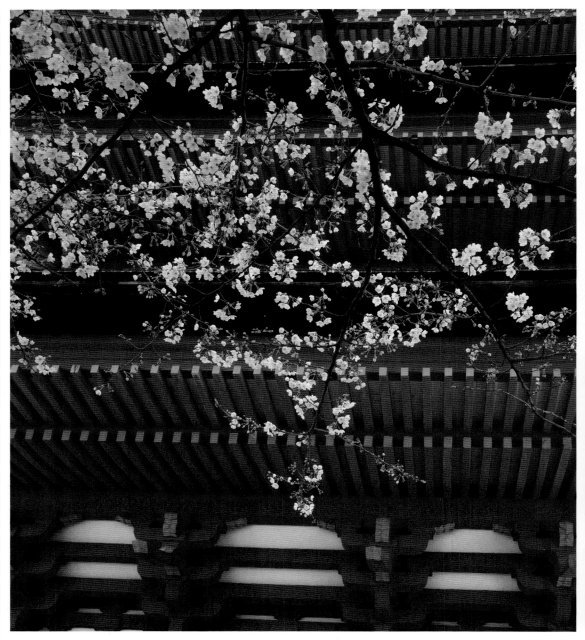

POWER OF PATTERNS

Any urban environment may offer regularly repeating patterns of simple shapes. Create strongly graphic images by isolating them in your shot.

ALTERNATIVE FOCUS

For an unusual take on a building, look for interesting contrasts. Here, the delicate cherry blossoms highlight the geometry of the temple's red eaves.

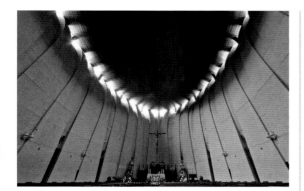

WIDE INTERIORS

Some interiors work best when photographed in wide angle. Alternatively, you can take a series of shots and stitch them together on a computer.

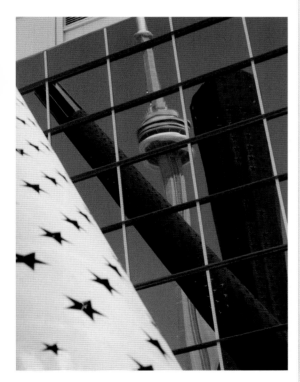

VISUAL INTEREST

Try showing modern buildings juxtaposed and overlapping with their neighbors to create a visual puzzle and, therefore, a more intriguing image.

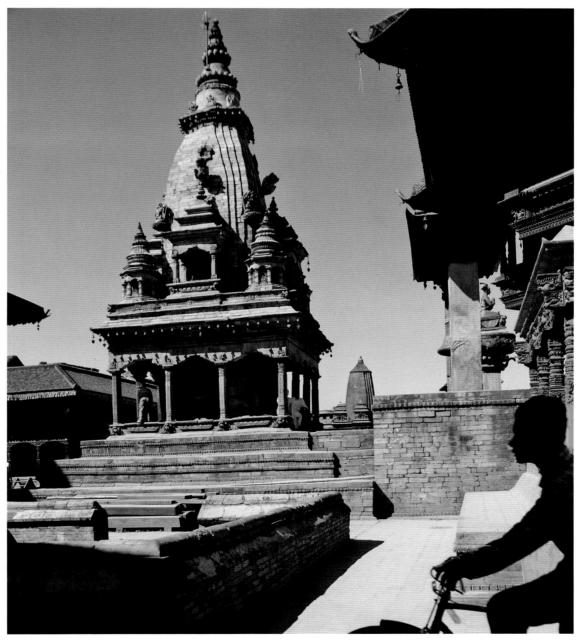

EXPLOITING NATURAL LIGHT

Taking photographs in bright sunlight can be tricky, but you can exploit its effects. Here, the hard shadows and the silhouette add depth and contrast.

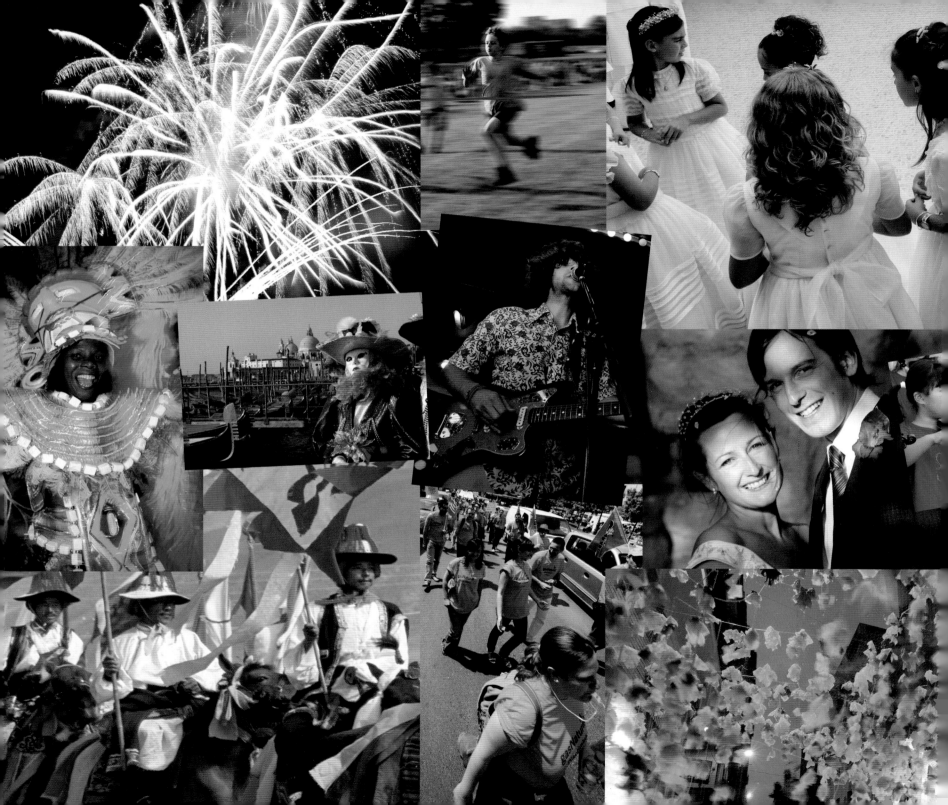

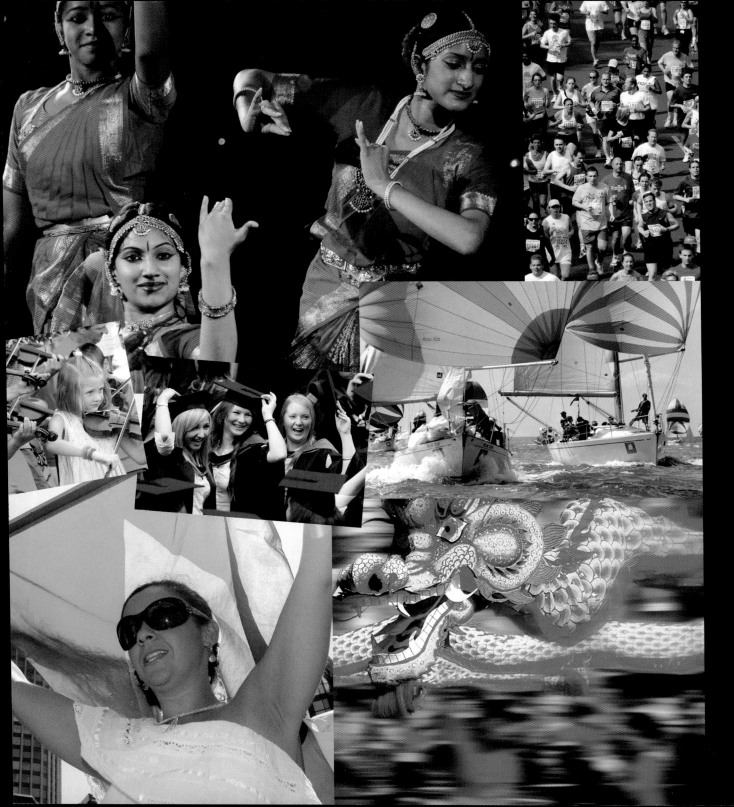

Events

12345678

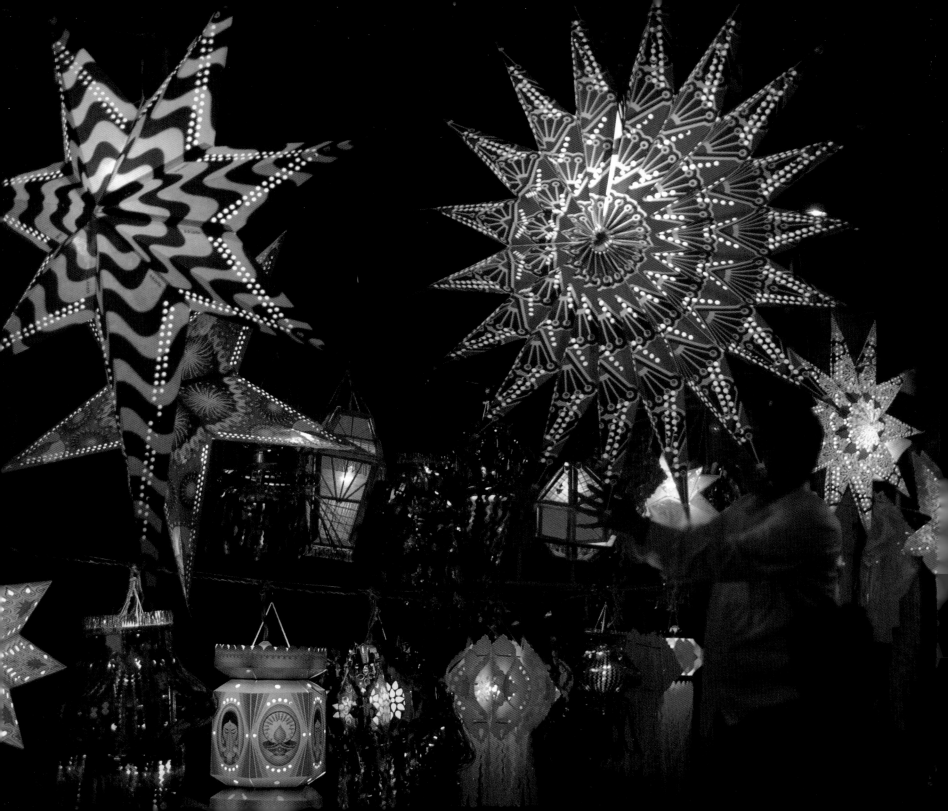

Events can be big or small, formal or informal. They run the gamut from a child's birthday party to a sporting spectacle. But regardless of the scale and type of event, cameras will always be present. Photography has become an essential part of any gathering. The ability of photography to transcend the documentary to enshrine, and even recapture in memory, the event being recorded means that the key moments in our lives all seem to call for a photographer. You will learn that to create successful images, not only will you use all the elements of photography such as color and light, composition and timing, focus and zoom, you must also plan for all eventualities and be able to rise to unexpected challenges.

An explosion of color

Still photography can be very successful at capturing the dazzling beauty of fireworks, for the same reason that these spectacular effects are stunning to look at with the naked eye. Against the darkness of the night sky, any sudden burst of bright light and vivid colors appears even more brilliant. Use a long exposure to capture the fireworks' trajectories, or a short shutter time to catch the exact moment the fireworks explode.

THE RIGHT EXPOSURE

A common problem when photographing fireworks is ending up with images that show illuminated smoke rather than an explosion of lights and colors. A long exposure will counter that issue – but not too long, or it can lead to blurred light trails, while too short an exposure leads to short light trails. Use the aperture to control the exposure.

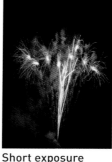
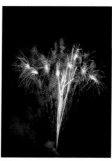

Short exposure　　**Long exposure**

CHECK THE LOCATION
Before the fireworks show begins, and while there is still some daylight, visit the location to find the best vantage points. Here, the lake offered a promising foreground.

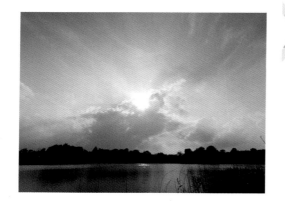

SET UP IN ADVANCE
For relatively long exposures, you will need to use a tripod to support the camera. Set this up while there is still light. Here I kept the camera fairly low to catch reflections from the fireworks in the lake.

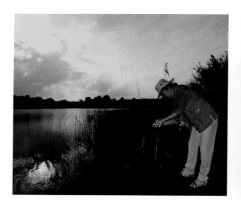

SET THE CAMERA
You will be working in the dark, so carry a small flashlight to help you make your settings. Turn flash and, if possible, auto-focus off. Use the manual exposure control.

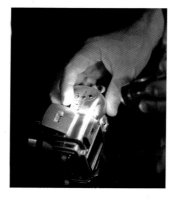

EXPERIMENT EARLY ON IN THE SHOW
Fireworks usually build up to a big climax, so use the early stages to perfect your framing and exposure times. Lean lightly on the camera and tripod during exposure to ensure a steady shot.

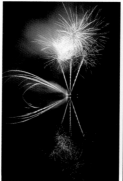
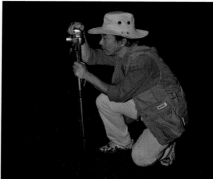

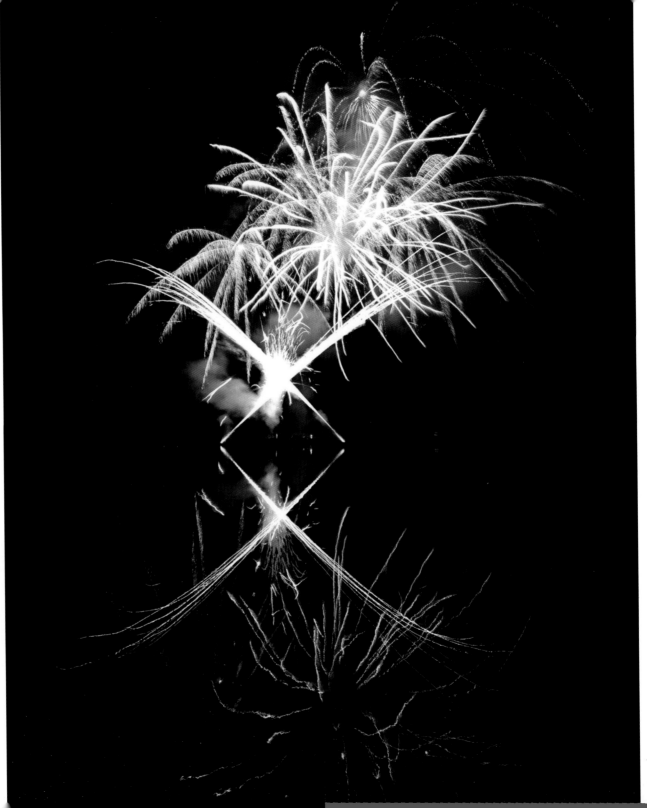

 FOR THIS SHOT
I set the zoom to normal, with a low to medium sensitivity to ensure the best image quality. With the autofocus switched off, I set the manual exposure mode to f/5.6 and ¹/₁₅ sec, then forced the flash off.

CAMERA MODE

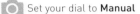 Set your dial to **Manual**

LENS SETTING

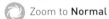 Zoom to **Normal**

SENSOR/FILM SPEED

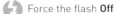 Use a **Low** ISO setting

FLASH

Force the flash **Off**

 GET THE TIMING RIGHT
Depending on your camera, you might need to press the shutter while the rocket is going up or at the moment it explodes, so that you catch the best effect.

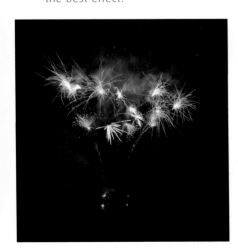

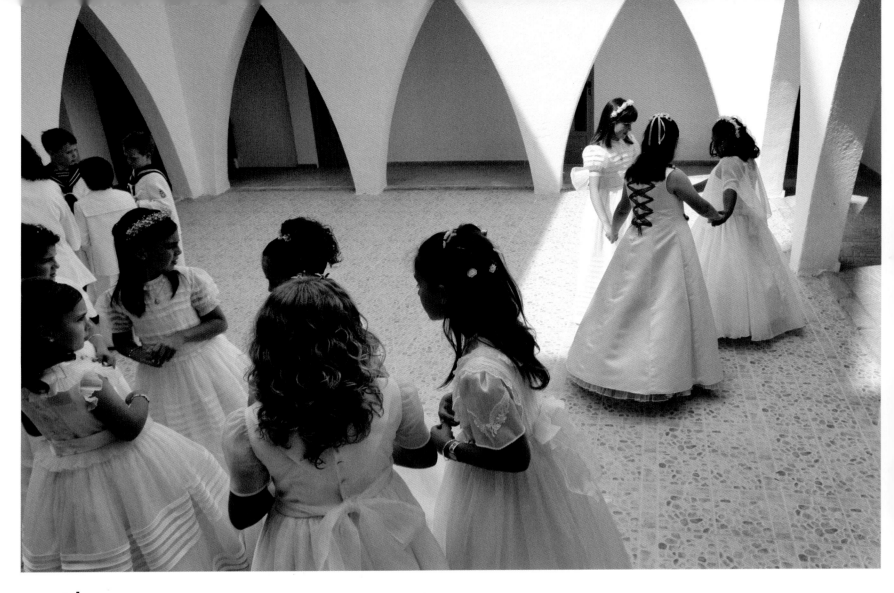

Milestone moments

In most cultures and religions, there are ceremonies and events in which children are dressed in special costumes and are the focus of attention for the day. Such occasions are as important for the rest of the family as they are for the children involved. Try to capture the event as a whole, showing the child taking part in a ritual shared with peers, friends, and classmates. This approach is demanding, but it will provide a rich, comprehensive record of the event.

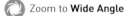
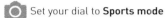
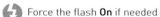
1 BE PREPARED

Investigate the venue before the event, so that you understand how the light falls, where people will enter or wait, and so on. While you are there, try to introduce yourself to someone official. This is also a good time to find out whether there are any restrictions on where and when to shoot.

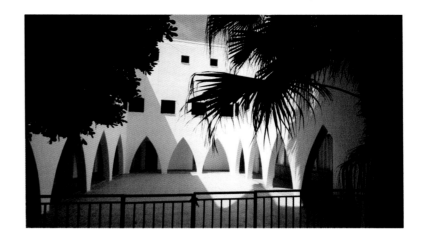

2 BE AWARE OF OTHERS

On the day, lots of friends and families will be trying to take pictures. Be considerate to others while still trying to secure the best position for your own photographic needs.

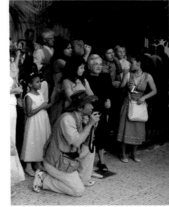

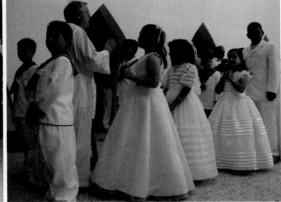

3 FIND THE LITTLE DETAILS

Look for telling moments that speak of the emotion, nervousness, or intimacy involved in the event being recorded.

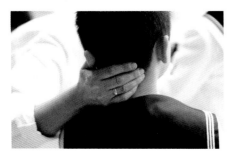

4 MOVE OVERHEAD

In crowds, a view from above is always an advantage. Hold the camera high above your head when shooting. With young children, this also emphasizes how small they are.

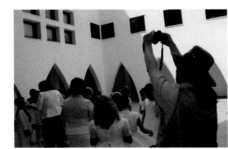

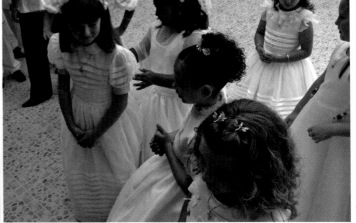

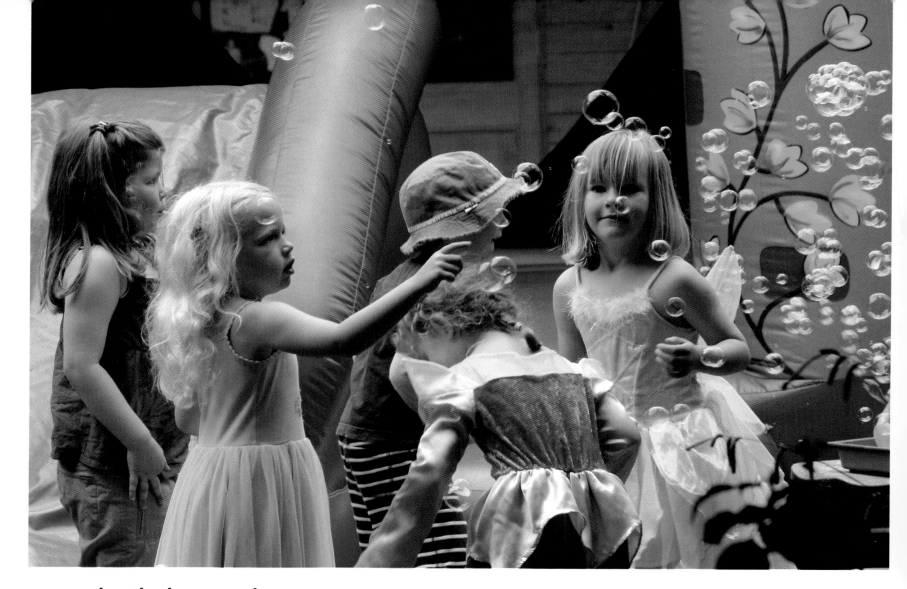

A children's party

As an adult at a children's party, it is likely that you will be banished to the sidelines. Use this opportunity to pay attention to the activities of the little ones, and you may be able to capture many delightful candid moments.

Keep an eye on the background or context in which the children are playing, and remember that there is a natural rise and fall in the intensity of children's games: watch the development of any activity so you can catch it as it peaks.

FOR THIS SHOT

I wanted to remain as inconspicuous as possible, so I set the zoom to maximum telephoto, which also flattened the perspective. With sensitivity set to medium-high because it was a slightly dull day, the flash was not necessary.

CAMERA MODE

Set your dial to **Program mode**

LENS SETTING

Zoom to **Maximum Telephoto**

SENSOR/FILM SPEED

Use a **Medium** ISO setting

FLASH

Force the flash **Off**

CONSIDER THE OPTIONS

Start by watching the proceedings from a distance rather than rushing into the thick of the action. Here, this approach enabled me to discover other appealing supplementary shots before moving in closer.

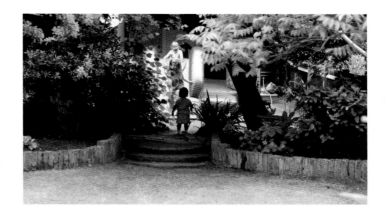

GET CLOSER TO THE ACTION

Move to where the main activity is taking place. Take individual portraits of the children, trying to capture amusing expressions, as well as group shots that reveal the fun of the party.

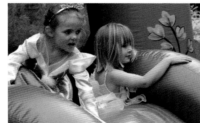
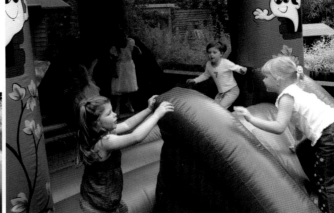

CHANGE THE SETTINGS

Once you find the close-up viewpoint you are most happy with, adjust your camera's settings accordingly—you may not have time to do so once the action starts to unfold. It is also a good idea to decide on a zoom setting and stick with it, changing it only if the situation changes.

MOVE PROPS AS NECESSARY

The bubble machine was a great attraction. In its original location, however, the background was rather dull. Moving it close to the bouncy castle, with its gaudy decoration, created just the right setting for the shot.

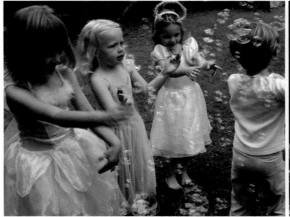
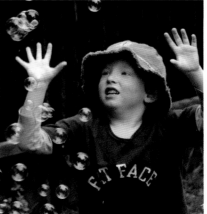

Wedding photography

Every married couple takes great pleasure in looking back at the photographs of their wedding day, so it is essential that these capture love, joy, and excitement. The bride and groom will be aware of their guests' desire to take pictures. However, to avoid the photography becoming a chore at a time of celebration, be sure to handle it with care and discretion. Planning ahead will help you get the best shots with minimal fuss—but keep the process light and fun.

1 POSITION THE COUPLE
If you have done your homework, you will have already established suitable locations. An archway, for example, can be used to frame the couple within a neutral background and offers soft curves and lighting variations.

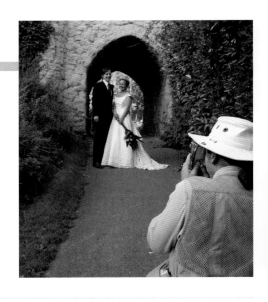

2 KEEP IT FUN
Encourage the couple to act naturally and spontaneously. Keep them amused with a little fun banter, but avoid photographing them while they are speaking, or you may end up with blurred facial features.

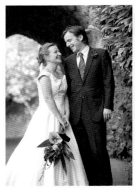
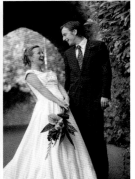

3 TAKE CANDID SHOTS
Keep shooting even when the bride and groom are not posing for you. What may initially look like an awkward composition through your viewfinder may candidly capture the affection between the couple more than a posed shot.

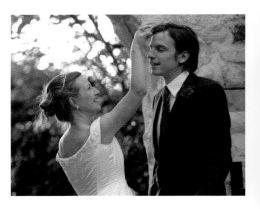

4 MOVE ON
Don't stay in one place, but stroll gently along to different locations, following the light. Try different perspectives as well, such as photographing from a higher viewpoint, through trees, or with a wide-angle zoom.

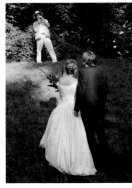
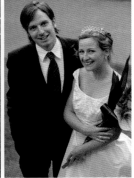

5 AVOID DISTANCE
Small differences in positioning that seem natural at the time may appear odd on closer inspection. This is because distances between people in pictures look greater than they really are. So ask the couple to stand as close to one another as possible.

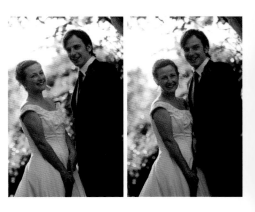

FOR THIS SHOT

A low to medium sensitivity ensured good picture quality, and I reduced the color saturation to give an accurate representation of the delicate flesh tones. I zoomed in to concentrate on the faces and used fill-in flash.

CAMERA MODE

 Set your dial to **Portrait mode**

LENS SETTING

Zoom to **Normal** to **Telephoto**

SENSOR/FILM SPEED

Use a **Low** to **Medium** ISO setting

FLASH

Force the flash **On**

PLAY WITH LIGHT

Experiment with available light. Soft, dappled sunlight produces an unusual and attractive effect, emphasizing only some features.

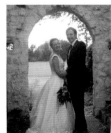

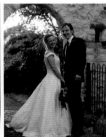

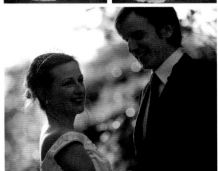

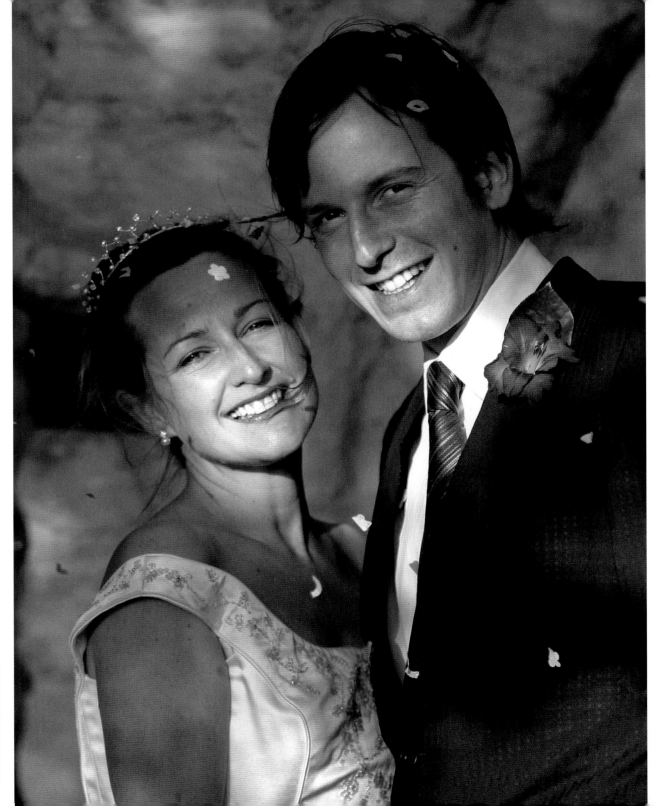

Wedding-day details

As a celebration that is central to most cultures, a wedding is full of rites, customs, costumes, and festivities. All of these elements provide the potential for a wealth of wonderful photographic compositions. Your coverage of a wedding, therefore, can document anything from details of dresses and decorations, to the spirit of celebration and the rituals and ceremonies that are central to the event.

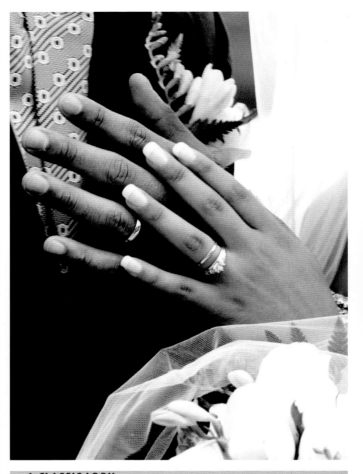

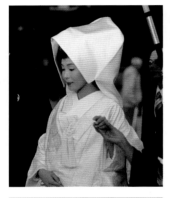

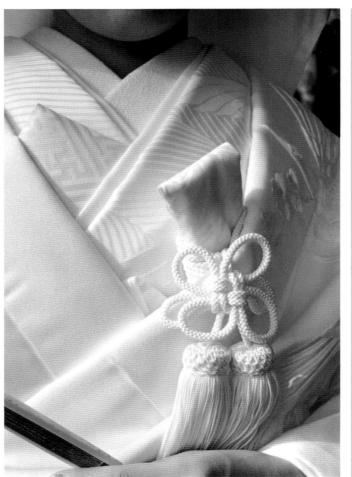

EXQUISITE DETAIL

The bride's dress is an important part of the wedding, so show it in its entirety, but focus on small details such as embroidery and trimmings, too.

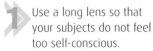 Use a long lens so that your subjects do not feel too self-conscious.

Expose for the skin tones to ensure accurate rendering of white fabrics.

A CLASSIC LOOK

It is always worth having some black-and-white images among your wedding pictures. The neutral tones confer a timelessness to the photographs.

Take photographs in color and convert a selection to black and white later.

Experiment with tone and contrast when converting images to black and white.

Ensure the blacks are dark and the whites carry some detail. Your mid-tones will then be accurate.

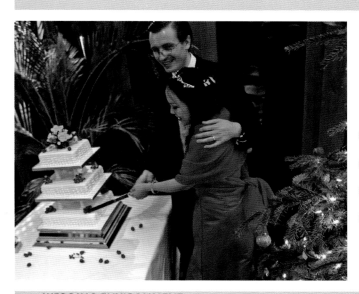

CRUCIAL MOMENTS

At key points in the day, such as the cutting of the cake, there is likely to be a rush for the best vantage points. You may even have to hold your camera above the crowd.

> Get into position early if it is possible without being unceremonious.

> Set a high ISO and turn off the flash for the best-quality lighting.

WEDDING ENVIRONMENT

As well as the participants, weddings also transform the space in which they take place, so take pictures of the decorations and table settings, too.

> Try using both maximum and minimum depth of field for different feels to the images.

> Use natural light to capture all the colors and details of the day.

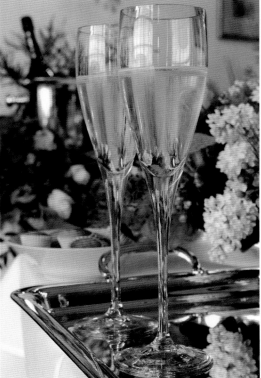

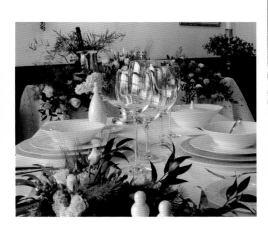

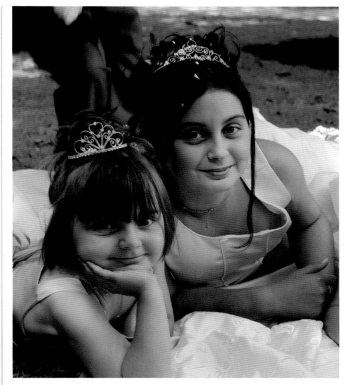

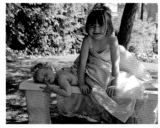

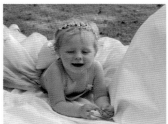

SECONDARY PLAYERS

Although children may play a relatively small role in the ceremony, they often provide the most delightful pictures, so be sure to photograph them.

> Avoid using flash: the light is unkind to the subtle tones of children's skin.

> Use a long zoom setting if you wish to minimize background clutter.

> Avoid taking portraits under trees, since this can give skin a green tone.

FOCUS ON THE FLOWERS

One of the most popular photographic subjects on the big day is the floral arrangement—in particular, the bride's bouquet. Make sure you capture it in a variety of pictures, along with other elements that embody the whole event.

1 Zoom into the flowers, but include the dress and the bride's hands for context.

2 On sunny days, use fill-in flash to help reduce the strength of shadows.

3 White dresses and black suits can mislead the camera: measure the right exposure from the skin tones.

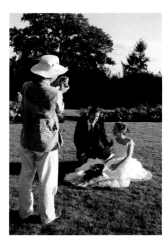

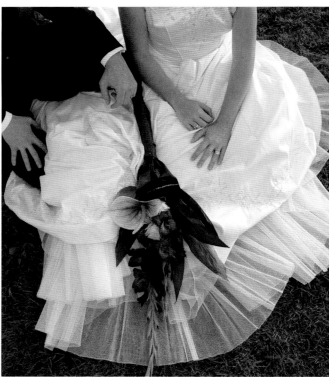

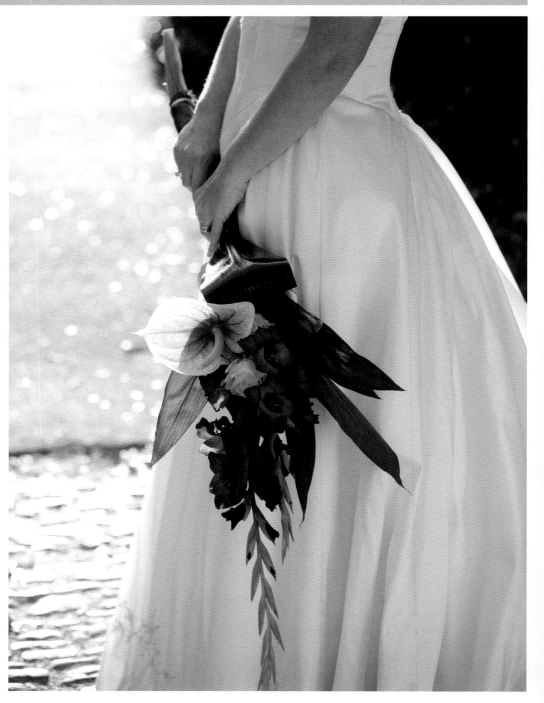

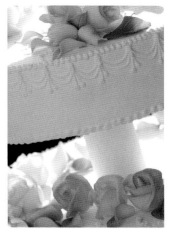

BACKSTAGE ACTIVITY

The preparatory activities before the wedding are ideal subjects for candid photography. Pictures of the bride in a reflective mood provide a nice counterpoint to more traditional wedding pictures.

> Use this opportunity to get close to the action, since there may not be enough room for a long zoom.

> Use the flash only if lighting conditions demand it.

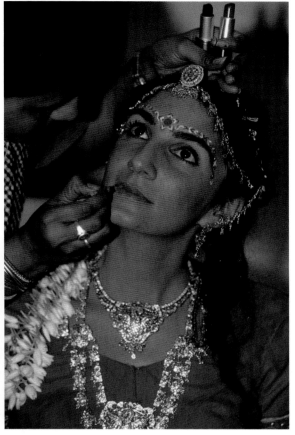

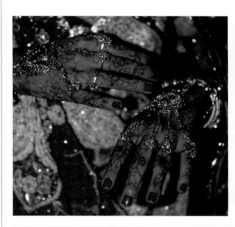

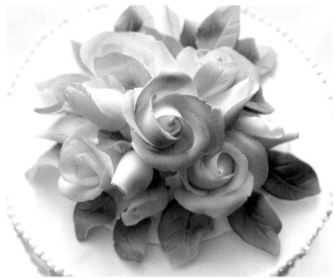

CAKE STUDY

Many wedding cakes are almost works of art. Approach this subject as you would a still-life project, and shoot from different angles and distances for a variety of compositions.

> Photograph the cake in soft, open light, such as that from a window.

> Overexpose a little to ensure pure white elements are rendered white.

> Set the highest image quality and low ISO for the finest details.

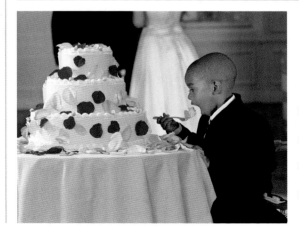

CANDID SHOTS

For really successful wedding photography, it is necessary to disengage from the festivities from time to time in order to observe the actions of some of the other guests.

> Use a long zoom to reach into a room without getting in people's way.

> Turn off the flash if you wish to avoid drawing attention to yourself and capture candid moments.

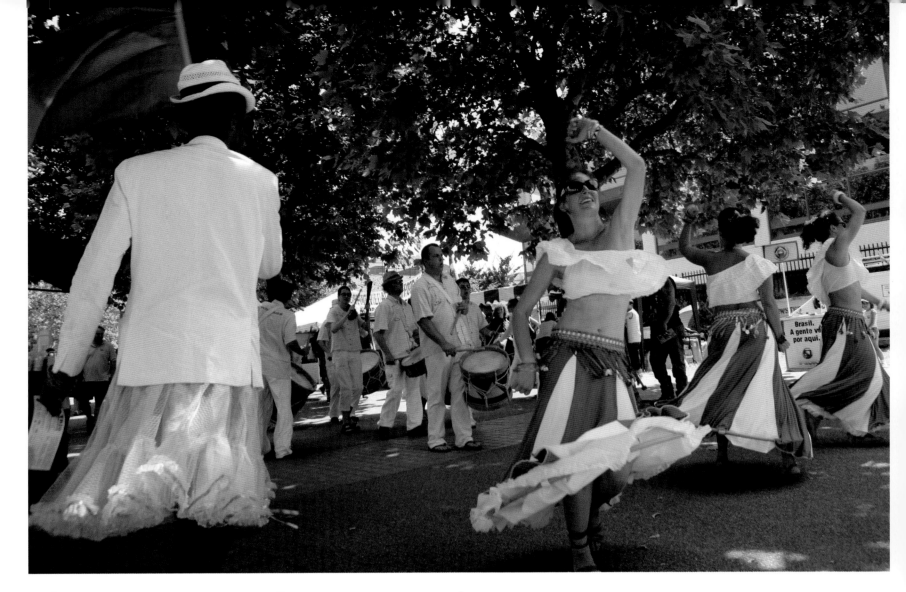

The spirit of carnival

Events such as carnivals, street parties, and parades create endless opportunities for lively, colorful images. Since everyone taking part in the celebrations expects to be photographed, you can almost guarantee interesting poses and smiling faces. In order to capture the truest spirit of the festivities, get into the middle of the action and just keep shooting. Your pictures will tap into the sense of fun that informs the occasion.

1 IMMERSE YOURSELF

Get right into the middle of the action, mingle, and move through the crowds. Most participants in the parade will be happy to have their picture taken, so you have no reason to feel inhibited. Smile and make eye contact with your subject: most people will smile back. If they don't, simply move on.

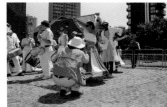

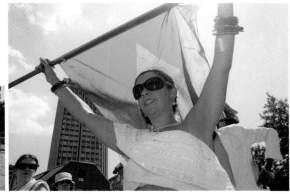

2 TAKE IT ALL IN

Photograph everyone: dancers, band members, and any flamboyant characters. You can also try various techniques, such as using the flash in the shade, or turning it off altogether. Consider taking shots from a higher vantage point, too.

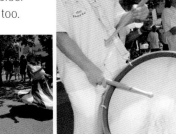

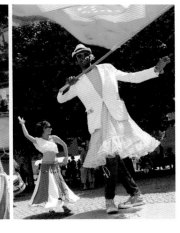

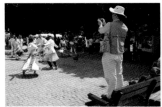

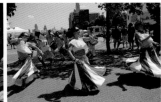

3 CHANGE YOUR POSITION

For variety, try shooting from a low viewpoint. This is especially useful for catching the swirling movement of the dancers' skirts.

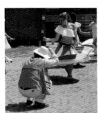

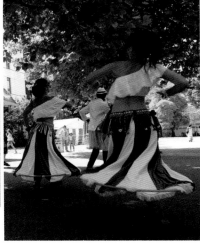

4 CAPTURE THE JOY

Make sure to get a sense of fun and celebration in your shots. Get up close to people enjoying themselves to capture their smiles. Use a wide-angle setting and do not worry about framing accurately—grabbing the moment is more important than careful composition.

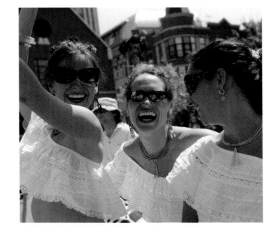

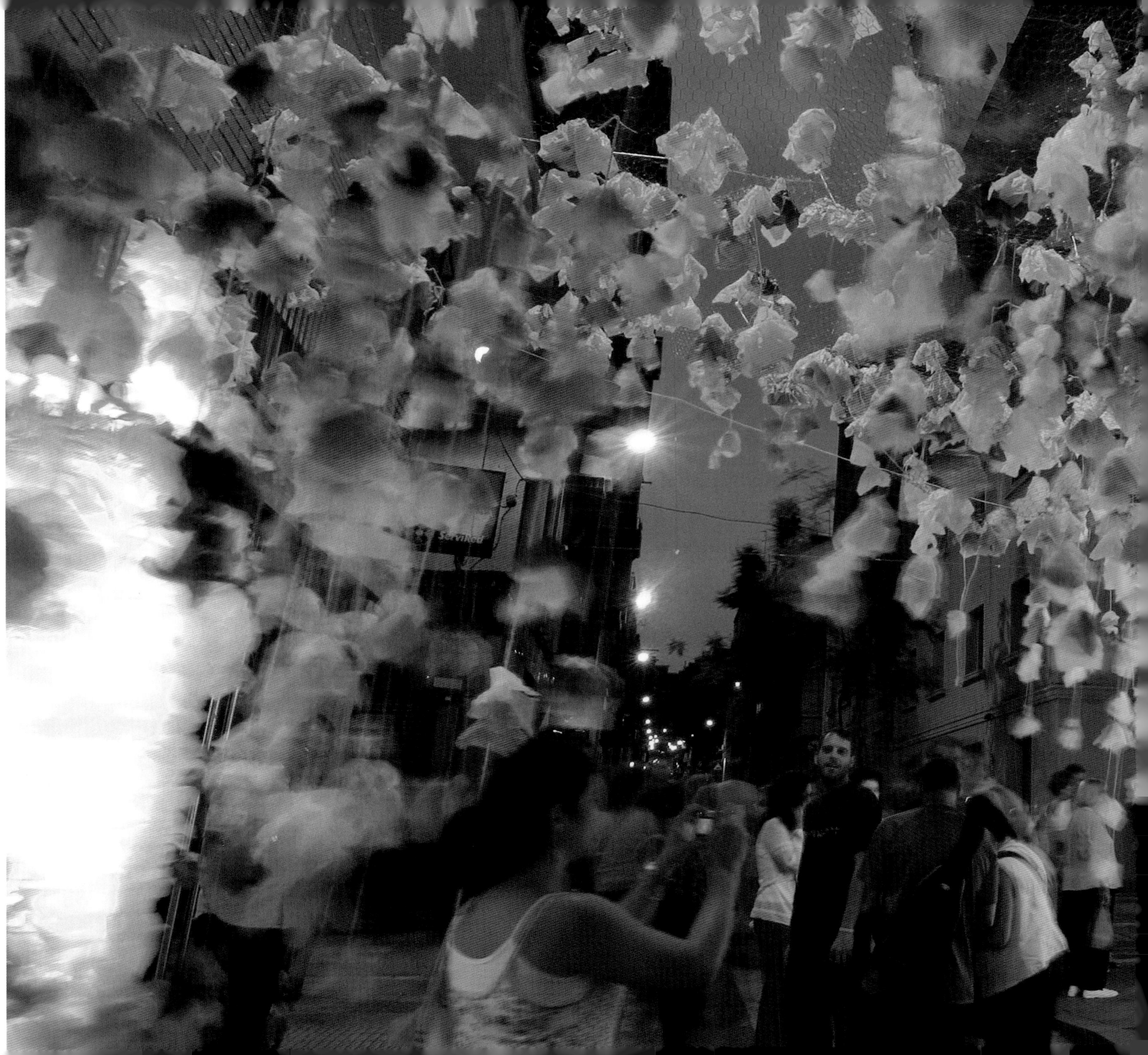

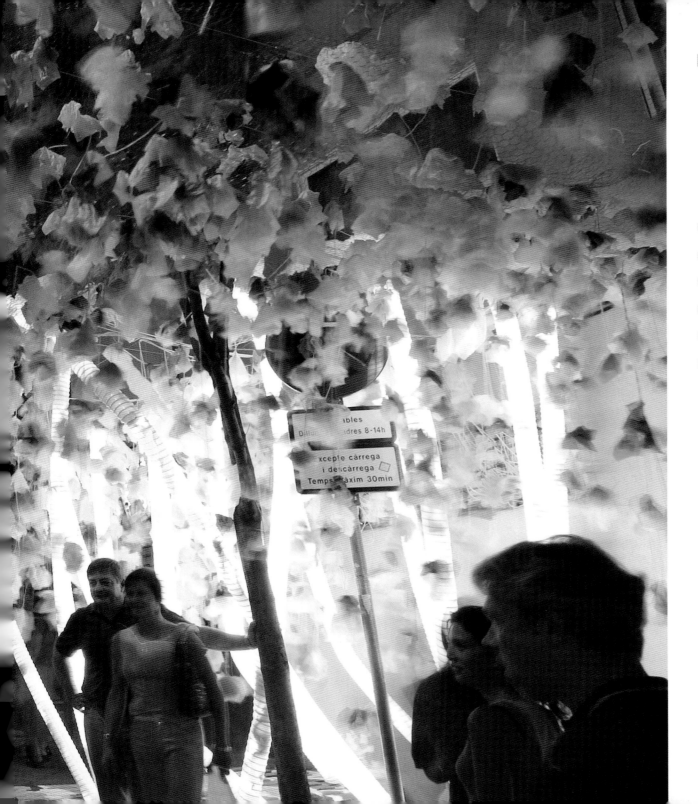

URBAN REVELS

There are many street festivals, such as Barcelona's Fiesta de Gràcia, that pit one street or one quarter of the city against another for the best, most colorful, and most elaborate decorations. These events are a gift to the traveling photographer.

1. Be sure to photograph people enjoying the festival, as well as the street decorations.

2. Use the full range of camera settings and try out lots of different viewpoints.

3. Use the LCD on your camera to show the locals your pictures. Some people may direct you to even better locations.

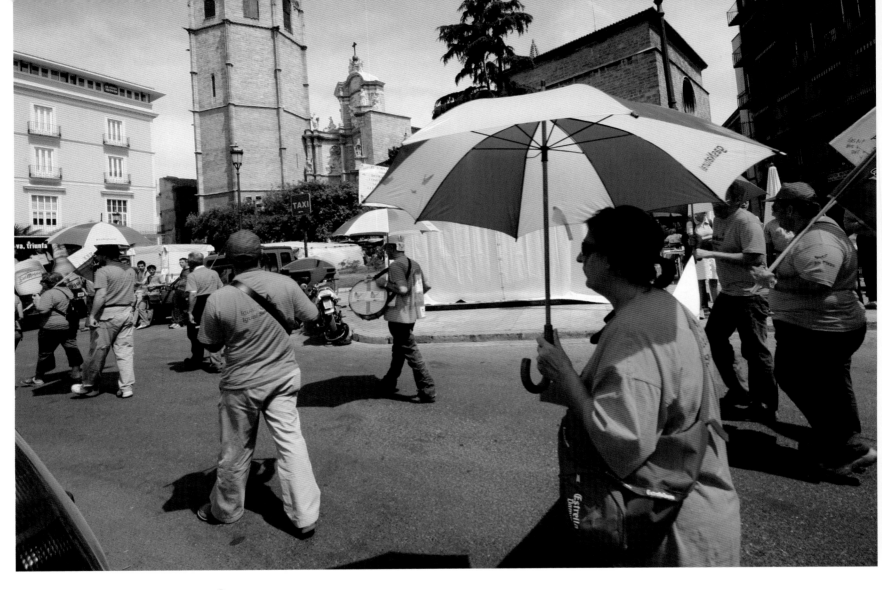

A street demonstration

You may be involved in a march because it highlights a cause that is close to your heart, or you may simply be an interested bystander. Either way, the chance to document a demonstration should not be missed. Those involved in the march can use the pictures on the campaign's website, in pamphlets, and to raise awareness in the media. The need, then, is to ensure that you obtain colorful, well-composed images that help promote the cause.

FOR THIS SHOT

I moved inside the procession and used a wide-angle zoom setting to capture the marchers and create a colorful, graphic composition. Flash helped fill in the shadows, but the bright sun ensured a good depth of field.

CAMERA MODE

Set your dial to **Sports mode**

LENS SETTING

Zoom to **Wide Angle**

SENSOR/FILM SPEED

Use a **Medium** to **High** ISO setting

FLASH

Force the flash **On**

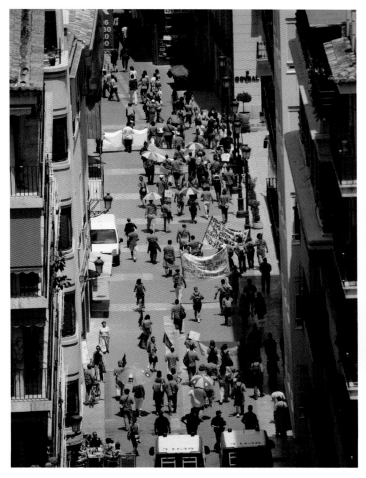

POSITION YOURSELF

If possible, reconnoiter the path that the march will take. High vantage points that offer good views are useful, but remember that you'll need time to return to street level. If you have just chanced upon the demonstration, it might be wise to stick with the crowd.

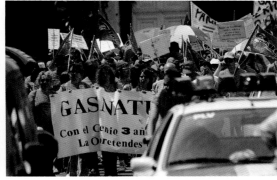

COMPRESS THE VIEW

Use a long focal-length setting and photograph from the front. The spatial compression gives the impression of greater numbers in a small group.

SHOOT FROM ABOVE

Take alternative views of the location and marchers by holding the camera high above your head on a wide-angle setting. Use a medium-high sensitivity setting to ensure extensive depth of field.

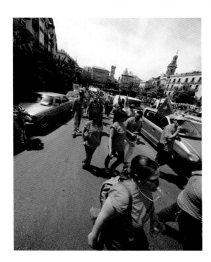

MIX WITH THE CROWD

To obtain a variety of images, you must mingle with the crowd, even if you are not involved. This calls for some physical fitness, since you will have to walk, stop, and perhaps crouch down to take a shot, then run to catch up and do it all again.

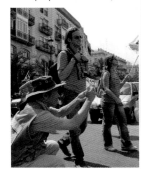

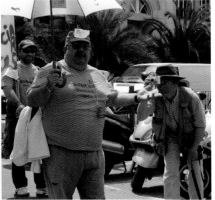

The magic of Christmas

Seasonal celebrations such as Chanukah, Diwali, Christmas, and Chinese New Year play an important cultural role in societies all around the world. These events also provide endless photographic opportunities, especially if you have children. You can capture the occasion just for the record, which will be valued by the family for years to come, or you could try to capture something of the sense of wonder and excitement experienced by the child.

FLASH OR NO FLASH?

The issue of whether to use flash or not must be considered on a case-by-case basis. If the mood and atmosphere are severely diminished or destroyed by flash, then do not use it. Christmas lights, for example, will look better in a dimly lit room with no flash, but you will have to work harder to obtain sharp pictures.

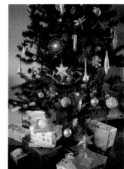
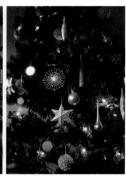

1 CHOOSE A VIEWPOINT
When photographing children, even small changes in viewpoint can make a big difference. From a grown-up height, the picture feels remote and impartially observed.

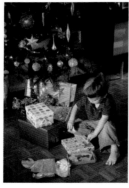
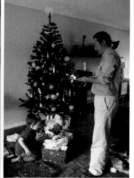

2 JOIN IN THE FUN
Move down to the child's level to interact with him and create some candid pictures. Join him under the tree with the presents, and help him with the wrapping paper.

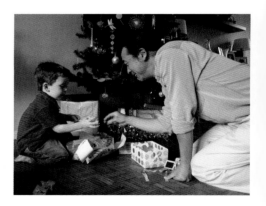

3 BE PATIENT
Some children are reluctant to be photographed. Do not insist on including them in every picture. Start wide to take in a general view, then move in on the details. The more photos you take, the less the child will notice that you are making him the star of your shoot.

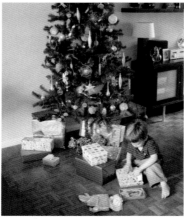
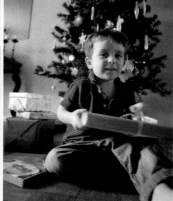
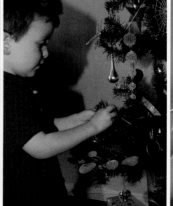
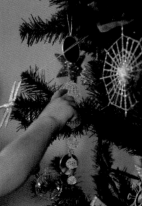

FOR THIS SHOT

I set a moderately long zoom to photograph the child without moving too close and disturbing him. I turned off the flash and used a high sensitivity for the sharpest results possible.

CAMERA MODE

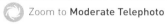 Set your dial to **Portrait mode**

LENS SETTING

Zoom to **Moderate Telephoto**

SENSOR/FILM SPEED

Use a **High** ISO setting

FLASH

Force the flash **Off**

DIRECT THE CHILD

To take a good close-up picture of the child and tree together, you may need to give the child some direction. Ask him to hang a few decorations, for example.

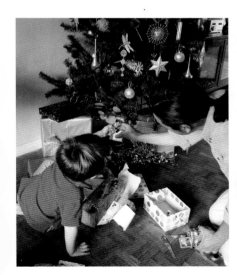

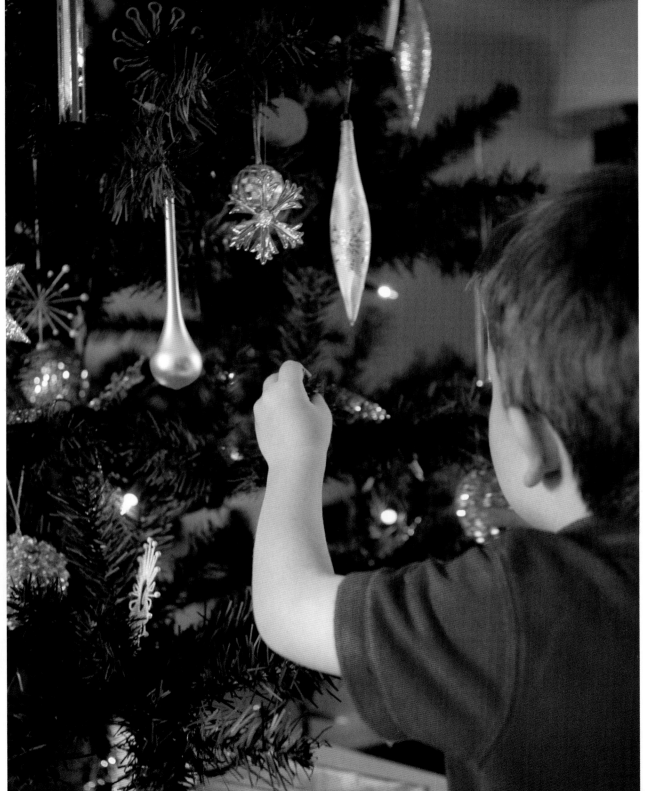

Festivals around the world

If you are traveling abroad, or even within your own country, try to time your visit with seasonal festivals. As well as stocking up on memory cards and spare batteries, your preparation should include learning about the festival in question and, if possible, taking a reconnaissance trip for the best vantage points beforehand. This way, you will know what to expect and where the best of the action is likely to take place.

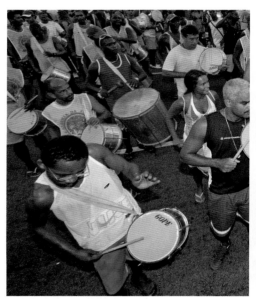

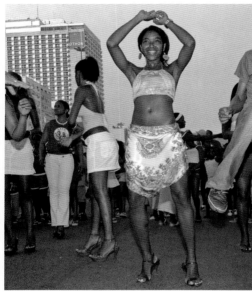

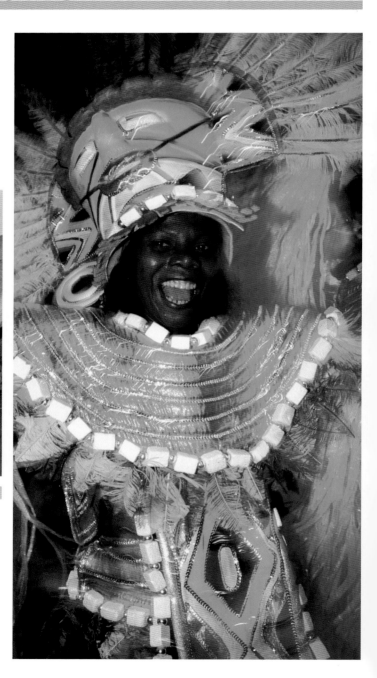

CARNIVAL EXCESS

Mardi Gras festivals are noted for their extravagance, high energy, and excesses, all in preparation for the abstinence of Lent. As a photographer, you will be as much part of the event as anyone else. Shoot freely and continuously: those reluctant to be photographed will be very few, and you will have no time to review pictures as you photograph.

1 Hold your camera high above your head to reach above the crowds and obtain a general view.

2 Shoot from street level too, since the low viewpoint helps to emphasize the liveliness of the dancing.

3 Use flash or short exposures to freeze the movement. You could also try longer shutter times for blur.

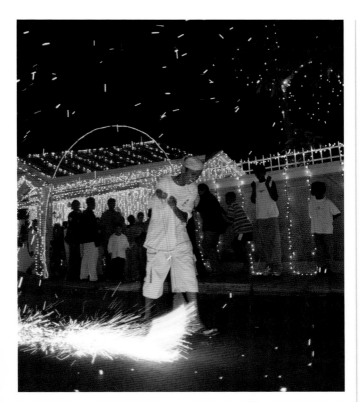

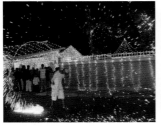

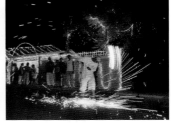

LIGHT IN DARKNESS

Nighttime festivals make full use of light—often as a symbol of the victory of good over evil. The dark background gives you the chance to write with light in a literal way, using long exposures for light trails. These pictures were taken at the Diwali Festival of Lights.

1 Use flash with long exposure to combine sharp elements and movement blur.

2 Check your initial shots: you may need to reduce exposure for solid blacks.

3 Use a small tripod to combine maneuverability with stability, if needed.

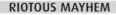

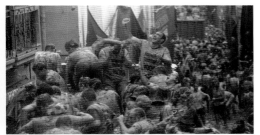

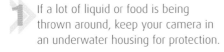

RIOTOUS MAYHEM

Some festivals take a few days to build up, but the climax may be over in under an hour. Such is the case with the Buñol Tomato Festival.

1 If a lot of liquid or food is being thrown around, keep your camera in an underwater housing for protection.

2 Capture the exuberance of the festival by getting right into the thick of the action.

3 Take general shots of the mayhem as well as portraits of individual revelers.

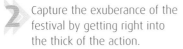

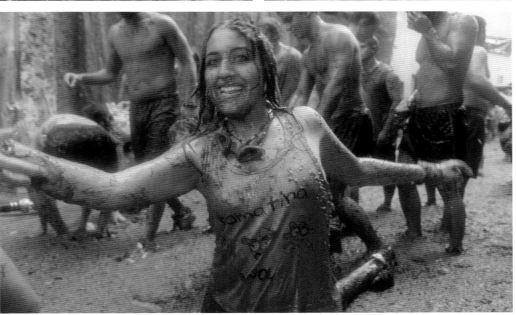

ACTION AND ANIMALS

Festivals involving horses – such as those held in Tibet, Mongolia, and parts of Central Asia – brilliantly combine local culture with the exciting display of sportsmanship. These images were taken at the Yushu Horse Festival in Tibet.

1 You may be quite far from the action, so use the longest zoom possible.

2 Ensure the sun is to one side or behind you when watching the main events.

3 Horses can kick up dust, so you need to protect your camera and replace the lens cap when not in use.

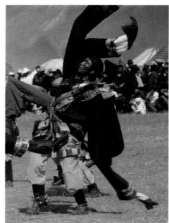
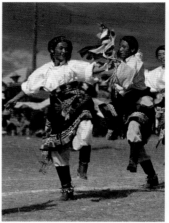
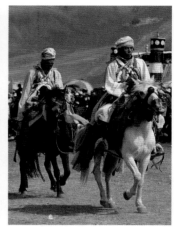

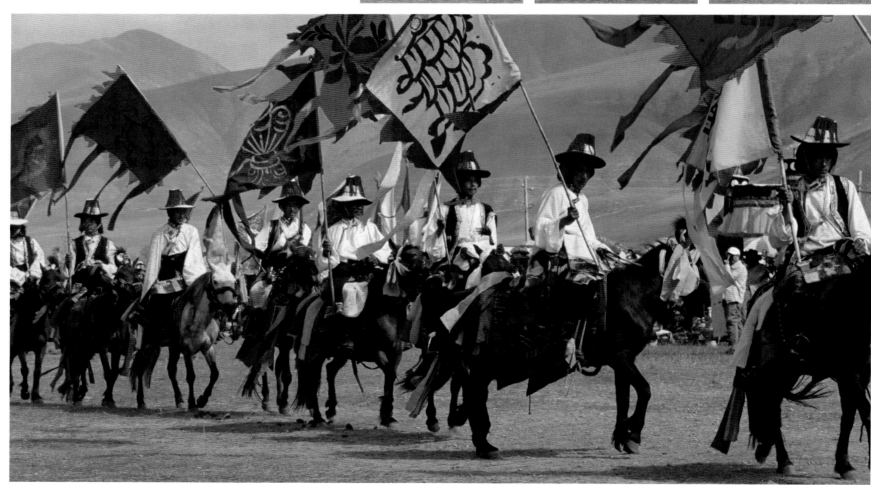

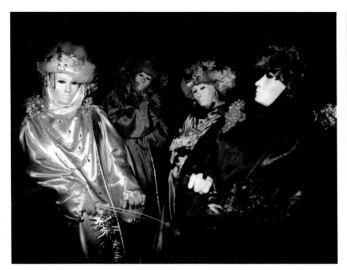

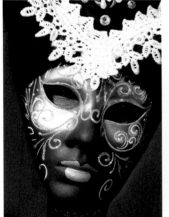

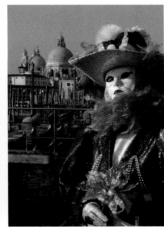

COLORFUL STREET PARTIES

Street festivities, such as the Chinese New Year revels, are easy to photograph because you are expected to take part. Follow the participants or focus on the decorations and banners.

> Experiment by strongly tilting the camera for unusual angles.

> To capture the sense of movement, try panning the camera during exposure.

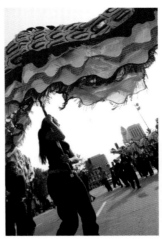

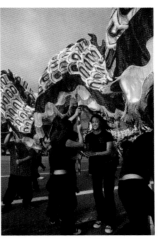

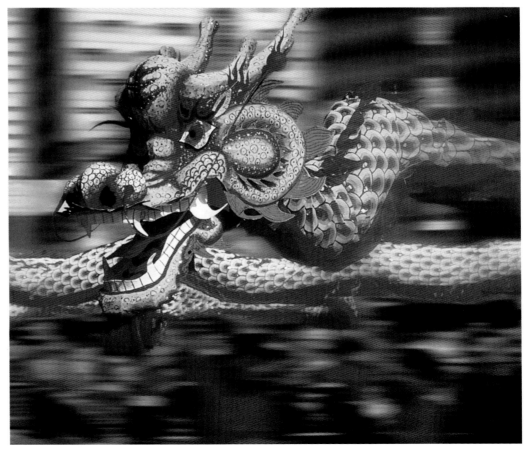

DRESSED TO IMPRESS

It is hard to go wrong with costume-based festivals, such as the Venice Carnival: everyone wants to pose for photographs, and the costumes are designed to be eyecatching.

> Use the flash to emphasize the graphic qualities of the costumes at night.

> Remember to include the context and the city in some of your shots.

> Get in close for dramatic portraits – this is one occasion when it is easy to do so.

Intimate music venues

While big-name music artists often ban photography at their shows, emerging musicians who play small concerts in the back rooms of bars usually have no objections to having their picture taken. If you are not a friend of the musicians, you can ensure a warm welcome by offering to give the management of the band or the venue a CD of your pictures. Once you develop a reputation, your passion for photography might even get you into concerts for free.

1 BE RESPECTFUL OF THE AUDIENCE

In a small venue, you can get very close to the artists on stage. Be aware of how your activities could impact on others' enjoyment of the show. Be as discreet and quiet as possible, changing position only between numbers.

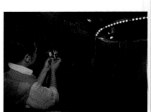
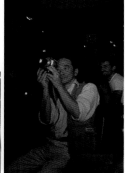

2 TAKE PICTURES OF THE CROWD

Intimate concerts are as much about the audience as the artists. For a well-rounded record of the evening, don't forget to turn around and capture a view of the crowd, or to take pictures from a vantage point at the back of the venue.

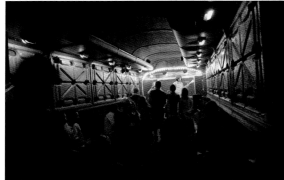
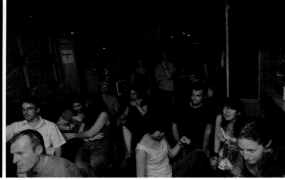

3 GET UP CLOSE AND PERSONAL

Get as close as you can to the stage. This will give you the chance to create individual portraits of the members of the band. Performers are rich subjects for photography, and your records could even become a valuable historical document of a band before it hit the big time.

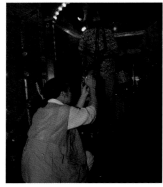
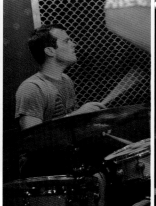
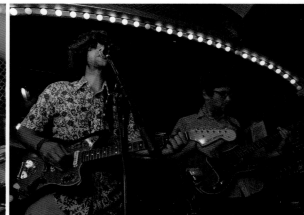

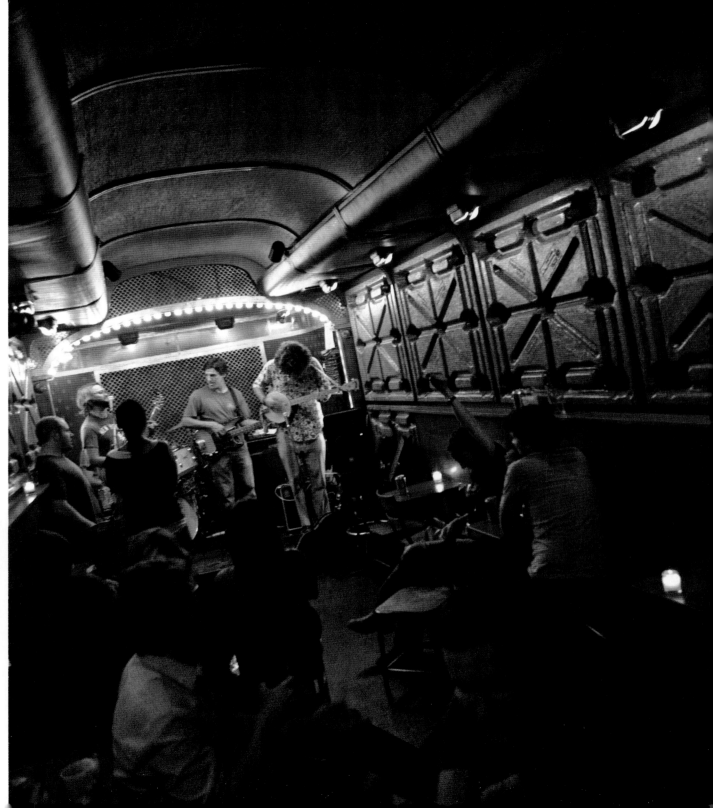

FOR THIS SHOT
I set the highest sensitivity available on my camera because the light levels were very low indeed. I used the lens at wide angle for maximum aperture and turned off the flash.

CAMERA MODE

 Set your dial to **any automatic mode**

LENS SETTING

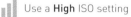 Zoom to **Wide Angle**

SENSOR/FILM SPEED

 Use a **High** ISO setting

FLASH

 Force the flash **Off**

4 AVOID USING THE FLASH
As well as killing the atmosphere, as in the image below, the flash is also distracting for both band and audience. Instead, rely on steady hands and a long exposure.

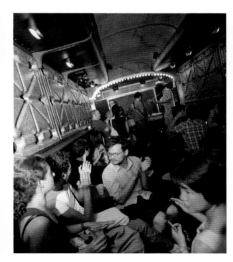

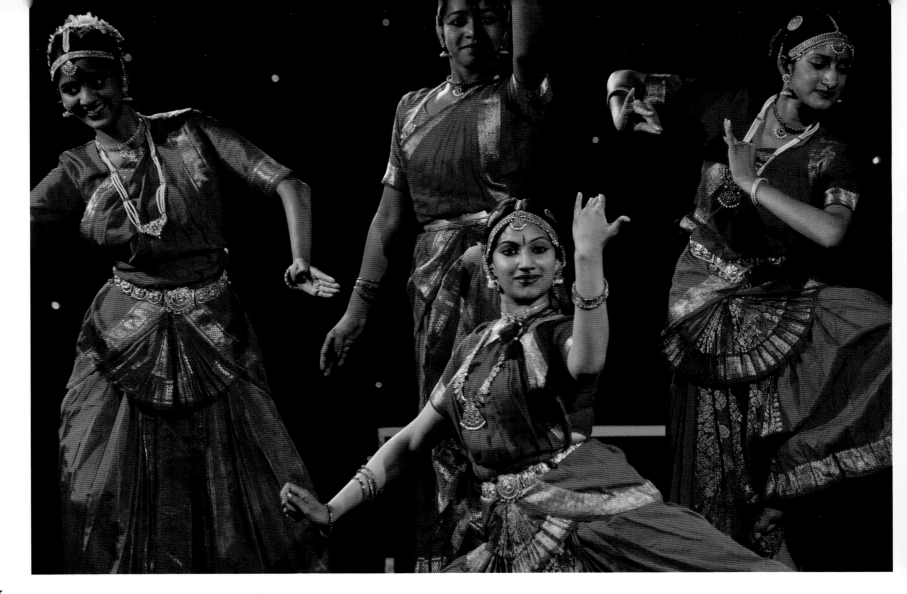

On-stage drama

Stage shows present several challenges to a photographer. Light levels are not as bright as they may seem, but contrast is so high that colors may be distorted. At most venues, even if you are allowed to take a camera into the show, you will not be allowed a tripod or flash. A long zoom is the solution for close shots, but its smaller maximum aperture may increase shutter times, so you will need to keep the camera steady to avoid blur.

FOR THIS SHOT

First I turned off the flash, as well as any camera sounds. Then, with a high sensitivity selected, I zoomed in to make a tight composition of the group, who were holding their pose for a few seconds.

CAMERA MODE

Set your dial to **Sports mode**

LENS SETTING

Zoom to **Medium** to **Long Telephoto**

SENSOR/FILM SPEED

Use a **High** ISO setting

FLASH

Force the flash **Off**

1 GET A CLEAR VIEW

Find a position that gives you a good view of the stage, while keeping out of other people's way. This may be at the back of the venue. Try to locate yourself centrally, since most of the action usually takes place center-stage.

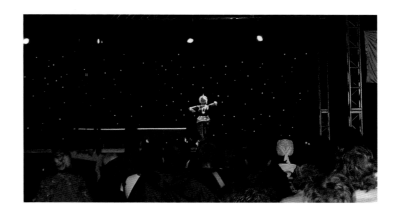

2 SET YOUR CAMERA

The single most important thing is to force the flash off. Use a high-sensitivity capture so that shutter times are short, and zoom to a medium-long telephoto.

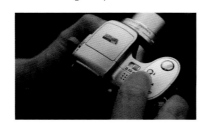

3 STEADY THE CAMERA

Whenever possible, hold the camera to your eye, since this helps keep the camera steady. If the audience's heads are showing up in your shots, lift the camera up for an unobstructed view, and use the LCD screen to compose your shot. You can also steady the camera by holding the strap taut.

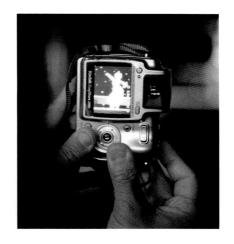

4 SHOOT THE SHOW

Once you are happy with your settings, focus on shooting the show. Follow individuals that attract your eye, or opt for a wider view of the whole stage. Indeed, try both. Review your images for quality at the beginning, but do not check your results as you shoot, since you will miss many photo opportunities.

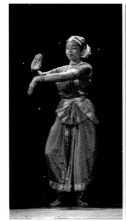

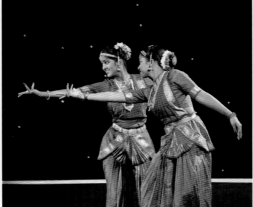

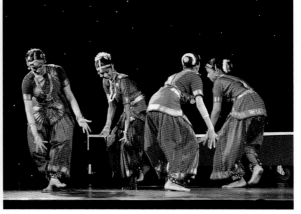

The thrill of the race

Any sports event with a large number of participants – a fun run, marathon, or triathlon – is a multilayered and adrenaline-fueled event that provides many photographic opportunities. There are several ways to approach this subject: you can capture the colorful masses of participants, the activities of the support teams, the bystanders, or individual portraits of the athletes. By that token, these events enable you to try out a wide range of photographic techniques.

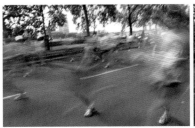 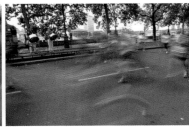

If you wish to freeze the motion of the runners, set very short exposure times. Exposures that are even only a little longer than normal will create a marked motion blur. If the shutter is open for too long, the runners all but disappear.

 ARRIVE EARLY
If you want to secure a prime location, get to the event with time to spare and work out where best to stand, taking trial shots to check composition.

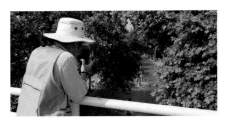

 TRY DIFFERENT SETTINGS
The lead runners will give you an indication of when the rest of the action will be passing. Try the effects of different zoom settings on an early group and pinpoint the best exposure to set for when the other runners arrive.

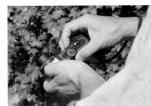 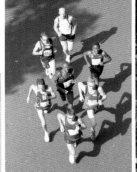 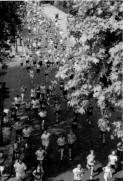

 EXPLORE DEPTH OF FIELD
For unusual effects, experiment with depth of field. For example, try focusing on a foreground element, this leaves the runners just distinct enough to make out.

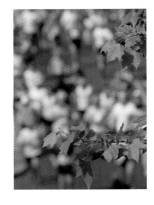

EXPLOIT YOUR POSITION
Shooting from a location above the action gives you the chance to try some unusual angles. However, when you are high up, never be tempted to lean over railings to get a shot.

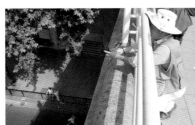 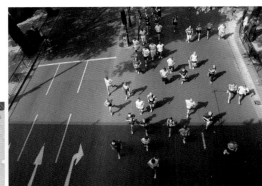

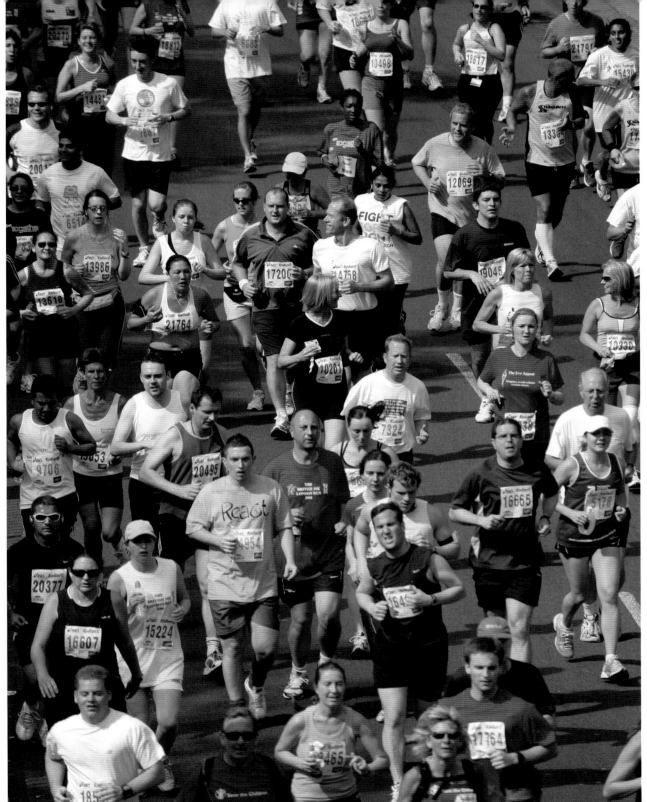

FOR THIS SHOT

In order to fill the frame with runners, I set the longest zoom on my camera. Sensitivity was set to low for high quality, but since the day was sunny, the exposure times were brief enough to freeze motion.

CAMERA MODE

Set your dial to **Program mode**

LENS SETTING

Zoom to **Maximum Telephoto**

SENSOR/FILM SPEED

Use a **Low** ISO setting

FLASH

Force the flash **Off**

5 FILL THE FRAME

Portray a sense of the masses by filling the frame with runners. Try to catch them exchanging glances and other such candid moments.

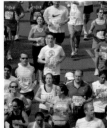
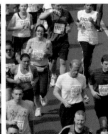
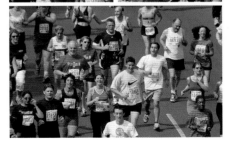

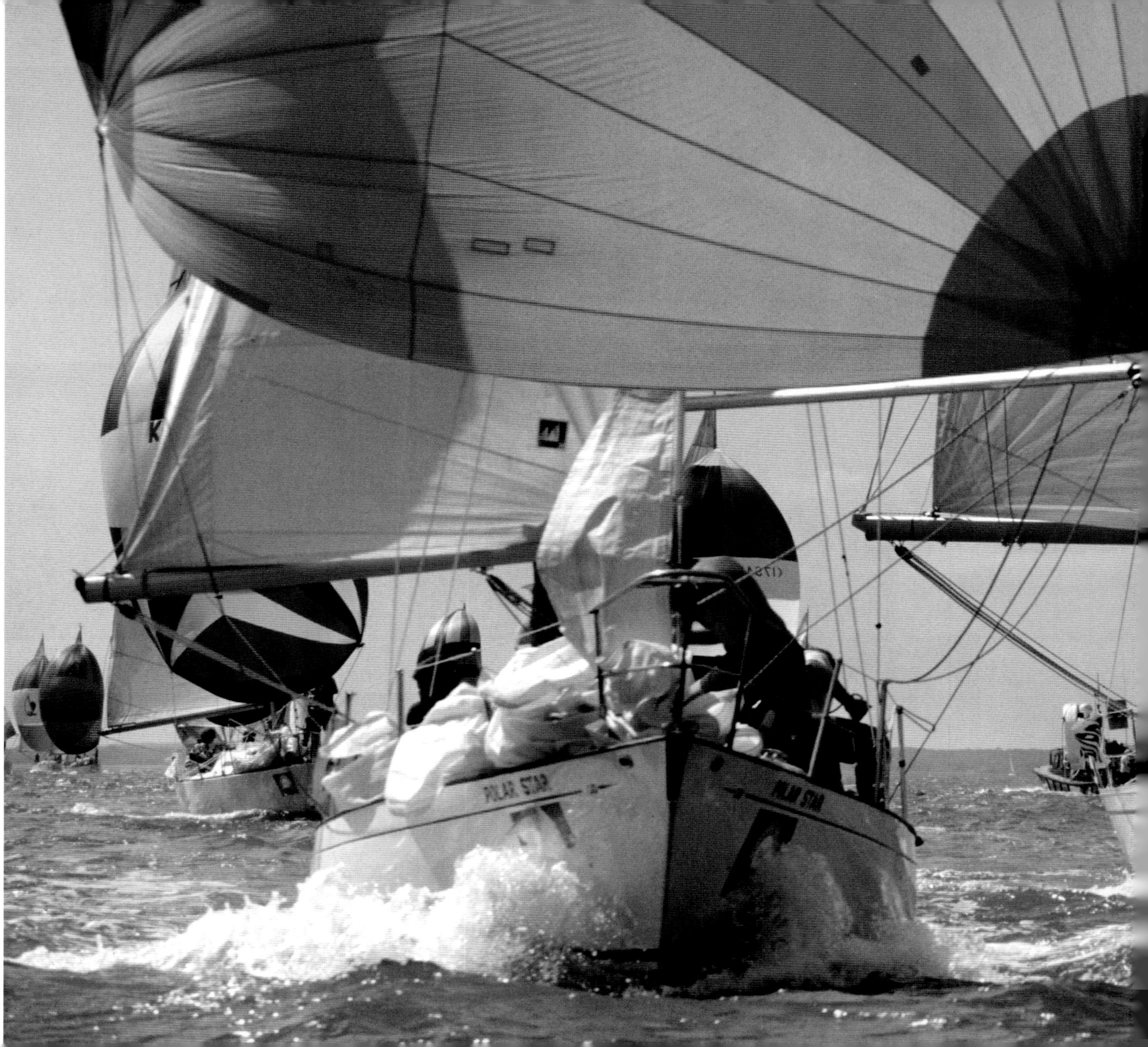
POLAR STAR

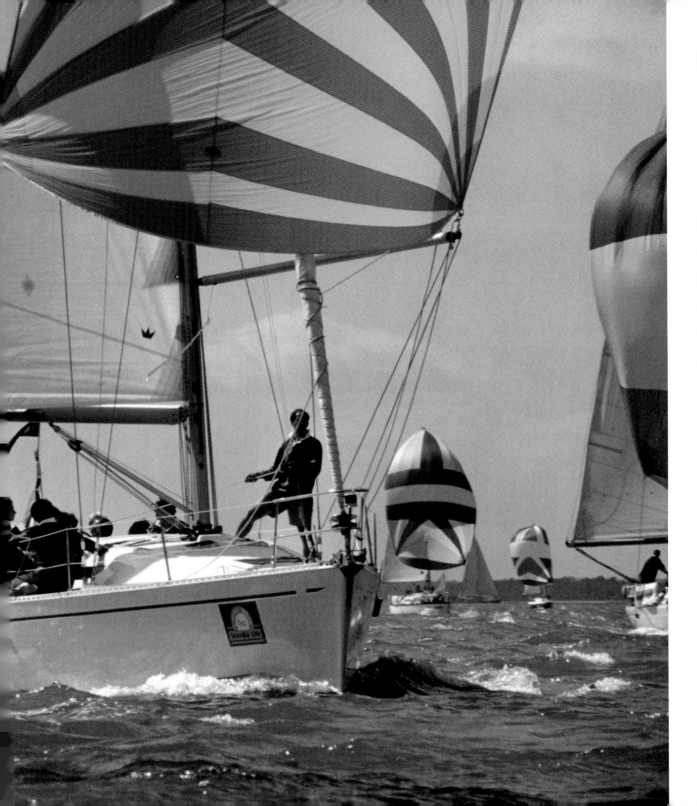

OPEN SAILS

The key to a stunning image such as this is all about access and little to do with photography. Once you have secured a place on a chase boat or a competing yacht, you need only adopt a good steady stance and keep taking pictures.

1 Set a long focal length for dramatic spatial compression of the elements of a scene.

2 Use a medium sensitivity for good image quality to allow short exposure times.

3 Protect your camera from water splashes by using a camera raincoat or a clear plastic bag.

A theatrical production

With their creation of parallel worlds, colorful spectacle, and intense emotions, plays offer a splendid opportunity for photography. However, it is extremely difficult to photograph theatrical performances successfully without upsetting other members of the audience and possibly the cast. The play's dress rehearsal is the best opportunity to capture a show: not only are the actors fully costumed, but at this stage, they usually enjoy a photographer's attention, too.

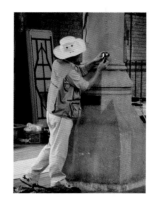

1 FIND STEADY SUPPORT
Try to be as inconspicuous as possible during the rehearsal. Turn the flash off and lean on any available support to keep yourself and the camera steady if the venue is dimly lit.

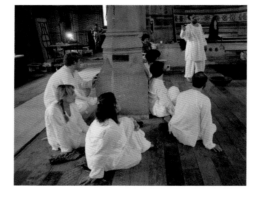

2 GET TO KNOW THE PLAY
Listening in on briefings and cast meetings will give you a good idea of what happens in the play and when. It will also help you determine the best positions from which to photograph the action.

3 GET CLOSE TO THE ACTORS
Take advantage of the fact that you don't have to worry about blocking the audience's view, but show respect for the actors' craft by turning off any camera sounds that might distract them.

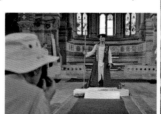

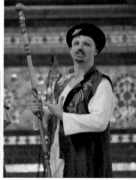

4 CAPTURE THE MOOD
As the actors become accustomed to your presence, you can move around more freely. Concentrate on capturing the atmosphere, the mood, and, indeed, the drama.

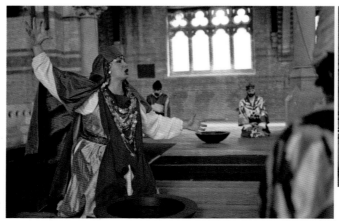

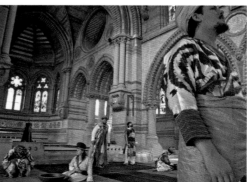

FOR THIS SHOT

I set a medium-long telephoto on the zoom and left it at that setting. With high ISO, no flash, and programmed auto-exposure, I could shoot rapidly. I waited for a dramatic moment with the actor against an interesting background.

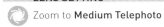 **CAMERA MODE**

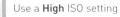 Set your dial to **Program mode**

LENS SETTING

Zoom to **Medium Telephoto**

SENSOR/FILM SPEED

 Use a **High** ISO setting

FLASH

Force the flash **Off**

5 BE AWARE OF SURROUNDINGS

You may want to include the venue in your compositions, especially if it's a photogenic location, since that will provide the most effective background to shots

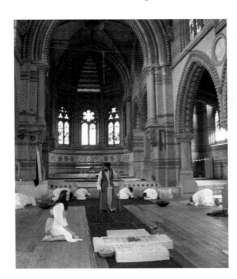

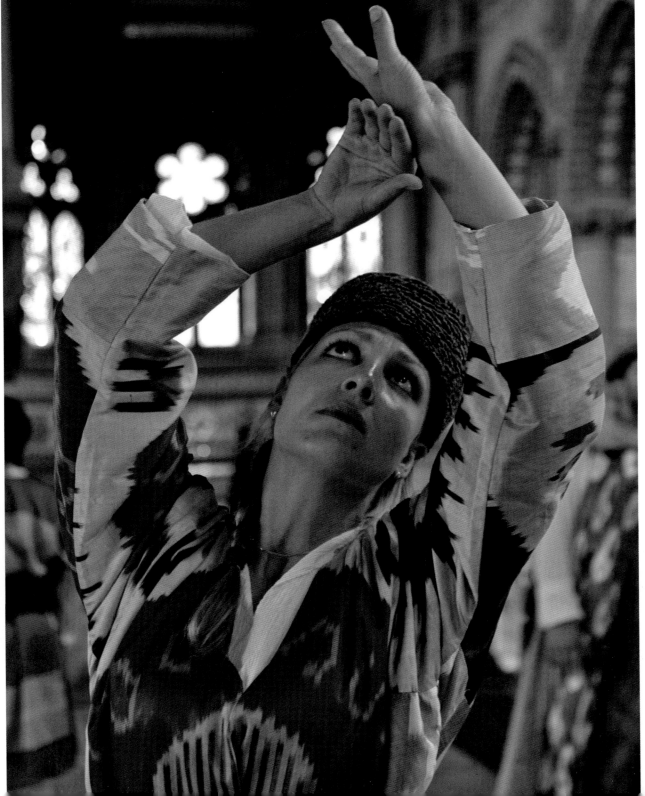

Events

Taking successful pictures of large gatherings of people celebrating a religious, sporting, or cultural event calls for a delicate balance between involvement and objectivity. Learn as much as possible about the festivities, so that your pictures highlight the most relevant aspects. You might also need to take time out from the event, so that you can capture images as a neutral observer.

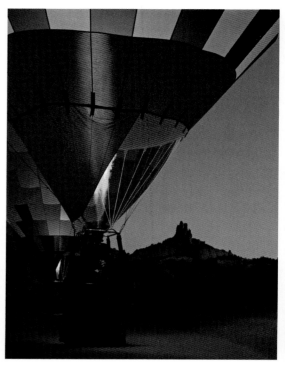

LANDSCAPE BEYOND
If a location is photogenic and interesting, such as the mountainous landscape in the background of this ballooning event, include it in the shot.

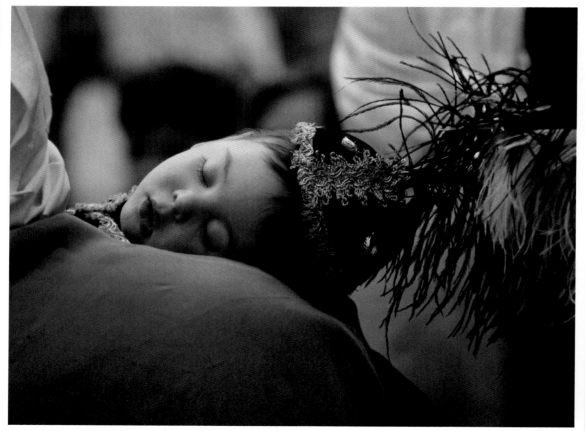

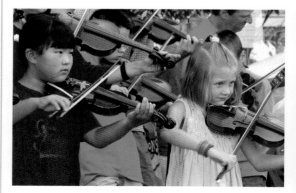

INDIVIDUAL FOCUS
Move close to the action—either physically or by zooming in—so that you can capture the facial expressions of individual characters.

CAPTURING SUBTLETIES
Keep your eyes open for scenes that may not be directly relevant to the event itself, but that add a touching or humorous element. After this child had taken part in a traditional Easter parade in Italy, the excitement of the day caught up with him, and he fell asleep in his mother's arms.

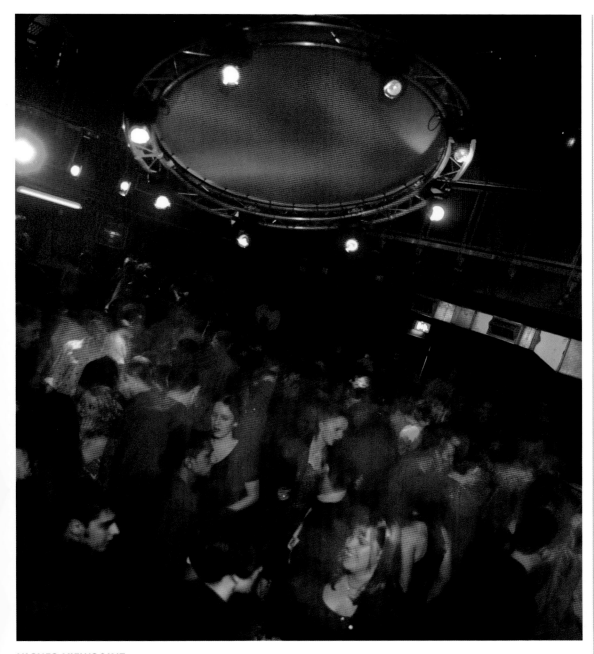

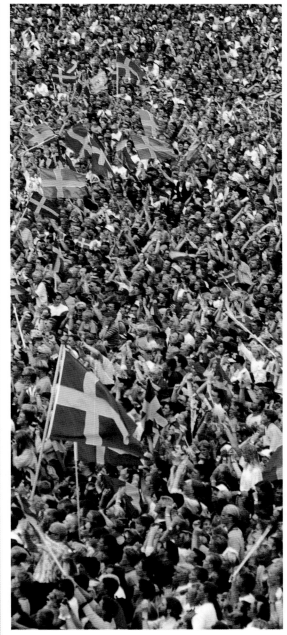

HIGHER VIEWPOINT

If possible, take photographs from a vantage point high above the crowds of party-goers to include as many people in the shot as possible. You can also exaggerate the party atmosphere of the occasion by using a long exposure and flash to create a blur of colorful lights and movement.

TELEPHOTO COMPRESSION

Try zooming in to compress the space between people so they appear even closer together than they already are, suggesting the press of a crowd.

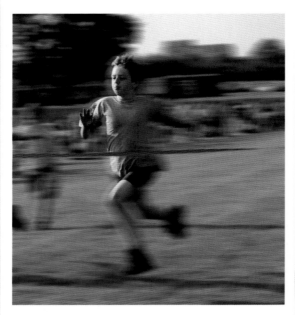

CREATING MOVEMENT

Position yourself just beyond the finish line for the best vantage point for school sports-day photos. Try panning the camera to create a sense of movement.

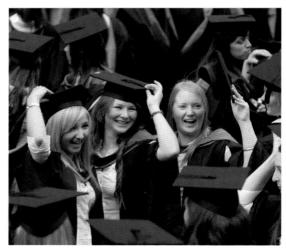

GROUP SHOT

On graduation day, as well as making the usual formal portrait, capture the elation shared by your subject and her colleagues. This enhances the sense of overall achievement and celebration.

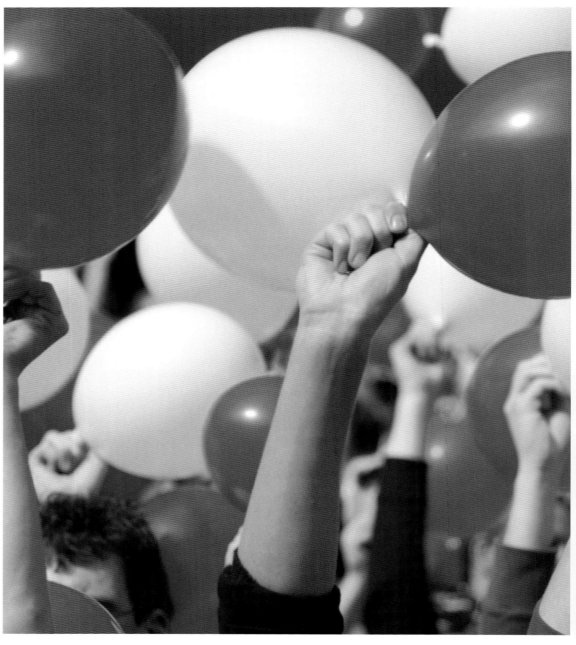

ABSTRACTING AN EVENT

At a sporting event, try turning your camera toward the crowds. The colorful display of balloons, flags, or streamers can make striking abstract compositions.

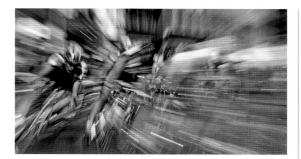

THRILL OF THE RACE
When photographing a bicycle race, try to convey the speed and thrill of the competition by using long exposures to create zooming streaks of color.

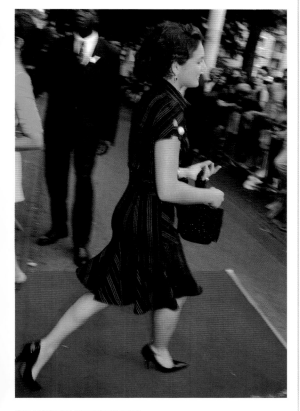

CELEBRITY ENCOUNTER
Big cities often hold film premieres with celebrity guests. Arrive early for a good spot, and use fill-in flash to balance available light for the best results.

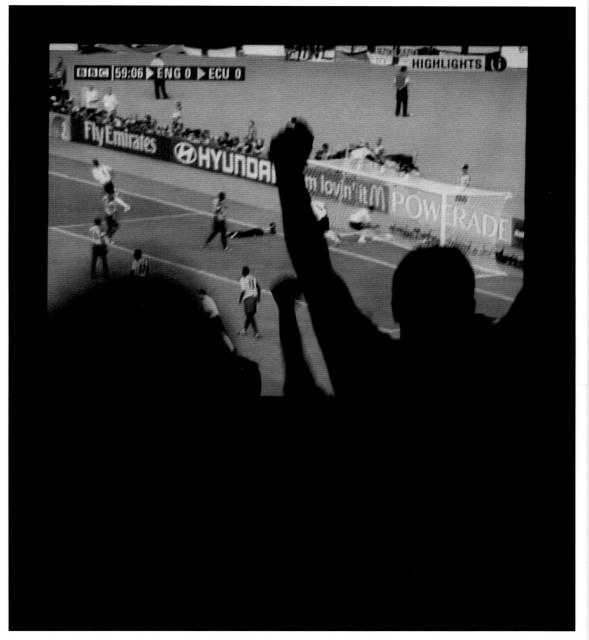

COVERAGE BY PROXY
Even if you are unable to attend the game, you can still capture the spirit of the event. Try contrasting silhouettes of cheering fans against the brightness of a big screen.

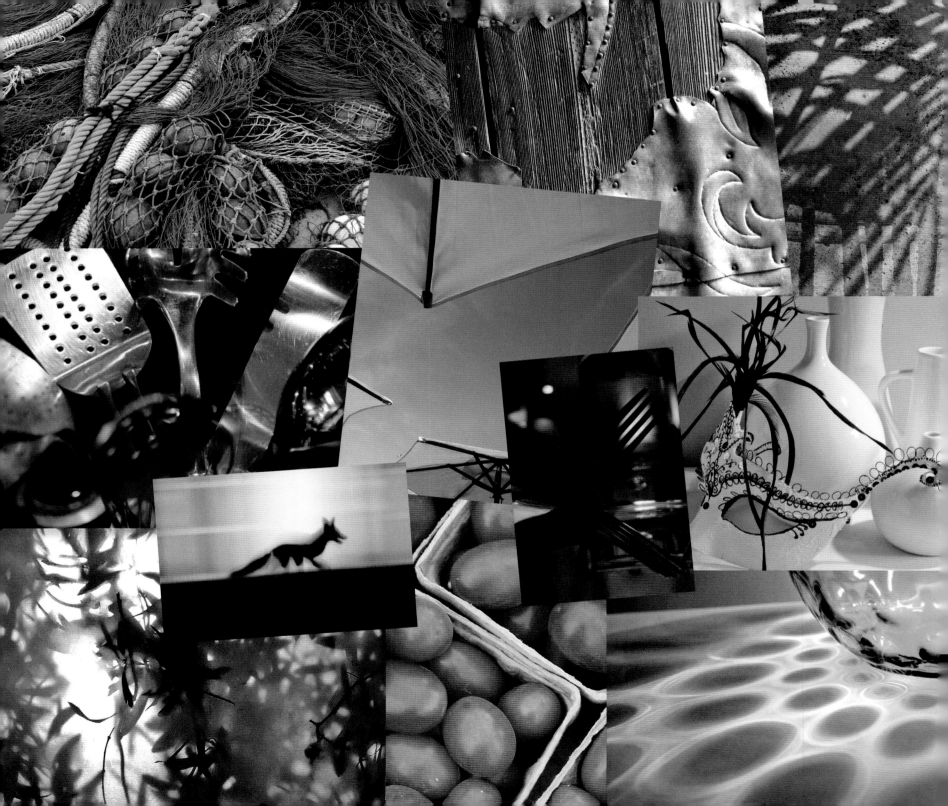

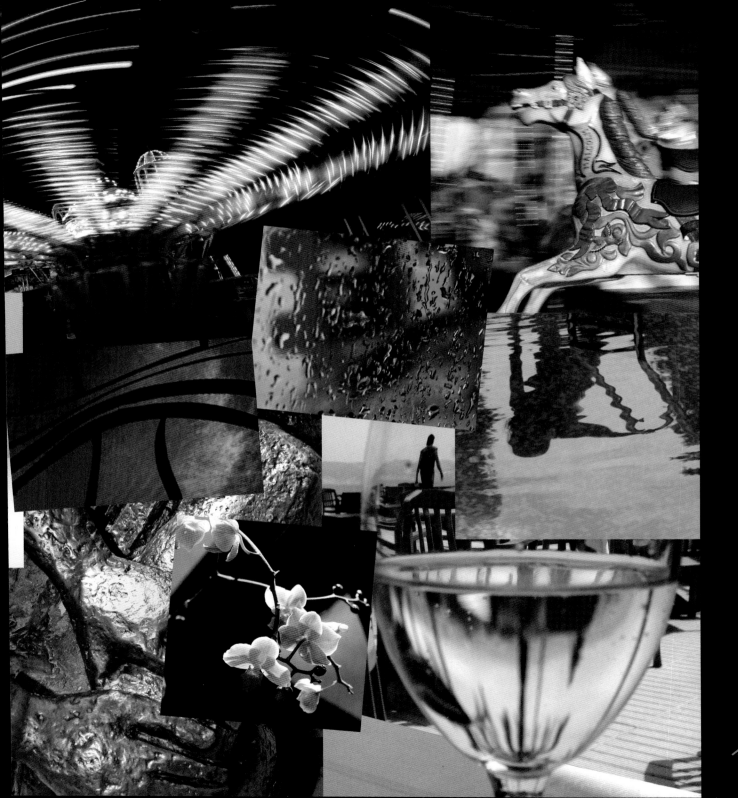

Artistic
expression

12345678

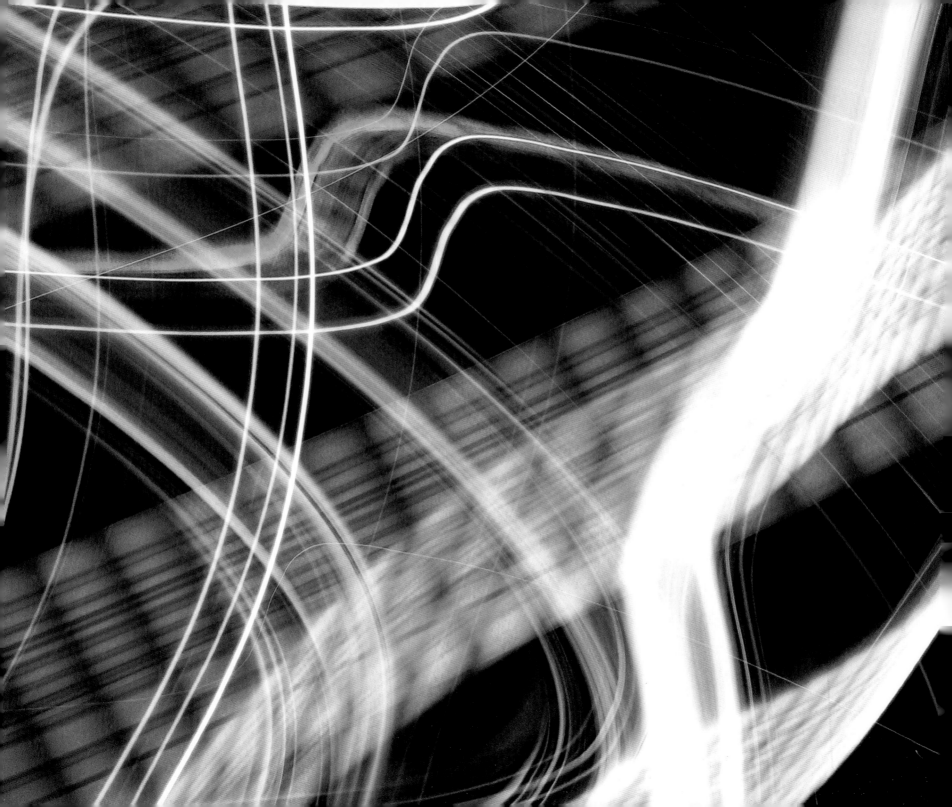

Artistic expression

refers to picture-making at its most relaxed—unconcerned for propriety, custom, or conscience. Here you allow yourself to be yourself: it is photography in which you aim to satisfy only your own visual curiosity, allowing your imagination to follow where the light leads you. According to your mood or inclination, you may capture the minutiae of ephemera or the mixed messages of urban decay, toy with optical effects or create still lifes, enjoy movement of light or find patterns in chaos. For this, all the techniques of photography are at your disposal. Use motion blur, use distorted colors and fragmented shapes, create arrangements that inspire you, or work with what you find.

Exploring art

The challenge for the photographer is to balance a view of an artwork that works as an image while conveying something of the spirit of the artwork as conceived by the artist. As three-dimensional artworks, most sculptures, for example, are designed to be viewed from all angles and to interact with their surroundings. Some statues invite a closer visual approach and tactile scrutiny—of the shape itself, the material, and the texture.

1 EXPLORE THE STATUE
When you first approach a sculpture, walk all the way round it to assess the way the light falls on it and the best view. Decide what to focus on: whether the shape as a whole or the surface textures.

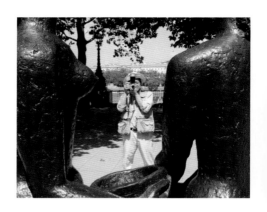

2 CHOOSE THE BACKGROUND
As you explore the sculpture, pay attention to how it relates to its environment. Some backgrounds might interfere with the shape of the piece, others complement and show off the form.

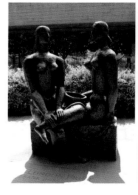 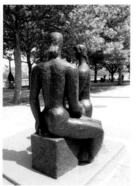

3 GET THE RIGHT LIGHT
Sculptures cast from metal are usually best photographed on overcast days to avoid glare. If you have to photograph on a sunny day, you may need the help of flash to fill in the shadows with light and soften contrast.

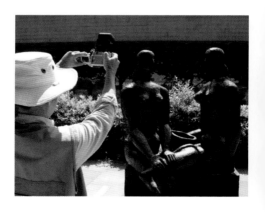

4 EXPERIMENT WITH COMPOSITION
Since they are immobile, sculptures are the ideal subjects for learning about composition. Try out the effects of different perspectives, zoom settings, and ways of framing.

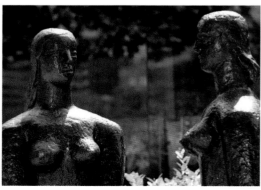 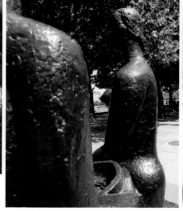 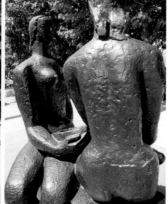

FOR THIS SHOT
I brought color to the textures and cast extra shadow on the ground by exposing with the flash on. I achieved an intimate perspective with a moderately wide zoom and near view. A low ISO setting helped reveal the subtle colors.

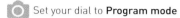

CAMERA MODE

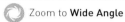 Set your dial to **Program mode**

LENS SETTING

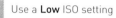 Zoom to **Wide Angle**

SENSOR/FILM SPEED

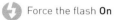 Use a **Low** ISO setting

FLASH

 Force the flash **On**

5 EXPLOIT THE LIGHT
Use the available light to help define shapes or show off texture. Supplementing natural light with flash or a reflector can also bring out other elements of the statue, such as color.

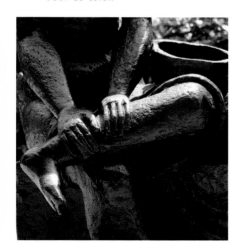

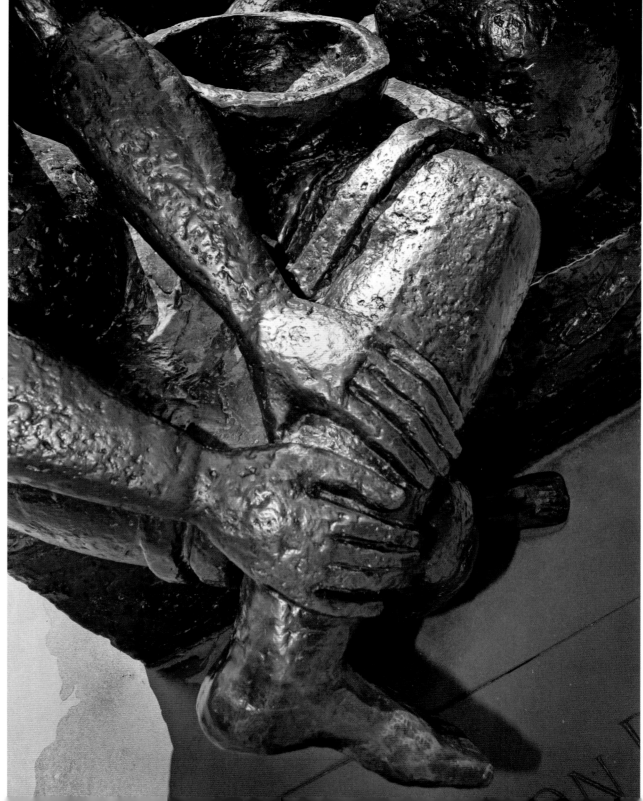

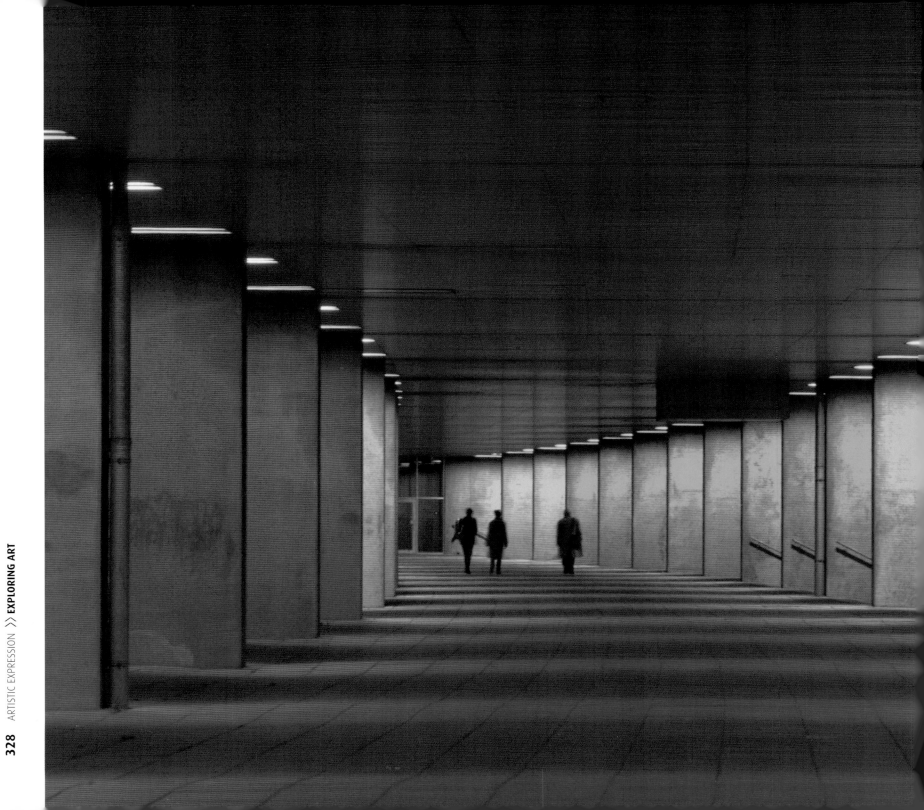

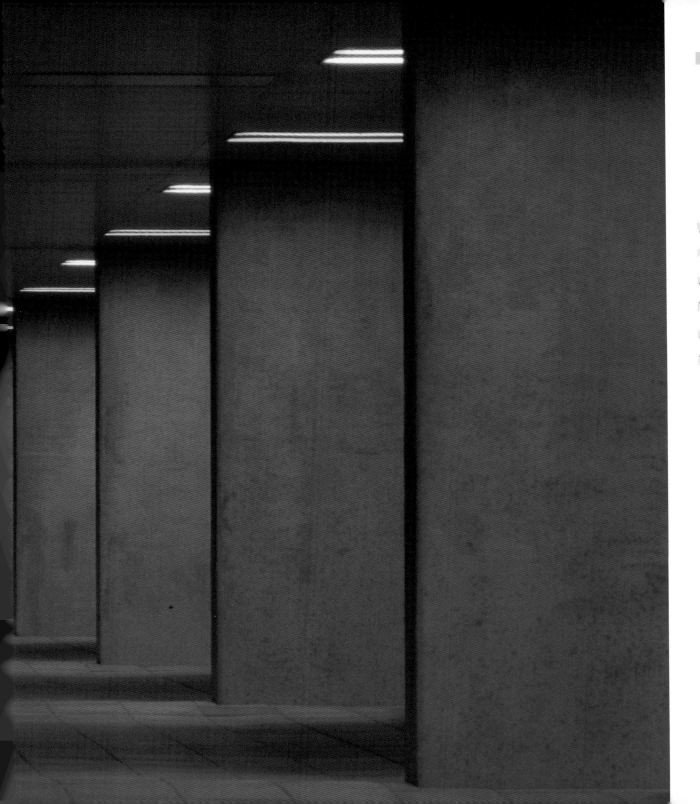

LIGHTS AND COLORS

Photographing in a strongly colored environment, such as this art installation, with its multiple colored lights, can be complicated by the camera trying to correct for the color. Check your images, and override this setting if necessary.

1 When photographing very large artworks, include people to give a sense of scale.

2 Try a straightforward, "objective" framing to present the art rather than your vision of it.

3 If necessary, adjust colors later, on a computer, for the most accurate results.

Sharpness and blur

With their vibrant colors, gaudy brilliance, and musical accompaniment, amusement-park carousels are a sensory door to a world of childlike innocence and giddy fun. Designed to catch the eye from a distance, carousels really come into their own when they are in full swing. Thanks to their cyclical motion, they are also excellent subjects for experimental exposures to help you learn about the effects of different settings.

1 POSITION YOURSELF
Stand near the carousel to get a sense of its speed and look at the various horses. Select the one you wish to capture, and then choose your position. In this case, one side of the carousel was lit by the setting sun, so it was obvious where to stand.

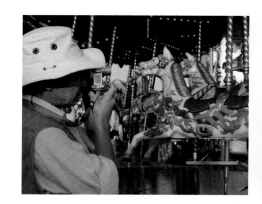

2 FREEZE THE ACTION
The motion of the carousel can be frozen if you expose with short exposure times. Movement is also more easily arrested if you position yourself so that the horses are coming directly toward you. Experiment by trying the same shutter time on different parts of the ride.

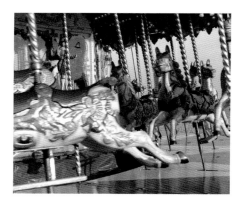

3 CHANGE YOUR SETTINGS
Set your camera to shutter priority so that you can control shutter times directly. If this option is not available on your camera, shift the programmed settings for different shutter times.

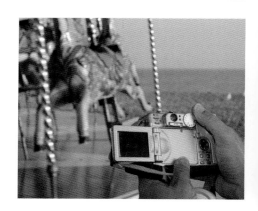

4 MOVE WITH THE FLOW
Release the shutter when your chosen horse is in position. Don't worry if you catch just its head or its hind legs at the start: you will have plenty of chances to get the timing right. Move with the horse as it passes you, so that some elements are sharp, and others blurred.

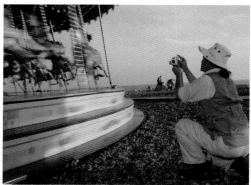
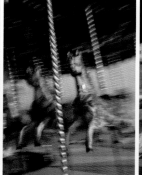
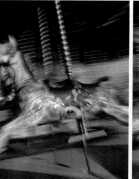
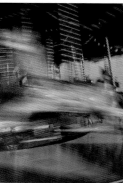

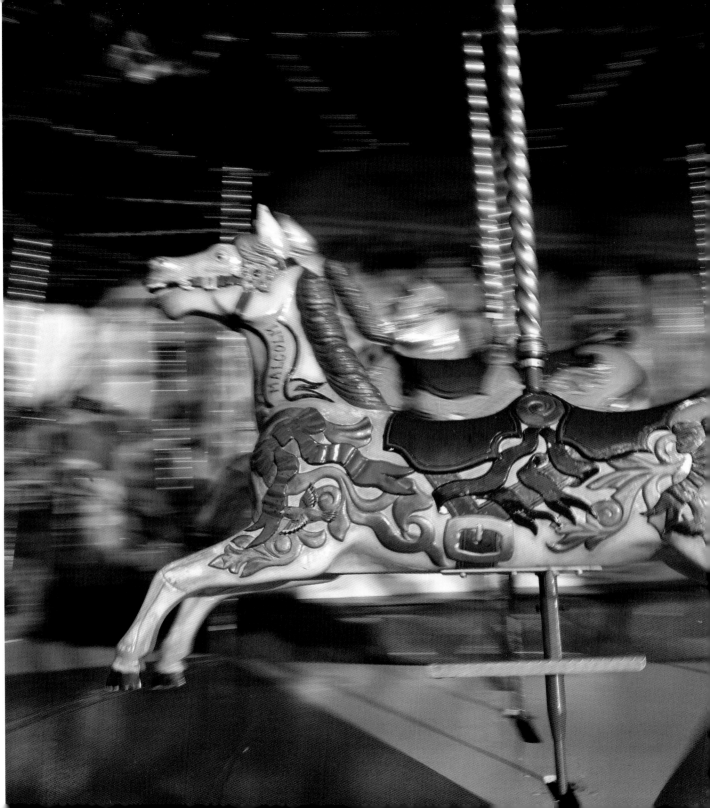

FOR THIS SHOT

With a shutter time of $^{1}/_{15}$ sec, I panned to follow the carousel's movement. This allowed me to catch one horse sharply while the rest are blurred. I varied the sensitivity to obtain the shutter time required.

CAMERA MODE

Set your dial to **Shutter Priority**

LENS SETTING

Zoom **as required**

SENSOR/FILM SPEED

Experiment with ISO **as required**

FLASH

Force the flash **Off**

5 EXPERIMENT WITH BLUR

When you use very long shutter times, you can reduce the horses on the carousel to a series of abstract colors.

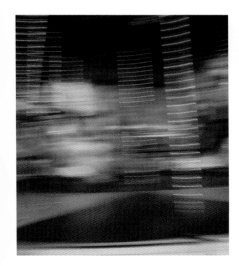

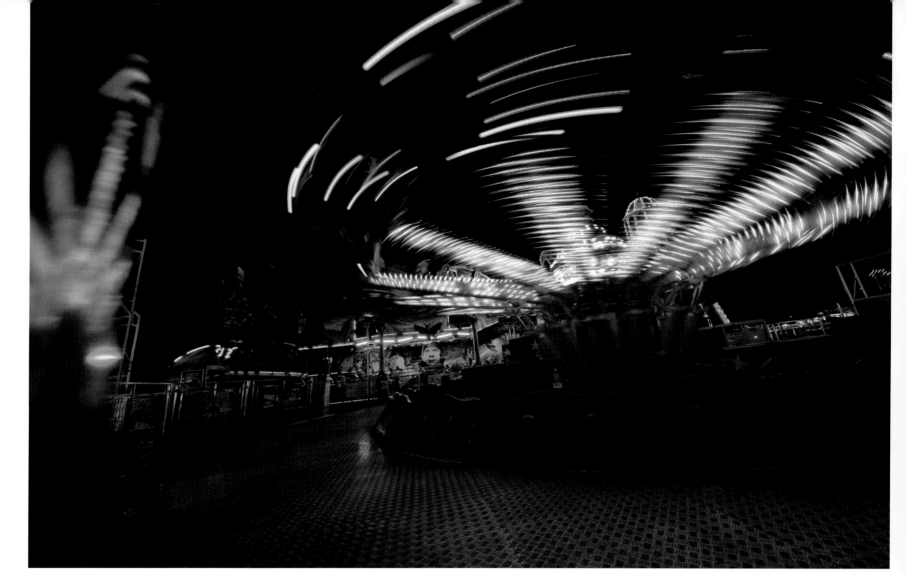

Light trails at night

Everybody loves a good, old-fashioned fairground, with its stomach-churning rides and multicolored lights. However, traditional rides like the ones offered by traveling carnivals are decreasing in popularity, unable to compete with the allure of high-tech theme parks. Many of us are nostalgic for the unique atmosphere of the fairground. You may wish to use your photography to capture this feeling, as well as the fairground's color and excitement.

FOR THIS SHOT

I set the zoom to the widest angle possible. I used a tripod and set an exposure of ⅓ sec with no flash to capture the movement. The emptiness of space all around made for an interesting contrast.

CAMERA MODE

Set your dial to **Night mode**

LENS SETTING

Zoom to **Wide Angle**

SENSOR/FILM SPEED

Use a **High** ISO setting

FLASH

Force the flash **On** if needed

1 START WITH A SHORT SHUTTER TIME

Fairgrounds at night are alive with bright moving lights. The easiest way to photograph the fairground is to use the shortest possible shutter time. This gives a static view, but one that is still full of interest due to the variety of lights.

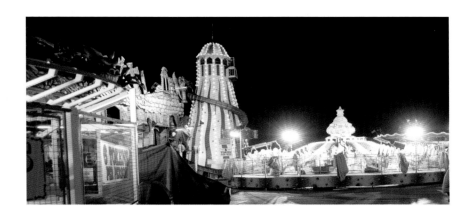

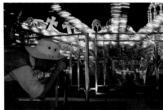

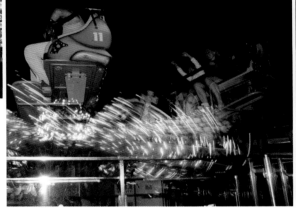

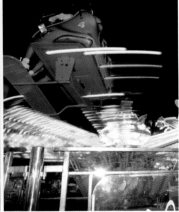

2 EXPERIMENT WITH FLASH

Using flash with a fairly long shutter time will lend your pictures both sharpness and blur – in this case, frozen revellers and light paths. You can make lights appear to trail from elements exposed with the flash in "second curtain flash" mode if available.

3 VARY SHUTTER TIME

For longer traces of light, use longer shutter time and a tripod. For these shots, I set speeds of 1 second (right) and 4 seconds (far right).

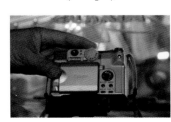

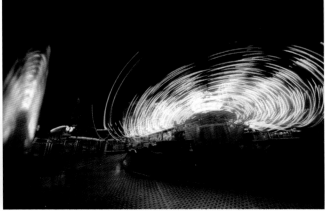

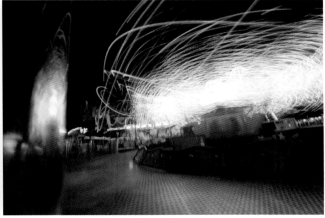

Abstracting the everyday

Fresh, colorful food is always a treat to the eye, and markets full of organic fruit and vegetables in different shapes, sizes, and textures are no exception. You may be so dazzled by all the incredible color combinations that you can't decide what to shoot. The best approach is to take your time and look at the produce as if you were shopping. By appreciating them as appetizing food, rather than as photo subjects, their photogenic qualities will shine through.

Outdoor markets are perfect places to pursue abstract themes—gathering objects by their color or shape, for example. Such arrangements make evocative images that can make a fun series of prints. Experiment with zoom settings: use wide for large masses and long for abstract close-ups.

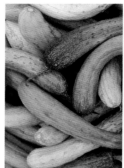
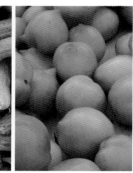

1 BE COURTEOUS

Produce in markets is positioned so that it looks at its most attractive to potential buyers. This layout makes it easy for you to photograph too, but make sure the sellers do not mind, and do not obstruct shoppers.

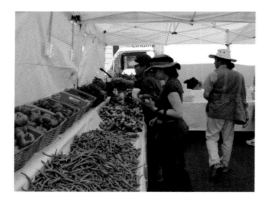

2 ADJUST THE SETTINGS

If the market is under cover, and especially if there is a color cast, be prepared to adjust your images on the computer later. Alternatively, use the white-balance feature on your camera if it has one.

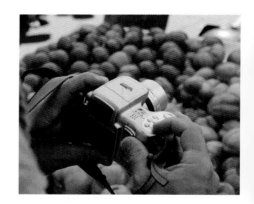

3 CONSIDER INCLUDING HANDS

You can make your pictures less abstract by including the hands of shoppers. This provides a contrast with the fruit, as well as context and scale. The hand can also be useful in helping you to create structure within the composition.

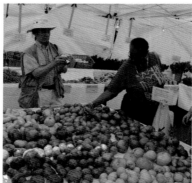
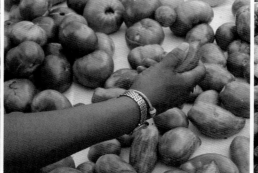
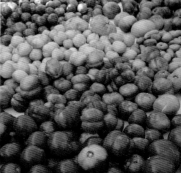

FOR THIS SHOT

I set the zoom to a normal to moderately wide angle, to give a natural perspective. A great depth of field was unnecessary since everything was on the same plane. Medium sensitivity helped ensure sharp images.

CAMERA MODE

 Set your dial to **Portrait mode**

LENS SETTING

 Zoom to **Normal** to **Wide Angle**

SENSOR/FILM SPEED

 Use a **Medium** ISO setting

FLASH

Force the flash **Off**

4 CREATE DIRECTION

While piles of fruit and vegetables are undoubtedly attractive, overhead shots of containers full of produce create successful images through the addition of rhythm and structure.

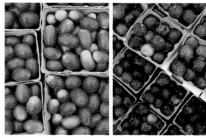

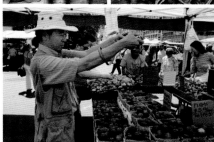

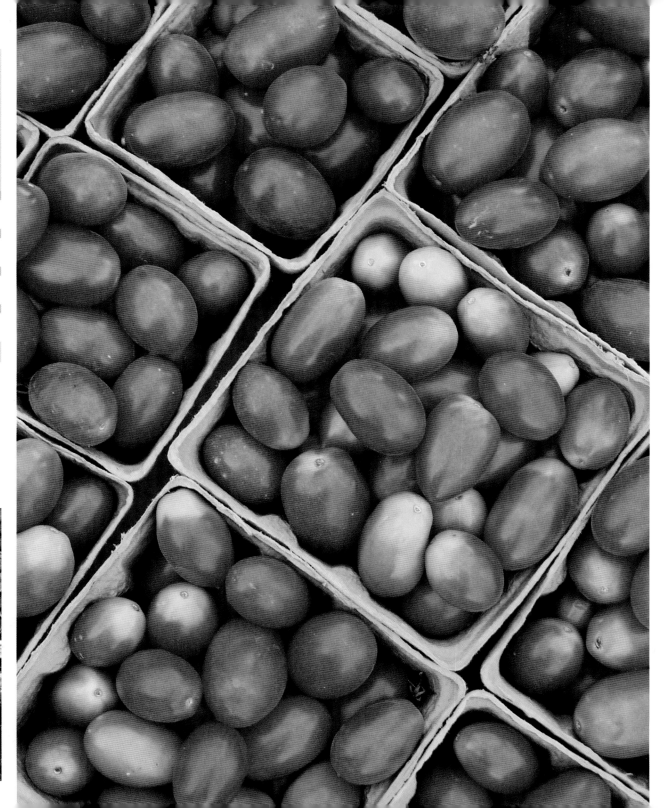

Color and light

One of the delights of photography is the way it can lead you to discover beauty in places and items you have been taking for granted—the road in front of your home, for example, or simple objects around the home. Learn to observe everyday things with different eyes. With only a little attentive application of light, that glass bowl that has been used as a receptacle for fruit or odds and ends for years might reveal itself to be a masterful player of color.

1 FIND A SUBJECT
Look around your house for suitable objects to photograph. If nothing catches your eye at first glance, look again, more closely: the point of this exercise is to discover hidden qualities in everyday objects.

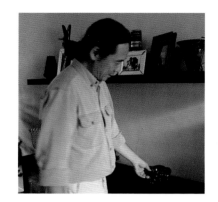

2 USE A TRIPOD
Once you have selected your item, set up your camera on a tripod. This will allow you to hold the camera steady.

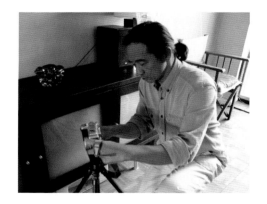

3 CHOOSE YOUR SETTINGS
When photographing items close up, set the lens to macro and turn off the flash. Select aperture priority and set the smallest aperture possible so that you can obtain the greatest depth of field.

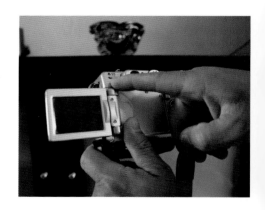

4 SELECT THE BACKGROUND
Allow your object to shine in front of a neutral or near-neutral background. Alternatively, try using colored backgrounds that contrast with the color of your object.

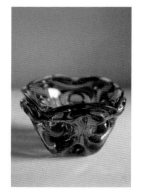

5 EXPERIMENT WITH LIGHT
Find a strong light source, such as a directional desk lamp. Play around with the position of the light and the object; this will reveal interesting effects that you might want to include in your shot.

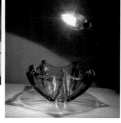
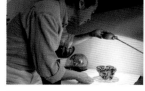
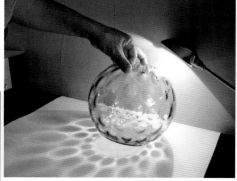

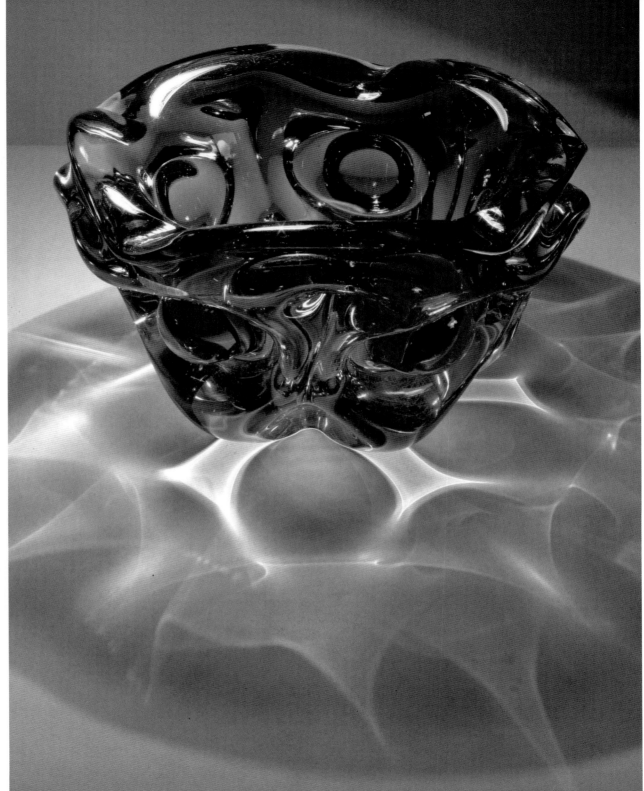

 FOR THIS SHOT
Using the zoom at a normal to moderate telephoto length and close-up mode, I selected the landscape mode and minimum aperture for the greatest depth of field. Low sensitivity ensured the best image quality.

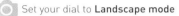

CAMERA MODE

Set your dial to **Landscape mode**

LENS SETTING

Zoom to **Normal**

SENSOR/FILM SPEED

Use a **Low** ISO setting

FLASH

Force the flash **Off**

6 POSITION THE LIGHT
Don't forget to light the background as well as the object itself. Here, I allowed a diagonal shadow to fall across the back of the vase to echo its shape.

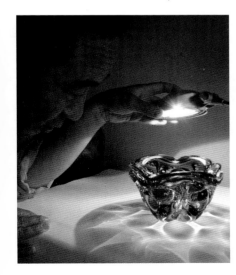

Reflections

Painters have long attempted to capture reflections—with varying degrees of success. Reflections are virtual images that cannot be directly projected on to a surface. As such, they are very difficult to paint. Photography, however, is perfectly suited to capturing their layering of light, color, space, and distance. Through this medium we are able to represent faithfully the full details of a reflected image.

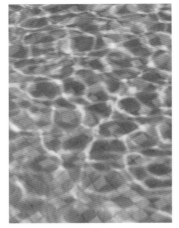

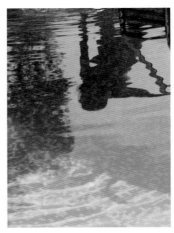

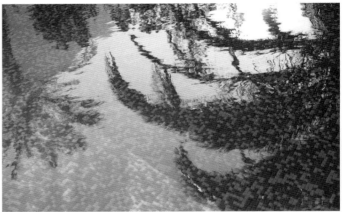

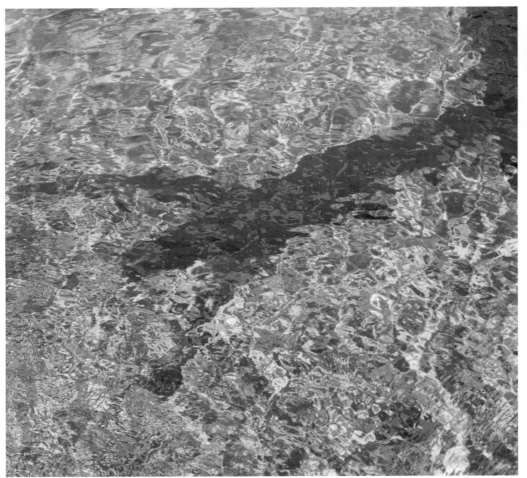

DAPPLED LIGHT AND SHADOW

A small swimming pool is a veritable laboratory of reflection effects. The surface does not always have to be glassy-smooth: the play of light and colored transparency is always interesting.

1 Achieve the smoothest tones by using the highest quality settings.

2 Use short exposure times to freeze any movement in the water.

3 To intensify colors, use a polarizing filter, but be aware that this may remove some reflections.

DISTORTED VIEW

The fluid lines of this metallic toy offer an abstract view of the street beyond. This shot is as much about the object as the image reflected in it.

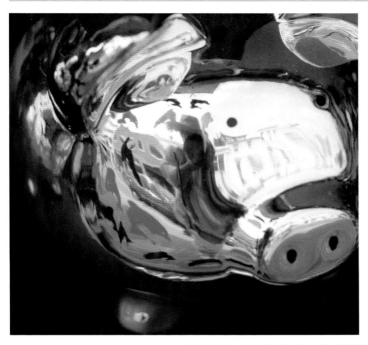

1 Use landscape mode or aperture priority for maximum depth of field.

2 Make and assess very small changes in position for the composition.

3 Stand at a distance and set a long zoom to minimize your own reflection.

RHYTHMICAL LINES

By including both the actual objects and their reflections in your shot, you can exploit strong symmetries to create powerful compositions.

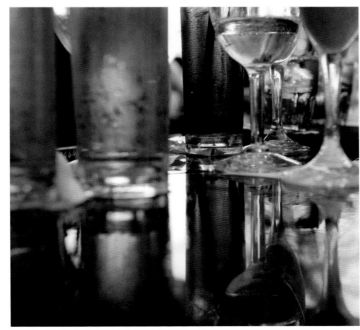

1 Place the camera as close to the reflecting surface as possible.

2 Use color contrasts and exploit shallow depth of field.

3 Try shots both with and without the flash to see which works best.

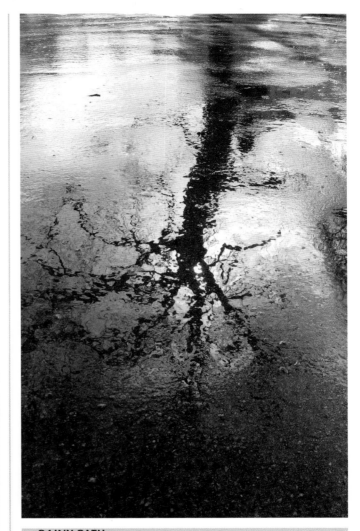

RAINY PATH

Reflections can bring a glow and lively light into an image even on dull, overcast days. Just work with the light that is available, and position yourself to maximize its reflection.

1 Set your lens to landscape mode to maximize depth of field.

2 If you want to improve the tones, set your camera to increase contrast.

3 Set your camera to increase color richness.

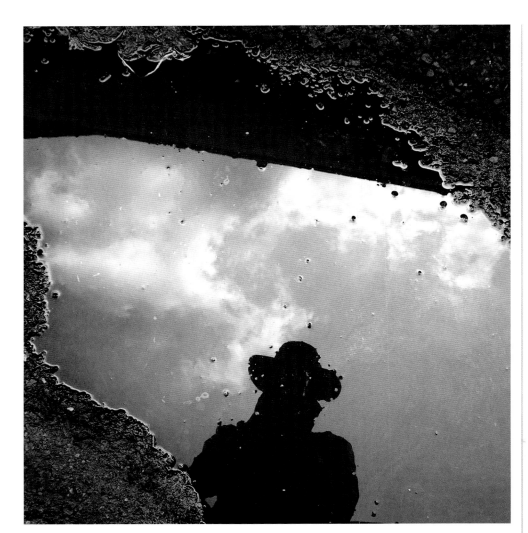

Sets of reflecting surfaces close together will fragment the reflected image to great effect.

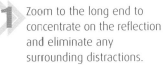

1 Zoom to the long end to concentrate on the reflection and eliminate any surrounding distractions.

2 Very small changes in position can make a big difference: compose slowly and with care.

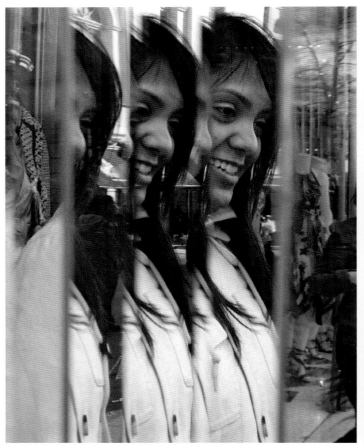

SILHOUETTE IN A PUDDLE

Within an urban environment, puddles of water may not appear attractive at first glance. But if you look closely, you may find textures, light, and reflections come together in an interesting composition.

1 Use a wide-angle view to capture both the context and the reflection.

2 Set the camera to increase color brilliance to improve the image.

3 For the best mirror effects, wait for any ripples in the water to disappear.

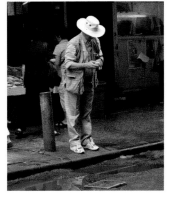

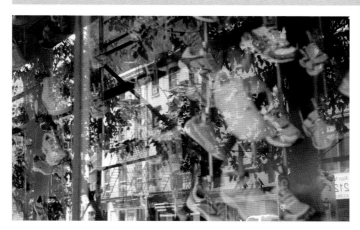

Reflections are visual multiplex systems, so your photographs can reveal intriguing layers.

1 To leave fewer visual clues to the location, use a concentrated view.

2 Add to the visual confusion by increasing the depth of field. This causes everything to appear on the same plane.

CONVEX MIRRORS

Photographing curved mirrors allows you to have twice the fun. They distort the world, giving unusual perspectives. Convex mirrors reflect a wider view than flat mirrors.

1 Photograph from the side to minimize your chances of appearing in the shot.

2 Use wide-angle views to record as much of the scene as possible.

3 Try to include both reflections and surrounding contextual elements.

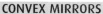

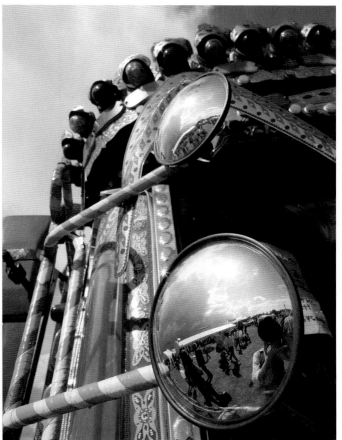

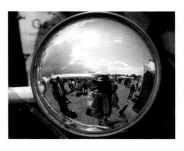

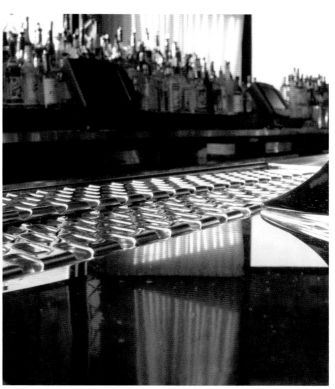

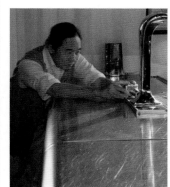

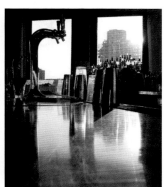

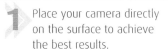

DESIGNER REFLECTIONS

The widespread use of polished surfaces—whether mirror-bright or softer and more subdued—for kitchens and bars is a gift to photographers.

1 Place your camera directly on the surface to achieve the best results.

2 Set a wide angle and landscape mode for the greatest depth of field.

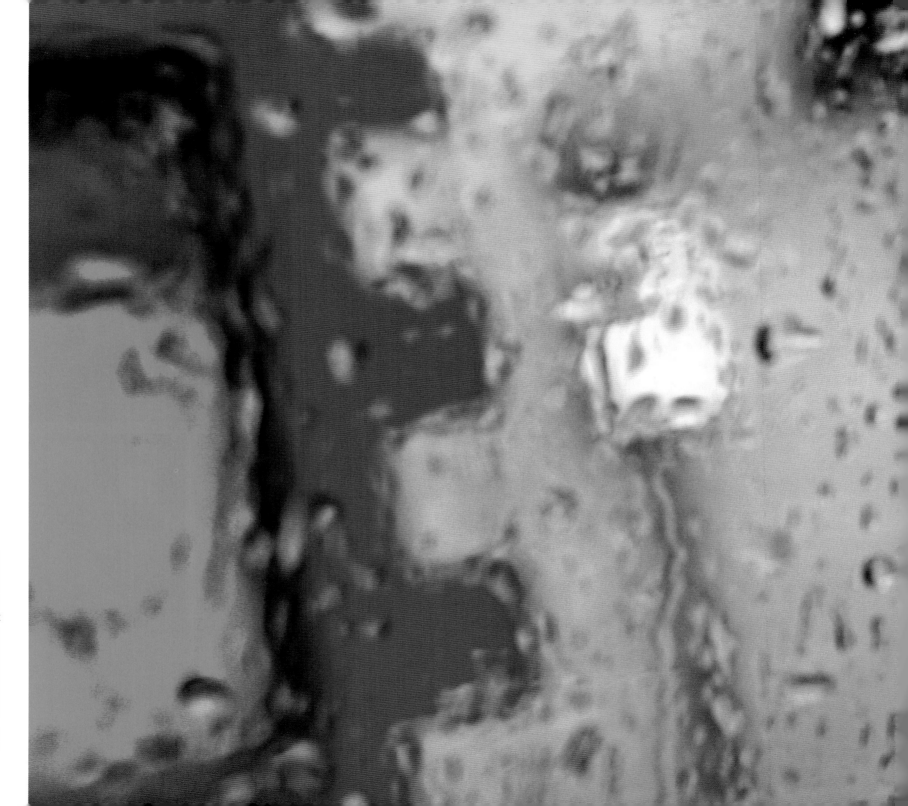

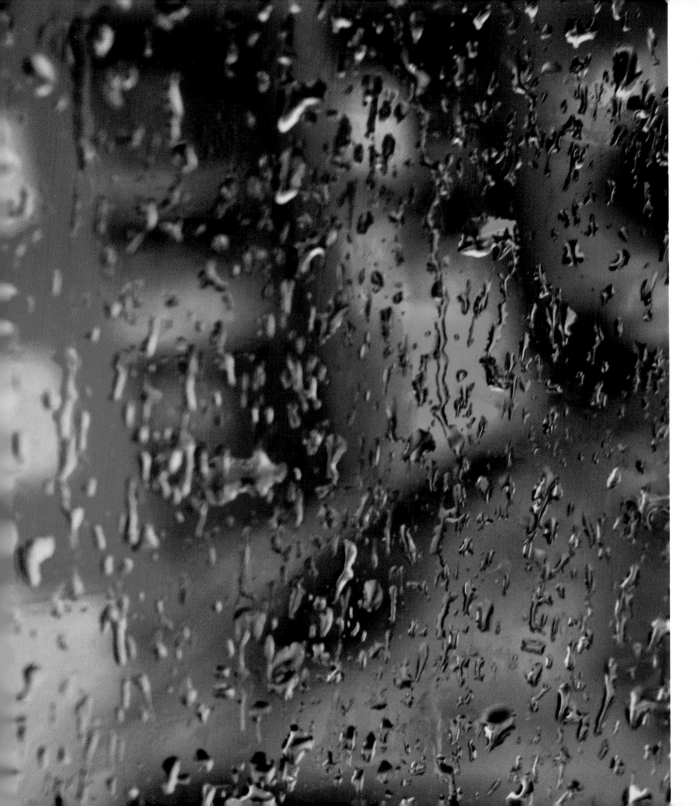

RAINDROPS AND NEON

Unless there is no light at all, you can usually find a subject worth shooting, so it pays to keep your camera with you at all times. This image is of shop fronts seen through a car window on a very wet, dark day. The diffused light helps intensify the colors.

1 Remember that, even in dim light, the camera captures the full intensity of colors.

2 For sharp results, use the highest sensitivity capture, even if colors may not be perfect.

3 You can focus on the water drops on the glass rather than the scene outside by setting close-up mode.

Impromptu still lifes

Still lifes have been a favorite artistic theme for centuries. This might have something to do with the fact that they are a static subject easily available to most people. Next time you're sitting in a restaurant waiting for your main course, try looking at the items on the table as a still life. If you keep a receptive mind and an open outlook, interesting arrangements will simply come up to you and quietly beg for attention. All you need is to have your camera ready.

1 ALWAYS BE READY
Keep your camera handy at all times and your mind on the look-out for photographic subjects. Many everyday objects have the potential to make an interesting shot.

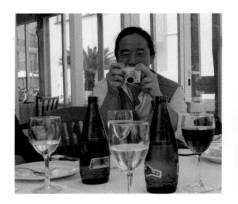

2 FIND CREATIVE SOLUTIONS
Don't disrupt anyone at the table by asking them to move so you can have a better shot. Rather, resort to unusual viewpoints such as resting the camera directly on the table, or simply take pictures of whatever is in front of you.

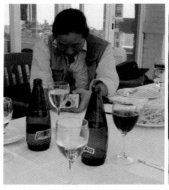

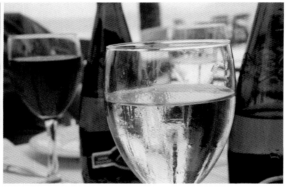

3 TRY DIFFERENT CAMERA SETTINGS
If you are at a leisurely lunch, use the time between courses to experiment with different focal length and aperture settings.

4 ARRANGE AND COMPOSE
Learn to see the array of bottles and glasses on the table less as a scattered mess and more as an opportunity. Try working with what is there, then adjust the positioning of the items to refine your composition.

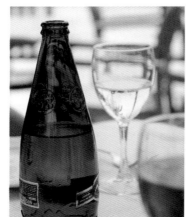

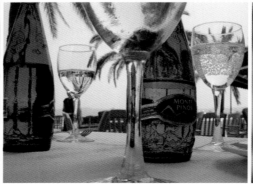

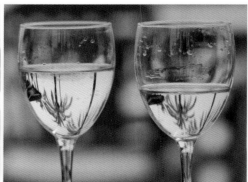

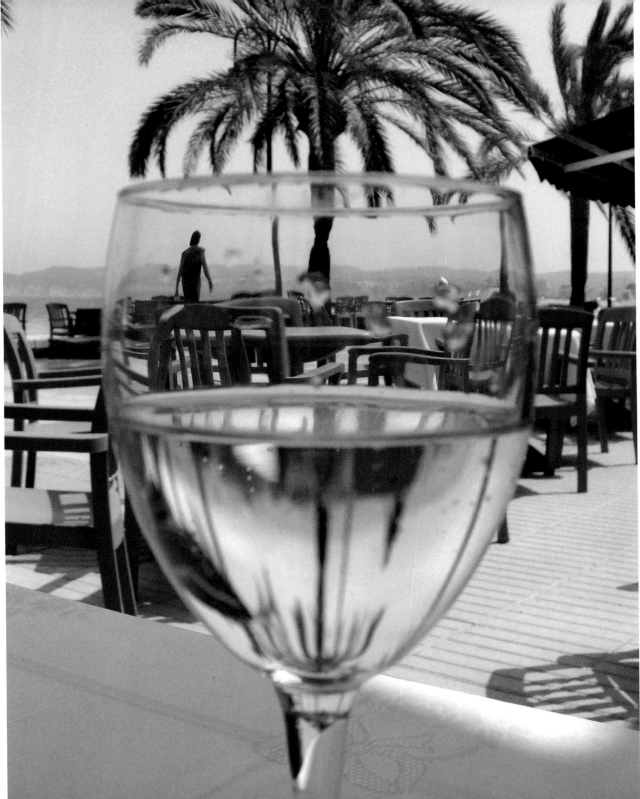

 FOR THIS SHOT
I set the zoom to a slightly longer-than-normal focal length and selected a medium ISO. The natural light of the sunny day allowed for an aperture setting that gave sufficient depth of field.

 CAMERA MODE
Set your dial to **Auto-exposure mode**

LENS SETTING
Zoom to **Moderate Telephoto**

SENSOR/FILM SPEED
Use a **Medium** ISO setting

FLASH
Force the flash **Off**

5 ADD SOMETHING EXTRA
Thanks to a happy coincidence of distance and dimensions, the glass of water created a lens effect, which inverted the tree. A passer-by completes the final shot.

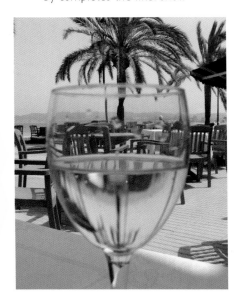

Still lifes

The beauty of still life is described by its very name: it is life that sits still for you to photograph. That means you can take your time, making all the adjustments you need, placing or removing elements, and fine-tuning the lighting until you obtain a result that holds together as a composition. Use a tripod so that you can leave the camera in position to concentrate on arranging the still life.

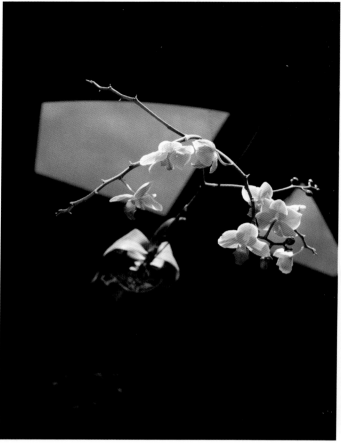

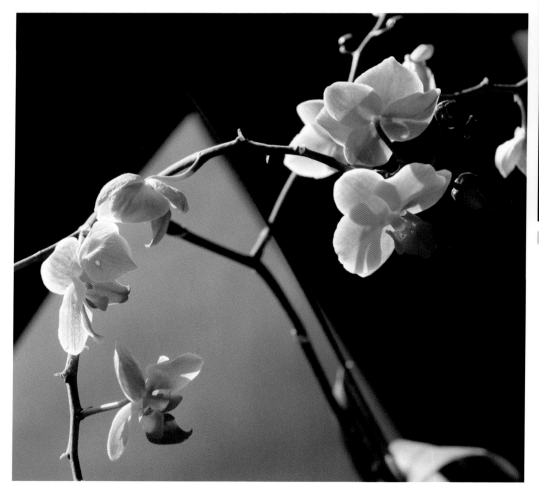

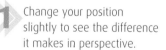

BURST OF COLOR

This orchid was placed on a black glass table to catch the evening light. The restrained color palette and simple arrangement make for a very effective composition.

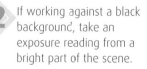

1 Change your position slightly to see the difference it makes in perspective.

2 If working against a black background, take an exposure reading from a bright part of the scene.

NATURE MORTE

Weathered stone is an ideal neutral background on which to display natural objects such as pine cones.

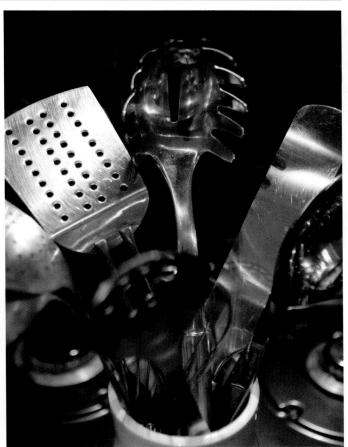

1 Use close-up mode to fill the frame with the object for the most detail.

2 To photograph objects with relatively little depth, use a normal zoom setting.

KITCHEN STILL LIFE

You don't need to leave the house to find subjects for your pictures. These kitchen tools offer much potential for still lifes, thanks to their varied shapes.

1 Make sure the utensils are clean: the camera will pick up even the smallest speck.

2 Turn on the lights to increase the number of highlights in the metal.

3 Use natural daylight as your main light source.

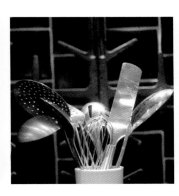

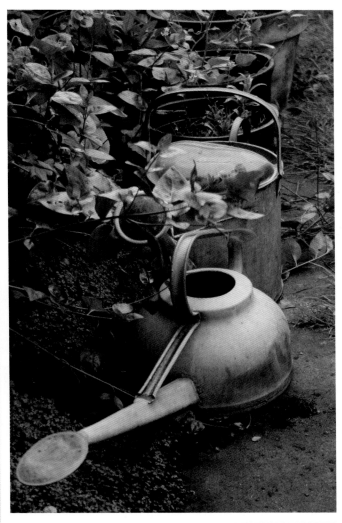

OUTDOOR ARRANGEMENT

This image works well because it uses a narrow range of colors, drawing our attention to the variety of shapes and textures in the composition. Even a small garden offers a wide range of photographic opportunities.

1 Overcast days are good for color photography; bright sunlight isn't always needed.

2 Use extensive depth of field to emphasize all elements equally.

3 Remove large distractions, but be careful not to lose the sense of character.

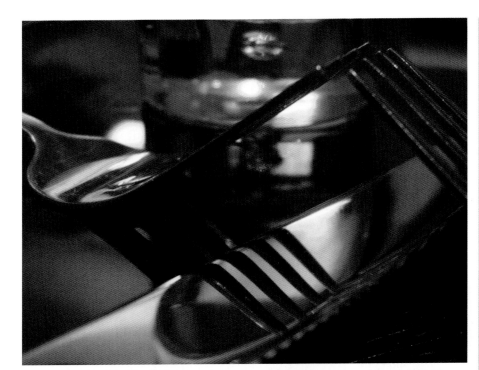

GLASSWARE REFRACTION

Glass objects such as vases, bottles, and glasses act like lenses and prisms. Looking at an object through glass – especially if it's patterned or cut – can magically transform both the glass and the object.

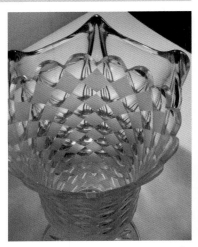

1 Use a wide angle and the smallest aperture to get as much depth of field as possible.

2 Use a table or reading lamp to introduce highlights.

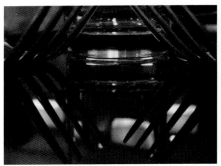 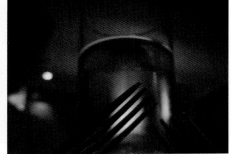

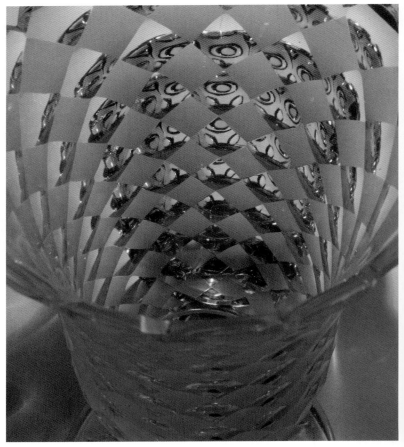

TABLETOP CLOSE-UPS

A set table can provide some intriguing photographic opportunities. Small digital cameras enable you to explore the visual secrets of a table setting and to get right into a still life in a way that would be impossible with larger equipment.

1 Set the camera to close-up, or macro, mode, and be sure to turn off the flash.

2 Rest the camera directly on the table to obtain unusual perspectives.

3 Take advantage of the fact that the camera is steadily supported to experiment with exposure times.

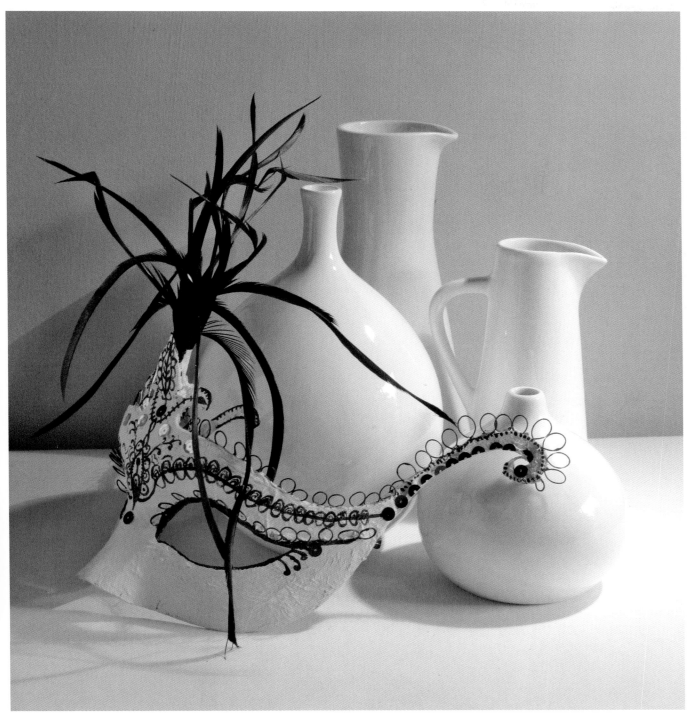

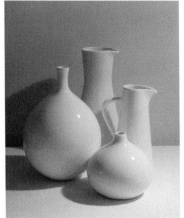

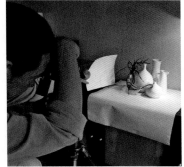

HIGH-KEY OBJECTS

Strangely, white objects are wonderful subjects for color photography. Adjust the white balance or try a few exposures to get the whites and any subtle tints right.

1 Check the image on the LCD screen for bright whites and light-gray shadows.

2 Experiment by adding props with contrasting textures to the main object.

3 Use a reflector or white paper to fill the shadows.

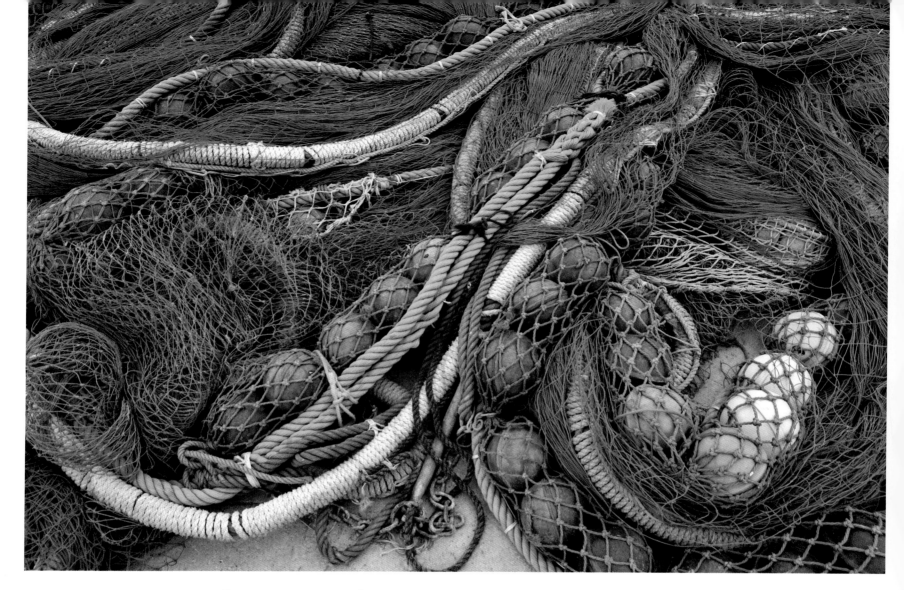

Patterns from chaos

It is notoriously difficult to paint or draw patterns from repeated fine details—the chaotic intricacy of fishing nets, for example, or the delicate precision of a spider's web. The ease with which photography captures such patterns, however, has made them much-loved artistic subjects, giving them a special place in the medium. The best thing about them is that interesting patterns and textures can be found anywhere, and often in the most unlikely places.

FOR THIS SHOT

I left the zoom set at normal to make framing simpler and quicker. For good image quality, I set the sensitivity at low to medium. Since this view is slightly angled, a good depth of field was needed, so I selected a small aperture.

CAMERA MODE

 Set your dial to **Landscape mode**

LENS SETTING

 Zoom to **Normal**

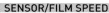
SENSOR/FILM SPEED

Use a **Low** to **Medium** ISO setting

FLASH

Force the flash **Off**

1 KEEP YOUR EYES OPEN

Even the most chaotic pile of clutter may—indeed, is likely to—offer potential for photographing patterns. Just because these items are lying around doesn't mean they don't belong to someone, so don't interfere with them.

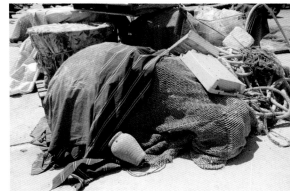
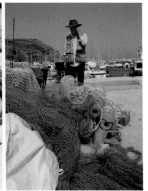

2 LET YOUR SUBJECT DICTATE THE LIGHT

The best lighting depends on the type of texture you intend to photograph. Strongly marked patterns with depth, such as these fishing nets, are best shot in soft light, but more delicate textures will benefit from harder, more direct light.

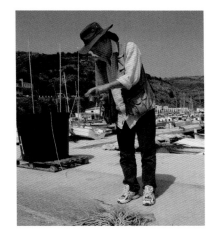

3 USE THE SCREEN TO COMPOSE THE SHOT

The external LCD screen of a digital cameras is a good tool for helping the search for textures. This is because it simplifies the image by showing only a rough approximation of the fine details. If the shapes and patterns look promising on the LCD screen, the image is likely to be effective.

4 SHOOT AWAY

Once you have found a promising source of textures and patterns, you can work at your leisure. Try photographing at differing scales, with and without color contrasts. Keeping the camera parallel with the surface of the texture will help ensure a good, "flat" pattern in the image.

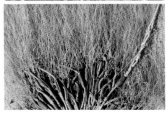
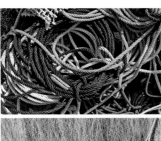
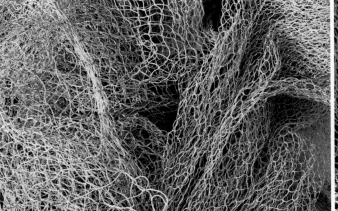
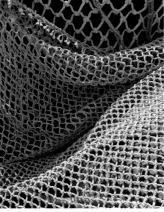

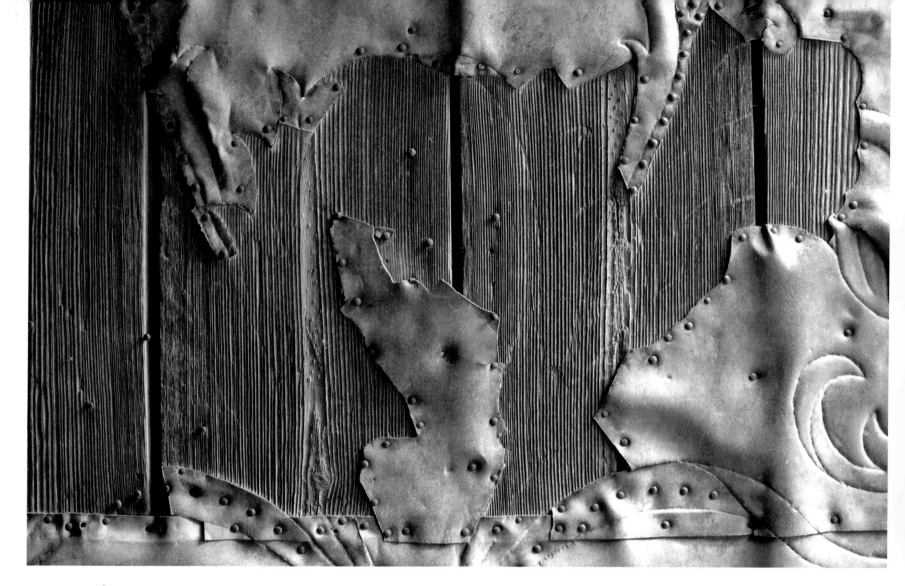

Exploring textures

Your primary photographic target may be a landmark building, but the greatest visual rewards may turn out to lie in the time-ravaged textures of its exterior. Indeed, the surface of a building can be a subject in its own right.

For the best results, compose the shot carefully to balance the different elements and to give a sense of scale. Choice of lighting is also important, since the more detail you manage to capture, the better the textures are revealed.

FOR THIS SHOT

I held the camera as square to the surface as possible, choosing a high-quality setting to capture all the fine details. Because I was very close up, I selected the macro setting. I forced the flash off to avoid flat lighting.

CAMERA MODE

Set your dial to **Program mode**

LENS SETTING

Set your lens to **Macro** mode

SENSOR/FILM SPEED

Use a **Low** or **Medium** ISO setting

FLASH

Force the flash **Off**

RELIEF LIGHTING

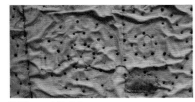

Diffused light

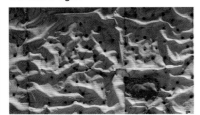

Direct light

To ensure the relief and fine details of a texture show up, light must come from one side. Depending on the texture, you may choose diffused light or hard, concentrated light. The best light is usually semi-diffused.

1 LOOK FOR UNUSUAL TEXTURES

Walk around the building, looking for interesting details and surfaces. In full sunlight, textures will be exaggerated, while in shady areas, they will be softened.

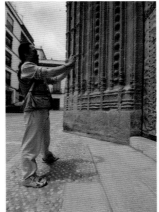
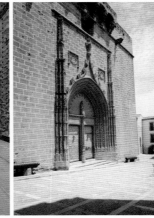
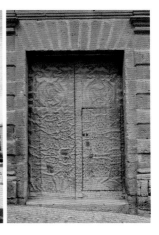

2 SET THE CAMERA

For distances closer than 2 ft (70 cm) or so, you may need to set your camera lens mode to macro or close-up. This is often shown as a flower symbol.

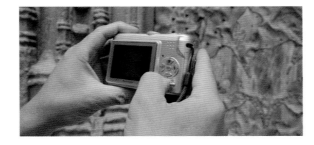

3 RAISE THE CAMERA

If the area you want to photograph is higher than eye level, you will need to hold your camera above your head. Remember to keep the camera square to the surface to prevent the image from becoming distorted.

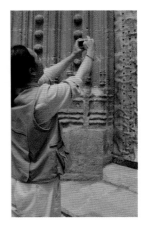

4 TAKE VARIOUS SHOTS

When photographing abstract details, it may not be obvious at the time which composition works best, so shoot lots. If nothing else, the textures may come in handy for backgrounds on websites, scrapbooking, or as frames for use with other images.

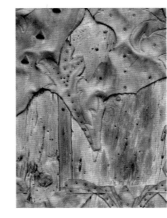
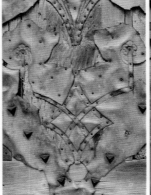
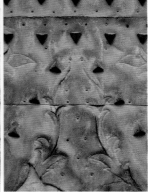

Art on the street

Urban landscapes are littered with elements that could be considered unsightly, including metal shutters, street furniture, and graffiti. Yet, any of these may be redeemed through photography. A camera can transform disorder, decay, and seemingly haphazard arrangements into pleasing visual compositions. The only requirements are the most basic: keep looking, and keep your camera with you at all times.

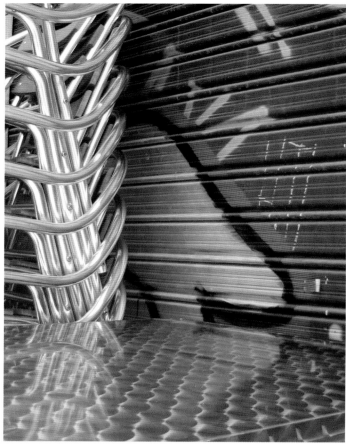

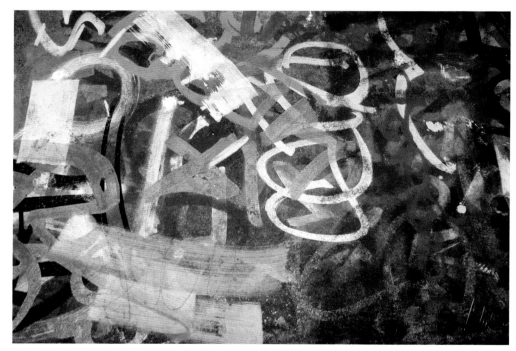

BLACK-AND-WHITE CONVERSION

You can take the abstraction of form and outline of graffiti to its extreme by removing the color from the image.

1 Select high color and high contrast for the strongest graphic impact.

2 For even distribution of sharpness, frame up square on to the surface.

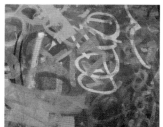

METALLIC SURFACES

The urban environment is full of metallic textures that enable you to explore quality of light. Here, the shiny tables contrast with the graffiti behind them.

1 When you see something promising, try out different viewpoints and framings.

2 Experiment with depth of field to discover which gives the best results.

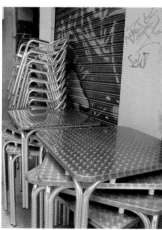

MIXED MESSAGES

Graffiti is often considered one of the first signs of urban decay. But it can be visually interesting. These open shutters, spray-painted while closed, have taken on a new quality.

1 Look for images that carry multiple meanings, since these are the most interesting.

2 Compose the image in a simple way, and let the situation speak for itself.

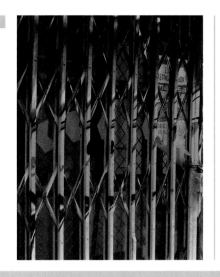

WARM LIGHTING

The visual appeal of many urban locations depends greatly on the quality of the light. Strong, warm light can lend beauty to even the most neglected corners.

1 Try a little intentional underexposure to intensify colors.

2 Select high ISO settings to add noise into textures that may be too smooth.

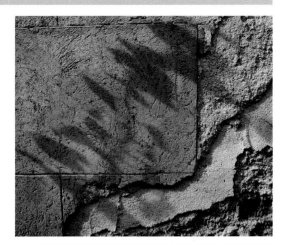

BEYOND THE MUNDANE

The best thing about carrying your camera with you at all times is that it helps to keep your mind attentive and open to photographic possibilities as they arise.

1 If in doubt about the composition, make the exposure anyway.

2 Avoid the temptation to tidy up the scene—the composition can end up looking staged and false.

3 Use the highest quality setting so that, if you wish, you will be able to make large, striking prints.

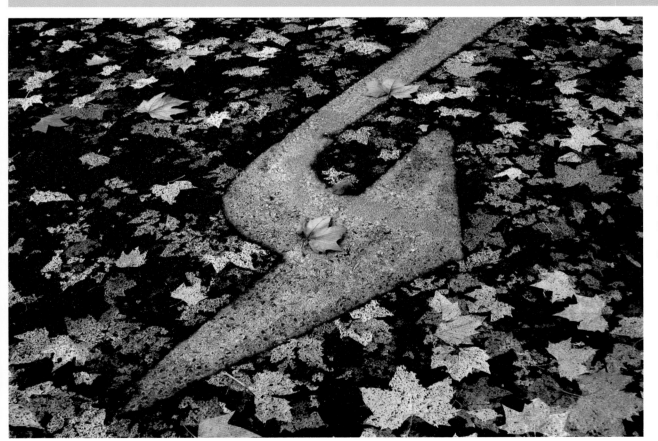

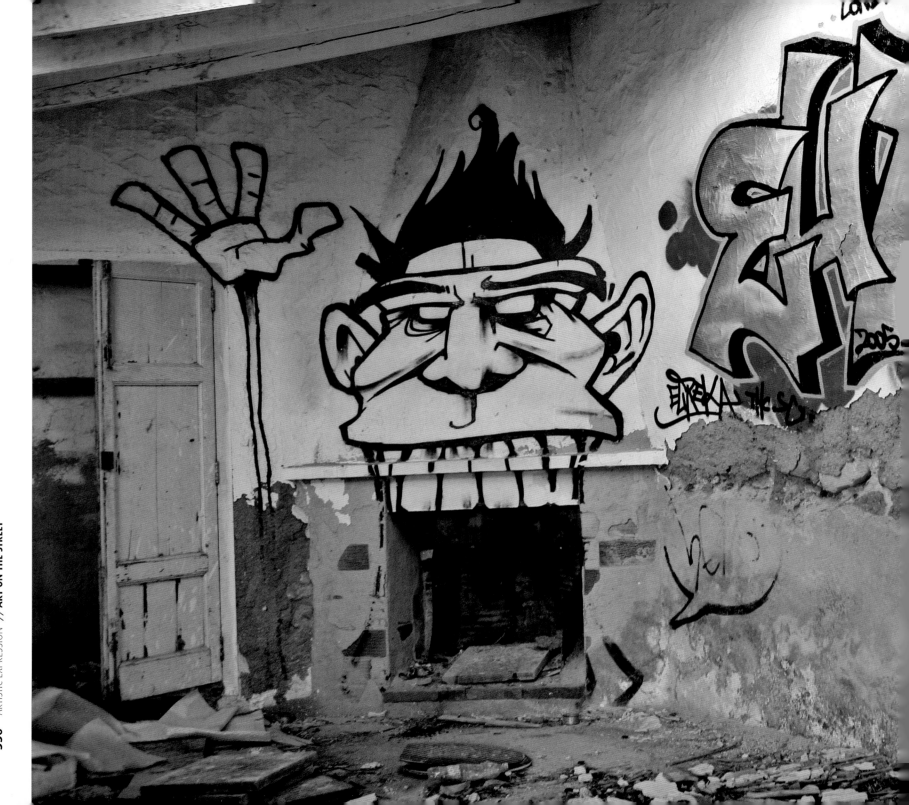

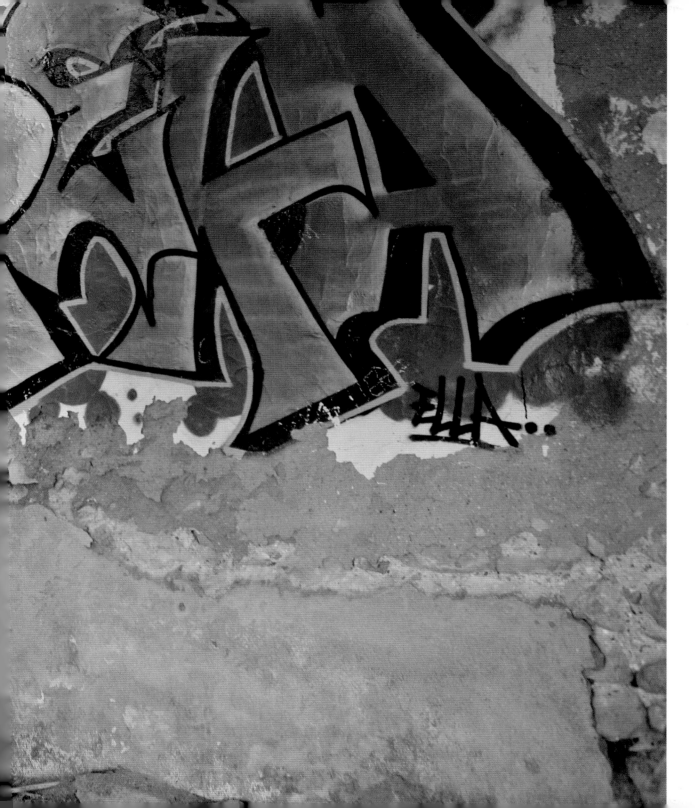

WRITING ON THE WALL

The most unlikely places—for example, run-down buildings or disused factories—can offer up the most surprising, interesting images. Photography can record all the scene in compelling detail and fidelity, in an instant.

1 Take all the necessary precautions when exploring areas that may be unsafe.

2 If your lens is not wide enough to take in the whole scene, try making a panorama.

3 In dim conditions, place the camera on a tripod or other support instead of using flash.

Artistic expression

One of the wonderful properties of photography is that you can use the camera for self-expression—framing photographs in the most subjective or instinctive way imaginable—yet it will still give you well-exposed, lifelike images, with sharp details. The camera allows you to indulge your love of color, of light and shade, or of intricate patterns.

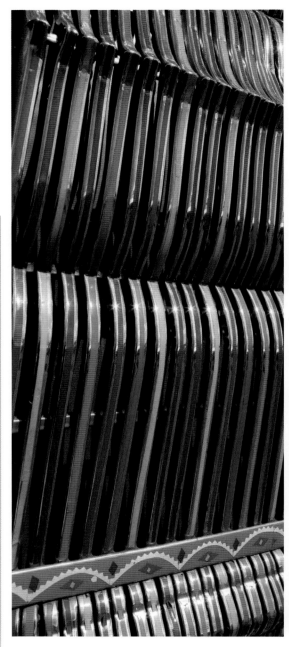

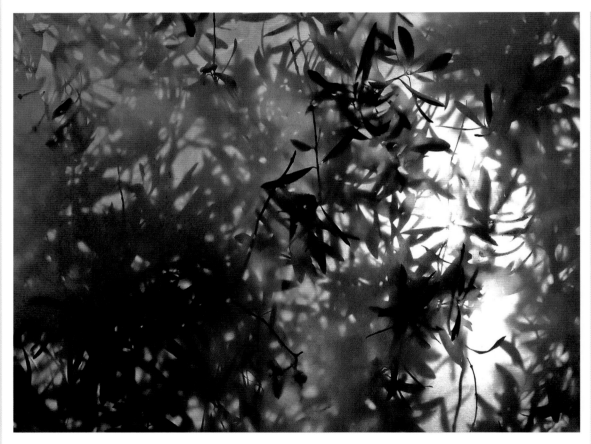

UNEXPECTED INSPIRATION
Train your photographic eye to look beyond the obvious: here, a simple pane of glass reveals silhouettes of olive leaves against the setting sun.

COLORS AND SHAPES
The radiator grill of a bus has been turned into a colorful work of art by a loving owner. Zoom in close and crop the image to create an abstract shot.

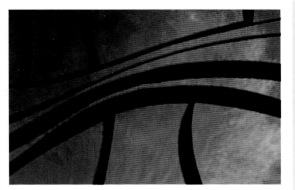

MODERN GRAPHICS
Indulge in the sheer enjoyment of light and color for their own sake by taking pictures of neon and plasma display screens.

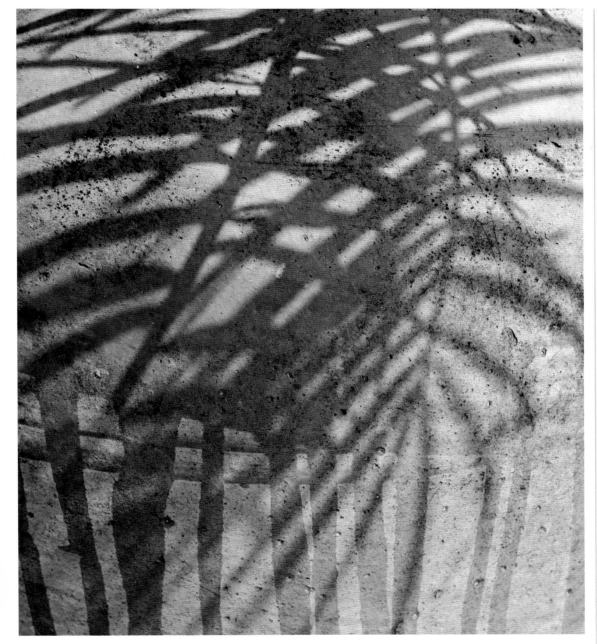

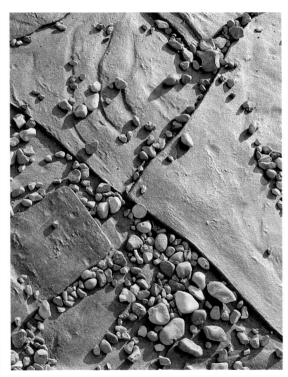

ART POTTERY
With its weathered surface and worn glaze, this terracotta urn is an intriguing subject in itself. Combine with shadows to add complexity to the composition.

NATURE'S COMPOSITION
The best artist of them all is Nature itself. Take time to explore the wonderful arrangements of pebbles on a rocky beach.

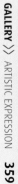

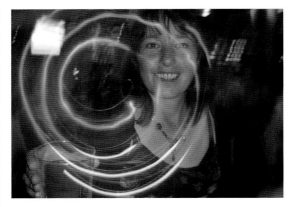

WRITING WITH LIGHT

To create a trail of light on a sharp image, simply combine a long exposure with flash while you wave a light in front of the camera.

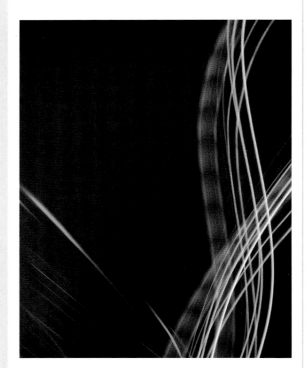

STREAKS OF LIGHT

When darkness is illuminated only by artificial lights, strap the camera to your wrist, set a long exposure, release the shutter, and throw the camera in the air.

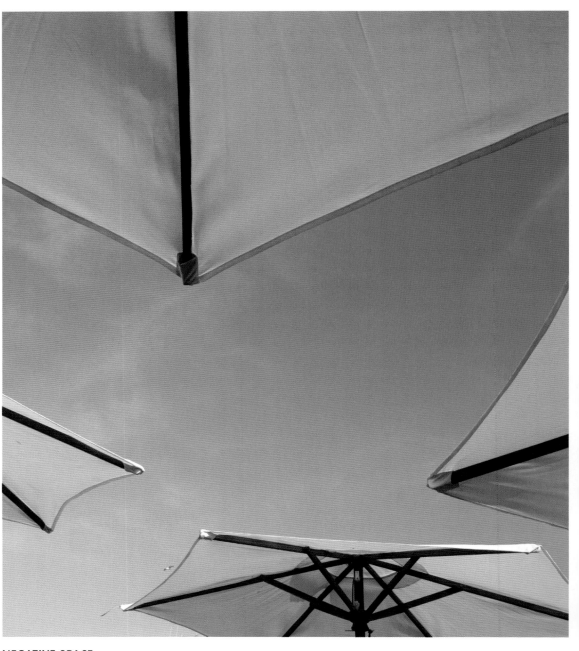

NEGATIVE SPACE

An empty area that defines the edges of objects is called "negative space." You can use it to positive effect by turning it into the subject itself.

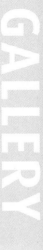

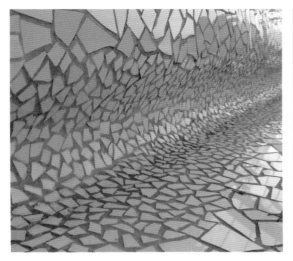

TEXTURED DETAIL
Unusual textures or views provide visual conundrums. What is it? How big is it? How was it shot? Such patterns do not need to be colorful to be effective.

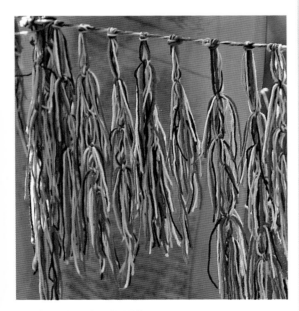

WORKING WITH COLOR
The materials threaded and knotted as prayers to the gods make intriguing patterns of colors, contrasting fine detail with broad areas of color.

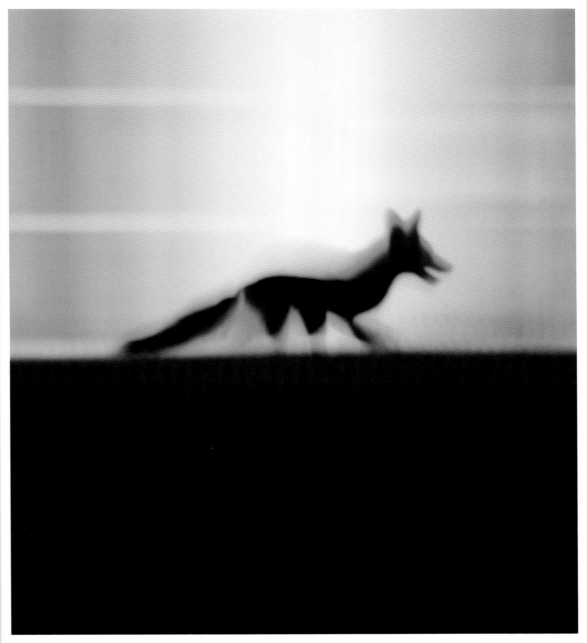

SHADOWS AND MOVEMENT
A running fox is caught in a blur of light by moving or panning the camera in the same direction as the animal's run during the exposure.

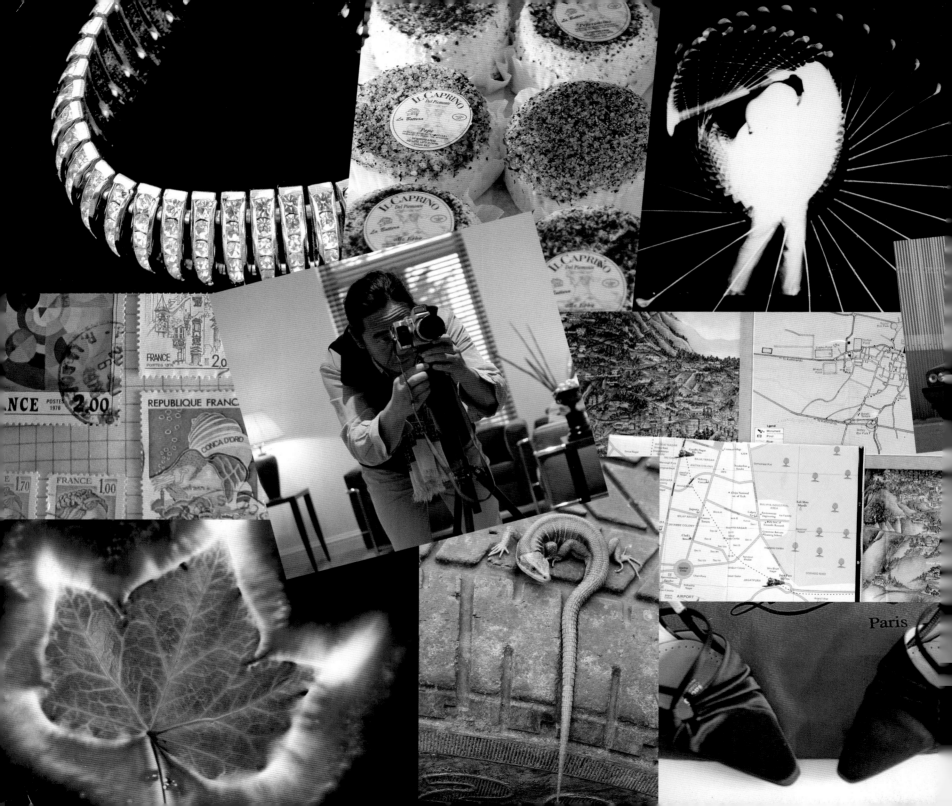

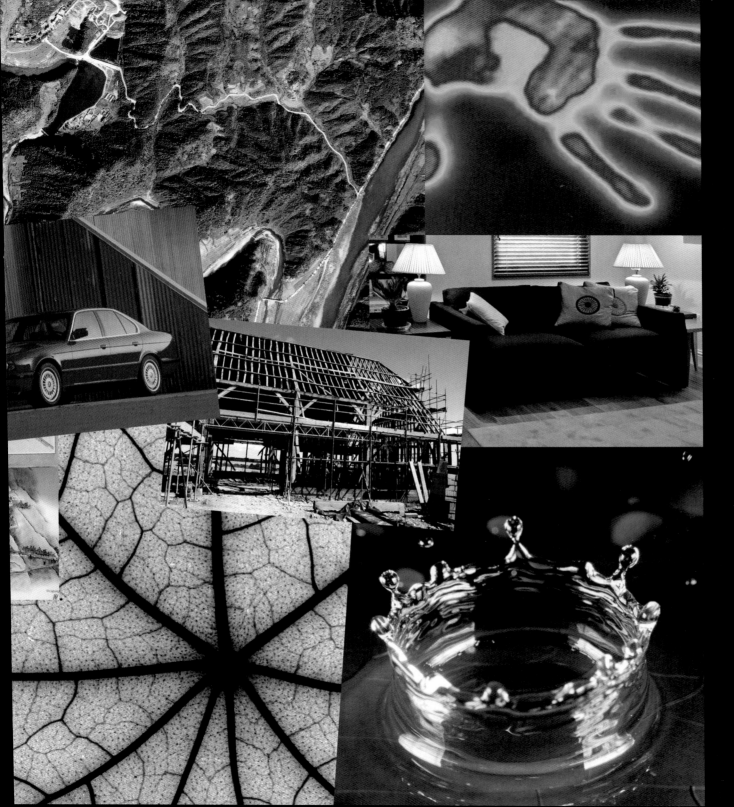

other
applications

12345678

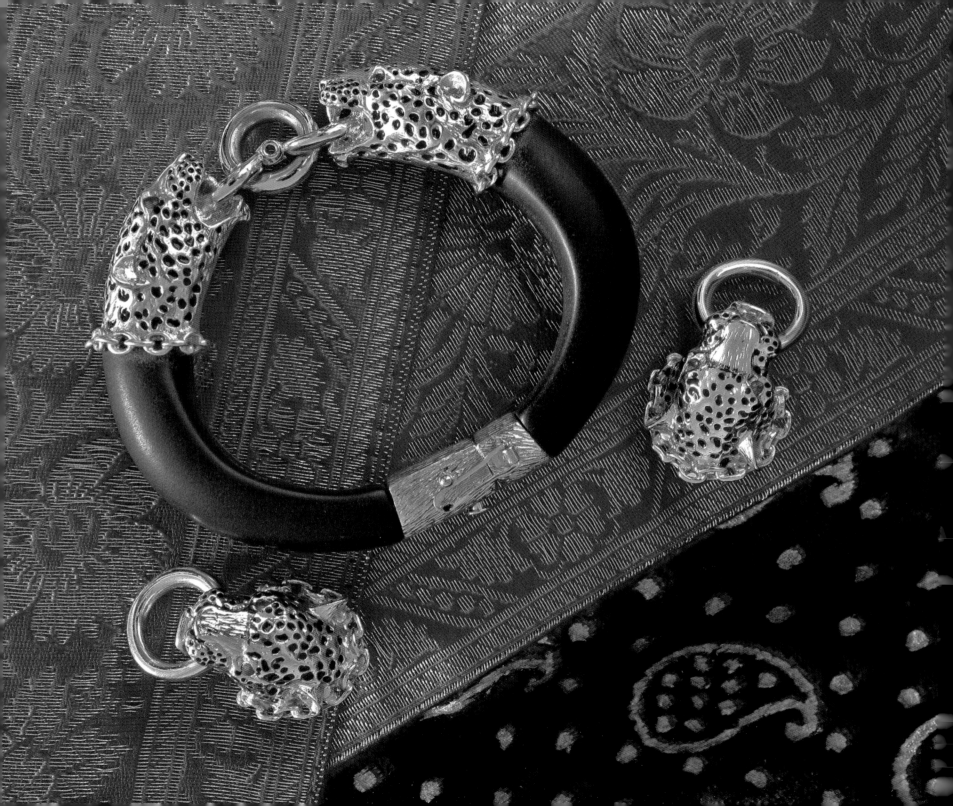

Other applications for photography include the all-important but often-ignored practical work. This is, in fact, one of the cornerstones of photographic practice. Businesses rely on photography in a multitude of ways—from presentation of products and services, to promotion and record-keeping. For similar reasons, individuals also rely on photographs: to record their collections, to sell unwanted items, and to document the progress of processes such as home renovations. At the same time, photographic records are vital to scientists, doctors, engineers, and surveyors, not only to facilitate detailed study within their field, but to uncover phenomena too subtle, too rapid, or too distant to be seen by the unaided eye.

Practical photography

Although photography was invented by artists for artists, its practical uses are socially crucial and perhaps economically far more important. While we see its professional application for use in advertising all around us, what is new and exciting is that everyone now can use photography as a business tool to sell products and services. Everyone can become their own professional photographer.

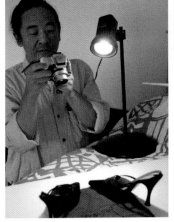

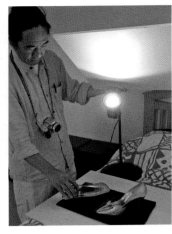

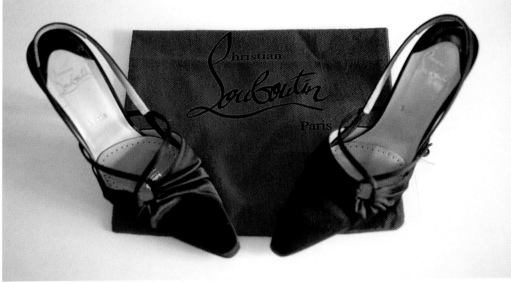

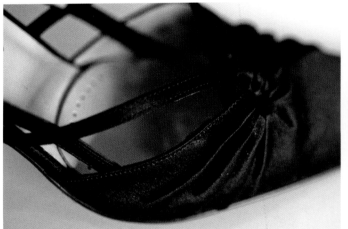

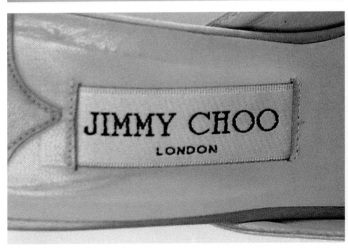

PHOTOGRAPHY FOR ONLINE AUCTIONS

eBay and other online-auction websites are among the largest users of images in the world. Bidders need clear, accurate, and truthful pictures of the items they are bidding for. The higher the quality of the images and the more angles you show, the more likely you are to achieve the best price possible.

1 To avoid casting dark shadows, flood your item with large amounts of soft light instead of strong directional light.

2 Arrange the item against a simple background, such as a board, pressed sheets, or its packaging, if appropriate.

3 Take close-up details of wear, designer labels, or ornamentation to prove the authenticity of the items.

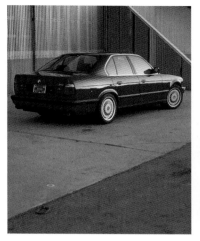

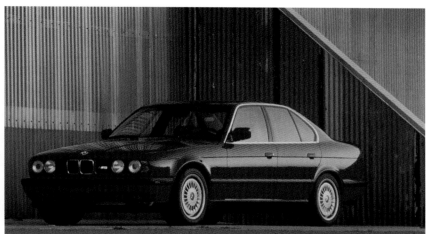

It works for the professionals, and it will work for you. The better the lighting and the glossier the car, the easier it will be to sell. Long shots from a distance emphasize sleek lines, while wider angle shots from close up suggest dynamism.

1 Clean and polish the car, and park it against a complementary background. Shoot it in soft light, preferably in the evening.

2 Angle the car so that the bodywork picks up neutral but attractive reflections. Add a little sparkle by turning on the lights.

PROMOTING A BUSINESS

Today, any company will benefit from illustrating its products or services, whether on a website or in a pamphlet. Colorful, well-lit, clear pictures can only help your business. Visualize how you want your customers or clients to respond to the images. For example, if you specialize in Italian delicacies, the pictures should make them feel hungry. You may wish to include a human element in your promotional literature too, but avoid showing staff, since they can quickly change.

1 Show the range of products you offer, and ensure the lighting makes them look their best.

2 Avoid including prices in the shots, or you will have to keep updating the pictures.

3 Make sure that colors and tones are accurate. Avoid exaggerating these important elements.

4 If possible, take shots of each of your products individually. This makes it easier when updating.

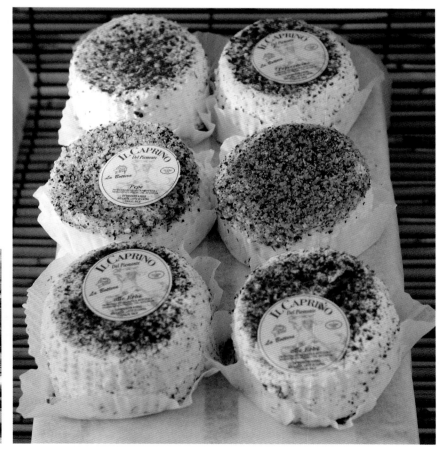

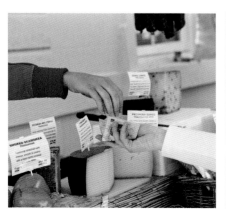

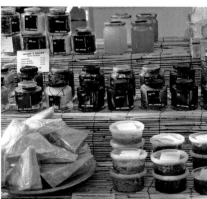

RECORDING YOUR BELONGINGS

Photographs of precious items such as heirlooms, jewelry, and ornaments are always useful for insurance records. They also help establish ownership, and may prove provenance if you sell any item. It can also be useful to take pictures of belongings you are putting into storage and attach them to the boxes. This will save time when retrieving an item.

1 Show jewelry items being worn: as well as recording their appearance, it will give an instant sense of scale.

2 Use contrasting backgrounds that show the item clearly – for example, a black background for silver jewelry.

3 Place a ruler, coin, or other familiar object next to the item you are photographing to establish its size.

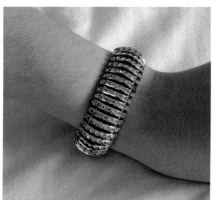

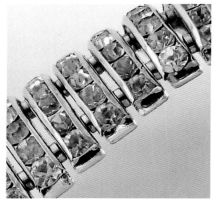

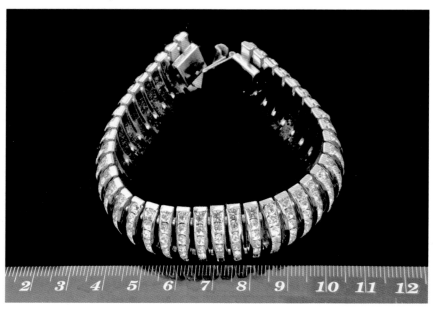

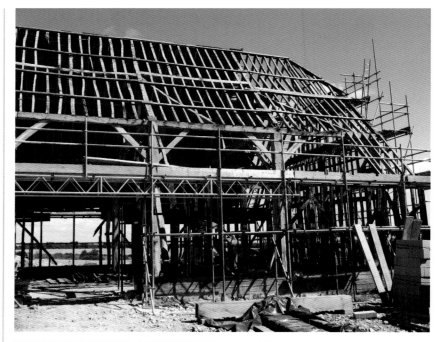

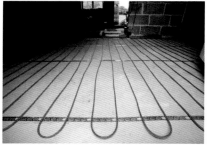

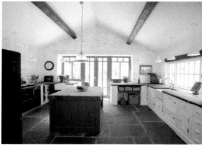

CHARTING A BUILDING PROJECT

Large projects, such as building or renovating a house, benefit from photography's powers of documentation. Record the progress made every step of the way. It can be worthwhile, too, to photograph things that will later be hidden, such as wiring or heating systems. Photograph everything you wish to comment on or correct, and document good points as well as bad.

1 To build a sequence showing the project's development, stand in the same position for each shot.

2 Ensure all images are date-stamped – some cameras have a setting that will put a date directly on the image itself.

3 If documenting a detail, be sure to photograph its context as well, or it may be difficult later to remember exactly where the shot was taken.

PHOTOGRAPHING HOME INTERIORS

High-quality images of a home interior can help when you wish to sell the property, or when you want to document the state of play before or after a makeover. While a view that includes everything in a single shot is impressive and exaggerates the feeling of spaciousness, it is also a good idea to take smaller, more intimate views that give a feel of the place.

1 Always use a tripod: it will enable you to line up the camera reliably, and to obtain good-quality, sharp images with good depth of field without a flash.

2 Set the lens to its widest angle. If this is insufficient, try making panoramas by stitching together two or more images on the computer.

3 Turn on all the house lights and bring in extra lamps to lighten dark corners. Work on cloudy days or when it is not too sunny outside, so that light from the windows is not too bright.

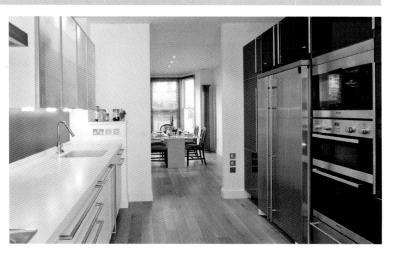

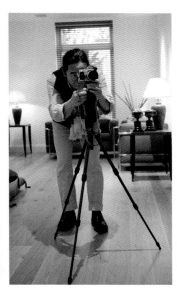

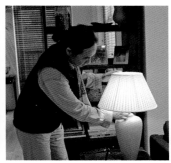

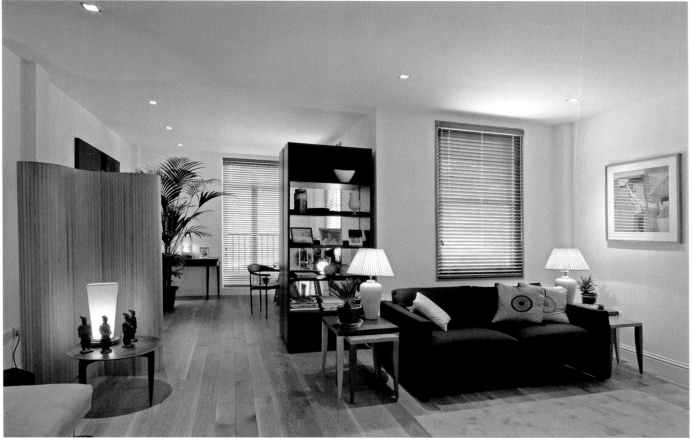

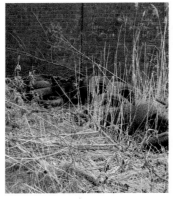

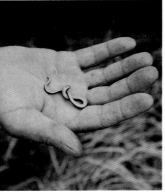

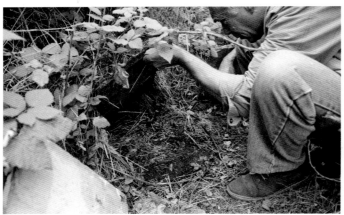

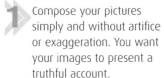

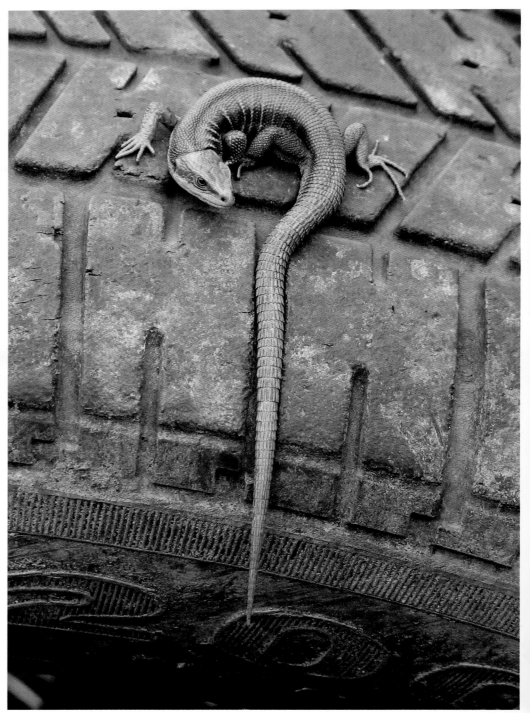

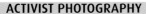

ACTIVIST PHOTOGRAPHY

One of photography's great contributions to making the world a better place is that it can be used by activist groups to communicate their concerns, to help raise awareness, and to share information. You can record the work of your group, for example, in preserving the habitats of local wildlife. For many people, your pictures will provide evidence they can relate to and will be a revelation.

1 Compose your pictures simply and without artifice or exaggeration. You want your images to present a truthful account.

2 Make before-and-after comparisons. These are effective at showing the benefits of the work that is being done.

3 Shoot everything at highest resolution, since you may be making an historically important document. Archive all your images.

SCRAPBOOKING

The question faced by many photographers at the end of a voyage of discovery is what to do with all the pictures. You can make simple albums for your photos, or you can go further and create scrapbooks. These combine all the memorabilia and ephemera collected on the trip with photographs to provide as complete a record as possible of the experience.

1. Keep all the tickets, maps, and leaflets that you pick up on your travels: they are useful for giving context to the pictures.

2. On your return, gather the materials together and photograph different compositions to use as backgrounds for your pictures.

3. Consider creating websites with your pictures, to share with the friends you made on your travels.

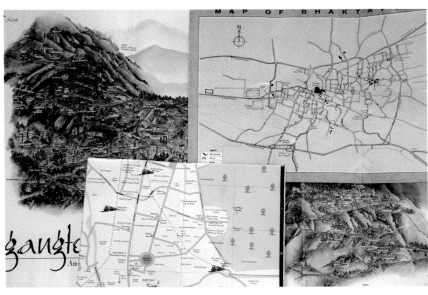

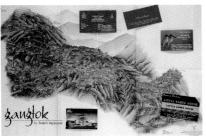

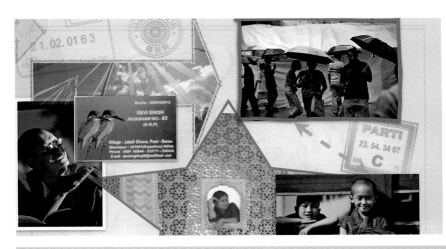

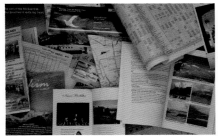

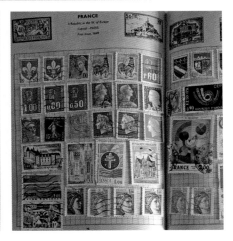

CATALOGING COLLECTIONS

Whatever you collect, and whether the items are of value or just of interest to yourself and fellow enthusiasts, photography is ideal for cataloging and keeping track of your collection. It also allows you to show it without exposing it to risk.

1. Make the highest-quality images possible of individual items. Also record larger groupings of items.

2. Use lighting appropriate to the object – side lighting to show the relief pattern on coins, for example, and overhead lighting for flat items such as stamps.

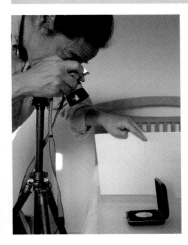

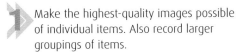

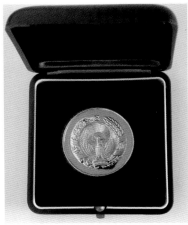

What the eye can't see

Even when handled by someone who is relatively inexperienced in matters of photography, a camera can produce visually pleasing results. It is no surprise, then, that in the hands of an expert with access to special equipment, it can create truly eye-catching images. These pictures reveal a world that is invisible to the naked eye: minerals in the ground, galaxies in space, and subtle phenomena beyond perception.

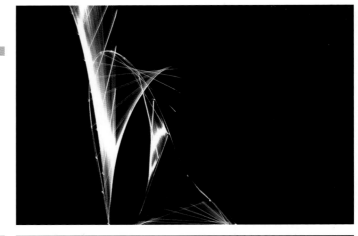

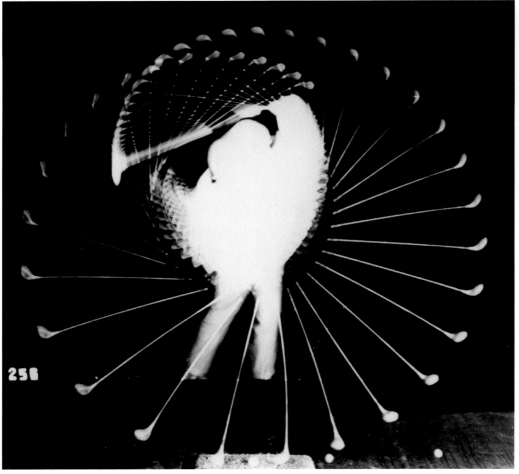

258

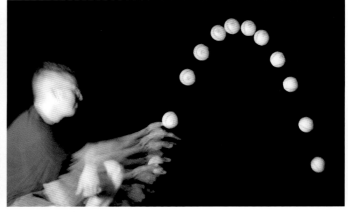

STROBE LIGHTING

The earliest type of flash photography used strobes—instruments that could produce brief, intense pulses of light. It took a surprisingly long time before a strobe's value in breaking down rapid movement into its constituent steps was appreciated. Some modern camera flash units can produce stroboscopic effects.

1 Shots have to be taken in complete darkness, so that the only thing recorded is the movement lit by the flashes.

2 The rate of flashing is adjusted to suit the movement: very rapid movements need a very high rate.

3 Digital advances revolutionized strobe photography, making it easy to review images and repeat movements if needed.

SATELLITE IMAGING

Our appreciation of the Earth has been radically transformed by satellites. Many of the technologies developed for satellite sensing have become the building blocks for digital photography.

1 Satellites work by analyzing different types of radiation to build up an image.

2 Colors are introduced artificially to emphasize different information.

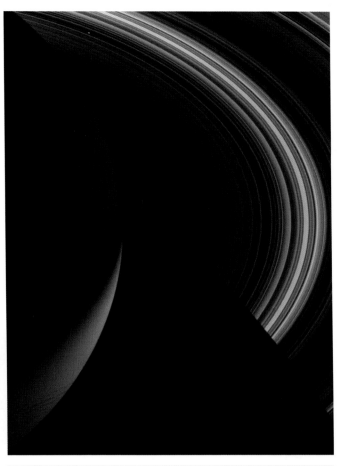

KIRLIAN PHOTOGRAPHY

Once thought to be documents of psychic energies, Kirlian images record the electrical discharge that takes place in a high-voltage, high-frequency field similar to the meteorological phenomenon of St. Elmo's fire.

1 This technique has been used to diagnose the state of health of people and organisms.

2 The object is placed directly onto a photographic emulsion; no camera is needed.

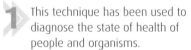

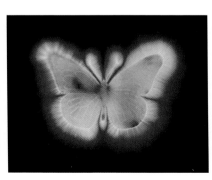

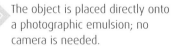

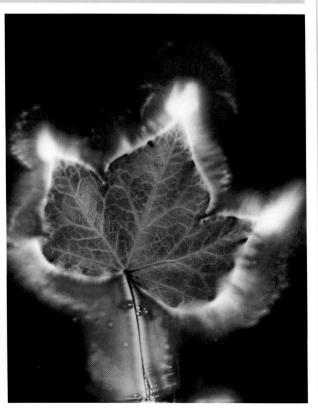

SPACE PHOTOGRAPHY

Interplanetary explorations by satellites have shown us the solar system in incredible detail, revealing stark and marvelous beauty. Each pixel in the images must be coded into a radio signal that is sent millions of miles back to Earth, where it is painstakingly reconstructed, a pixel at a time. Here, Saturn is lit by sunlight reflecting off its rings of dust.

1 Images are made by exposures through red, green, and blue to recreate natural color images. Other filters may be used.

2 Spacecraft cameras benefit from the vacuum of space to return extremely clear images: the above image was taken 900,000 miles from Saturn.

GALAXY PHOTOGRAPHY

The photography of galaxies, or collections of stars and planets such as our own, can produce some incredible images. Pictures of not-too-distant galaxies and nebulae are made by keeping a telescope/camera combination pointed to the same galaxy over a period of several hours.

1 Telescopes must be sited in areas with no light pollution and the cleanest air, such as that found in high deserts.

2 Shots need to be meticulously planned: galaxies must be in the right part of the night sky, and the weather has to be not only cloudless but also completely still.

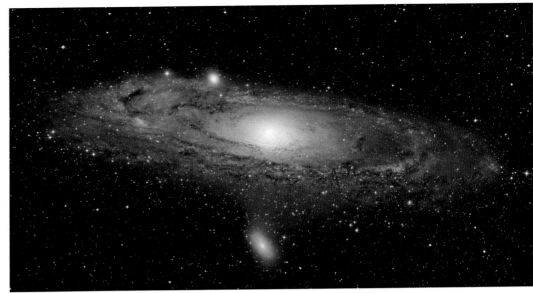

INFRARED IMAGING

We cannot see infrared radiation, the strength of which varies with the temperature of the subject. However, sensors can capture infrared and create an image. Such an image enables us to learn about the distribution of temperature within the subject. This information is normally invisible to the human eye.

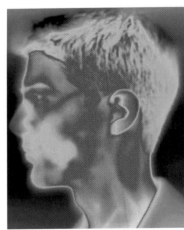

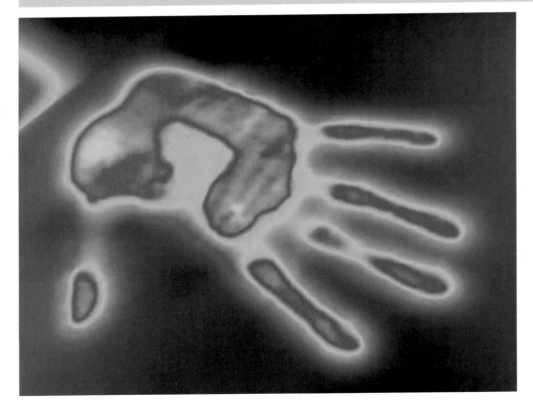

1 The allocation of colors to infrared is arbitrary but makes intuitive sense: cooler areas are blue, hotter ones are red.

2 Some night-vision optics and security cameras work by shining infrared light on the subject and reading the reflection.

3 It is difficult to create very sharp images because of the absorption of infrared radiation and problems with focusing.

X-RAY PHOTOGRAPHY

Although usually used for medical reasons, X-rays—high-energy radiation that can partially penetrate solid objects—can also be exploited for artistic purposes. The denser parts of the subject absorb more radiation, and this leads to the creation of the darkest parts of the image.

1 X-rays are essentially photograms: the object is laid directly on or close to the X-ray sensitive material.

2 X-rays are usually seen in negative. The images below have been printed, reversing the distribution of black and white.

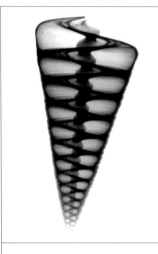
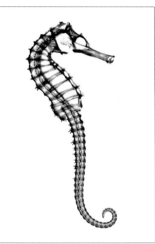

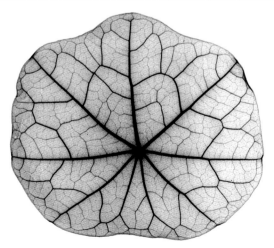

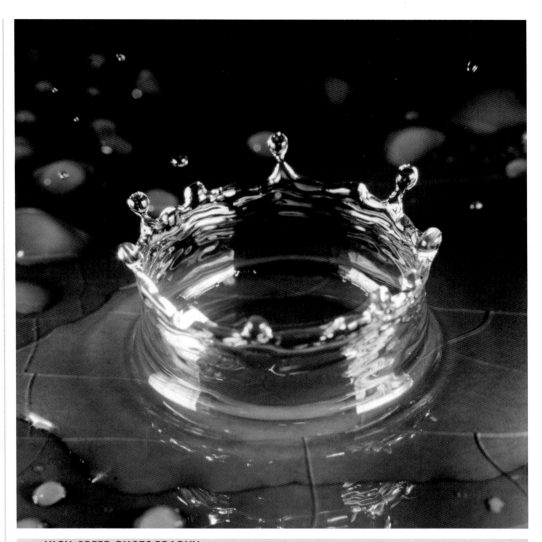

HIGH-SPEED PHOTOGRAPHY

The ultimate in flash-lit photography is the capture of events that are over in less than the blink of an eye—completed in just thousandths of a second or less. The main problem is not with providing enough light for the event, nor with the very brief time it lasts, but with timing the flash to catch the action at its peak. For this, specialist timing, switching, or tripping devices are needed.

1 The flash exposure should last for an even shorter duration than that of the event itself.

2 All the lighting should come from the flash alone, since the camera shutter must be opened before the event.

3 Because the flash must be extremely brief, it has to be extremely bright to make up for the short duration.

Glossary

32x speed The rate at which data is read to or from media such as a memory card or CD. For example, 32 times the basic rate of 150 kb/sec.

6,500 White balance standard that corresponds to normal daylight. It appears warm compared to 9,300.

9,300 White balance standard that is close to daylight. It is used mainly for visual displays since its higher blue content gives better color rendering in indoor lighting conditions.

analog A non-digital effect, representation, or record that varies in strength.

anti-aliasing A method of smoothing the "stair-stepping" diagonal lines sometimes seen in a digital image or computer typesetting.

aperture The narrowest part of the lens through which light passes. It is set by the lens diaphragm and determines the f/number.

attachment A digital file, such as an image, that is sent along with an email.

av (aperture value) setting Represented by the f/number, this controls the size of the aperture and how much light passes through a lens.

back-up To make and store second or further copies of computer files. Also, the copy made in backing up.

black An area that has no color or hue due to the absorption of most or all light.

bleed (1) A photograph or line that runs off the page when printed. (2) A spread of ink into fibers of the paper, which causes dot gain, in which dots print larger than intended.

BMP (Bit MaP) A file format for image files that are native to Windows.

brightness A quality of visual perception that varies with the amount or intensity of light that a given element appears to send out or transmit.

browse To look through a collection of material, such as images or web pages.

Brush An image-editing tool used to apply effects such as color, blurring, burn, dodge, and so on.

burning-in The act of giving a selected part of an image extra exposure, either in a darkroom or in image manipulation, making it appear darker.

byte A unit of digital information.

calibration The process of matching the characteristics or behavior of a device to a standard.

camera exposure The quantity of light reaching a camera's film or light sensor. It can be varied by adjusting the aperture of the lens and the duration of the exposure.

clone To copy or sample parts of an image for pasting on to another part of the image or another image.

CMYK (Cyan, Magenta, Yellow, Key black) A color mode used in printing in which inks of these four colors are combined to create all other colors.

colorize To add color to a black and white image without changing the original lightness values.

color A quality of visual perception characterized by hue, saturation, and lightness. It is perceived as attributes of things seen.

color balance Adjusting the white balance of an image to ensure correct color reproduction.

color cast A tint or hint of color that covers an image evenly.

color gamut The range of colors that can be produced by a device or reproduction system.

color management A system of controlling the color output of all devices in a production chain.

compression The process of reducing the size of a digital file by changing the way the data is coded.

contrast The measurement of the relationship between the mid-tones, with the brightest and darkest parts of a scene.

crop (1) To use part of an image in order to improve composition, fit the image into available space or format, or square up the image to correct the horizon. (2) To scan just the required part of an image.

dSLR Abbreviation for digital single lens reflex camera.

definition Subjective assessment of the clarity and quality of detail that is visible in image.

delete To remove an item from an image or a file from the current directory.

depth of field The measure of a zone or distance over which any object in front of the lens will appear acceptably sharp. It lies in front of and behind the plane of best focus.

direct vision finder A type of viewfinder in which the subject is observed directly—for example, through a hole or optical device.

display A device, such as a monitor screen, an LCD projector, or the information panel on a camera, that provides a temporary visual representation of data.

dodging A technique for controlling local contrast during printing by selectively reducing the amount of light reaching parts of the image that would otherwise print too dark. Also, its digital equivalent.

dpi (dots per inch) The measure of resolution of an output device as the number of dots or points that can be addressed or printed by the device.

driver Software used by a computer to control, or drive, a peripheral device such as a scanner, printer, or removable-media drive.

duotone (1) A photomechanical printing process that uses two inks to increase tonal range. (2) A mode of working in image-manipulation software that simulates the printing of an image with two inks.

electronic viewfinder An LCD screen, viewed through an eyepiece, that shows what is visible through the camera lens.

enhancement A change made to an image to improve one or more of its qualities—for example, increasing the color saturation or sharpness.

EVF *See* electronic viewfinder

exposure The process of allowing light to reach light-sensitive material or sensor to create an image.

f/number A lens diaphragm setting that determines how much light passes through the lens.

feathering Blurring a border or bounding line by reducing the sharpness or suddenness of the change.

file format A method or structure of computer data.

fill in To illuminate shadows cast by the main light by using another light source or reflector to bounce light from the main source into shadows.

filter (1) Part of an image manipulation software package that is used to produce special effects. (2) Software that is used to convert one file format to another.

flash (1) To illuminate with a very brief burst of light. (2) Equipment used to provide a brief burst of light. (3) Type of electronic memory used in, for example, digital cameras.

flatten To combine multiple layers and other elements together into a single background layer.

focal length The distance from the "center" of a lens to its point of focus on the film or digital sensor, when the lens is set to infinity. Usually measured in millimetres.

focus To make an image appear sharp by adjusting the distance setting of the lens.

frame rate The number of exposures that a camera can make per second (fps).

grayscale The term used to describe an image that is composed of discrete shades of gray. It is often synonymous with the terms monochromatic and black and white.

hard copy A visible form of a computer file printed more or less permanently on to a support medium such as paper or film.

histogram A graphical representation showing the relative numbers of something—an image, for example—over a range of values.

hue Name for the visual perception of color, in terms of the shade or complexion of the color.

ink-jet Printing method in which extremely tiny drops of ink are squirted on to paper or another medium.

ISO setting Measurement of a digital camera's sensitivity to light, equivalent to ISO ratings in film.

JPEG (Joint Photographic Expert Group) A data-compression technique that reduces file sizes with some loss of information. *See* lossy compression.

k (1) A binary thousand, sometimes used to denote 1024 bytes. (2) Key ink in the CMYK process. (3) Degrees Kelvin, which measure color temperature.

key tone An image's principal or most important tone. It is usually the mid-tone between white and black.

layer mode Picture-processing or image-manipulation technique that determines the way a layer in a multi-layer image combines or interacts with the layer below.

LCD (Liquid Crystal Display) A display using materials that can block light.

levels A display showing the distribution of pixel brightness within an image.

lightness The amount of white in a color. This affects the perceived saturation of a color: the lighter the color, the less saturated it appears to be.

lossless compression A computing routine, such as LZW, that reduces the size of a digital file without reducing the information.

lossy compression A computing routine, such as JPEG, that reduces the size of a digital file but also loses some information or data in the process.

mask Selecting parts of an image to restrict the area that digital manipulation will affect.

megapixel One million pixels. The term is used to describe a digital camera in terms of its sensor resolution.

mid-tone The gray that is midway visually between white and black.

monochrome Photograph or image made up of black, white, and grays. May or may not be tinted.

noise Irregularities in an image that reduce the information content.

opacity A measure of how much of an image can be "seen" through a layer or layers.

operating system The software program that coordinates the computer.

optical viewfinder A type of viewfinder that shows the subject through an optical system, rather than via a monitor screen.

out-of-gamut Colors from one color system that cannot be seen or reproduced in another.

output A hard-copy print-out of a digital file.

override A method of compensating for any over- and under-exposure produced by a camera's auto-exposure function.

paint To apply a color, texture, or effect with a digital "brush."

palette (1) A set of tools, colors, or shapes. (2) A range or selection of colors in an image.

pan To follow the motion of a moving subject with the camera during exposure.

peripheral A device such as a printer, monitor, scanner, or modem that is connected to a computer.

photomontage A composite photographic image made from the combination of several other images.

pixel A picture element. It is the smallest unit of digital imaging.

pixelated The appearance of a digital image whose individual pixels are clearly discernible.

ppi (points per inch) The number of points seen or resolved by a scanning device per linear inch.

RAM (Random Access Memory) A computer component in which information can be stored or rapidly accessed.

RAW An image file format that contains all the information captured by a camera in its un-processed form.

read To access or take information from a storage device, such as a hard disk or a CD-ROM.

red eye An image defect appearing as a red spot in the eye of a portrait subject. It is caused by the flash being reflected from the back of the eye.

resolution A way of describing the level of detail in an image. The higher the resolution of an image, the more detail it holds.

resizing Changing the resolution or file size of an image to suit its intended use.

RGB (Red, Green, Blue) The color model that defines colors in terms of relative amounts of red, green, and blue components. RGB is used to display colors on televisions, computer monitors, and LCDs.

scrolling The process of moving to a different part of an image that is too large to fit on to a monitor screen in its entirety.

serial exposure Making a series of exposures in quick succession for as long as the shutter button is held down, within camera's capacity.

single shot Making one exposure with a press of the shutter, even if the button is held down.

stair-stepping Jagged, rough, or step-like reproduction of a line or boundary, which was originally smooth.

synchro-flash Flash and exposure settings that balance with daylight to create a natural look.

telephoto An optical construction that enables the physical length of the lens to be shorter than the focal length.

thumbnail A representation of an image as a small, low-resolution version.

TIFF (Tag Image File Format) A very widely used digital image format that stores images without compressing them.

tint (1) Color that can be reproduced with process colors; a process color. (2) An overall, usually light, coloring that tends to affect areas with density but not clear areas.

TV (time value) setting Calculated in fractions of a second, this controls the length of time a camera's shutter remains open.

undo To reverse an editing or similar action within a software application.

upload The transfer of data between computers or from a network or peripheral computer to a central computer.

USB (Universal Serial Bus) The standard port design for connecting peripheral devices, such as digital cameras, printers, or telecommunications equipment, to a computer.

USM (UnSharp Mask) An image-processing technique that has the effect of improving the apparent sharpness of an image.

warm colors Hues such as reds, through oranges, to yellows.

white balance Matching the white of a scene to a standard white.

write To commit data on to a storage medium, such as a CD-R.

zoom A type of lens in which the focal length (field of view) can be altered without changing focus.

Index

a

abstract compression, landscapes 165

abstracts:
  abstract views (architecture) 226–7
  composing with light 359–61
  from events 320
  graffiti 354, 356–7
  monochrome (foliage) 122
  raindrops and neon 342–3
  texture 352–5, 358–9

action shots 58–63
  see also movement

Adobe RGB 19

advertising 366–7

aerial photographs 273

angle of shot:
  action shots 61
  architecture 251, 256
  gardens 116
  portraits 54

animals:
  gallery pictures 206–8
  pet portraits 172–5
  see also horses; wildlife photography

architecture:
  abstract views 226–7
  available light 222–3
  converging parallels 214, 223, 242
  focus on details 214–15, 227, 233

form and space 216–17
gallery pictures 276–9
iconic landmarks 236–41
low-light interiors 228–35
problems with tall buildings 237
supplying human interest 223
see also buildings; cities

art photography:
  lights and colors 328–9
  sculpture 326–7

assistance, with baby pictures 83

astronomy, galaxy photographs 374

auto-focus 21, 180

autumn colors 139

AV (aperture value) priority setting 19

available light see light

b

babies 82–5
  see also children

backgrounds:
  birds in flight 181
  children's parties 289
  flowers 122
  nudes 98
  open-air art 326–7
  portraits 54, 55, 71, 80, 108
  see also locations, choosing

beaches:
  color and texture 144–5
  holidays 92–3

silhouettes 107
sunset rider 178–9
see also sea

birds:
  exotic, in close-up 182–3
  in flight 180–81
  garden birds 184–5
  peacock close-up 197

black-and-white photography:
  city streets 268–9
  landscapes 130–31
  nudes 98
  portrait of boy 78–9
  weddings 292

blur:
  avoiding 61
  movement and 62–3, 321, 331, 333

bracketing setting 18, 35, 135, 231

bridges:
  character of 246–7
  in silhouette 248–9, 277

buildings:
  churches (exteriors) 214–15, 220–21, 226–7
  churches (interiors) 230–31, 242–3, 316–17
  home interiors 369
  illuminated 222–3
  modernist 218–19, 226–7, 232–5
  night shots 216, 218–19, 222–3, 266–7
  project documentation 368
  romantic ruins 224–5
  see also architecture

bulb setting, use of 33

business applications 367

butterflies, close-ups 188

c

cameras:
  accessories 16–17
  choice of 14–15
  settings 18–19, 57, 65
  time settings 19

campaign photography 370

candid and posed shots:
  parties 96–7
  portraits 70–73
  weddings 290–91, 295

carnivals and festivals 296–307

cars:
  cityscapes from 270–71
  photographed for sale 367
  reflections 255, 264–5
  wildlife shots from 195

ceramics, still life 349

chiaroscuro 74, 75

children:
  birthday party 288–9
  at events 318
  growing year by year 84–7
  informal portraits 68–9, 85–7, 106, 288–9, 302–3
  at play 56–61, 288–9
  posed portraits 76–7
  in wedding pictures 293, 295
  see also babies; portraits

Chinese New Year 307

Christmas 302–3

cities:
  black-and-white street photographs 268–9
  doors 257
  fountains 244–5
  hard and soft juxtaposed 260
  Manhattan from Staten Island ferry 252–3
  nocturnal cityscape 258–9, 266–7
  old and new juxtaposed 250–51
  rooftop views 272–3
  skyscrapers 260–63
  street demonstration 300–301
  streets and alleys 254–7
  unusual viewpoints 236–7, 264–5, 270–71
  Westminster 236–7
  see also architecture

cloudburst 166

clouds 160–63

color:
  Adobe RGB 19
  aquarium adjustments 204
  autumn leaves 139
  balance and saturation 42–3
  effect of mist and fog 135
  enhancing 103, 120
  exposure and 22
  firework display 284–5

Picture credits

p41 Dorling Kindersley © Barrie Watts tl; p59 © Doug Blane (www.DougBlane.com) / Alamy t; p61 Janeanne Gilchrist © Dorling Kindersley tl; p71 Amit Pashricha © Dorling Kindersley tr; p84 © Ace Stock Limited / Alamy bl; p84 © Mick Broughton / Alamy ct; p84 © D Hurst / Alamy tr; p85 © David Young-Wolff / Alamy tl, ct, cl; p85 © Robert Holmes / Alamy br; p92/3 Peter Mason; p98 © blickwinkel / Alamy tr; p98 © Rob Wilkinson / Alamy cc; p106 © Jennie Hart / Alamy bl; p108 Asia Images tl; p108 © Wolfgang Kaehler / Alamy tr; p109 © Alice & Max tr; p109 © Wendy Gray br; p136 © Jim Zuckerman / Alamy bl; p136 © John Terence Turner / Alamy cr; p136 © Ninette Maumus / Alamy tr; p137 © David Poole / Alamy tl; p137 © Thomas Hallstein / Alamy tr; p138 © ImageState / Alamy ct; p138 © AT Willett / Alamy tr & cr; p138 © ImageState / Alamy bl; p139 Jerry Young © Dorling Kindersley tr, cr; p139 © Gavin Hellier / Alamy tl, bl; p139 © Glen Allison / Alamy cb; p164 © Glen Allison / Alamy bl; p164 © Robert Harding Picture Library Ltd / Alamy tr; p165 © Hes Mundt / Alamy tr; p165 © Jerry Young br; p166 © Tom Till / Alamy l; p167 © Steven Poe / Alamy tl; p167 Shaen Adey © Dorling Kindersley bl; p167 © David Bowman / Alamy r; p178/9 © Mark J Barrett / Alamy; p185 © Chip Prager tc, bl; p186 © Chip Prager cr; p186 Dorling Kindersley © Rowan Greenwood tr; p187 © Arco Images / Alamy tl, tc, tr; p187 © Arco Images / Alamy bl; p188 © Juniors Bildarchiv / Alamy tl, ct, bl; p206 Dorling Kindersley tr; p207 Frank Greenaway © Dorling Kindersley; p208 © ImageState / Alamy tl; p209 © Images of Africa Photobank / Alamy; p238 © Jon Arnold Images / Alamy bl; p239 © Lightworks Media / Alamy cl; p239 Dave King © Dorling Kindersley ct; p239 © Liquid Light / Alamy tr; p239 Michael Moran © Dorling Kindersley bl; p239 © AA World Travel Library / Alamy cr; p240 © Graham Knowles / Alamy tr; p240 © Steve Allen Travel Photography / Alamy cr; p240 © Wendy Gray br; p241 Alistair Duncan © Dorling Kindersley tc, tr; p241 Nigel Hicks © Dorling Kindersley bl; p241 © JLImages /

Alamy cb; p241 © Jon Arnold Images / Alamy br; p244 © Kevin George / Alamy tr; p257 © Wendy Gray l; p276 Alistair Duncan © Dorling Kindersley tr; p276 © Scott Gregory Banner / Alamy br; p277 © Scottish Viewpoint / Alamy l; p277 © David Ball / Alamy br; p277 © Wendy Gray tr; p278 © David Ball / Alamy r; p279 Enrique Uranga © Rough Guides bl; p279 © Wendy Gray r; p292 © Royal Geographical Society / Alamy cl; p292 © J Marshall – Tribaleye Images / Alamy c; p292 Dennie Cody tr; p293 © Elvele Images / Alamy tr, cc, cr; p293 © Cephas Picture Library / Alamy bl, bc; p295 © Profimedia International sro / Alamy tl, tc, cl; p295 © Around the World in a Viewfinder / Alamy c, tr; p295 Nicholas Prior bc; p298/9 © Oso Media / Alamy; p304 © Peter Treanor / Alamy l, c; p304 © Donald Nausbaum / Alamy r; p305 © Fabrice Bettex / Alamy tl, cl, c; p305 © Andrew Watson / Alamy tr, cr, br; p314/5 © Patrick Eden / Alamy; p318 © adam eastland / Alamy l; p318 © Greg Vaughn / Alamy tr; p318 © Ilene MacDonald / Alamy br; p319 © Andrew Paterson / Alamy l; p319 © Chad Ehlers / Alamy r; p320 © M-dash / Alamy tl; p320 © John James / Alamy bl; p320 © kolvenbach / Alamy r; p321 © Action Plus / Alamy tl; p321 © Content Mine International / Alamy bl; p321 © Apex News and Pictures Agency / Alamy r; p328/9 © Apex News and Pictures Agency / Alamy; p367 © Transtock Inc / Alamy t; p372 © Prof Harold Edgerton / Science Photo Library bl; p372 © Edward Kinsman / Science Photo Library tr, cr; p373 © Garion Hutchings / Science Photo Library bl; p373 © Booth / Garion / Science Photo Library cb; p373 © Geoeye / Science Photo Library; p373 NASA / JPL / Space Science Institute; p374 © Robert Gendler / Science Photo Library t; p374 © Ted Kinsman / Science Photo Library b, cr; p375 © Bert Myers / Science Photo Library cl, c, bl; p375 © Adam Hart-Davis / Science Photo Library r.

All other images © Tom Ang.

Acknowledgments

AUTHOR'S ACKNOWLEDGMENTS

This book owes its production and creation, in crucial measure, to the Herculean efforts of project editor Nicky Munro; my warm thanks for her tireless contributions, which went a long way beyond the call of duty. Congratulations and thanks to Sands Publishing Solutions (Simon Murrell and David and Sylvia Tombesi-Walton), who turned a jumble of thousands of images and words into a clean, inspiring design.

I'm pleased to thank Andy Mitchell for the majority of photographs taken of me at work, but thanks also go to Wendy Gray, Nicky Munro, and Charlotte Crowther for the others.

I am also most grateful to those who modelled for me: Emma and John Owen; Joe, Annabel, and Bill Munro; Priscilla Nelson-Cole; Michelle Baxter; Su St Louis; James, John, Joe, and Ed Munro; Polly, David, Jack, Joe, and Billie Packer; Tracy, Peter, Hayley, and Ruby Miles; Wendy Gray, Wim Buying, Kyna Gourley, Jenisa Patel, Bronwen Parker-Rhodes, and Charlotte Crowther.

For their cooperation and access, many thanks to: Serafin Domenach of El Arca Animal Sanctuary, Guadalest, Spain; Yana Zarifi and her actors for access to *The Persians*; Jose Luis Quesada and Paula Albamonte at Ciudad de las Artes y las Ciencias, Valencia, Spain; Juan Llantada Sacramento of the Valencia Tourist Office and Jaime Samcho, counsellor of Valencia Cathedral for their help with the shoot at the cathedral; Steve Greenberg at 230 5th, New York; Jake at Pete's Candy Store, Brooklyn; Buffalino; Melinda Manning, assistant director for public relations at the New York Botanical Gardens.

For help during the New York shoot, special thanks to Su St Louis and staff of the Dorling Kindersley New York office, in particular Chrissy McIntyre and Michelle Baxter.

Many thanks to Kodak, Canon, Fujifilm, Panasonic, Nikon, and Ricoh for the loan of their cameras.

My special thanks to those who helped fill gaps in the photographic coverage, namely Chip Prager for his bird pictures; also to Wendy Gray, Andy Mitchell, David Summers, and Paul Self.

Above all, and as always, big thanks go to Wendy for her love and support, which make anything seem possible and enable much to be actual.

Tom Ang,
London

PUBLISHER'S ACKNOWLEDGMENTS

Dorling Kindersley would like to thank all those mentioned above and also: Tim Lane and Michael Duffy for design assistance; David Summers, Bob Bridle, Tarca Davison-Aitkins, and Simon Tuite for editorial assistance; John Noble for compiling the index.